SOLID GROUND

OTHER BOOKS BY MARK FINLEY:

2000 and Beyond
Angel Wars
Confidence Amid Chaos
Dark Tunnels and Bright Lights
Discover Jesus
Experiencing God
Final Days
God's Last Altar Call
Greater Expectations
Growing Through Life's Toughest Times
Hearts at Home
Hope for a New Century
Jerusalem Showdown
Jesus Face to Face
Lonely No Longer
Looking for God in All the Wrong Places
More Seeing Is Believing
Promise a Day
Questioning the Supernatural
A Religion That Works
Revelation Predictions
Revelation's Three Greatest Mysteries
Search for Certainty Bible Study Guides
Simply Salvation
Soul Care
The Stress Transformers
Strong Medicine for a Sick Society
Studying Together
They're Coming Home
Things That Matter Most
Thirteen Life-changing Secrets
The Thought Makers
To Hope Again
Unshakable Faith
What Happy Couples Know
What My Parents Did Right
What You Can Know for Sure
When Faith Crumbles
When Your Faith Is Shaken
Which Way America?
Why So Many Denominations?
Winning Your Biggest Battles

SOLID GROUND

Daily Devotional for Adults

MARK FINLEY

REVIEW AND HERALD® PUBLISHING ASSOCIATION
HAGERSTOWN, MD 21740

The author assumes full responsibility for the accuracy of all facts and quotations as cited in this book.

This book was
Edited by Tompaul Wheeler
Copyedited by Jan Schleifer and Jocelyn Fay
Designed by Willie S. Duke/Leumas Design
Cover art by Getty Images
Electronic makeup by Shirley M. Bolivar
Typeset: 11/14 Minion

PRINTED IN U.S.A.

07 06 05 04 03 5 4 3 2 1

R&H Cataloging Service
Finley, Mark A. 1945-
Solid ground.

1. Devotional calendars—Seventh-day Adventists. 2. Devotional literature.
I. Title.

242.2

ISBN 0-8280-1731-X

This book is dedicated

to Teenie,

a loving wife and companion in ministry,

who daily encourages me to keep following

the dreams God places in my heart.

to Debbie, Rebecca, and Mark, Jr.,

whose genuine friendship and care for their dad

mean more than words can express.

to Mom and Dad,

whose unwavering love through the years

has taught me what God's love is like.

FOREWORD

Jesus. That is what it is all about. That is what Mark Finley has been all about, and that is what this book is all about.

Mark Finley has spent his entire adult life leading people to Jesus in public evangelistic meetings and through the telecast of *It Is Written.* Now he has written this book with the same goal in mind. But this book is designed to help us start every day with Jesus. It is about spending every day with Jesus. The goal of Pastor Finley is that we will meet Jesus every day, spend at least some time in worship, and then spend the day with Jesus.

Nothing that I can think of would be more powerful for this church—or more powerful for our own lives—than to meet Jesus every day, and then invite Him to spend the day with us in our work, our home, our car, or wherever we are.

The devil doesn't care too much how we spend our time as long as we get too busy to have time for Jesus. I'd really like to encourage you to spend time every day with Jesus. Take the time to read one of these devotional pages, then allow Jesus to speak to you. Invite Jesus into your heart, as you start your day with Him.

I'm so pleased that Pastor Finley has provided this tool for us. I hope it will be valuable to you as you seek to know Jesus better during this year.

Don C. Schneider, President
North American Division of Seventh-day Adventists

ON SOLID GROUND

Therefore whoever hears these sayings of Mine, and does them, I will liken him to a wise man who built his house on the rock: and the rain descended, the floods came, and the winds blew and beat on that house; and it did not fall, for it was founded on the rock. Matt. 7:24, 25.

On July 28, 1976, the worst earthquake of the twentieth century, in terms of loss of life, killed 240,000 people in Tangshan, China. Most were villagers who lived in poorly constructed homes with weak foundations. This is also true of the massive earthquake in Gansu, China, which registered an amazing 8.6 on the Richter scale and took 200,000 lives on December 16, 1920. The pattern is the same everywhere in the world. Whether it is northern Peru, Central America, or southern Turkey, if the quality of the building is poor, the devastation is the greatest. Weak buildings do not survive earthquakes.

The same principle is true in our own spiritual lives. Some people do quite well when life goes well. They seem to thrive in life's good times, but when storms of difficulty crash on them, they fall apart. Why? Their spiritual experience is built on the weak foundation of their own human abilities. As long as their problems are no greater than their ability to cope, they do fine. When their problems grow larger than their inner strength, they crumble. Without a solid foundation they cannot cope with the seismic shocks of life.

God provides a solid foundation in His Word. As we meditate upon the truths of Scripture, we grow into mature Christians. God's Word gives our faith a strength and stability. It enables us to stand when the storms of life are fierce. It supports us when everything around is crumbling. Ellen White puts it this way: "Our bodies are built up from what we eat and drink; and as in the natural economy, so in the spiritual economy: it is what we meditate upon that will give tone and strength to our spiritual nature" (*Steps to Christ,* p. 88).

Fill your mind with God's Word. Open your heart to the influence of His Spirit through the Word. If you do, you will develop a solid, rock-hard faith that will meet the test of any storm.

PRECIOUS PROMISES

By which have been given to us exceedingly great and precious promises, that through these you may be partakers of the divine nature, having escaped the corruption that is in the world through lust. 2 Peter 1:4.

Millions around the world testify to the changes in their lives as a result of Bible study. The Bible's appeal is universal. It speaks to the hearts of men and women of all ethnic groups, all cultures, and all ages.

Reading its pages, drunkards become sober, thieves become honest, prostitutes become pure, and drug addicts become clean. Anger, bitterness, and resentment yield to loving forgiveness, mercy, and tolerance. Selfish greed gives way to unselfish service. Crumbling marriages are renewed. Broken relationships are rekindled. Shattered self-esteem is restored. In God's Word, the weak find strength, the guilty find forgiveness, the discouraged find new joy, and the despairing find hope. The same Holy Spirit who inspired the Bible's writers inspires those who read it.

In the early 1960s Tex Watson traveled to southern California in search of what he called "total freedom." He began hanging around an abandoned movie ranch with members of Charles Manson's "family." Tex proved an outstanding pupil, absorbing large quantities of drugs and imbibing the Manson philosophy of life. Manson told his followers they must be free, like wild animals, to live, lie, and kill.

What followed was the Tate-La Bianca killings in the summer of 1969. The calculated, grisly murders of seven people shocked the nation. Tex was convicted as one of the murderers. Psychiatrists diagnosed him as "insane, totally incapable of standing trial." While in the Los Angeles County Jail, he would throw himself screaming against the bars.

Today, all of that has changed. Tex Watson is a new man. He resides at a medium-security prison in San Luis Obispo, California, leading Bible studies and sensitively answering the questions of the inmates. Watson heads an organization called Abounding Love Ministries. This is no superficial jailhouse conversion. Tex has held "model prisoner" status for 15 years. The Holy Spirit, working through Scripture, has transformed his life. As Watson studied, meditated, and applied God's Word to his life, he changed.

If God did it for him, He can do it for us, as well. When the precious promises of God's Word become precious to us, they change us deep down inside. Discover this life-changing power for yourself.

THE SECOND TOUCH

Then He put His hands on his eyes again and made him look up. And he was restored and saw everyone clearly. Mark 8:25.

Which statement below most accurately reflects your feelings?

"Bible study is the most exciting portion of my day. I look forward to it as much as anything else I do."

Or:

"Bible study is rather boring, uninteresting, and certainly not exciting. I sort of force myself to do it because I know I should, but I don't enthusiastically anticipate it."

Sometimes we need the second touch. Today's Bible verse tells of the blind man whose eyes Jesus touched twice before his vision became crystal-clear. We too may need to see with new eyes. Here are two powerful Bible study techniques that will help you discover new gems of truth in God's Word. Applying these two simple principles will transform your attitude toward your Bible study time. The "eyes" of exciting Bible study are visualization and identification.

As you read the stories of the Bible, attempt to picture each scene in the narrative. Visualize the man stricken with palsy, shaking from head to toe as Jesus approaches. Picture the crowded marketplace in Jerusalem. Look through Jesus' eyes at the hungry multitude seated on the grassy slopes near the Sea of Galilee. Rather than hurrying through a passage to get to the point, pause for a moment to observe these important scenes. As you visualize each scene, picture it in your mind and try to identify with the Bible characters in the scene.

Imagine that you are the woman caught in adultery. Imagine that you are the thief on the cross. Imagine that you are the Roman centurion crucifying Christ. Get inside these characters. What would you feel if you were in their place? What would you be thinking if you were experiencing what they were going through? What if you were Daniel, unjustly condemned and thrown into the lions' den? How would you have felt if you were Moses, placing your feet in the Red Sea as it parted? Analyze the thoughts and feelings of the Bible characters. Put yourself in their places. Weep as they weep. Rejoice when they rejoice. Let your spirits soar with their triumphs and crash with their defeats. Seeing through new eyes will transform Bible study into an exciting adventure in faith.

January 4

THE LIVING WORD

For the word of God is living and powerful, and sharper than any two-edged sword, piercing even to the division of soul and spirit, and of joints and marrow, and is a discerner of the thoughts and intents of the heart. Heb. 4:12.

Helen Keller grew up in a world shut in by blindness and deafness. She became an almost uncontrollable "wild child" of intense passions.

One day while Helen was playing with a new doll her patient tutor, Anne Sullivan, placed the toy in Helen's lap and signed the letters d-o-l-l in her palm repeatedly. But Helen didn't understand. As the tutor tried to help her connect this thing in her lap with the signs on her palm the girl became agitated. She slammed the doll on the floor, breaking it to pieces.

Later Miss Sullivan took the unruly girl down the path to the well house. Someone was pumping water. Placing Helen's hand under the cool flow, the tutor spelled out w-a-t-e-r on her other palm. Suddenly it clicked in the girl's mind. Later Helen recalled, "The mystery of language was revealed to me. I knew then 'w-a-t-e-r' meant the wonderful cool something that was flowing over my hand. That living word awakened my soul, gave it light, hope, joy, set it free!"

The soul of this wild child, shut away in her own darkened world, was set free by the discovery of the living word. God's living Word, the Bible, illumines the darkness of our minds and sets us free as well. You can experience the exhilarating freedom that the living Word brings. Take a few verses at a time. Ask yourself these questions regarding the passage you are contemplating: What is God personally saying to me in this portion of Scripture? What does this passage teach me about the character of God? Is there anything in this passage that speaks to my own spiritual life?

Psalms is a great place to begin such reflections. Take one psalm at a time. Read a few verses. Allow the Holy Spirit to impress your mind. Pause, respond to God in prayer by communicating to Him regarding what He is saying to you in Scripture. Your prayer may take the form of praise, thanksgiving, requests, petitions, confession, repentance, or intercession. As you allow the living Word to shape your thoughts you will be set free to know God in a close, intimate way. Today, allow that living Word to truly set you free.

AMAZING ACCURACY

The words of the Lord are pure words, like silver tried in a furnace of earth, purified seven times. You shall keep them, O Lord, You shall preserve them from this generation forever. Ps. 12:6, 7.

What concrete evidence do we have that the Bible is historically accurate? Is there reliable information regarding names, places, and geographical locations in Scripture? Discoveries in the past 200 years demonstrate the validity of God's Word. Archaeology does not prove the Bible is divinely inspired, but it does provide a basis for belief. Demonstrating the accuracy of scores of biblical details, it supports our faith. The past two centuries have provided us with a number of remarkable archaeological finds. Here are just a few.

The Moabite Stone, discovered in 1868 in Jordan, confirms the Moabite attacks on Israel as recorded in 2 Kings 1 and 3. This is hard evidence from outside the Bible of a specific event recorded by writers of Scripture. Following the death of Israel's king Ahab in 853 B.C., the king of Moab attacked Jehoshaphat, king of Judah. Through the miraculous intervention of God the Israelites "rose up and attacked the Moabites, so that they fled before them" (2 Kings 3:24). The Moabite Stone precisely records the Moabite defeat and their subsequent retreat as outlined in the Bible.

One of the most amazing finds of the twentieth century was the Lachish Letters, discovered from 1932 to 1938. These incredible documents found 24 miles north of Beersheba describe the attack of Nebuchadnezzar on Jerusalem in 586 B.C. They detail Jerusalem's fall from the perspective of Babylon. The Lachish Letters confirm the historical accuracy of Jerusalem's fall. They testify to the truthfulness of the inspired prophets in Chronicles, Isaiah, and Jeremiah, who spoke of Babylon's attack on Jerusalem.

Another almost unbelievable find is the Cyrus Cylinder, made of clay. This record describes Cyrus, the Persian king, including his overthrow of Babylon and the deliverance of the Jewish captives in 539 B.C. This archaeological find is especially significant when one considers that Cyrus was named, more than 150 years before his birth, in Isaiah 44:27, 28 and Isaiah 45:1 as God's chosen "shepherd" who would carry out the deliverance of Israel.

These discoveries, along with scores of others, continue to confirm the accuracy and reliability of the Bible. They speak eloquently of a God who has not left Himself without a witness in the world. They testify powerfully that we can have absolute confidence in the integrity of the Scriptures. Praise God that His Word still stands.

PASSING THE TEST OF TIME

The grass withers, the flower fades, but the word of our God stands forever. Isa. 40:8.

The Word of God has stood the test through the centuries. It has proved trustworthy over time. Archaeological finds and discoveries of ancient manuscripts through the years have shed light on the authenticity of the Bible.

In 1798 Napoleon led 38,000 of his troops into Egypt. He also took hundreds of artists, linguists, and scholars to help him better understand the history of that intriguing land. Relics of the past were everywhere, with their hidden mysteries of a once-great civilization. Strange inscriptions decorated monuments and temple walls, leaving Napoleon and his brain trust wondering what secret messages they contained.

In 1799 one of Napoleon's soldiers unearthed a black stone about four feet long and about two and a half feet wide that would unlock the mystery of Egyptian picture writing and reveal secrets hidden for centuries. That slab, known as the Rosetta Stone, is now housed in the British Museum in London, England. The Rosetta Stone bears an ancient decree in three different languages: hieroglyphics (Egyptian picture writing), cursive Egyptian, and Greek. Scholars quickly translated the Greek text, but puzzled over the hieroglyphics. Twenty years later, in 1822, a brilliant young French Egyptologist by the name of Jean-François Chapollion startled the world by cracking the ancient code. With the language unveiled, scholars were able to verify biblical passages that had appeared questionable. Here is one striking example.

The Bible mentions a people called the Hittites about 50 times, discussing their dealings with Abraham, David, and Solomon. These biblical references picture the Hittites as one of the most powerful of ancient empires. Yet in all of the ancient historical records not a trace of them remained. Critics reasoned that it would be impossible for such a mighty empire to disappear from history without leaving a trace behind. They suggested that such a nation never existed. But then came the Rosetta Stone. The vast museum of monuments and pillars all along the Nile, its messages locked up in hidden languages for centuries, now opened its doors. Inscriptions on these pillars and palace walls speak repeatedly of the political and military conflicts between Pharaoh Ramses II and the "king of Hitti," or the Hittites. Today the Hittites' place in history is well established.

The Bible's claims are reliable. We can safely trust God's Word to reveal guidance, directions, instruction, faith, and hope for the future. In the shifting moral values of the twenty-first-century world, God's Word is still trustworthy.

January 7

THE SUSTAINING WORD

Your word I have hidden in my heart, that I might not sin against You. Ps. 119:11.

Dietrich Bonhoeffer was a courageous German pastor who resisted the Nazi regime. He was executed by the gestapo shortly before World War II ended. But before his death Pastor Bonhoeffer had time to send out a few letters from his prison cell.

Written just before his execution, these documents give us insight into the soul of a twentieth-century martyr. They show a man standing securely and confidently on the Word of God. After one terrifying experience when exploding shells nearly blew his cell apart, Bonhoeffer wrote, "The heavy air raids . . . led me back quite simply to prayer and the Bible."

In his last days, facing certain death, Bonhoeffer wrote of how much he enjoyed the Scriptures. Daily the Word of God nourished his spiritual life. In one of his last letters he wrote, "I am reading the Bible straight through from cover to cover." His words radiate with a joy in the Word. He added, "I read the Psalms every day, as I have done for years. I know them and love them more than any other book."

The Bible strengthened Bonhoeffer to face the greatest trial of his life. He received spiritual strength and indomitable courage through God's Word. His faith was unshakable because it was rooted in the God who reveals Himself through His unchanging Word. Ellen White writes, "If God's Word were studied as it should be, [men and women] would have a breadth of mind, a nobility of character, and a stability of purpose rarely seen in these times" (*Steps to Christ,* p. 90). The Bible gives an unusual spiritual strength. It brings depth to our spiritual lives.

Dietrich Bonhoeffer discovered the enormous benefits of prayerfully studying God's Word. God offers us the same opportunity. The spiritual giants of the past did not develop strong faith by chance. Their lives were rooted in God's Word. Their faith was strong because their devotional life was strong.

The same is true for us today. The same Holy Spirit who inspired the Scriptures inspires us as we read God's Word. As we meditate on God's Word today our faith will be strengthened too.

TRUTH WORTH EVERYTHING

Sanctify them by your truth. Your word is truth. John 17:17.

In the early 1400s a bright young lecturer at the University of Prague discovered the writings of the English Reformer John Wycliffe. As John Huss pored over the Scriptures, he became personally convinced that the church in Bohemia badly needed a reformation. Several years after taking priest's orders he was appointed rector of the Bethlehem Chapel in Prague. The founders of this chapel advocated the preaching of the Scriptures in the language of the people. Although Huss was of humble birth and was left fatherless at a young age, he had an insatiable desire for knowledge. He had an unusually bright mind and outstanding communication skills. He was admitted to the university as a charity case, but soon distinguished himself as one of the University of Prague's scholars.

After completing his college course, he entered the priesthood and soon became attached to the court of the king. He was also made a professor of the university where he had received his education. He became a powerful preacher renowned throughout Europe. When he began to preach that many of the church's beliefs could not be reconciled with Scripture, it sent shock waves throughout the church in Europe.

Standing on the authority of Scripture alone, he boldly called for reform in the life and beliefs of fellow church members. Huss staunchly defended his position that " 'the precepts of Scripture, conveyed through the understanding, are to rule the conscience; in other words, that God speaking in the Bible, and not the church speaking through the priesthood, is the one infallible guide' " (*The Great Controversy,* p. 102).

Huss's preaching led to violent opposition from the Roman Church. In 1415 he was burned at the stake in Prague, martyred for his faith.

Even in death John Huss had the absolute confidence that the truth that he believed, preached, and was willing to die for would one day triumph. God is calling us in our day to be passionate about obeying His truth in our age of moral decay. There are some things that are not worth compromising. The price is just too high.

STRENGTH FOR OUR DAILY NEED

Remember the word to Your servant, upon which You have caused me to hope. This is my comfort in my affliction, for Your word has given me life. Ps. 119:49, 50.

God's Word gives us hope in times of discouragement. It brings comfort in times of affliction. It imparts life in times of despair.

Pastor Pyoter Rumackik was imprisoned in a Soviet gulag for his faith. He discovered that even in our darkest times, God provides strength for our daily needs.

His experience became almost unbearable when prison officials took his Bible away. A few days later, a fellow prisoner handed him a notebook and said, "Here, read this poem." The pastor glanced up and couldn't believe his eyes. It was a poem about Christ's sufferings on Calvary. His spirit soared as he read it. He began flipping the pages and discovered more scripturally based poems and numerous passages of the Bible. They filled the entire notebook.

The unknown stranger announced, "It's yours; you can keep it," and walked away. That notebook filled with Bible passages and scriptural truth brought Pyoter great comfort during the next few years. It helped give him many precious moments of fellowship with God.

Later the Christian pastor discovered, to his surprise, that the prisoner who gave him the notebook was an atheist. While working alone as a shepherd late at night in the Mongolian highlands, he became fascinated with Christian radio programs. They lifted his spirits and provided inspiration during his solitary nights. He would tape programs and copy portions in notebooks to pass the time. Somehow he managed to smuggle one of his notebooks into the prison. He then felt inspired to give it to Pyoter. For the pastor, this Mongol shepherd seemed like the ravens that brought food to the prophet Elijah in the wilderness. God found a way to provide for his needs. All the power of the gulag guards could not keep God's Word from penetrating his heart. The bars of a cell could not keep God's Word out. The shackles of a prison could not chain the Word of God. God's living Word provides strength for our daily needs in all of the varied circumstances of our lives.

As we read the precious promises of Scripture we too will declare, "For Your word has given me life."

THE SCRIPTURES REVEAL JESUS

You search the Scriptures, for in them you think you have eternal life; and these are they which testify of Me. John 5:39.

Every book has a central theme. The central theme of the Bible is Jesus Christ. It is the story of the perfect world He created, sin's rebellion, the consequences of disobedience, and the efforts of a loving God desperate to save His lost children. The Bible is the story of Jesus plunging into the arena of human affairs to save a people who could not save themselves. In a world of self-centeredness, Jesus revealed the selfless love of God. In a world that did not love Him, Jesus loved unconditionally. "God demonstrates His own love toward us, in that while we were still sinners, Christ died for us" (Rom. 5:8).

I have seen this incredible love story touch the lives of millions around the world in our It Is Written evangelistic meetings. During our meetings in Madras, India, one of the local Bible instructors asked to be assigned to the worst area in town—a barrio known for its gangs, thieves, drugs, and drunkenness. One day while she was visiting people in that area, Jesus came face to face with the local gang leader. The gang leader confronted her and said, "Old woman, get out of here with your Jesus."

"Young man," she replied, "tell me why you don't love Him as I do." The gang leader began to curse and yell. She patiently listened. When he calmed down, she told him about the Jesus who changed her life. The Jesus who filled her heart with love and joy and peace. The tough, hardened gang leader began to weep. "Old woman, please come with me to all the gang members in this barrio to tell them about the love of Jesus too."

The Christ of Scripture transformed this doubter's heart. There is a love that flows from the pages of Scripture that changes our lives also. There is nothing we can do to change God's love for us. All of our sins will not keep Him from loving us.

The Bible speaks to us of a love so amazing, so incredible, so unparalleled, so matchless, so awesome that, if we let it, that love will change our lives.

ENEMIES NO MORE

But God demonstrates His own love toward us, in that while we were still sinners, Christ died for us. Rom. 5:8.

Martin Niemoller, a German Protestant theologian, languished for months in one of Hitler's prisons. During his imprisonment he spent days thinking about the questions of life and death. He reevaluated his life, meditating on God's enormous love for him. Quietly he prayed, "Lord, I cannot resist your love any longer. I accept your forgiveness. I believe I am your child." Niemoller had struggled with the thought of his own inadequacy and guilt. He felt unworthy, sinful, and distant from God. But in a wretched prison camp he was spiritually transformed.

At last released from prison, Niemoller made this penetrating observation: "It took me a long time to learn that God is not the enemy of His enemies." The apostle Paul outlines this truth marvelously: "But God demonstrates His own love toward us, in that while we were still sinners, Christ died for us. Much more then, having now been justified by His blood, we shall be saved from wrath through Him. For if when we were enemies we were reconciled to God through the death of His Son, much more, having been reconciled, we shall be saved by His life" (Rom. 5:8-10).

When we were His enemies, He was our friend. When we turned our backs on Him, He turned His face toward us. When we ran from Him, He ran to us. The glory of His grace is that He accepts the unacceptable, forgives the unforgivable, and loves the unlovable. Since we are forgiven, we can be forgiving. Since we are loved, we can be loving.

This thought is captured magnificently in *Steps to Christ,* page 15: "Such love is without a parallel. Children of the heavenly King! Precious promise! Theme for the most profound meditation! The matchless love of God for a world that did not love Him! The thought has a subduing power upon the soul and brings the mind into captivity to the will of God." This is the gospel and the good news of grace.

God's unconditional, changeless love is the central theme of the Bible. When we open His Word, we come face to face with His love.

January 12

LONELY NO LONGER

Since you were precious in My sight, you have been honored, and I have loved you; therefore I will give men for you, and people for your life. Isa. 43:4.

Clara Anderson was a maid in San Francisco. She was a very gentle woman and very conscientious. One day, after having worked for the same employer for 15 years, she disappeared. She seemed to have just dropped out of sight. Then miraculously, after days of searching, the city's Social Services Department found her.

Clara was in the process of starving herself to death in a mountain hideout outside of San Francisco. She said, "I want to die; leave me alone." When a reporter interviewed her, Clara said, "Look, nobody cares about me. I am just a maid, just one of thousands in society doing menial tasks. My life is of no value. I have no close relatives, no family, no friends. I'm so lonely that I don't want to live. There's no one I consider close to me, nobody I can talk to, nobody I can open my heart to. So just let me die, because nobody really cares."

There is good news for all the Clara Andersons of life. Somebody loves you more than you will ever realize. When God created you, He threw away the pattern. There is no one else like you in the universe. When the genes and chromosomes came together to form the unique biological structure of your personality, God made a one-of-a-kind you. You are special to Him. If He loses you, there is no way to replace you. God looks at you and says that you are precious. You are honorable. You are loved.

"He cares for each one as if there were not another on the face of the earth" (*The Desire of Ages,* p. 480), and "He watches over His children with a love that is measureless and everlasting" (*The Ministry of Healing,* p. 482).

On those days when you feel alone, remember that the Creator of the universe loves you with an immense love. In those moments of your life when you feel like all hope is gone, remember that the Creator of the universe is your best friend. He is committed to your eternal happiness. He is interested in every aspect of your life. He longs to fill your life with a sense of purpose.

His plans for your life are bigger, greater, and higher than you can possibly imagine. Choose today to come out of your dark dungeon of despair into the bright, warm sunshine of His love. Simply put, He cares. Let Him fill your heart, and rejoice.

BLESSED ASSURANCE

Let us draw near with a true heart in full assurance of faith, having our hearts sprinkled from an evil conscience and our bodies washed with pure water. Heb. 10:22.

One of the great Christian hymns is the well-known "Blessed Assurance." The melody was written by Mrs. Joseph Knapp. Her husband was the president of the Metropolitan Life Insurance Company. One day Knapp invited the prolific hymn writer Fanny Crosby to her home. Knapp wanted her to listen to a new melody she had composed.

Knapp sat down at the piano and began playing the melody. As she played she asked Crosby what thoughts were coming into her mind—what the melody suggested to her. Crosby responded, "Mrs. Knapp, your husband deals in life insurance. My heavenly Father deals in assurance. This melody suggests to me: Blessed assurance, Jesus is mine."

The word "assurance" means an inner confidence. Assurance is a sense of security. It also speaks of a sense of belonging and acceptance. In Christ we are accepted as children of God. In Christ we have the absolute confidence that our guilt is gone and our sins are forgiven. In Christ we have complete assurance that the gift of eternal life is ours.

The book of Hebrews reveals that as children of God we can have "the full assurance of hope until the end" (Heb. 6:11) and the "full assurance of faith" (Heb. 10:22). It is certainly not God's will for His children to be filled with uncertainty. The plan of salvation offers much more than nervous anxiety regarding our salvation. God longs for us to be filled with assurance.

Satan hates it when a child of God accepts Christ by faith and receives the blessed assurance of forgiveness, pardon, and freedom from guilt. Ellen White wrote, "Satan is ready to steal away the blessed assurances of God. He desires to take every glimmer of hope and every ray of light from the soul; but you must not permit him to do this. Do not give ear to the tempter, but say, 'Jesus has died that I might live. He loves me, and wills not that I should perish. I have a compassionate heavenly Father; and although I have abused His love, though the blessings He has given me have been squandered, I will arise, and go to my Father'" (*Steps to Christ,* p. 53).

In the parable of the prodigal son the father accepted his boy back home. With his father's signet ring placed on his finger, the wayward son received the absolute assurance of his father's love. Like the prodigal son, we too find love, acceptance, and forgiveness in the Father's heart. What confidence, what security, what hope, what blessed assurance.

FORGIVE AS YOU ARE FORGIVEN!

And be kind to one another, tenderhearted, forgiving one another, even as God in Christ forgave you. Eph. 4:32.

Jacquie sat on one side of the room, the board members on the other. The chasm between them seemed almost impossible to span.

Jacquie had grown up in her hometown church, but the ties were severed when she left her first husband and married another man. Now, 20 years later, she desired rebaptism. She sobbed out her repentance and asked for forgiveness.

Silence followed. The board knew her situation well, the pain it had brought the congregation. Could they bridge the chasm?

I knew I had to speak. I spoke kindly but directly. "She has suffered enough. Let's not give her any more pain. Paul's counsel is for us to be kind to one another, 'tenderhearted, forgiving one another, even as God for Christ's sake hath forgiven you' (Eph. 4:32, KJV). If God, in all of His perfection, accepts and forgives us, we can forgive Jacquie."

With quivering lips, her voice cracking, she responded. "I know I have done wrong," she said. "For years I have felt guilty. At times the guilt has almost driven me crazy. Please accept me."

I noticed a tear in the first elder's eye. Then I realized that most of the church board were crying. Soon a chorus of voices responded in unison, "Of course—of course we will accept you." Warmth, love, and acceptance filled the room. Board members reassured Jacquie of their love. Some hugged her. Others squeezed her hand in the warmth of Christian fellowship.

I stood back, recognizing again that our church was never more the church than at that moment. Here was the love of God in action. Here was Calvary demonstrated in the family of God.

As He hung dying on the cross Jesus prayed, "Father, forgive them, for they do not know what they do" (Luke 23:34). Forgiveness is an attitude of mercy toward those who have wronged us. It releases others from our condemnation because Christ has released us from His condemnation. It treats others as they do not deserve, because Christ treats us as we do not deserve. The essence of Christianity is forgiving as Christ forgives, accepting as Christ accepted, and loving as Christ loved.

NO EXCUSES

Therefore I abhor myself, and repent in dust and ashes. Job 42:6.

A company found itself in the middle of tense negotiations with union leaders. Company officials insisted that workers were abusing sick-leave privileges. The union denied it.

One morning at the bargaining table the company's negotiator held up the sports page of the local newspaper. He pointed to a picture showing an employee winning a golf tournament in town. "This man," the negotiator declared, "called in sick yesterday. But here he is in the paper beside a caption describing his excellent golf score."

After a moment of silence a union man spoke up. "Wow," he said, "think of the score he could have had if he hadn't been sick!"

Nice try! We can deny—we can try to cover up deceptions or our misbehavior. But it usually doesn't take us very far. Our sins have a way of finding us out. The wise man is abundantly clear: "He who covers his sins will not prosper" (Prov. 28:13).

Hollow excuses really don't provide many substantial answers. Flimsy reasoning is sometimes used to cover the grossest sins.

John Wayne Gacy, Jr., was convicted of murdering scores of children in his Chicago home. He claimed innocence despite the discovery of 27 bodies in a crawl space under the house. How did he respond as he faced death by lethal injection? Gacy said, "In my heart, as God is my witness, I haven't killed anyone."

"It wasn't really me." "I couldn't help myself." Such excuses have become all too common recently.

Scripture calls for something far different than lame excuses.

In a culture that often denies the reality of right and wrong, God calls for boldfaced, on-your-knees, heartfelt repentance. Repentance is a deep sorrow for sin. It is hurting because I have hurt the heart of God. It is weeping over my sins because God weeps over them. It is grieving over my sin because God grieves over it. It is feeling the pain of my sin because God has felt its pain.

Excuses produce only more guilt. Repentance leads to forgiveness. Forgiveness gives way to healing, and healing brings wholeness.

SOMEONE KNOWS YOUR NAME

To him the doorkeeper opens, and the sheep hear his voice; and he calls his own sheep by name and leads them out. John 10:3.

Peter Marshall, born in Scotland, was one of America's well-known ministers. He allowed God's voice to guide him throughout his life. One night in his childhood he decided to take a shortcut across the moors on his way home. The area was noted for limestone quarries. He was familiar with the terrain and felt he could safely navigate his way.

Though the night was starless and inky-black, he set out through the rock and heather. He could sometimes hear the far-off bleating of a sheep and the wind rustling through the heather. Occasionally a moor fowl fluttered up noisily. Otherwise, he was very much alone in the night.

Suddenly he heard a voice call out with great urgency: "Peter!"

Halting, he called back into the dark, "Yes, who is it? What do you want?"

There was no response, just a bit of wind over the deserted moorland. He concluded he'd been mistaken and walked on a few more steps. "Peter!" he heard again, this time with an even greater urgency. "Peter!"

He stopped in his tracks, squinted into the blackness of the night. Who was there? He leaned forward, stumbled, and fell to his knees. Reaching out a hand to the ground before him, Peter felt nothing but thin air. A quarry! Sure enough, as he carefully felt around in a semicircle, he discovered that he was on the brink of a limestone pit. One more step and he would have plummeted to his death. One more step—if he hadn't heeded God's voice, his life would have ended. Out there on the desolate moor Someone knew him, and Someone cared.

God knows our name. We are not some cosmic blur in the universe. God fashioned us. God made us. God created us. We are His. He cares. He loves. He knows us personally. We matter to Him. At times we may feel alone, but He is always there, calling our name, calling us into the security of His arms. Calling us home.

Ellen White writes, "Jesus knows us individually, and is touched with the feeling of our infirmities. He knows us all by name. He knows the very house in which we live, the name of each occupant. He has at times given directions to His servants to go to a certain street in a certain city, to such a house, to find one of His sheep" (*The Desire of Ages*, p. 479).

Jesus loves us that much. What troubles us troubles Him. What bothers us bothers Him. What hurts us hurts Him. We are His children. His interests are linked with ours. Nothing that in any way concerns us escapes His notice. Let your heart rejoice in His personal, intimate, loving concern today.

January 17

LOOKING UNTO JESUS

Looking unto Jesus, the author and finisher of our faith, who for the joy that was set before Him endured the cross, despising the shame, and has sat down at the right hand of the throne of God. Heb. 12:2.

Some time ago I received a letter from a mother who had lost two young sons, a 3-year-old boy and a 16-month-old baby boy. Both had drowned in a backyard swimming pool.

After a difficult period of grief she managed to refocus her vision. She began looking at Jesus intently.

She realized her life was worth living if God could use her in some way. She surrendered her life into His hands, placing her complete trust in Him. She began to experience an intense desire to get closer to God, to walk with Him each day. She found that this even made her feel closer to her two lost sons.

She wrote in her letter, "Now I hunger and thirst after God because of my love for Him. I know what it means to depend on Him fully, to seek Him with my whole heart, to love Him from my innermost being. I know how it feels . . . when God touches your soul and comforts you. I know how it feels to rest my head on His bosom."

This woman looked intently at Jesus in her darkest hour.

How can we look to Jesus? Seeing Jesus in Scripture brings spiritual vitality to our whole being. In the Gospels Jesus heals the sick, multiplies the bread, raises the dead, forgives sin, delivers demoniacs, and calms storms. He brings healing, happiness, and hope. He overcomes disaster, demons, and death. He defeats sorrow, suffering, and sickness. He triumphs over sin and Satan. His miracles reveal His power. His parables reveal the teaching of His kingdom. His sermons reveal His eternal principles.

His life reveals God's love for the spiritually bankrupt. It shows the redeeming quality of His grace. He seeks. He saves. He forgives. He transforms. He makes hearts new.

As we look unto Jesus God will fulfill His marvelous promise in 2 Corinthians 3:18: "But we all, with unveiled face, beholding as in a mirror the glory of the Lord, are being transformed into the same image from glory to glory, just as by the Spirit of the Lord." True, lasting character change comes as the Spirit of God impresses upon our minds the life-changing principles we are studying in Scripture. "It is a law of the mind that it gradually adapts itself to the subjects upon which it is trained to dwell" (*Patriarchs and Prophets,* p. 596). As the old hymn states: "Look upon Jesus, sinless is He; Father, impute His life unto me. My life of scarlet, my sin and woe, cover with His life, whiter than snow." Looking unto Jesus, we are changed. Let us look daily to Him, becoming more and more like the lovely Jesus we admire so much.

January 18

WIRED FOR GOD

This people I have formed for Myself; they shall declare My praise. Isa. 43:21.

In 1975 a Harvard physician named Herbert Benson wrote a best-seller titled *The Relaxation Response.* He had developed a simple technique to help people reduce stress. He taught them to relax by focusing on some positive mental image. For many people the results were remarkable. They had reduced heart rates, respiration, and stress-related hormones. Dr. Benson was even able to help people who had difficulty sleeping.

Then Dr. Benson began to notice something especially interesting. A certain subgroup of patients benefited from the "relaxation response" more than others. They had even better health, even more rapid recoveries. They were religious people, people who said they felt a sense of closeness to God as they fixed their minds on His goodness. People who meditated about the awesome love and power of God were healthier than those who did not.

Dr. Benson began to study exactly what was happening to these people when they experienced this closeness to God. Scientists took a new look at the brain's wiring. They observed how different parts of the brain react when stimulated. They pinpointed the headquarters of religious experience in the brain, a small almond-shaped structure called the amygdala.

Neuroscientist Rhwan Joseph concluded, "The ability to have religious experiences has a neuroanatomical basis." In other words, we have religion in our heads.

Dr. Benson puts it even more strongly. In his book *Timeless Healing* he writes, "Our genetic blueprint has made believing in an Infinite Absolute part of our nature." The doctor goes on to say, "We are wired for God." The Bible agrees. The prophet Isaiah exclaims, "This people I have formed for Myself; they shall declare My praise" (Isa. 43:21).

As our muscles are programmed to exercise, and our hearts designed to function efficiently on a low-fat diet, so our brains are wired to praise

God. Our brains are specifically designed for praise. When we praise God the electrical impulses of the brain stimulate the production of positive chemical endorphins. These endorphins are health- and life-giving. *The Ministry of Healing* states, "Nothing tends more to promote health of body and of soul than does a spirit of gratitude and praise" (p. 251).

We are programmed to praise. Today let your heart be filled with the life-giving, health-producing, wellness-stimulating attitude of praise.

January 19

GOD'S LOVE PENETRATES A RUSSIAN PRISON CAMP

Who shall separate us from the love of Christ? Shall tribulation, or distress, or persecution, or famine, or nakedness, or peril, or sword? . . . Yet in all these things we are more than conquerors through Him who loved us. Rom. 8:35-37.

God's love reaches people in every circumstance of their lives. In disappointment, disaster, and even in death God's love is there. In tears, tragedy, and terror God's love is there. In sickness, suffering, and sorrow God's love is there. In worry, want, and war God's love is there.

God's love penetrates prisons. In the Soviet Union God's love showed up in some unusual places. When Christians were imprisoned for their faith, God's love still triumphed.

In 1983 the Soviet Union charged 27-year-old Valentina with transporting Christian literature. The young believer with a charming smile and a strong faith found herself in a work camp in Siberia. The camp was known as the "Valley of Death" because of its high mortality rate. Its prisoners felt completely isolated from the rest of the world. It was a place designed to crush the human spirit.

But Valentina discovered that God was bigger than the gulag. She found a Christian sister, Natasha. In the middle of the night the two young women would sneak out of their barracks and meet under the open heavens. They had moments of beautiful fellowship.

The temperature was often 40 below zero, and their work boots couldn't keep their feet from freezing. But their hearts were warm.

"We would sing and pray for a few minutes, go back to our separate barracks to warm up a little, then meet outside again," Valentina remembers. "Sometimes we stood silently, just gazing together toward heaven. Nothing was dearer to us than heaven."

During her five years of imprisonment Valentina didn't feel abandoned by God. She felt Him come very close. Many times when someone sent her a letter with a quotation from Scripture, the verses seemed to answer a very specific question or need. It seemed as though God the Father was communicating directly with her.

When she was released in 1987, Valentina summed up her experience with these words from Romans 8:35-37: "Who shall separate us from the love of Christ? Shall tribulation, or distress, or persecution, or famine, or nakedness, or peril, or sword? . . . Yet in all these things we are more than conquerors through Him who loved us."

Valentina wasn't just a survivor. She was more than a conqueror. She experienced God's love in prison. It was bigger than the terrible isolation of the gulag. It was stronger than the hatred around her.

In the circumstances you face today God's love is there. Accept this divine reality, and live in the assurance of His care today.

January 20

A LOVE THAT GOES THE DISTANCE

For He made Him who knew no sin to be sin for us, that we might become the righteousness of God in Him. 2 Cor. 5:21.

On December 31, 1995, John Clancy, a veteran New York City firefighter, led his crew into a burning vacant apartment building in a lower Manhattan drug district. As the fire raged out of control the firefighters were concerned that someone might still be in the apartment building, although the only ones who used it were vagrants, drug addicts, alcoholics, and prostitutes. Nevertheless, Clancy and his colleagues decided to enter the inferno to conduct a search and rescue operation. Smoke reduced visibility to almost zero.

Suddenly the second-floor ceiling collapsed, trapping Clancy. His colleagues worked feverishly to deliver him, but when they finally pulled him out, it was too late. His body was burned beyond recognition. The last day of 1995 was the last day of this courageous firefighter's life. He left behind a wife who was six months pregnant and the future they were planning together.

John Clancy believed that all life was valuable, and was willing to risk his own to save whoever might be in the building. He left the safety of his own home for the danger of a raging fire. He entered the flames to save lives and lost his own. His devotion to duty cost him his life. He could not stand idly by when he knew others were dying.

Investigators discovered that the fire had been deliberately set. Edwin Smith, one of the "down and outers" who was reportedly in the building, set the fire. John Clancy was attempting to save the one who burned the building down. He gave his life for an arsonist.

Two thousand years ago another walked into the fires of death itself to save us. He delivered us from the blazing inferno of hell's fires. When Christ died He voluntarily took death's curse upon Himself. Today's text declares, "For He made Him who knew no sin to be sin for us, that we might become the righteousness of God in Him." Jesus never sinned, but He became sin for us. He voluntarily took upon Himself all of the shame and guilt for our sins.

He died the death we deserved so we could live the life He deserved. When Jesus suffered the excruciating death of the cross, He felt the separation from His Father. In the words "My God, My God, why have You forsaken Me?" (Matt. 27:46) Jesus expresses His sense of utter lostness. He could not see through the doors of the tomb. Sin shut out the Father's face. Our Savior experienced the death that sinners will die.

Jesus' love went the distance. He experienced the agonies of hell itself to save us. In the light of such love all we can do is fall at His feet and worship Him forever. He is worthy of our highest praise.

January 21

IN THE STORMS OF LIFE

Therefore, in all things He had to be made like His brethren, that He might be a merciful and faithful High Priest in things pertaining to God, to make propitiation for the sins of the people. Heb. 2:17.

A storm brewed just ahead of the English steamboat *Ariel.* The crew urged all passengers to safety below decks. But one passenger approached the captain with an odd request. He wanted to be lashed to a mast on the deck.

The captain stared in surprise at this small man with a weathered face. At length, crew members did as the man asked.

The steamboat sailed into the teeth of the storm. For four hours the wind drove waves furiously around the boat. And the passenger stood there paralyzed, helpless. He had known he would be terribly frightened. He knew he wouldn't be able to stay above deck if given a choice.

But he wanted, as he said later, to really see the storm. To feel the storm, to have the storm blow itself into him until he became a part of it. That's why he had himself bound to a mast.

After this experience the passenger, famed painter Joseph Mallord William Turner, went back to his studio and painted a remarkable picture that captured the awesome energy of the elements. It became one of the great artist's masterpieces.

Only after the artist had experienced the storm could he fully understand its fury. He painted a masterpiece because he personally had felt the fierceness of the wind, the pelting of the rain, the rocking of the boat, the salt spray of the waves, and the horrendous claps of thunder in the darkness of the night. Before Jesus could fully redeem us, He needed to experience what we experience in order to be our perfect Savior. He too needed to experience the fury of the storm. He needed to experience all of life's challenges. He needed to be wrenched with all of life's anguish and torn apart with all of life's heartbreak. If you are feeling lonely, Jesus understands, for He felt lonely too when His people rejected Him.

Has someone betrayed you? Do you feel hurt? Jesus felt hurt when one of His best friends betrayed Him. Is your body wracked with pain? His was as He hung on the cross. Do you face temptations that just seem to overpower you? Jesus experienced Satan's fiercest temptations. He understands. Through it all He was faithful. We can come to Him with all of our sorrows, disappointments, pain, and temptation. He will strengthen us to triumph just as He did. We have a sympathizing Savior who understands us and who is there to give us daily strength to meet life's greatest challenges.

January 22

SAVING GRACE

For all have sinned and fall short of the glory of God, being justified freely by His grace through the redemption that is in Christ Jesus. Rom. 3:23, 24.

Tuesday, September 11, 2001. Four teams of hijackers commandeered four separate airplanes and used them as instruments of death. An American Airlines jet streaked across the New York skyline and slammed into one of the twin towers of the World Trade Center. Minutes later another hijacked jet, a United Airlines flight, hurtled into the second tower. Another plane dove into the Pentagon, while a fourth crashed in a remote area near Shanksville, Pennsylvania.

One image indelibly impressed upon my mind is a group of weary firefighters, covered with soot, emerging from the smoke of the World Trade Center. They are carrying a frail old man away from the wreckage. The headline in huge red letters reads "Saving Grace." The caption: "Facing mortal danger, they risked their lives to save others."

That picture speaks to my heart. Those who were frail and weak could never have gotten out of the burning building alone. They needed a deliverer. They needed someone willing to risk life and limb. They needed a savior. Without someone who cared, someone willing to plunge into the flames, someone willing to die if necessary, the trapped had no hope.

We too are condemned to the flames. "For all have sinned and fall short of the glory of God" (Rom. 3:23), and "The wages of sin is death" (Rom. 6:23).

We cannot save ourselves. The incredibly "good news" of the gospel is simply this—Jesus leaped into the flames. He took on hell itself. On the cross He took upon Himself all of the condemnation of sin. My sin. Your sin. Jesus experienced all of the anguish that sinners will ultimately experience. He tasted "death for everyone" (Heb. 2:9). What a Savior! What a Deliverer! What a Redeemer!

In my imagination I see eternity's newspaper on our first day in heaven. Emblazoned across the front page is a huge picture of Jesus with blood-stained hands and a bruised brow, carrying me in His arms. When *you* see the picture, He is carrying you. The crimson headline reads "Saving Grace," and the entire host of the redeemed fall on their knees in praise. "Worthy is the Lamb who was slain to receive power and riches and wisdom, and strength and honor and glory and blessing!" (Rev. 5:12).

Forever and ever and ever. Amen.

January 23

DELIVERED

I can do all things through Christ who strengthens me. Phil. 4:13.

Anna was caught in the stranglehold of an intense struggle. Her modest apartment was located in the center of Honolulu's drug district. I met Anna while conducting a series of lectures on Bible prophecy in Hawaii. She seemed powerless to resist the drug dealers who daily urged her to buy another joint. Frequently she gave in, indulging her growing habit.

At the conclusion of one of my evangelistic meetings she pleaded with me for help. "Pastor, I'm so weak! I seem powerless to resist!"

I pointed her to God's promise: "I can do all things through Christ who strengthens me" (Phil. 4:13), and Anna made a marvelous discovery. A new sparkle flashed in her eyes. Jesus really would help her! He would actually supply His power to deliver her. Two of my associates visited Anna almost daily. The word went out in that drug-infested neighborhood: "Leave Anna alone! She's going straight."

Anna's discovery can make a powerful difference in your life, too!

The Christian life is not an initial commitment to Christ and then failure. It is not endless struggle against temptation on our own. Our Lord does not save us, then leave us helpless to battle with the devil. The Christ who redeems us from sin's condemnation delivers us from sin's power. The Savior who died to forgive us lives to empower us. We do not save ourselves; God saves us. We cannot deliver ourselves; Christ delivers us. "Many have an idea that they must do some part of the work alone. They have trusted in Christ for the forgiveness of sin, but now they seek by their own efforts to live aright. But every such effort must fail. Jesus says, 'Without Me ye can do nothing.' Our growth in grace, our joy, our usefulness—all depend upon our union with Christ" (*Steps to Christ,* p. 69).

Battling alone, we are powerless. The enemy is much too strong. His temptations are overpowering. The living Christ offers to do for us what we could never do for ourselves. He offers us His power, His strength. As we open our hearts to Him He will deliver us from the chains of sin that bind us. In Christ, through Christ, by Christ, with Christ, we are truly set free. He is our almighty Deliverer.

January 24

I OWE YOU MY LIFE

I have been crucified with Christ; it is no longer I who live, but Christ lives in me; and the life which I now live in the flesh I live by faith in the Son of God, who loved me and gave Himself for me. Gal. 2:20.

Stanley Praimnath sat at his desk on the eighty-first floor of the South Tower of the World Trade Center. Suddenly the nose of a 767 jet filled the sky outside his window. He dropped the phone and dove under his desk. Steel shrieked against steel as the ceiling crashed down. Electrical wires sparked. Desks and filing cabinets hurtled across the room. Smoke poured in. Stanley started sobbing and then praying.

People fled the building by the thousands. Horribly burned and profusely bleeding, they stumbled down darkened staircases.

Brian Clark was running down from the eighty-fourth floor when he heard cries for help. It was Stanley, who had somehow managed to crawl through the rubble but was now trapped under a fallen wall.

Brian pulled away charred debris and shattered doors. Finally he reached the desperate man. "You have got to make it through the wall," he yelled. "I can't," Stanley replied. "You have to do this," Brian shouted back. Stanley clawed his way until he was partly free, and Brian pulled him from the rubble. The two strangers hugged like brothers. When they finally got outside, with tears in his eyes Stanley looked at Brian and said, "Keep in touch, because I owe you my life."

When I think of the amazing love that saved me, my heart too cries out, "Lord, I want to keep in touch, because I owe You my life." The essence of the Christian life is fellowship with God. When two people are in love, they long to be together. Separation is painful. When we fully sense Jesus' love and commitment in saving us, our hearts respond in love. We long to be with Him. We want to spend time with Him in fellowship. We don't want to be separated from His love for an instant. "The price paid for our redemption, the infinite sacrifice of our heavenly Father in giving His Son to die for us, should give us exalted conceptions of what we may become through Christ. . . . 'Behold, what manner of love the Father hath bestowed upon us, that we should be called the sons of God.' 1 John 3:1. What a value this places upon man!" (*Steps to Christ*, p. 15).

God values us highly. He loves us immensely. He longs to be with us intensely. His love breaks our hard hearts and draws us to Him. Through Calvary, we owe Him our lives. The least we can do is to give back to Him the lives He redeemed and gave to us.

January 25

COUNTING THE COST

But what things were gain to me, these I have counted loss for Christ. Phil. 3:7.

No one can take from you what you have already given away. Paul consciously chose to give everything he possessed to Christ. Nothing was worth more to him than Christ. Nothing was more valuable than Christ's love or more precious than His grace. In comparison to His relationship with Christ, everything else paled into insignificance. When the apostle exclaims, "What things were gain to me, these I have counted loss for Christ," the word "loss" in the original language means "dung," "refuse," or "garbage." Christ is so incredibly precious that all of this world's treasures are garbage in comparison.

On December 8, 1934, Chinese bandits murdered two Presbyterian missionaries, John and Betty Stam. The thieves burned their home to the ground. Some days after the tragedy, Christian friends found Mrs. Stam's Bible among the charred ruins. On the flyleaf she had written: "Lord, I give up my purpose and plans, all my desires, hopes, and ambitions, and accept

Thy will for my life. I give myself, my life, my all utterly to Thee to be Thine forever. I hand over to Thy keeping all my friendships, my love. All the people whom I love are to take second place in my heart. Fill me and seal me with Thy Holy Spirit. Work out Thy whole life in my life at any cost now and forever. For me to live is Christ, and to die is gain."

Christ fills the empty heart. Christ enriches the poverty-stricken soul. Christ replaces the dung of this world with the priceless, matchless charms of His love.

Ellen White states it succinctly: "Whatever shall draw away the heart from God must be given up" (*Steps to Christ,* p. 44). The basic question in the Christian life is Who has your heart?

Jesus' teachings contain some amazing paradoxes. One incredible paradox is simply this: By giving all, we receive all. Today Christ offers us His all. His grace. His pardon. His mercy. His power. His courage. His comfort. His hope. His promise of eternity. The fellowship of His presence now and forever. In light of all He gives us, everything we give away is only garbage. What an exchange!

January 26

GOD EMPOWERS OUR CHOICES

And if it seems evil to you to serve the Lord, choose for yourselves this day whom you will serve. . . . But as for me and my house, we will serve the Lord. Joshua 24:15.

My friend Bill's father struggled with tobacco. Early in the morning Bill would see his dad pacing in front of the family farmhouse, fighting a terrible craving to chew tobacco. Often the old man took his chewing tobacco in his hand and threw it far out into the cornfield. Now he was free. He was done chewing tobacco.

But, as Bill tells the story, along about noon he would see his dad out among the cornstalks, head bent low, looking for something. What was he searching for? The tobacco he had thrown out in the morning!

Here's my question. If you were God, would you let him find it? "Oh no!" somebody says. "God would not let him find it!" But God did. Why? Because He gave Bill's dad the same power of choice in the afternoon that He did in the morning. God does not manipulate the will. God allows us to make choices. When we choose to put our will on the side of right, the Holy Spirit empowers our choices.

We do not overcome Satan's temptations through our willpower. We overcome them through God's power. Here is an often neglected, greatly misunderstood truth. We cannot overcome sin in our lives without God. And God will not overcome sin in our lives without us. In the plan of salvation our cooperation with God is imperative. As the Holy Spirit impresses our minds, we choose to surrender that specific sin that is offensive to God. Then the Holy Spirit gives us the strength to overcome. We do not overcome sin through our determined choice. Jesus made it plain when He said, "For without Me you can do nothing" (John 15:5).

Let's suppose I am in a large auditorium. The room is totally dark. It's impossible to find the exit. What if I had a shovel? How long would it take to shovel the darkness out? How much effort would it take to shovel all the darkness out? What if 100 people worked for three hours—could we push it out together? What if you guided my hand to a light switch on the wall? What if you helped me throw the switch? Immediately the room would fill with light. Why? The action of my finger, however small, threw the switch and connected the electrical wires with the source of power. When we place our will on the side of right, we connect with a source of infinite power. God's power flows into our lives. Dramatic, miraculous change occurs.

Christ longs to fill your life with His power. He longs to empower your choices. He will do it today. Why not yield to the impression of His Spirit now?

January 27

PRICELESS TREASURE

Again, the kingdom of heaven is like treasure hidden in a field, which a man found and hid; and for joy over it he goes and sells all that he has and buys that field. Matt. 13:44.

Colorado has a rich history of silver and gold mining. One of the most successful Colorado mining operators in the days of the early West was a man named Horace Tabor. He made millions from a site near Cripple Creek that he named Matchless Mine.

His wealth went to his head, and he began to do as he pleased. Tabor divorced his wife and married a beautiful socialite named Baby Doe. Soon misfortune overtook them. The price of gold and silver plummeted. Tabor incurred enormous debts. In the end he died a brokenhearted, poor man. But before his death he supposedly gave Baby Doe this admonition: "Have faith in the Matchless Mine; never give it up. It will give you back all that I have lost."

Despite this, the Matchless was soon lost to foreclosure; but for whatever reason, Baby Doe decided to live in a dilapidated storage shack near it, and continued there (at the generosity of the mine's new owners) until her death in 1935. The Matchless proved to have played out; if Baby Doe was hoping against hope that it would yet yield riches, her hopes were never realized.

One mine will never play out. There is one source of wealth that produces more and more. There is a mine of truth that is endless. The riches of His grace can never be exhausted. Jesus is the treasure hidden in the field. In comparison to all we have, our Savior is more precious still.

Someone has defined sacrifice as giving up something of lesser value for something of greater value. For example, when a person gives up smoking, they give up something of lesser value, cigarettes, which contribute to cancer and heart disease, for something of higher value, good health. Jesus' love is of inestimable value. His grace is incomparable. Receiving Jesus, we receive peace and pardon and power and purpose. Think of it. In Christ we receive an inner peace as He enters our life. He gives us a sense of calm security. He delivers us from the guilt of our past failures. He silences the accusing voices of a condemning conscience. In Christ we receive power. He imparts supernatural power to live. He is stronger than the habits that bind us.

The power of grace is greater than the power of sin. In Christ we have a new purpose for living. Christ gives us a new direction for our lives. He gives to life a new sense of meaning. There is no greater treasure. There is nothing of any greater value. There is nothing more precious. Christ is a mine that will never ever run out.

January 28

PAUL'S THREE "NOTS"

Not that we are sufficient of ourselves, . . . but our sufficiency is from God. 2 Cor. 3:5.

Therefore we do not lose heart. . . . The inward man is being renewed day by day. 2 Cor. 4:16.

We do not look at the things which are seen, but at the things which are not seen. 2 Cor. 4:18.

The apostle Paul was absorbed with Christ. In these passages he eloquently proclaims three "nots." In the first "not" the apostle declares that we are not sufficient.

The word "sufficient," as defined by *Webster's New American Dictionary*, means "adequate to accomplish a purpose or meet a need." It can also be defined as "capable of" or "able to do." Christ is the only one who can meet our deepest needs. Any attempt to meet the inmost needs of the soul outside of Christ is destined for bitter failure. Pleasure cannot satisfy our soul hunger. Popularity can't do it. Prestige can't accomplish it. Power won't meet the heart's needs. Only Jesus can truly satisfy. He is our sufficiency. Neither are we sufficient to save ourselves or fight the battle with our adversary alone. As the apostle states, "Our sufficiency is from God" (2 Cor. 3:5). Christ is our sufficiency. He is also our source of confidence.

In Paul's second "not," he exclaims that we do not lose heart. Our outward person may perish. Sickness may afflict us. Disease may ravage our frame. Old age may take its toll. Heart disease, cancer, or diabetes may devastate our body. In spite of what happens to us, Christ is working within us. He is our courage. He is our confidence. He is our comforter. He gives us hope for a brighter tomorrow. We do not lose heart. Christ lifts our spirits.

The apostle now comes to his final and third "not." "We do not look at the things which are seen." Christ is our vision. He lifts our sight from what is around us to what is above us. He lifts our vision from what is to what will be. He lifts our eyes from the things of time to the things of eternity.

During the London bombings of World War II, enemy planes pounded the city night after night. Fires blazed as whole neighborhoods turned into rubble. One little boy, peering out from a shelter, kept staring at the explosions in the distance. He stood there shaking and crying. But his father came quickly and turned his boy around and said firmly, "Face toward me. Face toward me."

The rest of the night, while bombs streamed down, the little boy would turn his face toward his father and stop shaking; the terror would drain from his face.

Today and each day Jesus appeals to us: "Face toward Me. Fix your eyes upon Me. Look at Me. I am your sufficiency. I am your confidence. I am your vision. Rest in My arms. Be secure in My love. Be hopeful in My embrace."

I AM PERSUADED

For I am persuaded that neither death nor life, nor angels nor principalities nor powers, nor things present nor things to come, nor height nor depth, nor any other created thing, shall be able to separate us from the love of God which is in Christ Jesus our Lord. Rom. 8:38, 39.

In 1556 a young man named Claes experienced a dramatic conversion. Studying Scripture in his Belgian home, he was overwhelmed with God's love. He concluded that salvation was through faith in Christ alone. Christ filled his heart and radiated from his countenance, and he just could not keep silent. The Christ whom he so passionately loved led him to share that love with others.

Church and state were united in sixteenth-century Europe, and the state church did not tolerate the slightest dissent. Claes was arrested and brought to Ghent because he challenged the church's view on salvation. The authorities tried to talk him out of his beliefs before burning him alive. He knew the only way he could avoid the stake was to give up those beliefs. But he held fast. Claes wasn't intimidated by the power of the state looming over him. He couldn't be coerced.

Claes was asked, "What is your faith?" He replied, "I believe only in Christ Jesus, that He is the living and true Son of God, and that there is no other salvation, whither in heaven or on earth." Claes kept his eyes on the Lamb of God, who had shed His blood for him. That was his security and strength. That was his purpose. He took great comfort in the promise Jesus made in Matthew: "Lo, I am with you alway, even unto the end of the world" (Matt. 28:20, KJV).

Jesus came through in Claes's darkest hour. And Claes could have joy in the Lord his God. In the last moments of his life, just before his execution, our Lord gave him an unusual peace. Claes wrote, "My heart kindled within me with joy to the Lord my God, so that all my trouble and anxiety were driven from me as dust is swept from the street."

Claes went to his death secure in Jesus' love. He was at perfect peace.

All the demons in hell cannot separate us from God's love. Sickness cannot do it. Tragedy can't accomplish it. Misfortune and mistakes are not powerful enough to separate us from God's love. Divorce, disease, discouragement, disaster, and death itself are not strong enough to separate us from God's love. In our darkest moments God's love is still there. Like Claes, you too can exclaim, "Lord, Thou art faithful to Thy promise."

TRIUMPH IN CHRIST

Now thanks be to God who always leads us in triumph in Christ, and through us diffuses the fragrance of His knowledge in every place. 2 Cor. 2:14.

Her name was Soetgen. She was arrested for her faith in 1559 and separated from her family, including her husband, Claes. When authorities executed Claes, Soetgen tasted fear and loneliness. From her prison cell in Ghent, Belgium, she looked out at life going by and knew she would never be a part of it again. She sensed that she would never again see her children. With tears in her eyes she wrote a letter of calm assurance and encouragement to them. This letter has been preserved down through the centuries, and it calls us to faithfulness today.

She wrote, "Since it pleases the Lord to take me out of this world, I will leave you a memorial, not of silver or of gold, for such jewels are perishable, but I should like to write a jewel into your heart, if it were possible, which is the word of truth."

In her final hours Soetgen did not think of her suffering and imminent death. She longed for her children to be faithful to the Christ she loved. She longed for them to experience His grace, to be faithful to His truth. Her letter continues with these powerful words: "I commend you to the Lord. . . . May He keep you to the end of your lives. May He lead you to the New Jerusalem, that we may see each other with joy on the day of the resurrection."

Helplessness could have overwhelmed Soetgen. She could have just fallen apart. Instead she wrote a letter full of love and confidence.

Just before her death, Soetgen received an encouraging letter from her daughter, Betgen. Yes, her precious little girl still clung to Christ. Yes, the same faith still burned in her heart. Yes, the same love for Christ still filled her life.

On November 27, 1560, Soetgen burned as a so-called heretic. Her parting words to her children, hastily written with a trembling hand, were "Herewith I commend you to the Lord, and to the work of His grace."

There is nothing more precious than our relationship with Christ. There is no other relationship more important. To know Him is life's most important priority. Echoing and reechoing over the centuries from a damp Belgian cell, the witness of a faithful martyr's life urges us to "seek first the kingdom of God and His righteousness" (Matt. 6:33).

January 31

HEARTILY UNTO THE LORD

And whatever you do, do it heartily, as to the Lord and not to men. Col. 3:23.

Pieter Beckjen made his living by ferrying people and goods on the river Amstel. Sometimes he would sail down the canals of Amsterdam with fellow believers—so they could worship in secret.

When Pieter and his wife had their first child, the couple tried to keep the infant hidden so they wouldn't be forced to have it christened in the state church. But neighbors eventually betrayed them to the magistrates.

Pieter was tried, convicted for "crimes against the divine and secular majesty . . . which disturb the peace," and condemned "to be executed with fire . . . and his entire property confiscated."

They put this earnest ferry operator on the rack in one last fiendish effort to bend his faith. But it proved unshakable. Pieter was burned in January of 1569.

A close friend of his, Willem Janss, heard about the planned execution and hurried to the site from a nearby town. Wanting to offer some encouragement, he arrived at Amsterdam's gate, but the bar had already been let down. Willem had to bribe the gatekeeper to let him in.

He rushed to the site of the execution and arrived just as Pieter was being led out to the stake. Willem called out, "Contend valiantly, dear brother."

What gave Pieter such death-defying faith? Why was he willing to stand "heartily" for the Lord without wavering? There is one significant reason. He believed that Jesus was more than a good man. He believed that Jesus was divine and that His offer of eternal life was real. To reject Jesus was to reject eternal life. Pieter accepted the Savior's words to Martha: "I am the resurrection and the life. He who believes in Me, though he may die, he shall live. And whoever lives and believes in Me shall never die" (John 11:25, 26). Eternal life is life forever in the joyful presence of God the Father, Jesus Christ His Son, the Holy Spirit, and all the heavenly hosts.

The martyrs of the past saw beyond the flames to eternity. By faith they grasped the promises of God.

The promise is ours today: "He who believes in Me . . . shall never die" (John 11:25, 26). Our lives are "hidden with Christ in God" (Col. 3:3). His promise of the resurrection is certain. We can have absolute confidence that He will fulfill His word.

MORE THAN CONQUERORS

Who shall separate us from the love of Christ? Shall tribulation, or distress, or persecution, or famine, or nakedness, or peril, or sword? . . . Yet in all these things we are more than conquerors through Him who loved us. Rom. 8:35-37.

A man named Dirk Pieters, awaiting his execution in prison, wrote a moving letter of comfort to the one he called "my most beloved sister and wife, Wellemoet." He tried to pour the hope that animated his heart into hers. He quoted Christ: "Therefore you now have sorrow; but I will see you again and your heart will rejoice, and your joy no one will take from you" (John 16:22).

Dirk helped his wife focus on the future joy of being reunited in the presence of Christ. He wrote, "I admonish you . . . my most beloved . . . let us draw near with a true heart in full assurance of faith . . . I commend you to God."

He fought through his anguish. He didn't allow his present circumstances to overwhelm him. And he quoted the reassuring words of Paul: "Who shall separate us from the love of Christ? . . . Yet in all these things we are more than conquerors through Him who loved us" (Rom. 8:35-37).

Dirk looked to eternal realities. He looked through the bars and through the prison walls. He was able to affirm that absolutely nothing, not life, not death, not anything in all creation, could separate the believer from the love of God in Christ Jesus. This is what Dirk was able to share in his darkest hour.

When we face life's end, Jesus' promise of eternal life is our only hope. Staring death in the face, we find that Jesus' promise of "forever" makes all the difference. Sensing that this life is not the end buoys us up with new hope.

Ellen White wrote, "Happiness that is sought from selfish motives, outside of the path of duty, is ill-balanced, fitful, and transitory; it passes away, and the soul is filled with loneliness and sorrow; but there is joy and satisfaction in the service of God; the Christian is not left to walk in uncertain paths; he is not left to vain regrets and disappointments. If we do not have the pleasures of this life we may still be joyful in looking to the life beyond" (*Steps to Christ,* pp. 124, 125).

In Christ we look to the "life beyond." We are more than conquerors through Him who loved us. Nothing can separate us from His love. Daily look to Him and let your heart be filled with courage. Daily look to Him and let your life be filled with joy. Daily look to Him and let your soul be filled with hope.

February 2

EVER INTERCEDING

Therefore He is also able to save to the uttermost those who come to God through Him, since He always lives to make intercession for them. Heb. 7:25.

When Jacob de Roore was brought to Bruges, Belgium, as a prisoner in 1569, he entered a doomed man. He had dared to share religious beliefs that didn't quite fit in with church tradition. And in 1569 the church had the power to snuff out the lives of those who threatened it.

Those who knew him described him as a God-fearing, intelligent, kind, and eloquent man. He worked hard at an honest job, loved his family, and had never harmed a soul. Jacob had earned his living as a weaver and then as a candlemaker. He had no formal theological education.

Jacob's principal interrogator was a Franciscan monk, Friar Cornelis. Jacob stood fast through the long interrogations that preceded his execution. He simply relied on the plain teachings of Scripture as his authority.

Jacob wrote these words as he awaited his execution: "My affectionately beloved and chosen wife, be pleased to know that my mind is tolerable well . . . except that I am very sorrowful for you and for the children's sake, since I love you and them from the heart, so that I know of nothing under heaven for which I would be willing to leave you; but for the Lord and His invisible riches we must forsake everything.

"Do not faint because of the tribulation which we must suffer, but remember how the innocent Lamb, Christ Jesus, had to suffer from the beginning in the faithful. Hence the Lord says: 'He that toucheth you toucheth the apple of [his] eye'" (Zech. 2:8, KJV).

Jacob died June 10, 1569. He was filled with courage, believing that Jesus interceded for him in heaven. Mocked and ridiculed like his Master before him, Jacob remained steadfast. Beaten and tortured, he remained faithful. Even in death Jacob drew his courage from his heavenly High Priest.

Jesus is more than our role model. He is more than our dying Savior. He is our living Redeemer, our Deliverer, our High Priest. He ever lives to intercede for us. He is your heavenly High Priest. His strength, courage, and steadfastness can be yours today. Let your faith grasp the reality of His promises. Open your heart to Him. Allow His strength to flow into your soul. Believe His power is yours right now.

Your all-powerful Intercessor is at your side. He is mightier than all the forces of hell. Rejoice in His all-conquering strength today.

WHY DOESN'T SOMEBODY DO SOMETHING?

But God demonstrates His own love toward us, in that while we were still sinners, Christ died for us. Rom. 5:8.

Young Braun lived in a village near London with his wealthy parents 100 years ago. Though agnostic, Braun's parents felt that he should attend church at least once in in his life. Dressing him up in his little black suit and bow tie, they asked the governess to take him. A horse-drawn carriage carried the boy down cobblestone streets for his first visit to a church.

The preacher talked about a man nailed to a wooden cross. He described the nails driven through the man's hands, the crown of thorns jammed upon his head, the blood that ran down his face, and the spear that ripped apart his side. The preacher described the agony in the man's eyes and the sorrow in his voice when he prayed, "Father, forgive them; for they know not what they do."

He described the Savior's overwhelming despair when He cried, "My God, my God, why hast thou forsaken me?" And he recalled Jesus' faith when in commitment He said, "Father, into thy hands I commend my spirit."

The sermon transfixed Braun. Wouldn't somebody do something? Wouldn't the congregation rise up in one accord and take the man down from the cross? Halfway through the sermon Braun sat crying. As he looked around in astonishment he saw that the congregation was complacent.

"What's the matter with these people, Nanny?" Braun asked. "Why doesn't somebody do something about that man on the cross?"

"Braun, Braun, be quiet," his nanny replied as she tapped him on the shoulder. "It's just a story. Don't let it trouble you; just listen quietly. You'll soon forget about this story when we go home."

Is the cross just a story to you? Is it something simply to sing about, write about, preach about, write poems about, with little power to change lives? What is the power of the cross? What is the meaning of it all? The cross reveals the depth of God's love, but it also reveals the terrible nature of sin. At the cross we see how ugly sin really is. Sin is so terrible that it destroyed the life of the innocent Son of God. God is so good that He accepts all of sin's horror to save you and me.

Sin destroys everything it possesses. When we really understand how sin killed the righteous Son of God, we will desire to turn away from it forever. Sin murdered our best friend. You don't play around with something that murdered your best friend. Sin took the life of someone who loves you more than anyone else in the world does. You don't embrace some-one who just murdered your beloved husband or wife.

Why not make the commitment today that you will surrender any-thing that separates you from Jesus? Sin will destroy you just like it de-stroyed Him. Since your Savior loves you so, choose to give up anything that brings Him pain.

February 4

THE FORGIVING HEART

And be kind to one another, tenderhearted, forgiving one another, even as God in Christ forgave you. Eph. 4:32.

Carol didn't want to believe that her husband was seeing another woman. Her emotions screamed against the prospect of a di-vorce. After 25 years of what she thought was a happy marriage, Tom was leaving her for a much younger woman. Her hus-band's affair left Carol emotionally devastated.

Their youngest son planned to be married within the year. Carol had looked forward to being home alone with Tom again. She saw it as a time to renew their love. And now she wondered why. Why had Tom chosen to leave her after she'd given so much, after she'd lived her life for him? Gradually her questions turned to bitterness, then to anger. It wasn't fair! It just wasn't fair!

Loneliness and deep depression overcame Carol after the divorce. The more she thought about what had happened, the angrier she became. One night, in deep distress, she cried out to God for strength to cope with this unbearable situation.

Soon she started sorting things out in her mind. Her husband had ru-ined her past, but she wouldn't allow him to ruin her future. In spite of what he'd done, in spite of her bitterness, she could *choose* to forgive him.

Carol recalled Ephesians 4:32: "And be kind to one another, tender-hearted, forgiving one another, even as God in Christ forgave you." She made a choice to let the words of this text seep into her soul, transform her heart, and make her a new woman.

If Christ could forgive *her* sins when she had been *His* enemy, she could forgive *Tom* even though he'd become *her* enemy. If Jesus could reach out to her when she didn't deserve it, she could reach out to Tom when he didn't deserve it. She could ask Jesus to give her a new attitude and a transformed spirit. Through Him she could become tenderhearted, kind, and forgiving.

With her new attitude of forgiveness, Carol experienced an incredible sense of inner peace. She was still lonely, but her troubled heart was at rest. She had a settled confidence that she could leave her life in God's hands.

An attitude of forgiveness is healing. When the boil of bitterness is lanced, and the pus of anger drains, God's therapy begins. His Spirit then makes something beautiful of our lives. Forgiveness is not justifying the wrong another has done to us. Forgiveness is releasing someone who has wronged us from our condemnation because Christ has released us from His condemnation. When we truly realize how much Christ has forgiven us, we cannot help but forgive those who have wronged us. When we understand His forgiveness, we forgive.

February 5

THE HEALING POWER OF FORGIVENESS

For if you forgive men their trespasses, your heavenly Father will also forgive you. Matt. 6:14.

Naomi had come to Dr. William Wilson for more than a year. Abused as a child, she struggled with uncontrollable anger, despite having reached middle age. Her outbursts were so violent and debilitating that at one point doctors had recommended psychosurgery.

One day Dr. Wilson listened to Naomi talk once again about all the people she was mad at. He felt helpless before this deep-seated hostility. But then it occurred to him—if this woman could somehow find it in her heart to *forgive* those who had wronged her, she just might find healing. He realized that the power to forgive came exclusively from God. Naomi needed God!

But this solution seemed wildly improbable. He was, after all, a sophisticated psychiatrist. Diplomas, awards, and professional certificates of merit decorated his walls. How could something so simple make the difference?

Still, he had to try.

Dr. Wilson talked to Naomi about how her own resentment and bitterness were imprisoning her. Naomi started to weep. Dr. Wilson asked about her religious convictions. Naomi was hungry to know Christ. She just didn't know how to accept Him.

Dr. Wilson explained how she could receive the forgiveness that Jesus offered from the cross.

Accepting Jesus' forgiveness, Naomi began to change. Now she and Dr. Wilson were able to work on forgiveness as a cure for her chronic anger. It was a painstaking process. Naomi had to confront painful things in her past, and she had to consciously forgive.

But now she had a means of healing. Now she had the forgiveness that Christ had given her. In time, Naomi was freed from the anger that had plagued her emotional life. She began to enjoy healthy relationships with coworkers and family members for the first time in decades.

The single most powerful principle in emotional healing is forgiveness. When we have been deeply hurt by someone else, our emotions are damaged. Our ability to trust is destroyed. Our security is shattered. Forgiveness is God's healing balm for broken hearts. When Jesus hung upon the cross, unjustly treated and cruelly crucified, He prayed, "Father, forgive them, for they do not know what they do" (Luke 23:34).

Forgiveness opens the door of the mind to receive God's love for those who unjustly treat us. Forgiveness is not an emotion; it is a choice. Is there someone who has wronged you, who has hurt you deeply? Are you harboring resentment toward another person? Now is the time to choose to forgive. The anger and resentment and bitterness will destroy you. If Jesus could forgive those who unjustly crucified Him, you can forgive those who have unjustly wounded you. Right now, will you ask the Holy Spirit to give you the spirit of forgiveness for anyone who has wronged you?

February 6

WHEN YOU CAN'T FORGIVE, PART 1

For You, Lord, are good, and ready to forgive, and abundant in mercy to all those who call upon You. Ps. 86:5.

In 1985 President Ronald Reagan visited a German military cemetery at Bitburg and laid a wreath at the monument there. He intended this as a gesture of reconciliation, a way to finally say goodbye to the painful memories of World War II.

But that wreath caused an international outcry, because 49 SS soldiers were buried there, and Hitler's SS was responsible for many atrocities against the Jews.

The gesture of reconciliation was fine, people said, but President Reagan had no right to forgive what had been done to the Jews. Only the Jews could do that. As the poet John Dryden once wrote: "Forgiveness to the injured does belong."

Only the injured have the right to forgive. Essayist Lance Morrow explained, "President Reagan could forgive John Hinckley for shooting him.

But he could not forgive, say, Ali Agca for shooting Pope John Paul II. Only John Paul could do that."

When we have wronged another person, the Holy Spirit often prompts us to ask their forgiveness. Some people carry a burden of guilt for years. There are barriers between them and other people. Their conscience condemns them for something they have done to offend a family member or friend. When we hurt someone else, we have really hurt one of God's children. In a very real sense we have wounded the Lord Himself. Remember: "Forgiveness to the injured does belong."

The first step in spiritual healing is to confess our sin to God. It is written, "If we confess our sins, He is faithful and just to forgive us our sins" (1 John 1:9). When we come to God in sorrow, asking Him to forgive us, He delivers us from sin's condemnation. Our moral guilt is gone. Paul states an eternal truth in Acts 24:16: "This being so, I myself always strive to have a conscience without offense toward God and men." There is a difference between moral guilt and psychological guilt.

God delivers us from moral guilt the instant we confess our sin. He does not wait until we make things right with another person. Often psychological guilt remains until, in God's forgiveness, we ask the person we have wronged to forgive us. Since we are already forgiven by God, we now have a new desire for the person we have wronged to forgive us. When an individual asks us to forgive them for some wrong, and we—the injured, bruised, hurt party—genuinely forgive, a new relationship is often forged. Barriers are broken. Walls come down. Together we rejoice in the healing balm of forgiveness.

February 7

WHEN YOU CAN'T FORGIVE, PART 2

So that, on the contrary, you ought rather to forgive and comfort him, lest perhaps such a one be swallowed up with too much sorrow. 2 Cor. 2:7.

Grief and rage consumed Elizabeth and Frank Morris after a drunk driver killed their son Ted. Their anger only grew as they followed the trial of Tommy, the young man accused of taking their son's life.

They learned how Tommy had drunk himself into a stupor one night, climbed into a car, swerved down a road, and then smashed head-on into Ted's vehicle.

Frank Morris became obsessed with every detail of the legal processing, living for the day when Tommy would be found guilty. And Elizabeth, when she wasn't contemplating suicide, fantasized about his getting the electric chair and about her throwing the switch.

The couple's torment didn't end with Tommy's jail sentence. They considered themselves Christians, but the depth of their hatred shocked them. Elizabeth began praying for a way out.

One day Elizabeth heard Tommy speak at Ted's high school as part of his rehabilitation. He seemed genuinely repentant, and Elizabeth mustered enough courage to speak to him afterward. When she learned that no one ever visited him in jail, she decided to visit him.

The visit began with a few moments of tense conversation. Then Tommy suddenly blurted out, "Mrs. Morris, I'm so sorry. Please forgive me."

Everything froze for Elizabeth as she stared at her son's killer. She wanted to let go of all the rage and pain. And yet every human instinct shouted, "Revenge!"

In that moment, however, something happened that moved her beyond the logic of refusing to forgive. She heard the words that a Man had spoken from the cross. They seemed to fall down around her: "Father, forgive them . . . Father, forgive them."

Suddenly she could forgive, because she was forgiven. Elizabeth found herself praying silently, "Dear God, You lost an only Son too. Yet You forgave those who killed Him."

Elizabeth Morris forgave Tommy and asked for forgiveness for the hatred she'd nurtured for months.

Christ's forgiveness is the gracious attitude that melts our hard hearts. Christ's mercy disarms us. His love, in spite of all we have done to hurt Him, wins us.

When we lovingly forgive someone who has wronged us, their heart melts. They are surprised by joy. They are overwhelmed by our graciousness.

Today, reach out in loving forgiveness to anyone who has wronged you. Graciously forgive anyone who has hurt you, and watch the barriers fall. You will be amazed at the healing power of forgiveness in your own life and in the lives of people around you.

FROM MURDERER TO SON

If You, Lord, should mark iniquities, O Lord, who could stand? But there is forgiveness with You. Ps. 130:3, 4.

Yesterday I shared the moving story of Elizabeth Morris's forgiving Tommy, the drunk driver who killed her son. Now, let me tell you the rest of the story. Elizabeth continued visiting Tommy in prison. This godly woman convinced Tommy that God could help him kick his eight-year addiction to alcohol. Tommy also began an intense course of Bible study.

One day Elizabeth's husband, Frank, had to pick Tommy up for a Mothers Against Drunk Driving program. Frank wasn't sure he could carry on a conversation with the young man, but as they drove along Tommy talked enthusiastically of all he was learning from the Bible. It became apparent that he'd made a commitment to Christ.

Suddenly Tommy said, "I wish I could be baptized." As it happened, they were just passing Frank's church. Frank himself had been authorized by his denomination to perform baptisms. It seemed a providential moment.

Slowly the two men walked inside the empty sanctuary. Frank ushered Tommy to the baptistry, and they slipped into the water. As Frank lifted his hand and repeated, "In the name of the Father, Son, and Holy Spirit," he couldn't help remembering that he had performed this same ceremony for his own son.

As Tommy came up out of the water he threw his arms around Frank and sputtered, "Please, I want you to forgive me too."

And still dripping with the water of baptism, Frank felt Christ's costly forgiveness flow through him as he whispered, "I do forgive you."

Tommy's chances of complete rehabilitation weren't good from a human point of view. He bore the psychological scars of growing up in a troubled family. He'd abused alcohol since the age of 16.

But Tommy succeeded against the odds. He kicked the habit for good. He found a steady job, and he developed a strong sense of purpose for serving the Lord.

Why? Largely because he found in Elizabeth and Frank Morris the parents he'd never had. Because Elizabeth kept visiting every day. Because they petitioned the judge to allow Tommy to spend every Sunday in their custody. Because he began to eat in their home, pray in their home, study in their home. Because Frank asked him to help with outdoor work around the house.

This grieving couple found a son again in one whom every human instinct had taught them to hate.

Does forgiveness cost something? Absolutely! But is it worth it? Ask Elizabeth and Frank Morris.

February 9

IN GOOD HANDS

Blessed be the God and Father of our Lord Jesus Christ, who has blessed us with every spiritual blessing in the heavenly places in Christ. Eph. 1:3.

William P. Wilson, professor emeritus of psychiatry at Duke University, is a world-renowned specialist in his field. His articles on psychotherapy have been published in major clinical journals. Numerous specialists in the medical community have carefully reviewed his work.

As a committed Christian, Wilson has attracted further worldwide attention by applying biblical insights to the field of psychotherapy. His clients often feel a need for acceptance, love, security, and joy in their lives. In his book *The Grace to Grow* he tells the story of Peter.

Peter was born with severe visual impairment. Even with glasses half an inch thick, he could make out only shadows. As a child he never learned to read. Constantly teased at school, he soon dropped out.

At 10 he began stealing inexpensive items out of small stores. By 21 he was a compulsive thief. Stealing gave him a sense of satisfaction, a sense of power, of being in control. By 30 he had filled his garage with items from hardware stores from all over town. Though he never used the items, and kept them in their original packaging, he kept stealing.

Carefully analyzing Peter's problem, Wilson worked to bolster his self-esteem by sharing scriptural insights. Within a year Peter had developed an entirely new self-concept. Courageously he returned the items he had stolen. He began to read a large-print Bible. Miraculous, unaccountable changes took place in his life.

At a Christian retreat for doctors, lawyers, and selected government workers, half-literate Peter shared the testimony of God's grace in his own life. Holding his large-print Bible six inches from his face, he began to read the reassuring message of Ephesians: "Having predestined us to adoption as sons by Jesus Christ to Himself, according to the good pleasure of His will, to the praise of the glory of His grace, by which He made us accepted in the Beloved" (Eph. 1:5, 6).

The spiritual insights in Paul's letter to the Ephesians changed Peter's life. They made a difference for him, and they can make a difference for you. Here are five incredible insights from Ephesians 1:

1. Our Lord chose us before the creation of the world (verse 4).
2. Our Lord predestined us to be His children (verse 5).
3. Our Lord accepts us (verse 6).
4. Our Lord has redeemed us (verse 7).
5. Our Lord will gather us together as one family (verse 10).

Let your heart rejoice. Let your spirit soar. You are chosen in Christ. You are accepted by Christ. You will be gathered together with Christ. This is something to sing about, for we are in good hands.

February 10

ANGER IS DEADLY

For as he thinks in his heart, so is he. Prov. 23:7.

John Hunter, a famous eighteenth-century British surgeon, suffered from attacks of angina. Outbursts of anger aggravated the condition again and again. But rather than deal with this problem, Dr. Hunter just lamented, "My life is at the mercy of any scoundrel who chooses to put me in a passion."

Sure enough, one day a "scoundrel" put him in a passion. A fellow board member of St. George's Hospital in London engaged him in a heated argument. Dr. Hunter stomped out of the meeting and dropped dead in the next room.

The Chinese philosopher Confucius once asserted, "An angry man is always full of poison." Confucius' statement is physiologically true. An angry, bitter, unforgiving spirit produces negative chemical by-products that are health-destroying.

How can we deal with anger? Are there any specific scriptural guidelines to assist us in overcoming the anger we feel? There are. Biblical principles help us in dealing with anger from a new perspective. Anger is an emotion. We cannot always determine if we will become angry. But we can choose not to allow anger to control us. The apostle Paul makes a fascinating statement regarding anger: "Be angry, and do not sin" (Eph. 4:26). In other words, when you feel the emotion of anger, do not allow it to control you. Don't be overcome by the anger. Openly acknowledge that you are angry. Be honest with God. Give your anger to God.

To deny we are angry and to repress the emotion of anger may produce only further physical and emotional trauma. To express our anger at others inappropriately will create only further barriers and alienate other people from us. To express our anger to God, honestly sharing the way we feel, opens our hearts to receive heaven's healing.

When Cain was filled with anger against his brother Abel, God asked, "Why are you angry?" (Gen. 4:6). It would be well for us to ask the same question. After honestly acknowledging our anger to God, we too might ask, Why am I angry? Identifying the source of anger, we are urged by the apostle Paul to deal with it quickly. He encourages us not to "let the sun go down on your wrath, nor give place to the devil" (Eph. 4:26, 27).

If we do not deal with our anger quickly, the devil will use our anger to control us. When you feel anger growing inside of you, take the anger to God. Ask Him to reveal the source of the anger. Confess your anger to Him. If necessary, go to the person you feel angry toward and make every effort to make things right. Remember that anger is not your friend. It will destroy you if it is uncontrolled.

Make things right if possible. Remember, it is not wrong to feel angry. It is wrong when that anger controls you and you do nothing about it.

February 11

HE RESCUED ME

And she will bring forth a Son, and you shall call His name Jesus, for He will save His people from their sins. Matt. 1:21.

During Sir Ernest Shackleton's expeditions to the Antarctic in 1914, his ship, the *Endurance*, was crushed in an ice floe in the Weddell Sea. The crew drifted for days until they could make a landing on Elephant Island.

Shackleton had the men set up camp where they could preserve their supplies and try to survive the coming winter. But he soon realized that no one would be coming to rescue them. No one had any idea where they were. They were cut off from the world by the freezing, stormy ocean. There was only one hope of a rescue: someone had to cross that hostile ocean and get help.

Shackleton prepared a 20-foot lifeboat for the voyage. From volunteers he picked a crew of five to join him. They would have to cross 800 miles of tempestuous sea in order to reach a Norwegian whaling station on the frozen island of South Georgia.

It seemed an impossible task in an open boat at the stormiest time of year. But Shackleton set out with his men. For days they huddled under a makeshift canvas covering, keeping the bow turned into the fiercest waves, praying that the wind wouldn't tear their small sail away. They endured bone-chilling cold, sleeping bags frozen stiff, icy water streaming down their backs, hunger, and thirst.

Seventeen days after their voyage began, when all were nearly dead of exposure and thirst, they spotted the black cliffs of South Georgia! Shackleton had made it through. Soon a ship would be on its way to rescue the rest of his stranded men.

When God looked down on our predicament and saw that we were isolated on our island, surrounded by a boundless sea of sin, He plunged into that hostile sea Himself. He took on Himself the icy vastness of the evil in humankind.

Jesus came on a rescue mission. We were helplessly lost. Marooned on this rocky, barren island called earth, we couldn't save ourselves.

Jesus left the security of home. He left the worship and adoration of the angels and the glory of eternity. Most of all, Jesus left the intimacy of His fellowship with the Father. Jesus had existed with the Father from eternity. Have you ever been separated from someone you love for days, for months, for years? You know how painful separation is. You know the inner emptiness it brings.

Jesus risked all to come to earth. He faced the full power of Satan's temptations. He experienced the enormous wrath of Satan's hatred. Jesus made this amazing sacrifice for one reason. He loved you too much to remain in heaven while you were lost. He loved you too much to remain with the Father while you were caught in the grip of sin. He plunged into the icy ocean of this sinful world to redeem us. What a Savior! What a Redeemer! What a Deliverer! He is worth serving and loving forever.

February 12

A BETTER TOMORROW

And if I go and prepare a place for you, I will come again and receive you to Myself; that where I am, there you may be also. John 14:3.

One of our greatest psychological needs is hope. Desperate people who feel trapped do unpredictable things to themselves and others. Someone has said, "You can live a few weeks without food, a few days without water, but only a few moments without hope." Hope lifts our spirits. Hope encourages our hearts. Hope inspires us to hang on in life's toughest times. Sometimes all we need to preserve us is a glimmer of hope that someday things will be better than they are today.

Jesus gave His disciples every reason to hope. Just before His crucifixion He encouraged them with these words: "Let not your heart be troubled" (John 14:1). In other words, don't be filled with anxiety. Don't let worry overwhelm you and fear control you, for "I will come again and receive you to Myself" (John 14:3).

Jesus promised to come again. Jesus promised to take us to a better place, to the better place He is getting ready. He is the one who holds the future. He will have the last word.

There is one event that is big enough, glorious enough, to overshadow our fears. There is one event bright enough to overwhelm all of our anxiety and overcome our worry—the second coming of Jesus Christ. He promised that we would see Him, "the Son of Man coming in a cloud with power and great glory" (Luke 21:27). Jesus will intercept history. He has promised to come again.

The promise of our Lord's return punctuates Scripture. For every Old Testament passage on the first coming of Jesus, there are eight on the Second Coming. The second coming of Christ is mentioned more than 1,500 times in the Bible. It is found once in every 25 verses in the New Testament. The promise of our Lord's return gives us an unshakable hope in a time of uncertainty. Scripture assures us that history will end in the glorious appearing of Jesus, not with some horrible nuclear, biological, or chemical war. It's not the mushroom cloud, but the cloud of Christ's glory, that will rule the future.

Read Paul's confident words in Titus 2:13: We wait "for the blessed hope and glorious appearing of our great God and Savior Jesus Christ." The blessed hope can keep us looking up when tragedy strikes. It can keep us looking up in disease and devastation, in disaster and death, discouragement and depression. The blessed hope lifts us from what is to what will be. It focuses our eyes on the glories of heaven above rather than on the difficulties of the earth below.

The return of our Lord plants the seed of hope in our hearts. Hold on to the hope. Nourish it. Cherish it. Let your heart soar with the reality of this thought: *Whatever I am facing today, my loving Savior has a much brighter tomorrow planned just for me.*

OWN A BRIGHTER FUTURE

Now He who has prepared us for this very thing is God, who also has given us the Spirit as a guarantee. 2 Cor. 5:5.

The New Testament writers give us a unique perspective on the coming kingdom, on eternal life. They look forward to eternal life as something that has already begun within them. The good qualities of love, joy, and peace they see as samples of the good life we will enjoy in the coming kingdom.

Paul sums it up in Romans 5:21. He contrasts the old, faithless life with the new. He writes, "As sin reigned in death, even so grace might reign through righteousness to eternal life through Jesus Christ our Lord."

Sin reigned before. Cruelty and hatred and selfishness resulted in death. But now grace rules. It rules through righteousness, through those good qualities the Spirit produces. And it leads to eternal life. That's Jesus Christ's quality of life. It's something we can begin to experience now. It is something that will take us through the fire and the smoke, all the way to Christ's second coming.

Twenty centuries ago the Son of the living God gave Himself up for weak and sinful human beings. He gave Himself up because this world was hostage to the terror of sin. All the tragedies of this world weighed on His shoulders and slowly crushed the life out of Him.

But by that great sacrifice Jesus nullified the curse of sin. He broke the chain reaction of hatred and cruelty and suffering.

This is the Savior who is coming! He is the one who will appear gloriously in the clouds. He is the one who offers us the brightest of all possible futures.

It's time to own that future. It's time to claim it for yourself. Don't let the threat of terror intimidate you. Don't let acts of hatred cause you to react in kind. Own a brighter future. God has gone to great lengths to make it possible. He has made the greatest sacrifice to put it in your hands.

It's up to you. You can choose that destiny with the beloved Son of God. You can decide right now that you will be among those who welcome His glorious return. You can open your heart to ensure that your arms will be open later, on that great day.

Seize the blessed hope. Put your life in the hands of this blessed Savior.

NEW TERROR, OLD WAR

And war broke out in heaven: Michael and his angels fought with the dragon; and the dragon and his angels fought, but they did not prevail, nor was a place found for them in heaven any longer. Rev. 12:7, 8.

The day passenger planes crashed into the World Trade Center and the Pentagon, the world changed. The indescribable sorrow of such an act stunned us all. September 11, 2001, propelled us into a new kind of fear, a new kind of sorrow, a new kind of war.

Government officials have dubbed it "the new war on terrorism." In truth, it is a very, very old war. Surprisingly enough, it began in heaven.

When we think of heaven, we think of peace, not war. We think of joy, not sorrow; of calm, not terror. How could war break out there?

In His infinite wisdom God gave freedom of choice to all beings created in His image. To take away freedom of choice would be to remove a part of us that makes us unique. It would remove a part of the image of God.

God values freedom. When there is no ability to choose, there is no opportunity to love. When there is no opportunity to love, there is no opportunity for lasting happiness. Love can never be coerced.

Thousands of years ago one of God's creatures began to develop strange feelings within. He began to question God's wisdom and justice. His name was Lucifer, "son of the morning." He had occupied a privileged place near God's throne. But now he allowed jealousy to seep into his soul.

Lucifer wanted all of God's perks—especially the applause and the glory. Lucifer became obsessed with his position. Jealousy turned to poison in his heart, and he began to believe that he could be completely fulfilled only if God was out of the way.

Lucifer's jealousy turned into such hatred that he was willing to go to war against God, against Christ and His angels. He persuaded other heavenly beings that God was holding something back; that He wasn't fair; that He couldn't really be trusted; that they would be better off on their own.

Lucifer pictured God as the enemy. All his discontent and frustration focused on one thing: getting out from under God's control. He talked himself into believing that overthrowing God's rule was worth any sacrifice. It was worth starting a conflict he couldn't hope to win. It was worth spoiling heaven itself.

Lucifer lost that first great cosmic battle. God cast him out of heaven. God won and Lucifer lost. Every time God and Lucifer battle, God wins and Lucifer loses. God has never lost a battle with Lucifer yet. There may be apparent setbacks, but God will win the war. You can stake your life on it. You are on the winning side.

February 15

FACING FEAR

Then He arose and rebuked the wind, and said to the sea, "Peace, be still!" And the wind ceased and there was a great calm. Mark 4:39.

The small fishing boat crossed the Sea of Galilee in the afternoon sun. Jesus and His disciples had made the trip many times, but today was different. A storm suddenly whipped the lake into a frenzy. Waves crashed over the boat as wind savaged their sail. The seasoned fishermen panicked, sure that they would all be drowned.

But Jesus stood up and put a hand against the mast. Facing into the fury of the wind, He calmly spoke three words: "Peace, be still!"

And suddenly everything changed. The dark clouds overhead cleared. The wind died down. The waves subsided. The lake became calm.

The disciples sat stunned, looking out at the glassy blue water. "Who can this be," they exclaimed, "that even the wind and the sea obey Him!" (Mark 4:41).

Who could this be? The one who wields the elements in His hands. The one who can transform the most perilous of situations. The one who is in control of all nature. The one who speaks a word and the wind and waves obey Him.

Jesus creates peace. And Jesus promises to bring peace to each one of us.

Scary things happen in this world. Troubles will come our way. But Jesus has overcome all the evil on the earth. He has overcome the chaos on the outside and the chaos on the inside. He's stronger than anything that might threaten us. That's the reason He can bring us peace.

There is great power behind Jesus Christ's peace. It's something we can claim in the most troubling circumstances, when we are seized with anxiety or tormented by worry.

Fear boils down to what we think about the most. And peace boils down to what we think about the most. That's why the apostle Paul passed on the great promise to us in his letter to the Philippians.

There is a peace that passes all understanding. Even when our minds cannot understand, our hearts can still trust. We can come to this Christ, who calmed the storm, and lay all of our worries, anxieties, fears, and tension at His feet. How do we do that? By simply making a conscious choice to trust Him fully with our lives. By focusing on His peace rather than our problems. By allowing faith to deflate our fear.

February 16

TRIUMPHING OVER TERROR

Then I said to you, "Do not be terrified, or afraid of them. The Lord your God, who goes before you, He will fight for you, according to all He did for you in Egypt before your eyes." Deut. 1:29, 30.

There is an old saying: "When we look at what's going on around us, trouble grows. When we look at Jesus, trouble goes." There is a lot of truth in that statement. It certainly does not imply that there will be no difficulties in our lives when we trust Jesus, but it does mean that the crippling fear that dominated our lives is defeated.

The best way to cancel out the negatives of our stressed-out lives is to focus on the positive. The biggest positive of all is God. He is bigger than our problems. He is better than our failures. He is more promising than our worries. He simply outweighs everything else if we get a close enough view to put Him in perspective. If we get close enough for Him to really touch us. If we get close enough to really hear His voice.

James Martin is a clergyman and writer in New York City who wanted desperately to do something after the September 11, 2001, terrorist attacks. He wanted to offer comfort and counseling to the survivors of the suicide attacks, so he waited at Chelsea Piers, a clearing facility. Informed that they had more than enough priests, ministers, and rabbis, James wandered outside to a lot filled with U.S. Army vehicles, police cars, fire engines, and dump trucks. Impulsively he asked a police sergeant if they might be able to use a member of the clergy downtown at ground zero.

As soon as James asked the question he felt something icy in his stomach, something unexpected: raw fear. He would be going to the scene of unimaginable carnage, of mangled bodies being recovered from ruins.

The officer did say yes. Immediately a police car appeared to take him to what had been the World Trade Center. James's fear increased with every block the vehicle traveled south. Fewer and fewer people walked the streets. Ahead, smoke still billowed from the terrorist strike.

Arriving at the burned, twisted ruins of the towers, James found people who needed to talk. He found exhausted volunteers and stressed-out rescuers who had a story to get out. He found people who just appreciated his presence with them at ground zero. James's fear had been swallowed up by something else. God was there. The qualities of love and grace and mercy were stronger than this smoking ruin. And that's what he chose to look at. That's what gave him perspective. That's what made him feel safe at ground zero.

How can you feel safe today? By keeping your eyes on the grace, on the peacemaker, on our all-powerful God who is our refuge in times of trouble.

Bring your anxieties and fears to the one who understands you best. Tell Him what you're feeling. He's big enough to take it all in. And then please keep looking His way. Don't let the threats out there set up camp in here. Don't let the dangers in the world block out the one who so loved the world.

February 17

A REFUGE IN A TIME OF STORM

I will say of the Lord, "He is my refuge and my fortress; my God, in Him I will trust." Ps. 91:2.

It is a day I will remember as long as I live, though it began as any other Friday in June, in my hometown of Norwich, Connecticut. The sky was bright and clear. Puffy white clouds calmly floated overhead in a sea of blue sky.

I was in my early teens, whiling away the afternoon fishing with a friend. But that afternoon the fish weren't biting. Maybe the fish knew something we didn't.

Toward midafternoon the sky darkened. Suddenly, seemingly without notice, the winds picked up. The once-bright sky darkened. Loud rolling peals of thunder exploded above our heads. The lightning flashed as rain poured down in sheets. In a matter of minutes we were soaked to the skin. We knew this was no ordinary storm. With the heavy rain and the higher than usual water, the river overflowed its banks. Flash floods covered the roads. The winds reached gale-force proportions. We were trapped in a fierce hurricane with no place to hide.

We searched for safety. Finally we discovered shelter under a large bridge. The water levels were still low enough for us to find some temporary security there.

Our natural instinct in any storm is to find security. We long for a place of refuge. This is especially true when we face life's overwhelming storms. Make no mistake, there is a promised place for ultimate security. God Himself promises to stand beside us. The Hebrew prophets discovered that long ago. Look at Psalm 91:2-5: "I will say of the Lord, 'He is my refuge and my fortress; my God, in Him I trust.' . . . He shall cover you with His feathers, and under His wings you shall take refuge; His truth shall be your shield and buckler. You shall not be afraid of the terror by night, nor of the arrow that flies by day."

What a beautiful, reassuring picture of our mighty Lord. We find refuge under His wings. His faithfulness is like a shield. He is the one who can neutralize "the terror by night."

The psalmist chose ancient military terms to describe our God's protection. Living life in His care is more secure than the strongest military fortress. Trusting His power provides more defense than the mightiest army. His love surrounds us with a defense shield stronger than any ancient armor.

Although at times we may have some fears, we are not crippled by fear. Although at times we may have some worries, we are not paralyzed by worry. Although at times we may have some anxieties, we are not seized by anxiety. In the Father's hands we are safe and secure now and forever.

February 18

FAITH IN A FAST-FORWARD WORLD

For we walk by faith, not by sight. 2 Cor. 5:7.

The fast-forward world of the twenty-first century seems to have been blown to a much stormier place. In my home state of California, commuters have taken to solving traffic disputes with handguns. Freeway etiquette is a life-or-death issue.

Designer drugs are reaching junior high students. Crudity and violence crowd the spotlight. Hard-core porn has moved from the back alley to our living rooms. International terrorist groups are turning deadly biological viruses into weapons of mass destruction. And one little computer virus can bring an entire economy to a standstill.

As cartoon character Charlie Brown once declared: "I have a new philosophy. I'm only going to dread one day at a time."

How do we live one day at a time in the middle of a storm? How are we to grow healthy families? How are we to find a measure of peace?

In the New Testament we do find a command that is offered as the antidote to stress and anxiety. It's something the apostles repeat again and again: live by faith.

The New Testament addresses faith more than any other quality, with 483 references. Jesus Christ kept pointing the lame, the blind, the proud, and the broken to it as their only hope. The apostles centered their gospel around it. For example:

- "The just shall live by faith" (Gal. 3:11).
- "My righteous one will live by faith" (Heb. 10:38, NIV).
- "I live by faith in the Son of God" (Gal. 2:20).
- "We walk by faith, not by sight" (2 Cor. 5:7).

What is faith? How do you define it? What did the Bible writers mean when they used expressions such as "the just shall live by faith" or "walk by faith"?

In the New Testament the word for faith is a strong, dynamic, vibrant word. It means trust, belief, confidence in. The Bible writers always speak of faith in the sense of someone to place our faith in. Faith might be defined this way: Faith is a God-given gift that leads into a relationship of trust with our heavenly Father as a friend well known. It is the settled confidence that He will always do us good and never harm. It leads us to believe He will ultimately bring the best, even out of the worst possible circumstances, because He cares for us so much. The life of faith is a life of hour-by-hour, day-by-day continual trust. It is into this life of trust that I invite you today.

February 19

WHEN GOD GOT HIS HANDS DIRTY

To demonstrate at the present time His righteousness, that He might be just and the justifier of the one who has faith in Jesus. Rom. 3:26.

After the September 11, 2001, attacks the United States began to prepare a response. At first some Americans imagined that a few well-placed cruise missiles might do the trick. We had aircraft carriers with lethal war planes heading toward the Persian Gulf. We had spy planes we could deploy over Afghanistan that can track a single camel plodding down a mountain trail.

But soon we realized this wasn't going to be just a quick strike. We weren't going to win the war against terrorism from a distance. We were going to have to get close. We were going to have to get our hands dirty. There would be casualties.

The new war on terrorism requires an investment of time. It requires a major commitment. And that points to the heart of God's response to terrorism, His response to Lucifer's challenge. This is the key component to success in dealing with evil in our world today. This is God's answer. This is His move against jealousy and resentment and hatred. This is how He reacts to being regarded as the enemy.

To put it simply, God didn't fight the war from a distance. He came close. God got His hands dirty. That's the commitment He made in the person of Jesus Christ. And that is the good news we can cling to in the face of terror. The apostle Paul says, "Grace to you and peace from God the Father and our Lord Jesus Christ, who gave Himself for our sins, that He might deliver us from this present evil age" (Gal. 1:3, 4).

God wants to deliver us "from this present evil age." He wants to deliver us from its terrors. How does He do that? He gives Himself up for our sins. He does that in Christ on the cross. He becomes a casualty. He absorbs in His own body all that we fear. He absorbs in His own flesh all the world's misdirected hatred.

Does God simply order us around from a distance? By no means! He came to shed His blood for us! Is God looking for a way to condemn, to keep us in our place? By no means! He died to pay the penalty for our sin.

Does God have to control everybody to be happy? By no means! He gave up His life in order to give us our freedom. God made a spectacle of His love and mercy and justice on the cross. It was His ultimate act of counterterrorism. He exposed the ugliness of sin for what it is.

As a victim of violence on the cross, God demonstrated that violence and coercion are not the answer. He shows us why He has the right to be our sovereign Lord. It's His love that gives Him that right, His sacrificial love.

So the real question for us today is: Where do we stand when it comes to God's love?

Has God's love filled your life? Do you reveal His love in your family, at school or work, and in your daily relationships? God's love will win in the end. Let His love fill your life today and flow out to each person around you.

February 20

COMMITMENT: A FADING TRUTH

Whoever desires to come after Me, let him deny himself, and take up his cross, and follow Me. Mark 8:34.

Sociologist Stephen Cohen recently completed an in-depth study of contemporary secular culture in America. In his sample, he concentrated on what he called "moderately affiliated" Jews, the vast majority of whom are neither atheists nor strictly observant. What stood out most in all his interviews is something he calls "the sovereign self." Today the self rules; the self is the measure of all things. There are no higher commitments.

Other sociologists have discovered identical attitudes among the vast majority of Christians today. It's just the way people think. The self is sovereign. We don't look for great causes or great truths anymore. We don't look for something bigger than ourselves to belong to. We look for something that will fit our size, something that will feel comfortable. The self is sovereign today in ways our grandparents would have a hard time understanding.

And we've lost something in all this. There's a truth that has been fading from the landscape, a missing element in our lives. It's called *commitment.* Real commitments are hard to come by these days. We shy away from big promises. We avoid serious investments of ourselves.

One thing is certain: Even a casual reading of the New Testament reveals that Jesus called His followers to commitment. He called Matthew from his lucrative, powerful position as a tax collector with these two compelling words: "Follow Me." Scripture records, "So he [Matthew] arose and followed Him" (Matt. 9:9). Christ appealed to His disciples: "Whoever desires to come after Me, let him deny himself, and take up his cross, and follow Me" (Mark 8:34). Commitment, self-denial, and surrender are often overlooked in today's crossless, easygoing, accommodating Christianity. A compromising Christianity without commitment lacks substance. It lacks genuineness. It lacks power. It lacks real joy.

Jesus stated it well: "For whoever desires to save his life will lose it, but whoever loses his life for My sake and the gospel's will save it" (verse 35). Lasting satisfaction flows from a definite purpose. There can be no real purpose without commitment to a cause larger than ourselves. When we become absorbed in something bigger than we are, we discover the key to life's true happiness.

There is no greater commitment than to the cause of Christ. There is no greater purpose than to reveal God's love to others. We discover life's true meaning when we give ourselves away. The deeper your commitment is, the larger your life is. People committed to Christ live life to the fullest, because they are totally absorbed in Him and His mission to the world. Surrendered to Him, encircled by His love, they are motivated by a larger vision.

Today I invite you to this larger vision of faith.

February 21

COMMITMENT AND CHURCH ATTENDANCE

And let us consider one another in order to stir up love and good works, not forsaking the assembling of ourselves together, as is the manner of some, but exhorting one another, and so much the more as you see the Day approaching. Heb. 10:24, 25.

Commitment is a fading truth in our world today. Commitment to a church is disappearing. And yet it's one of the things we need the most. In fact, we're starving for it.

The author of Hebrews writes, "Let us consider how we may spur one another on toward love and good deeds. Let us not give up meeting together, as some are in the habit of doing, but let us encourage one another" (Heb. 10:24, 25, NIV).

Don't give up meeting together. Why? Because that's one of the ways in which you are built up spiritually. That's how you are encouraged to pursue "love and good deeds."

You have to make a commitment in order to get fed. You won't get fed driving by churches. You won't get fed hanging out in the foyer. You won't get fed sampling sermons.

You have to *belong* to a fellowship in order to be truly nurtured. You have to stick with a group through thick and thin, for better and for worse, in order to grow, in order to develop the kind of relationships that support you, that keep you accountable, that inspire you.

We've lost sight of that today. We don't want to submit to the guidance of others. We don't want to conform to the rules of a church body.

We've got a lot of freedom, but we're starving in it. Our souls are living on a subsistence diet. We're not getting the solid food we need. We're not hearing what we need to hear (but don't want to hear).

Here are three specific things you can do to receive the greatest spiritual blessing from church:

1. Commit to attend every week. Sporadic meals don't nourish your body, and sporadic church attendance will not nourish your soul.

2. Prepare your heart for worship by praying. God will give you the spiritual blessing your heart needs most. Anticipate a blessing. Believe that God is going to speak to you through the music, the prayers, and the sermon. Attend church with a joyous sense of expectation, not a dreary sense of obligation.

3. Be an active participant in worship, not a bored spectator. Bring your Bible. Concentrate on the words in the hymns. Enter into the spirit

of the prayers. Take notes on the pastor's sermons.

Commit yourself to receiving a blessing this week. God will surprise you with far more than you could ever imagine.

February 22

THE SEEDS OF TERRORISM

Let all bitterness, wrath, anger, clamor, and evil speaking be put away from you, with all malice. Eph. 4:31.

What makes a terrorist? How do terrorists think? What is their mind-set? Terrorists are people who have learned to hate. They focus on an enemy. They believe this enemy is responsible for their ills. They see their enemy as the source of all of their difficulties. Bitterness, resentment, and anger are the seeds of terrorism. When these seeds are fanned by the flames of hatred, terrorists will make any sacrifice to destroy their perceived enemy. Terrorism begins in the mind. When hatred lodges in the heart, terrorists are born.

We can give the devil a place in our hearts just as Adam and Eve gave him a place in the Garden of Eden, with disastrous results. He gains a place when we buy into hatred, when we center our lives around ourselves instead of God. Paul gives this urgent appeal: "Let all bitterness, wrath, anger, clamor, and evil speaking be put away from you, with all malice" (Eph. 4:31).

Put hatred and resentment and jealousy away. The expression "put away" is one of the strongest expressions in the Bible. It means "divorce yourselves from." God is saying, "Get a divorce from bitterness, anger, and hatred." Terrorists are people who express these qualities on a larger scale, a global scale. They are simply people who have the means to express their hatred dramatically.

The cosmic war between good and evil is going on right now in our own innermost thoughts, our own impulses. And we need to decide for sure where we stand when it comes to God's love.

The book of Hebrews tells us exactly what to do in order to stand in the right place. It pictures Jesus Christ as a great high priest, the one who justifies those who respond in faith, the one who can deal with the sin inside us. And then it gives us this invitation: "Let us draw near with a true heart in full assurance of faith, having our hearts sprinkled from an evil conscience" (Heb. 10:22).

Let us draw near. We need to get close to the one who can cleanse our hearts from animosity and jealousy. We need to get close with a true and honest heart. God didn't battle evil from a distance. He didn't just send a surgical strike from heaven. God came close. God got involved.

We need to respond in kind. Have you been keeping God at a distance? Have you just been nodding your assent to the right beliefs? It's time to do more than that. There's a war going on. And it's a war that must be won in our own hearts.

I challenge you to draw near. Get involved with God; start a real, openhearted, straight-talking, eye-to-eye relationship with God. Dealing with the stuff in our innermost hearts is a struggle; it's a fight. But it's a battle Jesus promises to win on our behalf. It's part of a war in which the enemy has been decisively defeated at the cross. So please, draw near. Draw near to the one who has earned the right to be your Rescuer, your Champion, your Savior.

February 23

RESILIENCE: THE ABILITY TO BOUNCE BACK

I can do all things through Christ who strengthens me. Phil. 4:13.

In recent years we've learned about the harmful effects of stress on the immune system. Stress breaks the body down. But did you know there is also research that shows something else? It shows that stress, coupled with a belief that a problem can be overcome, actually *strengthens* the immune system. The same stress accompanied by a different attitude makes a totally different physical impact.

Michael Rutter followed the progress of 125 kids on the Isle of Wight, off the British coast, and in inner-city London. Each was a child of people who'd been diagnosed as mentally ill. How could they possibly survive growing up in an environment that was, literally, crazy?

After 10 years Rutter found that many of these kids did just fine. The resilient children took positive action to address a stressful situation. They did something. Vulnerable young children managed to grow beyond a horrible situation because they believed their actions would produce results.

Two major studies looked at African-American and Hispanic adolescents in Chicago. Researchers analyzed the key difference between those who showed resilience and those who didn't. What was it? They called it "having a stronger cognitive motivational pattern." In plain English, they had more positive attitudes. They believed they could change their environment.

Did you know that this same essential quality, this same belief, is highlighted in the New Testament? Yes, Christ and His apostles understood what resilience is really about long before these psychological studies. And they shed a very special light on the subject. Paul was a man who knew plenty about adversity. "I can do all things through Christ who strengthens me" (Phil. 4:13).

The apostle's confidence was firmly grounded in his faith in Christ. Christ strengthened him to meet challenges such as imprisonment and shipwreck with cheerful resilience.

According to the New Testament, it's faith that enables us to keep believing that our actions will produce positive results in even the worst of circumstances. Faith is the key ingredient in resilience. Faith is the confidence that God is bigger than our problems. Faith is trusting not only that God is able and willing to solve our problems but also that He *will* solve them.

Your environment may be forbidding. You may have obstacles all around you. You may come from a dysfunctional family. You may have handicaps or addictions. But God is bigger than all that. Are you feeling helpless? God is bigger than your habit. Are people putting you down? God believes in you much more. Have you been labeled a loser? God has high expectations. Do you feel abandoned? God gave up everything to claim you as His own. You just can't have a better person on your side. Isn't it time to respond with a little faith? Isn't it time to respond with whatever faith you can muster? Tell God, "Here I am. I'm willing to act. I'm willing to take responsibility. I'm willing to make better choices. I'm willing, because You make good things happen."

February 24

GETTING PAST OUR GRIEF

Blessed are those who mourn, for they shall be comforted. Matt. 5:4.

In the aftermath of September 11, 2001, people across America looked for ways to get past their grief. The pain for many seemed unbearable. Spouses lost their mates, children lost a parent, and parents lost their children. Friends, colleagues, and neighbors intimately knew people whose lives were snuffed out in an instant.

Although there are no quick-fix solutions to the excruciating pain of such a terrible loss, Christian counselors share at least three fundamental principles that can hasten emotional healing. Here they are:

1. *Talk it out.* Find someone you can discuss your inner feelings with. Mourning is the natural response to loss. In the Old Testament tragic loss was usually accompanied by weeping and wailing. The Israelites expressed their grief dramatically. In today's more restrained society such public outbursts of sorrow are generally inappropriate. However, finding a

shoulder to cry on, expressing our sorrow, sharing our inner feelings, is a vital part of getting past our grief.

2. *Understand the cycle of grief.* Most people experience a range of emotions that are fairly predictable and normal. A few weeks after September 11, 2001, I spoke to a woman whose husband had died on one of the flights. She described how at first she had denied it. She didn't want to believe that her husband had been on one of the planes that had gone down. She experienced anger at the airlines. Discouragement overwhelmed her. Denial, anger, discouragement, and often guilt are normal emotions at a time of tragic loss. Expect this cycle of emotions. They do not always come in the same order. Their pattern is not always predictable, but generally they surface. Anticipating them ahead of time helps us cope with them when they do come.

3. *Accept the reality.* God does not always step in to prevent evil, but He is still in control. We live in a world where bad things happen to good people. In the war between good and evil there are casualties. He is allowing evil to run its course, but He is there in the midst of suffering. He is there to comfort those who mourn. He is there to encourage the discouraged. He is there to strengthen the weak. He is there to inspire hope in the downhearted.

Through our grief we can take hold of His hand by faith. We can let His light penetrate our darkness and His promises encourage our hearts. We can look for the better day to come.

February 25

A GOD OF NEW BEGINNINGS

For I know the thoughts that I think toward you, says the Lord, thoughts of peace and not of evil, to give you a future and a hope. Jer. 29:11.

God's plans for us are better than we can imagine. He is the God of a bright tomorrow. He is the God of a promising future. God can take over shattered dreams and make something beautiful out of our lives. He has the amazing ability to rebuild our lives. He is the God of new beginnings. A young woman whom I will call Leslie sent this incredible letter to our It Is Written office. It testifies to God's power to completely transform our lives.

"I am a committed child of God, but it wasn't always this way. My parents divorced when I was 10. I was abused and finally left home at age 14. I was in and out of mental and penal institutions until 18. I married, but after a few years was divorced from my first husband. I fell heavily into drug and alcohol abuse. I suffered through abusive relationships. I hated myself and didn't trust God, either. I used prostitution to get drug money. In 1993 I was homeless and married to a drug addict. At different times I contemplated suicide. In 1994, after another divorce, I came to the end of the line. I decided to check myself into a drug rehabilitation facility.

"There I met John. When we left the facility, we moved into an apartment and both got jobs. We seemed to be doing fine. The only problem was that there was nothing to take the place of the drugs and alcohol. Four months later we were consuming them again.

"One night after an argument we discussed what we had learned about a 'higher power.' We got down on our knees and said the most sincere prayer of our lives! The next day, when John was tempted to take a drink of alcohol, he heard a voice say as plainly as if someone were right next to him, 'You asked Me to take it away, and I took it away.' That began our journey home. From there we began reading our Bibles and watching Christian television. Our offerings were being sent to different ministries we saw on TV, one of which was *It Is Written!*

"The journey to the truth began in July 1995. In August we received a flyer in the mail for a Revelation Seminar at a local hotel. Much to our delight, everything taught came strictly from the precious Word of God. We didn't miss one night. We accepted with open arms, minds, and hearts all the truths placed before us. Learning of the Sabbath was such a joy. It all made sense, and we rejoiced that God would share His love, His truth, with people as unworthy as we are. The hand of Providence had led us to His remnant, the Seventh-day Adventist Church. We were married and baptized at the end of 1995. We are enjoying our new lives together in hopeful anticipation of Christ's second coming. Thank you for having a part in our conversion story."

What a testimony. God can do "exceedingly abundantly above all that we ask or think, according to the power that works in us" (Eph. 3:20).

His power is greater than the evil chains that bind us. His power is greater than the ugly habits that enslave us. Open your heart to Him today. Let His power flow in. He is the God of new beginnings.

MORE THAN SKIN AND BONES

But now, thus says the Lord, who created you, O Jacob, and He who formed you, O Israel: "Fear not, for I have redeemed you; I have called you by your name; you are Mine." Isa. 43:1.

Have you ever wondered how God could love you so much? Would God miss you if you were lost for all eternity? With millions upon millions of angelic beings, and the countless number of the saved, would God even notice if you were lost?

You are one of a kind. You are not merely skin covering bones. You are not a biological accident. When the genes and chromosomes came together to form the unique biological structure of your person, God threw away the pattern. There is no one else like you in the universe. If God loses you, there is no one else who can replace you. There would be an emptiness in His heart forever. God is lonely for your love. No one else can love Him like you. There is a place in His heart that can be filled only by your love.

Let's suppose a woman has 10 children. One of those children, a 7-year-old boy, is playing baseball on the front lawn. His older brother hits the ball out into the street. While the 7-year-old is running after it a speeding driver hits his brakes too late. He skids and strikes the boy, killing him.

As a pastor, I'm called to have the funeral for the child. Wondering how I might help the mother, I come up with what I believe is a brilliant idea. To help her overcome her grief, I decide to discuss all the advantages of the boy's death. Placing my hand upon her shoulder, I say, "Mother, I'm really sorry for what's happened to your boy. I know it must bring you grief. But I understand you had 10 children. You have only nine left now? With nine, you'll have more money and more time.

"Estimate that you're now going to have 10 percent more time to rest, 10 percent more money, 10 percent more dessert to go around, 10 percent more of everything. Think of what that child cost you in time and energy. Certainly your nine other children will make up for your lost boy." Would that mother agree?

She might respond, "I don't want just anybody. I want Joey. It's Joey I miss. It's Joey my heart longs for. It's Joey's chair at the table that is empty."

If a mother has 10 children, does she love each of them any less than if she has only three? How many does a mother's heart have the capacity to love? One? Two? Twenty? Who put that capacity to love in the mother's heart? A loving God. And the same loving God who placed it in a mother's heart to love has an infinite capacity to love.

God's love is infinite. There is enough to go around. Enough for you. Enough for me. Enough for all of us.

February 27

THE ROYAL LINE

To Him who loved us and washed us from our sins in His own blood, and has made us kings and priests to His God and Father, to Him be glory and dominion forever and ever. Amen. Rev. 1:5, 6.

A story is told of the death camps of World War II. At the train terminal in one of the camps the officers began separating able-bodied men from the women and children. One father, a member of a royal family, gazed on this scene and heard the fearful voices of families torn apart. He realized he might never see his young son again. He knelt down beside the boy and held him by the shoulders. "Michael," he said, "no matter what happens, I want you always to remember one thing. You're special; you're the son of a king."

Soon father and son were separated by the soldiers and marched off to different sections of the camp. They never saw each other again. Michael learned much later that his father had perished in a gas chamber. He had to go out alone and try to make his way in the world.

But his father's last words would always stay with him. They became a guiding beacon in his life. "You're the son of a king."

Michael determined that whatever came, he would behave like the son of a king.

Has the reality of this enormous truth hit you yet? Does it guide your actions? Does it mold your behavior? You are a child of the King of the universe. Royal blood runs through your veins. You are part of the royal family of heaven. When we accept Jesus as our personal Savior, we are "born again" into the family of God. Through Christ we are adopted into heaven's royal line. The apostle Paul states this truth eloquently: "Now, therefore, you are no longer strangers and foreigners, but fellow citizens with the saints and members of the household of God" (Eph. 2:19).

What a privilege! We are members of God's household. What a calling! We have a new identity.

A portion of God's family is in heaven, but there is also a portion right here on earth. Scripture refers to those who have accepted Jesus as a definite part of God's family. The third chapter of Ephesians makes the point plain:

"For this reason I bow my knees to the Father of our Lord Jesus Christ, from whom the whole family in heaven and earth is named" (Eph. 3:14, 15).

Let your spirit soar. You are a part of God's family. Let your soul grasp this glorious spiritual truth today. Your heavenly Father is the Creator of the universe.

You are the son or daughter of the King. Why not behave like the prince or princess you are?

February 28

WHEN GOD LIGHTS REVIVAL FIRES

And when they had prayed, the place where they were assembled together was shaken; and they were all filled with the Holy Spirit, and they spoke the word of God with boldness. Acts 4:31.

Prayer is powerful. As the disciples prayed, the Spirit of God descended upon them. Filled with the power of God's Spirit, they shared His Word everywhere. Merchants and farmers, peasants and soldiers, tax collectors and fishers were converted. Thieves became honest. Prostitutes became pure. Murderers became gentle. New Testament Christianity made a dramatic impact on the first-century world.

Throughout history spiritual revivals have made a life-changing difference in society. Let me give you an example of what can happen when God's Spirit really gets hold of a place.

It all started when a young Welsh ministerial student named Evan Roberts had trouble sleeping. In the spring of 1904 he was repeatedly awakened in the wee hours of the morning by "a sense of God's presence and communion with Him." As he began praying regularly with a few friends it became evident that God was up to something. One of the group stated the conviction that God would give them 100,000 souls in Wales.

Evan Roberts began preaching at young people's meetings. The Christ-centered message he and others proclaimed ignited the whole country.

In some towns every church was packed from 6:00 in the evening to 1:00 in the morning every night for a year. People confessed their faults to God and to one another. Wrongs were righted, property and money restored. In an 18-month period, from 1905 to 1906, crime seemed almost nonexistent. At one rare trial the judge interrupted the proceedings and led the defendant to Christ. The prosecuting police officer and the jury sang hymns.

The revival even reached down into the Welsh mines. The swearing of the miners disappeared. The pit ponies had to learn to respond to a whole new vocabulary. Gentle words replaced the cursing of their handlers.

The Welsh revival sent waves of spiritual renewal through the whole world.

God longs to pour His Spirit out upon you. He longs for you to be a world-changer. You can change the world around you. The Spirit working through you will make a difference. The Spirit who transforms your life transforms other lives through you. When God lights a revival fire in your life, the sparks of revival are blown by the winds of His Spirit to light people around you.

During the Welsh revival two reporters traveled from London to report on the events. When they arrived in a quaint Welsh country village, they asked a police officer for directions to where the revival was occurring. The officer straightened to his full six-foot-two-inch frame and simply stated, "If you want to find the site of the revival, look within this uniform. It is in my heart."

Revival always begins in someone's heart. Today it can begin in your heart. Today it can begin in your life. Today the Spirit desires to do something special in you.

February 29

THE POWER OF INTERCESSION

The effective, fervent prayer of a righteous man avails much. James 5:16.

Some time ago a member of the clergy tried to comfort a woman whose husband had left town during a revival. He was a bitter agnostic and had said he wouldn't be back until "the religious flurry" was over. The wife had hoped the revival would finally convert her husband, but now there seemed little chance.

The minister invited the woman to attend a morning prayer group he was leading. She dried her tears and determined to attend.

The prayer group quickly agreed to pray together over the man's departure. They tackled the challenge with great gusto, asking God to overtake the wayward husband, bring him back, and lead him to Christ.

The same night he astounded everyone by showing up at the revival meeting. He had quite a story to tell.

He'd ridden 18 miles into the hills when he was suddenly stopped in his tracks. He couldn't go on. Suddenly he was made to feel how horribly he had behaved. He sensed he was a sinner in need of God's grace. A deep conviction came over him to return.

The man told the congregation, "I now know that I must be born again, or I can never see the kingdom of heaven." This unmistakably rescued man took his seat amid the tears and sobs of the whole congregation.

That very night he accepted Christ as his Lord and Savior.

Intercessory prayer is powerful. It changes things. God values human freedom. He is doing everything He can to reach every single person before we even pray, yet God is limited by people's choices. He will never violate any individual's freedom of choice. He influences but never coerces. He convicts but never compels.

When we pray for someone else, God pours out His Spirit through us to reach them. Intercessory prayer opens up new avenues for God to work. It provides God with another opportunity. Ellen White states it well: "It is a part of God's plan to grant us, in answer to the prayer of faith, that which He would not bestow did we not thus ask" (*The Great Controversy,* p. 525).

Something happens when people pray. Two or three people earnestly praying make a difference. God hears. God answers. God moves. God touches lives. Do you have a prayer partner? Do you regularly meet in a small intercessory prayer group? Why not ask God to help you find a prayer partner? Why not begin a ministry of intercession in your own life? If you are an intercessor already, encourage other people to join you in interceding. Find someone to pray with and write out a prayer list and watch what God does. You will be amazed.

A NEW TOMORROW

Looking for the blessed hope and glorious appearing of our great God and Savior Jesus Christ. Titus 2:13.

We need a strong hope today that can sustain us when uncertainty clouds the horizon. Unnerving threats have invaded our world. Just opening a package, or taking a plane or train ride, or going downtown have become newly stressful events. We look over our shoulders with uncertainty.

We need hope today, for questions loom large in our minds: Who holds the future? Will terrorists have the last word? Or someone else? Will the world end with a bang or with something better?

I believe that someone else holds the future. That someone has been planning a better ending for some time. Jesus Christ made a promise to His disciples near the close of His earthly ministry. It was recorded: "The Son of Man will send out His angels, and they will gather out of His kingdom all things that offend, and those who practice lawlessness" (Matt. 13:41).

Jesus promised to come again and destroy all evil, replacing it with righteousness. He holds the future in His hands.

Why do I believe this, even in a time of terror and tragedy? Because He held lepers in His hands and gave them back their health. Because He touched the eyes of the blind and gave them sight. Because He touched the paralyzed and the demon-possessed and restored them to wholeness. Because He spoke a word, and the dead came to life.

Yes, I believe He is the one who holds the future. He will have the last word.

One event is big enough, glorious enough, to overshadow anything terrorists can do. One cloud is bright enough to overwhelm all the smoke and fire of suicide attacks. Jesus promises that we will see "the Son of Man coming in a cloud with power and great glory" (Luke 21:27).

The world has not been the same since the first time Jesus interrupted history. When He comes again, His kingdom will take over the whole world. This time *all* the sick and suffering will be healed. This time *all* the "dead in Christ" will come to life.

This is the promise that can give us an unshakable hope for the future. Scripture assures us that earthly history will end in Jesus' glorious appearing. Not the mushroom cloud, but the cloud of Christ's glory will rule the future. We can rejoice in the certain hope of our Lord's return.

March 2

LESSONS FROM A BOLOGNA SANDWICH

I do not seek My own will but the will of the Father who sent Me. John 5:30.

The story is told of a construction worker who ate a bologna sandwich each day for lunch. Day after day he ate the same kind of sandwich. One day, as he ate with a friend, the guy stopped in the middle of a half-eaten sandwich and grumbled, "I hate bologna sandwiches!" After a moment of deathly silence he repeated, "I hate bologna sandwiches!"

"Why don't you ask your wife?" his friend asked meekly. "I'm sure she would fix you something else."

The man snorted, "I pack the bologna myself!"

Most of the bologna in our lives we pack ourselves. Contrary to some popular theories, we are not primarily victims of society's ills. God created us intelligent thinking beings. He has given us the power of choice.

When God placed our first parents in their garden home, He gave them the power of choice. They were not predestined to fail, victims of some cosmic plot, or puppets manipulated by divine strings. The essence of the image of God is the ability to make moral choices. The freedom to choose and the taking of responsibility for the choices we make are the heart of what it means to be human. God so values our freedom of choice that He allows us to make wrong choices, in order to preserve our ability to choose. Positive choices bring positive results. Negative choices bring negative results.

Bible history is littered with the shattered lives of people who made poor choices. Cain's uncontrollable anger led him to murder his brother. He spent the rest of his life running. David's uncontrollable lust led him to adultery with Bathsheba. Although he experienced forgiveness, his actions shattered his family relations. Judas's uncontrollable desire for money led him to sell his Lord cheap. His unusually talented life ended much too soon. Poor choices lead to disastrous results.

Think of Joseph, Daniel, and Paul. Their positive choices led to incredible results. Joseph's choice to resist the advances of Potiphar's wife changed the course of Egyptian history. Daniel's choice to refuse the Babylonians' wine changed the course of Babylonian history. Paul's choice to refuse to bow before Caesar's idols changed the course of Roman history.

God gives no greater gift than the power to choose. Right choices can change your life for the better. Today, remember that we pack most of life's "bologna" ourselves. Determine to make good choices and live the abundant life God wants you to live.

LET THE FIRE FALL

But who can endure the day of His coming? And who can stand when He appears? For He is like a refiner's fire. Mal. 3:2.

One of America's famous attractions of years gone by was the firefall of Yosemite National Park.

On a summer evening tourists from around the world would gather below Glacier Point for the dramatic show. At precisely the stroke of nine a voice rang out across the waiting camp, "Let the fire fall!"

And 3,000 feet above the floor of the valley, a voice answered, "The fire falls!"

Flaming embers poured over the precipice into the darkness of the summer night. They cascaded down the sheer white granite of the mountain wall. No one who saw the firefall would ever forget it.

Throughout Scripture, fire symbolizes the presence of God. When you encounter God's fiery presence, your life is changed forever. Moses entered the presence of God at the burning bush (Ex. 3:2-6). The high priest experienced the presence of God between the cherubim in the Most Holy Place of the earthly sanctuary (Ex. 25:22). Elijah challenged the prophets of Baal on Mount Carmel, and the fire fell. First Kings 18:38 describes the scene with the words "Then the fire of the Lord fell." The fire of God's presence consumed Elijah's altar. The people fell on their faces and cried out, "The Lord, He is God."

The fire of Pentecost transformed Peter into a powerful proclaimer of the gospel. More than 3,000 were baptized in one place in one day. The fire continued to fall on these early disciples until the "word of God spread, and the number of the disciples multiplied greatly" (Acts 6:7). The disciples turned the world upside down. The Spirit's power transformed not only them but their families, their friends, and their communities.

God longs for His fire to fall again. He longs to consume the dross of sin in our hearts so the fire of His presence can light the world. He longs for the day when the world will be aflame with His love. It happened at Pentecost and it will happen again. Oh, God, let the fire fall!

MIRACLE ON DEATH ROW

Therefore, if anyone is in Christ, he is a new creation; old things have passed away; behold, all things have become new. 2 Cor. 5:17.

Sam Tannyhill, a criminal who told his story on death row, is a dramatic example of the power of God's Word to change a man's life completely. Sam's childhood was far from ideal. His parents divorced when he was 5 years old, and he was shuttled to a dozen different homes, leaving him feeling bewildered and unwanted. At the age of 10 Sam began a series of minor offenses—pocketing dime store items, trespassing on private property—that led to greater acts.

Eventually Sam was convicted of forgery and sentenced to prison. After five years he was released, only to rob a small restaurant in Ohio two weeks later. Forcing a server into his car, he sped out of town. Her badly beaten body was discovered the next day.

In time, Sam was captured and sentenced to die in the electric chair. While in prison he was visited by several Christians. One held out a Bible, a gift from his 9-year-old son. The Christian told Sam, "My boy says you can have it on one condition: you must read it."

Although at first Sam had little interest in the Bible, he eventually opened it out of sheer boredom. Soon he became absorbed. His own words reveal his spiritual journey.

"So I started at Matthew, and I read all the part called the New Testament. . . . I was . . . a murderer, but yet I read where people in the Bible were also outside of the law. Then I was troubled; I wanted that peace of mind this God was giving away, but how could I get word to Him? Can He really hear you when you pray? And will He answer a man who has never heard of Him? . . .

"So I tried praying. My prayers never got out of my cell. I prayed for help, but hung on to the world with both hands. . . . I decided to . . . give it one more try. . . . For three days there was no more miserable soul on this earth than I. . . .

"I got on my knees and truly confessed every wrong I could think of, and asked that God please help me. I told Him that if I had forgotten any of my sins to have mercy on me and add them to the list, because I was guilty of them too.

"Let me tell you, I never had such a wonderful feeling in my life. I wanted to shout it to the world. Yes, I felt the Spirit of God as He truly brought His love into my heart. . . .

"I am in a cell in death row, but I am more free here than I ever was in the streets. I have no fear of death whatsoever. To me death is one step closer to my Jesus. . . .

"I can truly say there is no sin too black that the blood of Jesus Christ can't wash as white as snow."

Christ still accepts sinful desperate human beings. He still assures us that "the one who comes to Me I will by no means cast out" (John 6:37). Today, if you have already committed your life to Him, will you rededicate yourself to Him? If you haven't yet committed yourself to Him, why not do it today? His arms are wide open for you.

March 5

THE LIFE-GIVING POWER OF THE WORD

Having been born again, not of corruptible seed but incorruptible, through the word of God which lives and abides forever. 1 Peter 1:23.

Robert Wong is one of the most radiant, cheerful people I've ever met. I had the chance to talk with him on a trip to Hong Kong. He told me a remarkable story of 15 years in a Communist prison. He'd been sentenced because of his activities in Christian outreach.

Mr. Wong spent the first four years in solitary confinement. During the next four years he was allowed a five-minute visit with his family once a month.

As he told me of his ordeal I was struck by how cheerful and positive he seemed about life. I caught no trace of bitterness or anger. This man just seemed to exude the spirit of Christ.

Why? I wondered. What had sustained him during his years of isolation?

Mr. Wong told me what it was. He said prisoners were never referred to by their names. Each prisoner was given a number. It was part of the effort to erase their identities. One day, while walking in the prison yard, Mr. Wong heard a guard call out, "Prisoner 105."

For some reason that number kept going around and around in his mind. Suddenly he remembered number 105 was the number of one of his favorite hymns in the Chinese hymnal, "Give Me the Bible." Once a month he was allowed to write to his family a short message consisting of 100 Chinese characters. The next time he was able to send a letter, Mr. Wong ended it with the number 105.

The next time they visited Mr. Wong, one of them managed to smuggle a Bible to him.

I'll never forget what Robert Wong said to me: "That is what sustained me!"

The copy of the Word kept him going. Before that, he repeated only memorized texts again and again. But now he had the precious book in his hands. God remained very real to Robert Wong. He remained a radiant presence, even in those years of captivity.

There is incredible life-changing power in the Bible. The Holy Spirit speaking through God's Word transforms our lives. The Word of God strengthens us in life's trials. It empowers us to overcome life's obstacles. It encourages us in life's disappointments. It inspires us in life's challenges. It lifts us in life's heartaches. God's Word is the spiritual bread that nourishes our souls (see Matt. 4:4). It is the water of life that satisfies the raging thirst within (see John 7:37). It is the light that illuminates the darkness and guides us on life's journey (see Ps. 119:105).

Robert Wong found incredible strength in God's Word, and you can too. Why not set aside 30 minutes today to simply meditate upon the life-changing passages of God's Word?

March 6

FOUR THINGS CHRISTIANS DON'T HAVE!

He who did not spare His own Son, but delivered Him up for us all, how shall He not with Him also freely give us all things? Rom. 8:32.

Many years ago an ordinary factory worker saved up enough money to go on a luxury cruise. Purchasing the ticket consumed all his savings. Anxiously he awaited the date of his departure.

Having used all his money for the ticket, he realized he could not afford to eat in the ship's dining hall. He purchased some cheese and crackers before departure.

The first few days of the cruise, things went well. He enjoyed the magnificent ocean views, marveled at the brilliant sunsets, and relaxed by the ship's swimming pool. But he was definitely tiring of cheese and crackers. The aromas wafting from the exquisite dining hall, along with the comments of other passengers regarding the delicious meals, enticed him. He could stand it no longer.

With cautious hesitancy he inquired of the chief steward, "Sir, how much are the meals?"

"May I see your ticket, please?" the steward asked. Examining the ticket, the steward replied in surprise, "Didn't anyone tell you the meals are part of the package? They come with the ticket!"

The poor man was living below his privileges. Like him, many Christians are living below their privileges. Countless Christians feel guilty, insecure, and fearful.

Our Lord offers us much more.

The apostle Paul describes these Christian privileges in terms of four things Christians do *not* have.

In Christ there is no condemnation. Romans 8:1 declares: "There is therefore now no condemnation to those who are in Christ Jesus." In Jesus all condemnation is gone. The accusing voices are silenced. We are acquitted, pardoned, forgiven, set free from sin's devastating guilt. Since Christ bore our guilt on the tree, we need not bear it in a condemning conscience. He was condemned so that we need not condemn ourselves.

In Christ there is no bondage. Romans 8:15 declares: "For you did not receive the spirit of bondage to fear." As Christians we may fail, but we are no longer in bondage to sin. We have a new master. Sin no longer dominates or controls our lives. Christ has broken the bondage.

In Christ there is no ultimate defeat. Romans 8:28 declares: "And we know that all things work together for good to those who love God." As Christians we are not in the hands of the evil one. We are not like leaves blown in the autumn breeze, with no direction. God is in control and will work all things out for good.

In Christ there is no separation. Romans 8:35 asks: "Who shall separate us from the love of Christ?" The apostle lists tribulation, distress, persecution, famine, nakedness, peril, and sword. Christ's love penetrates our darkest, most trying moment. In Christ guilt is gone and bondage is broken. In Christ all things work for good, and nothing can separate us from His love.

March 7

THE MASTER STRATEGIST

I have set the Lord always before me; because He is at my right hand I shall not be moved. Ps. 16:8.

Brother Andrew, they called him. Andrew's business was smuggling Bibles through what was known as Europe's iron curtain.

One day back in 1961 Brother Andrew loaded up his little old Volkswagen and headed east from Holland with his friend Hans. As they wound their way through Germany's lush valleys and meadowlands they prayed that the hidden Bibles they were carrying would find their way safely into the hands of the Russian believers.

As they passed through Poland their pulses picked up. Could they really slip their sacred cargo past the snarling guard dogs and bristling rifles of the Soviet border guards?

Yes! They made it through! With hallelujahs in their hearts Andrew and

Hans hurried on toward Moscow. Arriving at their destination, they located the Baptist Church and showed up for Thursday night prayer meeting.

Now they had to be really careful. Whom could they safely entrust with their smuggled treasure? They suspected that the KGB had informants in the audience. Sometimes even pastors were under pressure to report Bible smugglers. Silently they prayed for guidance. After the service Brother Andrew and Hans lingered in the lobby, studying the faces of the 1,200 worshipers who were shuffling out the door. Suddenly they saw him, a thin balding man in his 40s.

"There's our man!" Hans whispered. Brother Andrew nodded.

Hearts thumping, they approached the stranger and cautiously introduced themselves. And what a surprise they got! The man had come all the way from Siberia in hopes of finding a Bible for his church. In fact, he had been instructed in a dream to make the long journey to Moscow.

At first he hesitated, for Bibles were scarce. But the dream had been authoritative. Without further delay he obeyed.

After hearing the incredible story, Hans observed, "You were told to come westward for 2,000 miles to get a Bible, and we were told to go eastward 2,000 miles, carrying Bibles. And here we are in Moscow tonight, recognizing each other the instant we meet."

The Siberian brother was excited—too excited, in fact. They had to calm him down quickly lest he betray their glorious secret. Can you imagine the joy in his heart as he set off for home the next morning with a dozen precious Bibles?

God is a master strategist. He leads seekers for truth to His witnesses for truth. When we come to Him with sincere hearts, we too can know with absolute certainty that He will guide us. With steady hearts we can place our lives in God's hands.

March 8

IN THE END: JESUS

The Revelation of Jesus Christ, which God gave Him to show His servants—things which must shortly take place. And He sent and signified it by His angel to His servant John. Rev. 1:1.

The artist and cartoonist Thomas Nast performed an interesting feat in public exhibitions. He took a canvas six feet long by two feet wide and placed it horizontally on an easel. Then he rapidly sketched a landscape with green meadows, cattle, fields of grain, a farmhouse, bright sky, and fleecy clouds. It was the usual cheery scene. When he stepped aside, the audience applauded.

Then Nast began to dab in a few darker colors, as if touching up the painting. Soon his strokes appeared reckless. He blotted out the bright sky, the fields, and meadow. Dark slashes of paint obliterated the whole composition. It looked like something angry and abstract. Nast stepped back and declared, "It's finished." The audience didn't know what to do. Should they applaud, or should they weep? Then Nast asked stage attendants to turn the canvas to a vertical position. And suddenly there stood a painting that depicted a beautiful waterfall plunging over a cliff of dark rocks bordered by shrubs and trees. It was a stunning composition.

The picture of the end times can look quite scary and chaotic, with all those woes poured out, trumpets of doom blasting, and plagues devastating the earth. It can appear like a dark series of clouds and slashes on the canvas.

But Jesus turns the picture right side up. He turns the whole planet right side up. Jesus standing tall as the Alpha and the Omega, as the Bright and Morning Star, as the Leader of the armies of heaven coming to the rescue—that's what makes the picture of the end so glorious and hopeful.

Jesus is the hero of the book of Revelation. Revelation 4:11 presents Him as the all-powerful Creator. All heaven sings praise to Him in these words: "You are worthy, O Lord, to receive glory and honor and power; for You created all things, and by Your will they exist and were created." In Revelation 5:6 Jesus is the "Lamb" that was slain. He is the one who has "redeemed us to God by Your blood out of every tribe and tongue and people and nation, and have made us kings and priests to our God; and we shall reign on the earth" (Rev. 5:9).

Here is the Christ of Revelation. He is the all-powerful Creator. He is the loving, sin-pardoning Savior. He is the sympathetic, righteous Judge.

Best of all, He is the glorious coming King.

In Revelation Jesus turns the picture right side up. All of human history is moving toward one grand, glorious climax. History had a beginning point, and it will have an ending point. It is not merely a collection of accidental events. Our planet has a date with destiny. Jesus is the beginning of all history and the end of it. Jesus is the one who sets all things right. Praise His name.

MORE THAN A MERE MAN

"I tell you the truth," Jesus answered, "before Abraham was born, I am!" John 8:58, NIV.

Years ago, when Lew Wallace was practicing law in the midwestern United States, an atheist friend told him that within a few years all the little white churches dotting the Indiana countryside would be only a memory. Religion had no future.

Wallace didn't know what to say. He realized that he knew almost nothing about God or the Bible. He had no convictions on the subject. He determined to study the matter firsthand for himself. He decided to examine the Bible, using his legal training to look for credible evidence, and reach a proper conclusion.

Since he supposed this would be a rather dreary study, Wallace thought he might add some interest by creating a story about Jesus out of the materials he uncovered. At first he intended to present him as a man, an extraordinary man to be sure, but just a human being. However, as he studied the historical background of Jesus' life and looked at the narratives in the Gospels, Wallace began seeing much more than he bargained for. The story he found in the Bible had a more-than-human design. The more he studied, the more convinced he became of the divinity of Christ. Certainly the world needed a Savior, and Wallace couldn't imagine a better one than this Jesus.

In his study Wallace found not only a story; he found Jesus. He did go on to write the intended story about Christ, in part to express his new convictions. He called it *Ben-Hur*. It became a best-selling novel and was later turned into one of Hollywood's biggest motion pictures.

For Wallace, the discovery that Jesus was more than a mere man meant all the difference. If Jesus is only a man, He is our example and little more. If He is only a man, He has no power to forgive our sins, transform our lives, or resurrect us from the dead. Jesus' statement to the religious leaders in His time is one of the most significant He ever made about Himself. "Before Abraham was [born], I AM" John 8:58. The expression "I AM" means the self-existent one. The one with no beginning or ending. The eternal one. When the all-powerful God manifested His glory to Moses in the burning bush, He declared that His name was "I AM" (Ex. 3:14). This expression uttered by the divine Christ is a declaration of all He is to us.

He personally reassures each of us:

I AM the forgiveness your mind seeks.

I AM the assurance your soul longs for.

I AM the love your heart craves.

I AM the power to break sin's bondage.

I AM the hope to lift your spirit.

I AM the supplier of every need.

Whatever you need, the divine Christ says today, "'I AM' that very thing. Seek Me, and you will discover everything you long for."

March 10

SOMEWHERE I CAN BELONG

The eternal God is your refuge, and underneath are the everlasting arms; He will thrust out the enemy from before you. Deut. 33:27.

Something happened inside me the first time I saw her. She moved down the street with a peculiar shuffle, her eyes glued to the sidewalk. Her gray hair and deep wrinkles spoke of years gone by. But there was something more. She was weathered, worn, and dirty, her clothes unwashed, and her hair unkempt. Her body emanated a foul odor as she pushed a battered shopping cart filled with plastic bags and cardboard.

I see her regularly in our suburban community of Thousand Oaks, California. Each time I feel a tinge of pain. My college-age son tells me she wanders aimlessly from Ventura to Newbury Park, on to Thousand Oaks and Westlake, and back again. She has no place to live, no place to belong.

I do not know her particular situation. Perhaps alcoholism consumed all her money. Perhaps she is mentally ill. Perhaps she was severely abused by a parent or a husband. Whatever the cause of her homelessness, her plight haunts me. Here's why. Inside each of us is the need to belong somewhere. Homeless people have no place. They don't belong anywhere. You know that instinctively. That's why it is hard to turn our eyes away.

Sometimes, even if we live in a beautiful four-bedroom dream house, we still find ourselves looking for that place to feel secure, to feel contented. We are restless for home, longing for that somewhere to belong.

Throughout Scripture God invites us to find our true home in Him. In Him we find refuge, safety, and security. Listen to these reassuring words: "The eternal God is your refuge" (Deut. 33:27). "God is our refuge and strength" (Ps. 46:1).

We are not homeless wanderers. We are not unwanted street people. We are not restless vagabonds. There is a place in Christ's heart just for you. You can find comfort and security in Him. In Him our restless longings cease. I love that old hymn:

"In the heart of Jesus, there is love for you,

Love most pure and tender, love most deep and true;
Why should you be lonely, why for friendship sigh,
When the heart of Jesus, has a full supply?"
—Alice Pugh and C. H. Forrest

In Jesus we are truly at home, and our restless longings cease.

March 11

WHEN ACCUSING VOICES ARE SILENCED

For if our heart condemns us, God is greater than our heart, and knows all things. 1 John 3:20.

Johanna is a successful businesswoman in her mid-80s. She has a great job, a gorgeous home, and a wonderful family. But something is eating away inside of her. She is restless, discontented, and guilty. The guilt of her past haunts her. The accusing voices in her head never seem to be silenced. An unwanted pregnancy that led to an abortion still greatly troubles her. Fractured relationships cause constant emotional trauma. Her moral failures as a young woman are always with her. Johanna wonders at times, Will I ever have peace?

Here is an awesome truth about God's amazing love: His love is greater than our failures. His grace is greater than our sin. His mercy is greater than our mistakes. His forgiveness can quiet the accusing voices within our minds.

Christ came to save sinners. Only sinners qualify for His grace. Only those who have fallen need to be picked up. Think of Mary Magdalene. She failed multiple times. Mary was notorious for her moral laxity. Even Jesus declared, "Her sins are many" (Luke 7:47). Nevertheless, this adulteress found forgiveness in Jesus. Think of Peter. He denied his Lord three times. The disciple who would preach to thousands on the day of Pentecost openly cussed, swore, and denied his Lord, yet he found forgiveness.

God's mercy in no way minimizes sin; it maximizes God's grace. There was forgiveness for Mary and Peter and a dying thief. There is forgiveness for you and Johanna, too. The accusing voices can be silenced. He loves us too much to allow us to be lost without fighting to save us. His love is still there wooing our hearts. Will you surrender to His love today?

GETTING THE MESSAGE THROUGH

But God demonstrates His own love toward us, in that while we were still sinners, Christ died for us. Rom. 5:8.

A fascinating painting hangs in the National Gallery of Art in Washington, D.C. In a moving World War II scene the artist depicts a battlefield with two groups of tanks moving toward one another. Two divisions of Allied forces are attacking the Nazi forces. The tanks are firing their guns. Ground troops are in full battle. One lone soldier in the center of the picture captures your attention. Two sets of Allied soldiers have been cut off from each other. An enemy bullet has pierced their telephone communication line. In the midst of heavy gunfire a lone soldier is responsible for repairing the severed phone line. His hands are outstretched over his head as he works on the wire.

Just as he completes the job bullets rip through his uniform, and his chest is splattered with blood. The artist has chosen one word to describe the picture: *Through.* A lone soldier gave his life for the message to get through. Communication is reestablished!

A lone Man hung on a cross, suspended between heaven and earth to get the message through. God loves you! A rebel angel declared that God's law was unjust. This angel claimed that God was arbitrary and His requirements were unfair. He claimed that God did not really love His creatures.

The cross eloquently answers Satan's most blatant arguments. The cross reveals two eternal truths: how deadly sin is and how good God is. Sin destroyed the most innocent man ever to live. Sin killed the Son of God. Sin destroys all those who play with it. Sin is deadly. If it is so bad that it killed Jesus, shouldn't we consider that it might destroy us, too, if we embrace it?

The cross reveals how incredibly good God is. It reveals His amazing love. It speaks eloquently to the entire universe of a God whose love goes the limit. A God whose love goes to any length to save us. God's message came through on the cross. Heaven values you so much that Jesus Himself would accept all of sin's condemnation to save you. It is incomprehensible, but still true. Jesus would rather accept the full penalty of sin Himself, even if it meant eternal separation from the Father, than for us to be lost. He would rather miss out on heaven Himself than for us to.

I cannot resist that love. All I can do is yield to the love that speaks from the cross and worship Him forever.

CONDEMNED NO LONGER

Blessed is he whose transgression is forgiven, whose sin is covered. Blessed is the man to whom the Lord does not impute iniquity, and in whose spirit there is no deceit. Ps. 32:1, 2.

In the late 1960s American news focused on veterans returning from the Vietnam conflict. But a veteran of another war was returning home as well. For 25 years he had hidden in the mountains of the Philippines. This Japanese World War II veteran, still clad in the ragged fragments of his uniform, was a frail, emaciated specimen of humanity. For 25 years he had lived in fear, not knowing that the war was over. Cut off from civilization, he had wandered through the jungles in isolation, barely surviving.

When finally found wandering the Philippine jungles, he could hardly believe that the war was over. He thought that this news was merely a deceptive ploy of the enemy.

Other imprisoned souls still live in dungeons of unbelief today, carrying huge burdens of guilt. But the war is over, friend. Jesus sets the condemned captives free.

Unresolved guilt is destructive to our physical, mental, and spiritual health. Like a pebble in our shoe it will rub our conscience raw unless dealt with.

Sometimes accusing voices inside may torment us like demons. There is a way to deal with guilt. It is helpful to realize that there are at least three kinds of guilt. There is the guilt that occurs because I have not reached the goal that I have set for myself or I've failed to reach another's expectation. Second, there is the guilt that occurs when I have failed in a relationship with another person. I may feel guilty because of something I have said or done to offend someone else. Third, my guilt feelings may also come from knowing I have sinned or broken God's law.

I call these three kinds of guilt psychological guilt, relational guilt, and moral guilt. Psychological guilt occurs when I do not meet the standards I have set for myself. Relational guilt occurs when I fracture a relationship with someone I value. Moral guilt occurs when I violate my conscience by breaking God's law. Sin brings guilt.

Jesus is the answer to each of these three types of guilt. He is my perfection. When I fail to meet impossible standards I have set for myself, I trust in Him. He is my comfort when I have wounded another with my words or actions. I ask Him to give me the grace to ask for forgiveness. When my heart condemns me for breaking God's law, I fall on my knees in confession and repentance.

When we take these three steps, guilt will go. Acknowledge your sin. Confess it to Jesus, and accept His forgiveness. He sets the captives of guilt free. He replaces our guilt with His forgiveness. He replaces accusation with acceptance. He replaces condemnation with mercy. His promise is still true. "He will again have compassion on us, and will subdue our iniquities. You will cast all our sins into the depths of the sea" (Micah 7:19).

March 14

THE TRUSTING HEART

Many sorrows shall be to the wicked; but he who trusts in the Lord, mercy shall surround him. Be glad in the Lord and rejoice, you righteous. Ps. 32:10, 11.

In the days of the Counter-Reformation in England the government executed Richard Cameron for his beliefs.

Officials cut off Cameron's head and hands and brought them to his father, imprisoned in Scotland for the same crime. The officials asked, "Are these the hands and head of your son Richard? Do you recognize them?"

With tears streaming down his cheeks, the father gently reached out and embraced the arms and head of his son. His lips quivered. Gently he spoke: "I know them, I know them. They are my son's, my own dear son's. But it is the Lord who grants me mercy all the days of my life. Good is the will of the Lord, who cannot wrong me or mine."

Even the work of the enemy, in destroying his son, could not shake the faith of the elder Cameron in his God.

He had a trusting heart. He accepted God's promise in Psalm 31:24: "Be of good courage, and He shall strengthen your heart, all you who hope in the Lord."

How is it possible for a father to see the mangled, bloody body parts of his son and not fall apart himself? How is it possible to survive such awful emotional trauma? There is only one way. It is not some incredible inner strength. It is not some unusual power. It is a trusting heart. It is the absolute confidence that one day God will make all things right.

When we place our absolute trust in God, He imparts unexplainable spiritual strength. Divine power flows from the throne of the universe to empower us. In Him we receive spiritual strength to survive the enemy's attacks. A life of trust is a life of power, strength, and unshakable faith. It is a life of immovable resistance against evil. It is a life of living in God's presence by God's promise through God's power. It is this life of trust that

He invites you into today. It will enable you to face anything the devil thrusts upon you.

March 15

FROM ANXIETY TO PRAISE

Be anxious for nothing, but in everything by prayer and supplication, with thanksgiving, let your requests be made known to God. Phil. 4:6.

On Thanksgiving Day, 1961, businessperson and gospel singer Merrill Womach took off in his small private plane from a little airport near Beaver Marsh, Oregon. While barely airborne, the plane suddenly whipped around and plunged a hundred yards through icy tree branches to the ground. When Merrill regained consciousness, he saw flames all around him. He managed to scramble out of the wreckage, but not before his legs, arms, chest, and head were badly burned.

He couldn't see, but he stumbled through deep snow toward the sounds of a nearby highway. Fortunately, two men had seen his plane go down and rushed to the scene in their station wagon. As Merrill staggered toward them he looked like a monster, without eyes, nose, or mouth. His head was charred and swollen.

The men placed him gently in the back of the car and headed toward a hospital. Merrill lay there, feeling the incredible pain sweep over him. But, as he later recalled, "an incredible thing happened. I felt like singing."

Forcing one eye open, he looked down at his hands and began to realize how badly he'd been burned. But the feeling of wanting to sing persisted as the car rolled down Highway 97. "My head was swelling, and the pain grew more and more intense," he remembered. "Still I felt like singing! It was an old gospel song I had learned as a child. I don't know why that song came rushing out of me instead of cries of pain and self-pity, but it did."

As the two men in the front seat listened in disbelieving silence, these words emerged from a crack in Womach's blackened face: " 'I've found the dear Savior, and now I'm made whole; I'm pardoned and have my release. His Spirit abiding and blessing my soul; praise God, in my heart there is peace.' "

An ambulance met the station wagon at Collier Memorial State Park. The attendants transferred Womach to a stretcher and sped away. Through the scream of the siren and through Merrill Womach's own loud pain, the song still emerged unchanged—a wonderful anthem of praise: "Wonderful peace, wonderful peace. Peace that the world cannot give. When I think how He brought me from darkness to light, there's a wonderful, wonderful peace."

The presence of peace does not mean the absence of pain. There are times God gives us deep peace at a moment of deep pain. In the midst of our times of greatest need God supplies His greatest peace. Peace is a gift that God freely offers. Whatever our life's circumstances, we can claim God's peace by faith. Believing that He is the author of peace, we open our hearts to receive it.

Do you feel restless today? Is your heart filled with anxiety? The apostle Paul speaks to your heart this very day from Colossians 1:2: "Grace to you and peace from God our Father and the Lord Jesus Christ." Rejoice today; God's gift of peace is yours. Rejoice; your anxiety can give way to praise in the light of heaven's peace.

March 16

DANGER! DO NOT TOUCH!

The Lord is my light and my salvation; whom shall I fear? The Lord is the strength of my life; of whom shall I be afraid? Ps. 27:1.

A supply clerk checking in for the graveyard shift at his factory was warned of a small box that had been left on the loading dock. Printed on all sides were the words "DANGER! DO NOT TOUCH!" Everyone had been told to stay clear of the parcel until management could check out the situation. The night clerk didn't even want to breathe near the thing. He was greatly relieved when a supply foreman arrived in the morning.

The foreman put on gloves and safety glasses. Slowly, carefully, he opened the box. Inside he discovered 25 signs that read "DANGER! DO NOT TOUCH!"

Imagine all the stress that mysterious box caused those dock workers. They spent their time imagining the terrible toxic compounds it might contain. The little box grew into a great burden of anxiety. But often, when we analyze our problems, we realize they are a lot like that box. They look forbidding, but they aren't fearful after all.

Occasional fear is a normal part of life. Any one of a number of things might trigger these fear mechanisms. We may fear the worst when we discover an otherwise unnoticed lump under our arm. Unusual heights, fierce storms, air turbulence, or excessive speed may frighten us.

Although everyone is afraid sometime, some people's lives are dominated by fear. Boxes labeled "Danger" seem to be filling their lives. Their lives seem controlled by the negative emotion of fear.

God is certainly not the author of fear. The apostle Paul makes this point clear. "For God has not given us a spirit of fear, but of power and of love and of a sound mind" (2 Tim. 1:7).

Excessive fear, continually imagining the worst, is unhealthy. God is daily planning the best for us. He is fully capable of taking every experience in our life and working good out of it (Rom. 8:28). Since He is in control of every circumstance of our lives, we can trust Him to work all things for good. Fleeing in the wilderness alone, fearing death at Saul's hand, David wrote: "I sought the Lord, and He heard me, and delivered me from all of my fears" (Ps. 34:4).

Give God your fears. Bring Him all that troubles you. Allow Him to deliver you from crippling fears. What are you afraid of today? Kneel before Him. Present Him with everything that makes you afraid. You will be glad you did.

He will replace your fears with faith. He will replace anxieties with assurance, your worries with wisdom. He will replace your troubles with His tender touch.

March 17

THE DEVIL'S NAIL

Buy the truth, and do not sell it, also wisdom and instruction and understanding. Prov. 23:23.

A certain Haitian man wanted to sell his house for $2,000. Another man wanted very badly to buy it, but he was poor and couldn't afford the full price. After much bargaining, the owner agreed to sell the house for half the original price, with just one stipulation. He would retain the ownership of one small nail protruding from over the door. After several years the original owner wanted the house back, but the new owner was unwilling to sell. So the first owner went out and found the carcass of a dead dog and hung it from the single nail he still owned. Soon the house became unlivable. The dead dog's stench was unbearable. The family was forced to sell the house to the owner of the nail.

If the devil has a nail to hang his temptations on in your heart, he can take possession of your life. If you give the devil room to operate, he will do everything he can to destroy you.

Consider Cain. He allowed the emotion of anger to get out of control. His uncontrolled anger erupted into violence. He murdered his own brother. Anger was the nail in his heart that the devil hung the outburst of violence upon.

The apostle Paul makes this insightful statement: "'Be angry, and do not sin': do not let the sun go down on your wrath, nor give place to the devil" (Eph. 4:26, 27).

We give place to the devil when we allow compromise to govern our actions, when we cherish sin in our hearts. We give place to the devil when we fail to deal with some sin God is pointing out, and instead justify the sinful behavior in our life.

Compromise is deadly, not merely because the individual act is wrong, but because each compromise allows the devil another nail to hang further temptation upon in our hearts. The only solution to compromise is Jesus' attitude when He joyously proclaimed, "I always do those things that please Him" (John 8:29).

Jesus' joy was to please the Father. His one goal was to do the Father's will. His chief ambition was to bring joy to the Father's heart through obedience. He resisted the devil's attempts to place one nail in His heart. Let Jesus wield the hammer of truth and pull out all of the devil's nails today.

March 18

THE MASTER'S VOICE

And the peace of God, which surpasses all understanding, will guard your hearts and minds through Christ Jesus. Phil. 4:7.

I climbed into the attic, where my grandfather kept the canaries he raised. I watched amazed as he placed a canary in a cage alone, then covered it, leaving the bird in total darkness. He began to whistle. Hearing its master's voice, the canary picked up the tune. Learning the song in the darkness, the bird remembered it ever after.

God is teaching you and me to trust as He taught Jesus to trust. One of the greatest lessons of life is to learn to trust when we cannot understand, when it seems dark, when the journey seems long and the way seems hard, when there is no way around, over, or through the mountain.

In the book of Philippians the apostle Paul discusses a "peace . . . which surpasses all understanding" (Phil. 4:7). When the perplexities and trials of life confuse us, our faith can still cling to God's promises. It is not necessary to understand why things happen. Often we will not understand what's going on in our lives. Life has its joys and sorrows, its victories and defeats. Trying to understand why God allows heartache and suffering may only leave us confused. Though the Christian life is not one that we will always understand, it is one in which we can always trust.

Trust includes the inner conviction that God is at work in our lives.

Like the canary, we are learning a song in the darkness. We are learning to respond to the Master's voice. We are learning a song of trust. Think about Jesus hanging in the darkness on the cross, suspended alone between heaven and earth. He cried out, "Father, into thy hands I commend my Spirit" (Luke 23:46, KJV). Though ridiculed by the mob, betrayed by Judas, denied by Peter, forsaken by His disciples, rejected by the Jews, and crucified by the Romans, Jesus lived the life of trust.

Jesus teaches lessons of trust in every experience. Ask God to deepen your trust through your circumstances. Ask Him to increase your faith, to help you hang on to His love even when you cannot understand. Pray, "Lord, I do believe. Teach me to fully trust."

March 19

STRENGTH FOR OUR DAILY NEED

Remember the word to Your servant, upon which You have caused me to hope. This is my comfort in my affliction, for Your word has given me life. Ps. 119:49, 50.

God's Word is powerful. It gives us hope in times of discouragement. It brings comfort in times of affliction. It imparts life in times of despair. It brings guidance in time of confusion and peace in times of doubt. It encourages our hearts in life's darkest moments.

Recently I interviewed Pastor Mikhail Kulakov, once the leader of the Seventh-day Adventist Church in the former Soviet Union. Pastor Kulakov's testimony had a profound effect on my own life. This godly, deeply spiritual giant of the Word has now devoted his life to overseeing the translation of the Bible into modern Russian.

During the oppressive Communist regime, Pastor Kulakov was sentenced to prison, labor camps, and eternal banishment by the Soviet government. Sometimes he went for weeks with no contact with his family. At the time he was a young man in his 20s. He wondered if he had any future at all.

One day a parcel arrived at his labor camp addressed to him. His mother had sent him some simple food stuffs. Hidden within the parcel was a New Testament. When the censor opened the package and rummaged through it, he discovered the old Bible. When he yanked it out, the cover fell off, and the pages flew in every direction. Of course the censor denied Pastor Kulakov the privilege of keeping the Bible. In the confusion of picking up the scattered pages, though, he failed to see Pastor Kulakov quickly slip one page into his pants pocket.

Back at the barracks, Pastor Kulakov eagerly read the sacred page of Scripture. His eyes fell on John 17:24: "Father, I desire that they also whom You gave Me may be with Me where I am." His heart leaped for joy. This single passage of Scripture encouraged him for weeks. Jesus, his loving Savior, didn't want him to be in that filthy, rat-infested barracks. Jesus longed for him to be in heaven. One verse made a difference.

One verse will make a difference for you. Let God's promises encourage your heart and lift your spirits today.

March 20

WHEN GUILT IS GONE

If we confess our sins, He is faithful and just to forgive us our sins and to cleanse us from all unrighteousness. 1 John 1:9.

Conducting an evangelistic campaign in Stockholm, Sweden, I spent an evening visiting with one of the city's travel agents. She had been attending our meetings in the heart of the city. As we discussed spiritual things she said, "Pastor, I have a question I've always wanted to ask a minister. Is abortion murder?" With tears in her eyes, she blurted out a story of thwarted love, of an unwanted pregnancy, and of her hasty decision to abort her baby after carrying it for four months.

After the breakup of her first marriage, she met a man she believed was the man of her dreams. She fell in love. They dated for six months, and he promised to marry her. She found herself pregnant by him, but one day he told her that he was already married and had three children in another country. He said he now needed to leave and return to his family.

The sudden news devastated her. With the collapse of this second relationship, she could not stand to bear a child by a man who had so used her. She had the child aborted, yet she never felt comfortable with her decision. An inner restlessness plagued her, a sense that she had taken an innocent life.

She bore the heavy, oppressive burden of that guilt for the next 18 years. Now, as we talked together, I gently explained that when Christ cried out, "Father, forgive them; for they know not what they do" (Luke 23:34, KJV), His forgiveness was for her. His forgiveness had been there all along. It was rooted in Christ's very nature. Together we read 1 John 1:9: "If we confess our sins, He is faithful and just to forgive us our sins."

"Does the text say," I asked, "'If we confess our sins . . . except abortion'?" "Oh, no!" she responded. "Would you like me to write in your Bible, 'If we confess our sins . . . except abortion'?" I asked. "Certainly not!" she said.

Tears filled her eyes. She began to realize that what God promises is really true. She grasped His promise by faith. "If we confess our sins, He is faithful and just to forgive us our sins." A new peace flooded her soul. Forgiveness had been available for 18 long years, yet she received its benefit only when she opened her heart to receive it.

Here is an eternal truth: forgiveness is rooted in God's very nature. It is part of who He is. The cross reveals God's loving character of mercy, providing forgiveness for the entire human race. Though we do not receive God's forgiveness until we confess our sins, our confession does not earn God's forgiveness. Rather, our confession opens our heart to receive the forgiveness that was there all the time. It is there for you and me today.

Open your heart to God's amazing forgiveness. Let Him silence every accusing voice in your head. Let Him wash away your guilt with the wonders of His love today.

March 21

GET UP . . . GO ON

Do not rejoice over me, my enemy; when I fall, I will arise; when I sit in darkness, the Lord will be a light to me. Micah 7:8.

On May 7, 1824, a gifted composer conducted the first performance of his Ninth Symphony in a Viennese theater. The crowded auditorium received the program with enthusiasm. This man seemed to put so much emotion in his music, so much that was passionate and heroic. At the end of one movement the audience broke into thunderous applause.

But the conductor just stood there, his back to them, calmly turning the pages of his score. Finally the contralto on the stage had to pull him by the sleeve and point him to the audience. Only then did Ludwig van Beethoven, totally deaf, turn and bow.

He could not hear any of the clapping, and he could not hear a note that he was conducting. But the whole symphony was there in his head, and he was giving it dramatic, glorious expression.

Beethoven had good reason to enjoy that unforgettable evening. In a way, he had been composing against his past, turning ugliness and disappointment into something beautiful.

Perhaps he remembered a scene from years before. It's midnight; a little boy is fast asleep in the Beethoven home. His father stumbles in from a tavern with a drinking buddy and roughly shakes young Ludwig awake. Father demands that he play the piano for his guest. And so, gathering his wits and brushing tears from his cheeks, the boy makes his way to the piano and begins to play for hours.

Ludwig's father could be harsh and even cruel to his son. A childhood companion recalled that Ludwig's father often compelled him to the piano by beatings. Some believe that Beethoven's later deafness may have resulted, at least in part, from the abuse he received as a child.

Beethoven's music is not all sweetness and light. It is also thunder and longing. Beethoven had plenty of opportunity for anger and resentment, yet he found a way to express his feelings positively. Expressing the deepest parts of himself, he turned his life experience into a gift.

The God of heaven is fully capable of lighting up the darkness of our lives. The light of His love penetrates our moments of darkest despair. His light leads us out of darkness.

When we are crushed by sadness or broken by grief, God picks us up. He is there when we stumble. Our fall may result from our own mistakes or from the decision of someone else. A dysfunctional family situation, oppressive boss, or the betrayal of friends may beat us down. Disease or debt may oppress us, yet God's Word is still true. The prophet Micah cries out, "Do not rejoice over me, my enemy; when I fall, I will arise" (Micah 7:8). In His strength you can rise and rejoice today.

March 22

STOPPING THE DOWNWARD SPIRAL

The Lord will give strength to His people; the Lord will bless His people with peace. Ps. 29:11.

Jan's parents brought her up in a Christian home, but she rebelled against their values. Believing them manipulative and controlling, she set out to explore the world on her own. By age 15 she had slipped into alcohol and drug abuse. These became addictions that she could never quite shake.

Jan tried to find the love she needed with a succession of men. She lived with several boyfriends but could never settle down, never experience a truly stable relationship.

Sometimes Jan would visit the church of her childhood. I remember her at some evangelistic meetings I conducted. Jan was interested, but she could never quite grasp the real power and presence of God. Several times she came forward after an appeal; several times she determined to stop abusing drugs. But each time she went back to the old life. The pull was just too strong.

Trying to help Jan was terribly frustrating. I wanted her to experience God's love, to grasp what a relationship with Him could mean, but it kept slipping through her fingers. It remained painfully out of reach.

Life just kept spiraling downward for Jan. It had started with typical adolescent rebellion, but one problem led to another. The problems grew and grew until her life was out of control.

We have a word for people such as Jan. It's not a very kind word. We dismiss them as "losers." They're messed up. They've got all kinds of problems. They never get their act together.

Why did Jan keep failing? Why couldn't she find a way out of her problems? Could some basic lifestyle decisions have made a major change in her life?

I believe God's grace is greater than any habit that binds us. As Scripture states, "But where sin abounded, grace abounded much more" (Rom. 5:20). Grace is much stronger than sin. God's power is greater than our adversaries. Here is how you can personally receive it:

1. Acknowledge that you are weak and incapable of battling the enemy on your own (see John 15:5).

2. By faith, believe that God's power is sufficient to deliver you (see Phil. 4:13).

3. Determine to cut off all pathways of sin. Resist the devil (see James 4:7).

This last point is where many people fail. Determine to separate yourself, by God's power, from the source of your temptation. Whatever trips you up, avoid it. Guard the pathways of temptation. Though you cannot avoid all temptation, you can choose to avoid positions in which you know you will be tempted. You can win the battle before the temptation comes by not making yourself vulnerable. Make the choice beforehand. You will be glad you did.

March 23

EMBRACED BY LOVE

In this the love of God was manifested toward us, that God has sent His only begotten Son into the world, that we might live through Him. 1 John 4:9.

Kim was excited! Maybe excited is too mild a word. She was euphoric! She was wild with delight. Her husband, Steve, had just won the Ohio state lottery of several million dollars—$107,000 per year for 20 years. To top it off, he won the lottery a second time to the tune of $100,000. This Dayton couple could live the life of their dreams. Incredible pleasures lay at their fingertips.

There was only one problem. Kim was having an extramarital affair, and she knew the win would cause only greater problems. She didn't want to walk away from millions, but certainly didn't want to end the affair, either. She wanted Steve's money, but had no interest in his love. The lottery winnings dominated Kim's mind. She plotted to get the money, and finally came up with a plan to hire a hit man to kill her husband.

While she discussed her plan on the phone with her lover, her 21-year-old son listened to the entire conversation. Soon police arrested Kim for plotting her husband's death—for a mere $500. She had put $25 down, with the balance to be paid when the job was done.

Surprisingly enough, Steve repeatedly visited Kim in prison. "You don't wash 22 years under the bridge," he explained. Their relationship grew. He diligently fought to have her sentence reduced. He dropped all his charges against her. His love broke her heart. His loving initiative touched something deep inside. Kim saw her affair for what it was—a cheap imitation of the real thing. How could she resist the real, genuine, authentic love of one who would not let her go? How could she be unfaithful to somebody so faithful to her? How could she turn her back on one who embraced her with his love? She couldn't. She wouldn't. When she finally got out of prison, she threw her arms around him, sobbing, "Please, never, never, never let me go!"

Their friends call them crazy, and Steve and Kim don't disagree. "Love is a state of insanity anyway," Steve said. "You just cannot explain it."

God's unconditional love is certainly unexplainable. Unconditional love is a love that perseveres no matter what. It is a love that is not dependent on the one being loved. Here is an almost unbelievable thought.

There is nothing you can do to get God to love you any less. Our actions do not determine His love—His heart does. When we turn our backs on Him, He loves us still. When we reject His invitation to follow Him, He loves us still. When we violate His will, He loves us still. Our actions may bring Him pain. Our wrong choices may break His heart. Our bad decisions may give Him deep grief, but nothing we do can change His steadfast love.

I can't turn away from that love. All I can do is fall at His feet and thank Him forever for loving me so.

POWER FROM INSIDE OUT

I can do all things through Christ who strengthens me. Phil. 4:13.

Treena Kerr lived in a beautiful colonial mansion on Chesapeake Bay. She seemed to have just about everything. Her husband was the famous Galloping Gourmet on television, Graham Kerr. The couple had worked hard. They'd become very successful. They could afford a lavish lifestyle. They had wonderful friends.

But Treena was dying inside. The center wasn't holding. Those on the outside saw a cheery, glamorous woman. But those close to Treena knew she struggled with serious emotional problems. In fact, she'd been going downhill for years.

At one point Treena had been judged incapable of managing her life. Doctors considered admitting her to a mental institution for an undetermined period. Only a high daily dose of Valium kept her going.

Treena had a young maid named Ruthie, who began praying for her. Ruthie told fellow believers at her church, and they began to pray for Treena too.

Ruthie knew that everything else had failed to help Treena. Her husband had just taken her on a dream cruise around the world in a beautiful yacht to see if that would help, but she'd come home more miserable than ever.

One day, after three months of prayer, Ruthie found Treena screaming at the ceiling in her bedroom. She got up enough courage to suggest, "Why don't you give your problems to God?"

Treena angrily took up the challenge. She shot back, "All right, God, if You're so clever, You deal with it, because I can't."

A week later Treena found herself in Ruthie's church. Before she knew it, she was responding to an altar call. Treena knelt and began weeping. "I'm sorry, Jesus; forgive me, Jesus" was all she could say.

Treena left that church feeling like God had touched her. Back home she started seeking to know this God who saved her. She started reading a Bible Ruthie had given her.

Treena read until late into the night. As she reached for her sleeping pills an inner voice said, "You won't want anything like that anymore." She poured her drugs down the bathroom sink. Most people don't just quit taking that much Valium cold turkey, but Treena slept soundly and woke refreshed, invigorated, and clear-eyed.

God's power working in her gradually transformed her life. The Christian life is not a matter of gritting your teeth and holding on for dear life. It's not a matter of feverishly struggling to obey God's will. Christianity is a relationship with God that is life-transforming. As Paul so poignantly puts it: "That He would grant you, according to the riches of His glory, to be strengthened with might through His Spirit in the inner man" (Eph. 3:16).

The Spirit strengthens us within. Treena Kerr discovered the secret to wholeness in her own personal life. The Holy Spirit living within brings an amazing new spiritual power into our lives. God offers you this life-changing power today.

March 25

DON'T GET STUCK IN A RUT

But the path of the just is like the shining sun, that shines ever brighter unto the perfect day. Prov. 4:18.

Dwight L. Moody, one of modern times' most prolific evangelists, always had an eagerness to learn. He had an intense desire to daily grow in Christ.

During one long preaching tour Moody traveled by train with a singer named Towner. A drunk with a badly bruised eye recognized Moody and started bawling out hymns. The evangelist didn't want to deal with the man and said, "Let's get out of here." But Towner told him that all the other cars were full.

A conductor came down the aisle. Still irritated, Moody stopped him and pointed out the drunk. The conductor went over and gently quieted the man. He bathed and bandaged his eye, then led him back to his seat, where he fell asleep.

After reflecting on this for a while, Moody told his companion, "This has been a terrible rebuke to me." The conductor had acted like the good Samaritan, Moody said, while he had responded like an indifferent Pharisee. Moody shared the humbling story each day for the rest of his preaching tour.

Although Moody was a powerful preacher, he regularly sat at the feet of guest speakers, his Bible open, taking notes. Moody is an outstanding example of being teachable, of one who was willing to learn, to grow, to discover more and more of God's truth.

God may be trying to reveal something to you today.

The circumstances we face each day reveal whom we really are, as well as shape who we become. If there is no anger inside of us, no circumstance can bring it out of us. If there is no bitterness inside, no amount of injustice can stir it. If there is no lust inside, no amount of flirtation can arouse it. If there is no dishonesty inside, even the opportunity to cheat will not prompt it.

Every day life's circumstances show us what is really in our hearts. God wants our issues out in the open so we can deal with them honestly. Sometimes He allows us to see painful revelations of who we really are so we can bring everything inside of us to Him. He is fully capable of handling it. Allow His Spirit to reveal what's really inside today, and determine to keep growing in Jesus.

March 26

A FAITH WORTH DYING FOR

He who has an ear, let him hear what the Spirit says to the churches. He who overcomes shall not be hurt by the second death. Rev. 2:11.

The bloodstained sands of time speak of a New Testament faith worth dying for. Phileas, executed for his faith in A.D. 306 in Alexandria, was one of these. But before he died, he left a beautiful testimony for his faith, recorded by eyewitnesses.

The young and wealthy Phileas, a product of the upper class, had served honorably in public affairs. A wife and children brought him much happiness. Though becoming a Christian involved risking everything, he gladly took that risk.

After his arrest the Roman prefect of Egypt tried to persuade him to give up his faith: "Free your mind of this madness that has seized on it," he urged Phileas.

Phileas calmly replied, "I have never been mad and am quite sane now."

"Very well then," the prefect replied. "Sacrifice to the gods." Phileas answered that he could sacrifice to only one God.

"What kind of sacrifices does your God like?" he was asked.

"Purity of heart, sincere faith, and truth."

Throughout the interrogation, as Phileas stood before the judge, his weeping family behind him, he testified eloquently for his faith.

When pressed again to give in, Phileas said, "The Savior of all our souls is Jesus Christ, whom I serve in these chains. . . . I have given much thought to my situation, and I am determined to suffer for Christ."

Shortly afterward Phileas was beheaded. People such as he challenge us to be faithful to the purity of the gospel. They call us back to the bedrock faith of the New Testament believers, to the commitment of the disciples, to the steadfast faith of the martyrs. Today's Christianity is often an easygoing, accommodating, crossless Christianity that costs little. It is a spineless, soft faith that requires little real sacrifice, or a superficial faith promising its adherents health, wealth, and status. Yes, Jesus offers us the abundant life (see John 10:10), but He also offers us the cross. The Master said, "If anyone desires to come after Me, let him deny himself, and take up his cross, and follow Me" (Matt. 16:24). Jesus is the pearl of great price (see Matt. 13:46). Anything we give up for Him is well worth it. His incalculable worth, His unsurpassed loveliness, His inestimable value, makes all of our sacrifices pale into insignificance. He is worth the cost.

March 27

OUR GUIDE EVEN UNTO DEATH

For this is God, our God forever and ever; He will be our guide even to death. Ps. 48:14.

Lizzie Atwater, expecting her first baby, waited in agonizing suspense as bands of marauders closed in on her compound. A missionary to China during the Boxer Rebellion of August 1900, she faced the prospect of a brutal death at the hands of fanatics who had sworn vengeance on all foreigners.

But in time of terror Lizzie found a way to hope. This is what she wrote to her sister and her family shortly before her death:

"I long for a sight of your dear faces, but I fear we shall not meet on earth. I am preparing for the end very quietly and calmly. The Lord is wonderfully near, and He will not fail me. I was very restless and excited while there seemed a chance of life, but God has taken away that feeling, and now I just pray for grace to meet the terrible end bravely. The pain will soon be over, and oh, the sweetness of the welcome above!"

In Ecuador, January 1956, Roj Youderian was killed while trying to share the gospel with Auca Indians in the jungle. Days after his body was found, Roj's wife, Barbara, wrote this in her private journal: "God gave me this verse in Psalm 48 two days ago: 'For this God is our God for ever and ever: he will be our guide even unto death' [Ps. 48:14, KJV]."

In the Belgian Congo, September 1956, missionary Lois Carlson strained to listen to the static from a shortwave radio. Simba nationalists had overrun Dr. Paul Carlson's hospital.

Once in a while Dr. Carlson could sneak out a brief message on the shortwave. Lois caught this sentence: "Where I go from here I know not, only that it will be with Him."

Days later, another message: "I know I'm ready to meet my Lord, but my thought for you makes it more difficult. I trust that I might be a witness for Christ."

When witnesses discovered Dr. Carlson's body, slain at the hospital, they found a New Testament in his jacket pocket. Inside, the doctor had written the date—the day before his death—and a single word: "Peace."

Peace in the face of the worst of circumstances. Peace in the most troubling times. Peace in despair, peace in disaster, peace in the face of death. God's peace is His special gift for you today. Whatever the circumstances of your life, whatever situation you find yourself in today, whatever troubling thoughts are racing through your mind, grasp this simple promise by faith: "I will hear what God the Lord will speak, for He will speak peace to His people" (Ps. 85:8).

Open your ears. Listen for His voice. Hear His word of peace to your soul today.

March 28

THE FLAG OF ALLEGIANCE

Hallow My Sabbaths, and they will be a sign between Me and you, that you may know that I am the Lord your God. Eze. 20:20.

In the early 1600s Dorothy Traske conducted a private preparatory school in London. A lengthy waiting list testified to her popularity as a teacher.

Mrs. Traske and her husband, John, were Puritans. Puritans believed that the Church of England needed to be purified and brought back to its New Testament roots. Seeking to order their lives after the clear principles of Scripture, the Traskes ran across the Bible commands regarding the seventh-day Sabbath.

The Traskes determined to conform to this clear biblical command. Mrs. Traske closed her school on Saturday.

When pupils' parents asked why, Mrs. Traske explained her convictions. Authorities investigated, and they threw her into London's Gatehouse prison. They considered her actions a defiance of the state.

Mrs. Traske languished in prison for some 15 years. Not wanting to burden those on the outside with her needs, she subsisted for the most part on bread, water, roots, and herbs. Finally, shut away inside gray walls, she sickened and died. She was carried out of Gatehouse prison and buried in a field.

For Dorothy Traske the Sabbath was a sign of loyalty. More than just another day, it was a command from God. To reject the Sabbath was to reject the Lord of the Sabbath and the Creator who so designated it. She faced imprisonment and death, not out of loyalty to just a day, but out of her faithfulness to God's command. In theory one 24-hour period is the same as any other. But according to God's Word, the Sabbath is decidedly different.

God's command says, "Remember the Sabbath day, to keep it holy" (Ex. 20:8).

The Genesis account records: "God blessed the seventh day and sanctified it, because in it He rested from all His work which God had created and made" (Gen. 2:3).

The seventh-day Sabbath is God's blessed and sanctified symbol of loyalty. Fly His flag. Worship His name this very Sabbath. If Dorothy Traske was willing to die rather than compromise her Sabbath allegiance, should we not be willing to worship Him each Sabbath rather than compromise ours?

March 29

HERALDS OF TRUTH, PART 1

And you will seek Me and find Me, when you search for Me with all your heart. Jer. 29:13.

Attending St. Patrick's School in Norwich, Connecticut, as a boy, I had little idea that Patrick of Ireland laid the foundation for Sabbathkeeping in the British Isles.

As a young man in the fifth century, Patrick heard Christ's gospel preached in the Roman province of Gaul. He accepted this as God's truth and soon felt called to share this good news in Ireland, where he had spent some years as a slave.

Patrick's powerful biblical preaching led thousands to bow the knee before a new Lord, Jesus Christ. Included in those baptized was King Niall's descendant, Columba, who became another of Christianity's great pioneers. Like Patrick, Columba upheld the Bible as the only foundation for faith, and emphasized the blessing of obeying the Ten Commandments, which he called "Christ's law."

About A.D. 563 Columba sailed to the small island of Iona, just off the British coast. There he founded a Christian school and missionary center. Missionaries from Iona preached God's Word powerfully throughout the British Isles.

Columba also concluded something very interesting: that unconditional allegiance to God's Word meant he should observe the Sabbath of the Bible. On his deathbed Columba said, "Truly this day is for me a Sabbath, because it is my last day of this present laborious life. In it, after my toilsome labors, I keep Sabbath."

Now read what historian Andrew Lang wrote about the Celtic church, which Columba and Patrick founded: "They worked on Sunday but kept Saturday in a sabbatical manner."

Throughout history some Christians somewhere have kept the Bible Sabbath. Through careful Bible study they discovered God's true holy day. David's words in Psalm 42:1 certainly apply to this group of searching believers: "As the deer pants for the water brooks, so pants my soul for You, O God."

God blesses with precious gems of truth those who sincerely seek in His Word. The Sabbath is an untarnished truth that has been uncovered by Bible students in all ages.

It is a truth that was uncovered at a price. Many were tortured, beaten, imprisoned, and sentenced to death because of their faithfulness to the Lord of the Sabbath. As Sabbathkeepers we stand on the shoulders of such giant stalwarts of the faith as Patrick and Columba. They have left on the pages of history a legacy of commitment that we would do well to follow today.

March 30

HERALDS OF TRUTH, PART 2

If you love Me, keep My commandments. John 14:15.

In 1662 a minister named Francis Bampfield landed in the Dorchester jail, condemned for his nonconformist beliefs. Bampfield had become one of the most celebrated preachers in his area of England. He was a scholarly, generous, and devoted man. But none of that mattered to the authorities. He had to conform to the traditions of the established church.

While in prison Bampfield became convinced that the seventh day is the Sabbath. After all, the Puritans emphasized the importance of God's moral law, the Ten Commandments. It didn't make any sense to keep all but the fourth.

It's interesting to note how Bampfield tried to persuade his fellow Puritans. Many didn't want to accept the seventh-day Sabbath because they regarded it as a Jewish institution. Bampfield pointed out that humankind and the Sabbath were created in the same week. It happened in the Garden of Eden, long before Abraham.

Genesis describes this as God's crowning act of Creation. "Then God blessed the seventh day and sanctified it, because in it He rested from all His work which God had created and made" (Gen. 2:3).

Driven by such clear Scripture texts, Bampfield had to conclude, "While weeks do last they [humankind and the Sabbath] will live and stand together."

Bampfield's contemporaries kept pointing out that Sunday was the *Christian* holy day, but he just couldn't get around the clear example of Christ. Bampfield combed the New Testament but could find no evidence that Christ ever kept any day of the week holy but the seventh.

He carefully examined the New Testament evidence for Sabbath-keeping. Texts such as these persuaded him that Jesus was a Sabbathkeeper:

"If you love Me, keep My commandments" (John 14:15).

"And as His custom was, He went into the synagogue on the Sabbath day, and stood up to read" (Luke 4:16).

Bampfield reasoned that if Jesus worshiped on the Sabbath, it was a good enough reason for him. The fact that Jesus kept the Sabbath is a compelling reason for us to worship on it too.

Some feel corporate Sabbath worship makes little difference. They reason that they can get just as much blessing from reading at home. They see little reason to attend church on Sabbath morning. They forget one vital truth: Jesus considered Sabbath worship extremely important, so important that He made it His custom.

March 31

HERALDS OF TRUTH, PART 3

There remains therefore a rest for the people of God. For he who has entered His rest has himself also ceased from his works as God did from His. Heb. 4:9, 10.

During the Reformation period many accepted the truth of the Bible Sabbath. Another distinguished Dissenter who became so convicted was Theophilus Brabourne. In the 1650s he pastored a church that kept the seventh day. To those who insisted that keeping Saturday holy meant a return to Judaism, Brabourne asked, "Will you reject the gospel because it was first given to the Jews? Why then do you reject the Sabbath because it was given to the Jews?"

Brabourne carefully linked the gospel and the Sabbath.

Brabourne's opponents argued that the Sabbath had been discontinued in favor of the first day, to honor Christ's resurrection. But Brabourne pointed to something Jesus had said shortly before He ascended to heaven. Warning His disciples about a time ahead when they would have to flee persecution, He said, "Pray that your flight may not be in winter or on the Sabbath" (Matt. 24:20).

Brabourne could only conclude that Christ believed His followers would be observing the same Sabbath that He had. He wrote, "Christ allowed of the ancient Sabbath as a Christian ordinance in the church all the times of the gospel after His death."

Many Sabbatarians were accused of legalism, of returning to the old ceremonial law. But Brabourne pointed out that keeping the Sabbath on the seventh day was no more legalistic than keeping Sabbath on the first day of the week. It was possible to observe either Sabbath or Sunday for the wrong reasons.

The Sabbath is not a symbol of righteousness by works. It is a symbol of righteousness by faith. Each Sabbath we rest as a symbol that we cannot save ourselves. We rest in Jesus' love, in His care. We rest in Jesus' salvation.

As Hebrews 4:10 puts it: "For he who has entered His rest has himself also ceased from his works as God did from His." The Sabbath is a symbol of rest, not work. When another day is substituted for Sabbath by a human decree, that day is a symbol of righteousness by works. Salvation by works substitutes man's way for God's. Righteousness by faith exalts God's way of salvation. When Christ died on the cross, He rested in the tomb over Sabbath, revealing His complete work of salvation, providing grace for all.

This Sabbath, rest in God's love, in His salvation. The Sabbath speaks in clarion tones today. There is enough saving grace for all of us.

HERALDS OF TRUTH, PART 4

Behold, You desire truth in the inward parts, and in the hidden part You will make me to know wisdom. Ps. 51:6.

John James established a Seventh Day Baptist Church in Bull Stake Alley, on Whitechapel Road in London. It became known as the Mill Yard Church.

On Saturday, October 19, 1661, while James preached, officers of the law walked into the church, interrupted the service, and demanded that the preacher come down from the pulpit. James, however, wanted to finish his sermon. He may have had an idea it would be his last. The officers promptly dragged him from the platform and took him outside, charging him with uttering treasonable words against the king.

James was confined to Newgate Prison. A month passed, and he was brought before the judges in Westminster Hall. The court condemned him, without real evidence, for trying to overthrow the government and slandering the king. He was sentenced to be hanged.

On November 26, 1661, James was bound to a sled and dragged through the streets to Tyburn, the place of execution. As the executioner prepared to do his duty, James began to speak to the crowd looking on. They would never forget his words.

He spoke powerfully about his hope in Christ, then prayed passionately for all gathered there. Witnesses remembered how gentle and loving his remarks seemed, set against this terrible place of death.

John James is not a figure who stands out in history. He founded no religious movement. He did not rediscover the central truths of the gospel like John Wycliffe or Martin Luther. He is just one of the many believers who, in their own way, expressed an unconditional allegiance to Jesus Christ.

John James was a man of integrity. He could not compromise his conscience. In today's world of moral irrelevance and compromising Christianity, God is calling for men and women who "desire truth in the inward parts." Few people in today's world of opinion polls have the conviction of conscience to be different from the majority. Moral anarchy reigns. Many Christians have little real spiritual backbone. Their Christian character lacks the steadfastness of a John James.

Echoing and reechoing through the centuries comes the witness of a life given for truth. The message is carried on the sacred winds of time. Keep the faith. Keep the faith. Keep the faith.

STEADFAST UNDER PRESSURE

If indeed you continue in the faith, grounded and steadfast, and are not moved away from the hope of the gospel which you heard, which was preached to every creature under heaven. Col. 1:23.

Georgio refused to compromise. Discovering the Ten Commandment law, the Sabbath truth convicted him. He decided that although, to his knowledge, there were no other Sabbathkeepers anywhere in the world, he would be faithful to his conscience.

Since he lived in an Orthodox state, Georgio was ultimately excommunicated from the church. No one in his community could buy anything from him, and no one could sell to him. His children couldn't attend school, because all schools were Orthodox schools. He was isolated within his own community.

Yet he believed that the things he read in the Bible were right. He determined to follow Scripture at any cost. Three years later representatives from the British and Foreign Bible Society visited his country. Georgio inquired regarding the Bible Sabbath. They gave the usual arguments against it: that we are not under the law but under grace, that the day one keeps is not important. Still, they did not dissuade this man. To him their arguments seemed weak.

Through careful questioning he finally discovered that there were a small number of Sabbathkeepers in Turkey. Since he did not have their address, he merely wrote to "any Sabbathkeepers in Istanbul, Turkey." He continued to press for a response and over a six-month period wrote letter after letter.

Finally, after months, a letter was delivered to a small Sabbathkeeping church in Istanbul. Contact was set up, and this man learned of the worldwide movement of Seventh-day Adventists and became an Adventist. Ultimately he had to move from his village. God blessed him. His children attended non-Orthodox schools. He started a little business, which prospered. He eventually became a leader of a small Adventist church in Greece.

Georgio's story is not unique. There are many around the world whose commitment to truth is steadfast. The word "steadfast" means to gallantly hold on, to not yield, to cling to truth. In an earnest heartfelt prayer David declared: "My heart is steadfast, O God, my heart is steadfast" (Ps. 57:7). Is your heart steadfast? Are you shaped by the environment around you? Are you molded by the popular culture?

Georgio made a single-minded decision. This decision influenced everything else he did. Frankly put, Georgio decided to do nothing that would in any way displease God. He determined to allow God's Word to shape his thoughts, the Holy Spirit to guide his actions, and Christ's will to influence his behavior. Why not make Georgio's choice your choice today.

April 3

IS THE MAJORITY ALWAYS RIGHT?

Enter by the narrow gate; for wide is the gate and broad is the way that leads to destruction, and there are many who go in by it. Because narrow is the gate and difficult is the way which leads to life, and there are few who find it. Matt. 7:13, 14.

God can surprise even pastors by the way He works. Sometimes He confronts us with truth. Shakes us up. Jars us from our complacency.

Ray Holmes pastored a 500-member Lutheran church in the upper peninsula of Michigan. His wife, Shirley, confronted him with the question of the seventh-day Sabbath. At times he'd felt uncomfortable in his denomination, out of harmony with those who believed that the Bible's concrete teachings needed updating. He longed to base his faith on biblical truth, but the seventh-day Sabbath? It didn't seem possible that so many leading scholars could be wrong!

Pastor Holmes was committed to the supremacy of Scripture. His attitude was "If God's Word says it, I believe it." His faith was built on the solid truths of God's Word. But this time he was shaken to the core. He'd been brought up in his denomination's tradition of keeping the first day. He'd assumed that since Christ rose from the dead on the first day, the true Bible Sabbath was indeed Sunday.

Responding to his wife's challenge, Pastor Holmes pored through the Bible, attempting to unravel the truth. Ultimately his discovery led him to resign his position as pastor of the Lutheran congregation and become a Sabbathkeeper. Pastor Holmes discovered that the majority isn't always right.

What did Jesus mean by His statement "Broad is the way that leads to destruction"? Why did He declare "Narrow is the . . . way which leads to life"? God is certainly not trying to hide truth from us. The narrow way is not narrow because it is difficult to find. It is narrow because it is difficult to follow. The reason many people cannot find truth is because they are not willing to follow it. The price of truth is surrender. The surrendered heart discovers more and more truth in God's Word. It is God's plan for us to keep growing in our Christian walk. When was the last time you were confronted by some Bible truth that necessitated a change in your life?

Is your Christian life stagnant? Does truth challenge you? Are you regularly challenged by the Spirit to make changes in your life? Pastor Ray Holmes was challenged by the truth. His response was "God, whatever You impress me to do, I am willing." Can our response be any less?

April 4

GOD'S CALL TO RETURN

I will arise and go to my father, and will say to him, "Father, I have sinned against heaven and before you. Luke 15:18.

Lisa lived on the beautiful island of Oahu in Hawaii. Life on the island paradise was a dream until the morning that her husband said, "Honey, I'm going for a hike," and never returned.

Alone in an isolated mountainous region, along a volcanic ridge, Hank slipped. The loose gravel gave way beneath his feet. He plunged headlong into a 500-foot ravine, broke his neck, and died. It took authorities three days to find him.

Lisa had a hard time getting over her loss. Even with the passing of weeks and months, it still hurt. And as Lisa worked through her pain, she heard the call of Another: "Come to Me, all you who labor and are heavy laden, and I will give you rest" (Matt. 11:28).

Lisa had been brought up to keep the Bible Sabbath. As she sensed God's call to her heart, she believed that only by returning to her roots could she find rest. To Lisa, keeping the seventh-day Sabbath symbolized resting in God's loving arms. Resting from her care, her anxiety, her burdens, her troubled heart.

To Lisa, the Sabbath symbolized home. In a very real sense the Sabbath is home. It calls us back to our Eden home, where God set the Sabbath aside as a day of fellowship with Him.

Adam and Eve spent their first Sabbath with God and with each other. Linked in a fellowship of love, they rejoiced in His presence. Bonded intimately, they were drawn to their Creator and to each other. The central purpose of the Sabbath is relationship. In the hurried, hectic pace of life, relationships often do not take priority in our busy lives. The Sabbath calls us to pause and to reflect on what is really important. It speaks to us of the intimacy our hearts long for. It is a weekly invitation to place priority on our relationship with God, our family, our friends, and the people close to us.

Lisa found rest and renewed relationships in the Sabbath, and you can too. God invites you to experience the most fulfilling relationship this very Sabbath.

April 5

REST FOR WORKAHOLICS

Come to Me, all you who labor and are heavy laden, and I will give you rest. Take My yoke upon you and learn from Me, for I am gentle and lowly in heart, and you will find rest for your souls. Matt. 11:28, 29.

Henry was on a fast track to the very top of Chicago's business world. He marketed condominiums in a downtown high-rise, and he could barely keep up with demand.

Henry worked seven days a week. With hardly time for sleep, he certainly didn't have time for God. Henry had turned his back on his religious upbringing many years before. It just didn't work for him. It just didn't make the difference everyone said it was supposed to make.

But now Henry thought he'd found something that really worked. He was completely caught up in his business.

In fact, the weekends were the busiest in the real estate business. But one day Henry's parents recommended that he watch an *It Is Written* program called "Rest for Workaholics." It described how the Bible Sabbath is an ideal remedy for the stress-filled, hectic lifestyle.

The program hit close to home for Henry. He started to realize that he needed spiritual rest, Sabbath rest, in his own life. Religion had never worked for him before. It had always seemed like a bunch of trivial rules. He had never been able to build a genuine relationship with Christ. But maybe, just maybe, he had never invested the right kind of time in that relationship. Maybe he had never given Jesus Christ a real chance.

After the program Henry called our 800 number to locate Adventist churches in the Chicago area. The next Saturday Henry walked into a Seventh-day Adventist church not far from his home. The warmth of these believers enveloped him. The pastor made a powerful appeal at the end of his sermon, and Henry found himself standing in the aisle, breaking up inside emotionally.

It was time to make a decision. Would he keep on with his nonstop business venture? Or would he invest time, quality time, in a relationship with Christ? Standing in that sanctuary, the arms of his new friends around him, Henry made his choice.

In the Sabbath Henry discovered an oasis from his workaholic ways. Moses called the Sabbath "the Sabbath of rest" (Ex. 31:15).

The Sabbath is not a recommendation; it is a command. It is not a yellow blinking light at the crossroads of life, which we may choose to recklessly speed through. It is a red light. A stoplight. God loves us too much to merely recommend that we pause to refresh and rebuild our minds, bodies, and souls. In the Sabbath our all-powerful Creator, our loving Redeemer, and our coming King commands us to stop the frantic running in our lives, stop the incessant working in our lives, and find rest in Him. What an invitation! What a command! What a God!

April 6

NURTURED IN TRIAL

Oh, love the Lord, all you His saints! For the Lord preserves the faithful. Ps. 31:23.

The authorities found young sailor Gerrit Corneliss working on a barge. Taking him to the city hall, they interrogated him and told him to give up his New Testament beliefs.

Gerrit refused. He would give them no information that might lead to the arrest of his fellow believers. They blindfolded him, drawing him up by his hands and leaving him suspended for long periods. They beat him with rods and laid him on the rack.

The torturers threatened to keep it up until he gave in. But Gerrit remained silent. It was reported that he thanked God for keeping his lips shut.

When they took him out to be burned, they had to carry him in a chair because he could no longer walk. Arriving at the stake, Gerrit finally opened his lips. But it was only to pray fervently. "Father and Lord, be gracious to me. . . . Thou knowest my simple love toward Thee; accept me, and forgive them that inflict this suffering upon me."

In the Middle Ages the church had become powerful, usurping the authority of the state. No clear distinction separated the authority of the church and that of the state. Holding a belief different from one prescribed by the state church was considered treason. Believers in variant tenets were fiercely persecuted.

During this time of persecution God made this remarkable promise to His faithful followers. "But the woman was given two wings of a great eagle, that she might fly into the wilderness to her place, where she is nourished for a time and times and half a time, from the presence of the serpent" (Rev. 12:14).

Amazing! God nourishes His people in the wilderness. Oppressed, persecuted, tormented—but nourished. Harassed, hunted down, tried, sentenced to death—but nourished.

In all of their trials, God's people are spiritually fed. God does not leave us alone in our most difficult periods. He does not abandon us when the going gets rough.

Like the faithful Christians of the Dark Ages, we too are nourished in truth. God uses the troubles we face to teach us. He uses life's stresses to strengthen us, the hard knocks to nurture us.

In the difficulties you face today, God's promise is yours. Look to Him, and you too will be nourished in the wilderness.

April 7

THE SANCTUARY'S SERENITY

We might have strong consolation, who have fled for refuge to lay hold of the hope set before us. This hope we have as an anchor of the soul, both sure and steadfast, and which enters the Presence behind the veil. Heb. 6:18, 19.

A few years ago medical researchers studied the effect of the shocks of life on the central nervous system. They took one lamb and placed it alone in its pen, with electric shock devices hooked up around it. As the lamb wandered to one side of the pen the researchers threw a switch, shocking the lamb. Immediately it twitched and scampered to another part of the pen. Soon the researcher shocked the lamb again. Again it ran.

The scientists discovered that the lamb would never return to a place where previously it had been shocked. After a series of shocks the little lamb stood quivering in the center of its pen. It had no place to run, nowhere to go. The shocks were everywhere. Completely overcome emotionally, filled with anxiety and stress, its nerves gave way. The lamb had the equivalent of a nervous breakdown and died in the middle of the pen.

The researchers then took this lamb's twin and placed it in a pen. This time they put the lamb's mother in with it. Presently they shocked it. Again the lamb ran, but this time it ran to its mother and snuggled up to her closely. Evidently she reassured it, because it left her side to begin eating again. The researchers threw the switch again, and once again the lamb ran to its mother. Reassuringly she consoled it again. The researchers then noted a remarkable difference in the two lambs. The second lamb had no fear of returning to the spot where it had received the shock. To the amazement of the researchers, future shocks no long disturbed it. It showed none of the symptoms of nervousness, stress, or anxiety that its twin had shown under the same circumstances. What made this remarkable difference? The lamb had the assurance of someone to flee to. It had confidence and power in someone outside of itself to cope with stress.

Everyone needs such confidence. Even the atheistic philosopher Julian Huxley admitted: "Man does better if he believes as if God is there." The human heart has a deep need for someone to place confidence in, someone to go to in trouble, someone who will offer reassurance in the stresses and strains of life.

There is a place we can flee to for refuge, a place of calm assurance where we can feel secure. The living Christ ministers as our high priest in heaven's sanctuary. He is just as alive today as He was when He walked on earth 2,000 years ago. He is as truly with us as He was with the disciples. By faith we can enter into the presence of God. By faith we can flee for refuge into the security of the sanctuary. By faith we can lay hold of the secure hope we have in Jesus. By faith we can be unmoved, anchored in the presence of Christ within the veil. Triumphantly we can sing, "On Christ, the solid Rock, I stand; all other ground is sinking sand, all other ground is sinking sand."

April 8

HE RESTORES MY SOUL

He restores my soul; He leads me in the paths of righteousness for His name's sake. Ps. 23:3.

The door of my office suddenly flung open. A tough-looking young man with a scruffy beard burst into the room. Believing he might attack me, I stepped back. My Russian translator stepped between us. The man began waving his arms and talking animatedly in Russian.

It was March 1992, and I was in the midst of a series of evangelistic meetings in Moscow's Kremlin auditorium. Now my translator explained that this man was one of Moscow's notorious criminals. He had been in and out of jail 28 times. Filled with guilt and hopeless about his future, he longed to find peace.

I picked up my Bible and read 1 John 1:9 to him: "If we confess our sins, He is faithful and just to forgive us our sins." I told him the story of the thief on the cross who found forgiveness.

With tears running down his face, this guilty young Russian knelt and received God's forgiveness.

I left Moscow and didn't return for almost a year. When I returned to conduct an evangelistic follow-up meeting in a large civic auditorium, my Russian translator commented, "You will really enjoy our choir this evening. Each choir member was baptized last year during your evangelistic meetings." I enjoyed the choir immensely. I couldn't help noticing one clean-shaven, radiant young man in his early 30s. It was the notorious criminal I'd prayed with the year before. His face beamed with God's love. His eyes sparkled with a sense of wonder at God's grace. The hymns he sang flowed from a converted heart.

God longs not merely to forgive us. He longs to restore us—our joy, our peace, our purpose—into His image. The apostle John puts it this way: "Beloved, now we are children of God; and it has not yet been revealed what we shall be, but we know that when He is revealed, we shall be like Him, for we shall see Him as He is" (1 John 3:2).

If we allow Him to, He will restore us into His image. He will make us "like Him." What a privilege, what a promise, what a destiny.

April 9

TAKE RESPONSIBILITY

For we must all appear before the judgment seat of Christ, that each one may receive the things done in the body, according to what he has done, whether good or bad. 2 Cor. 5:10.

Billy was a 4-year-old terror in his church kindergarten. He pushed the other children, knocked them down, tripped them, and generally kept things upset.

One day the teacher said to him, "Billy, would you like to pray?" The little fighter prayed a simple prayer: "Jesus, please help those little children not to fall down so much."

What a masterful request! In one statement he absolved himself of all responsibility for the other children's falling down and getting hurt.

Change and responsibility go together. We can have no real behavioral change unless we take responsibility for our actions. If we are merely victims of our environment, the environment becomes responsible, not us. If we are simply the product of what others have done to us, then they are responsible.

All change begins with a sense of personal ownership of our actions. Unless we own our actions, we will excuse our behavior. God has given us the power of choice and has promised to empower our choices. His spirit impresses us to do right and enables us to do it. Accepting that we are morally responsible for our behavior, confessing our sins, and choosing to change allows us to receive God's pardon and power. God's grace saves us from sin's guilt and grip. As the old hymn says, "Rock of Ages, cleft for me . . . be of sin the double cure, cleanse me from its guilt and power."

Our environment influences our behavior. Our choices determine it. No one chooses for us. God has given us the capacity to make our own moral decisions.

We will not be judged based on others' decisions. We will be judged on our own. Moses' appeal to Israel millenniums ago speaks to our hearts today. "I call heaven and earth as witnesses today against you, that I have set before you life and death, blessing and cursing; therefore choose life, that both you and your descendants may live" (Deut. 30:19).

The choice is ours. His voice still speaks today. Choose life.

April 10

A DEADLY DELUSION

As the cloud disappears and vanishes away, so he who goes down to the grave does not come up. He shall never return to his house, nor shall his place know him anymore. Job 7:9, 10.

In the 1960s James Pike, an Episcopal bishop in New York City, thought he could communicate with the dead. He could not reconcile himself to the suicide of his son Jimmy, and thought the dead boy might try to contact him. Bishop Pike believed the Bible contained good moral principles, but he rejected its teaching authority. He thought Christ was a good man but not the Son of God, and he rejected the Bible instruction about what happens after death.

Bishop Pike moved to England to spend time at Oxford and Cambridge universities, where he studied biblical manuscripts. Upon returning to his room one day, he noticed a number of bizarre occurrences. Cards containing Jimmy's picture, which he'd placed on the nightstand, were opened. The clocks in the room had stopped at 8:20, precisely the time his son had committed suicide. Safety pins he'd left closed on his dresser were opened at odd angles. The mirror tilted at an angle. Jimmy's clothes were taken from a box and strewn around the room.

Bishop Pike felt that Jimmy was trying to contact him, so he visited one of London's spiritists. The medium brought up the form of the bishop's son, with this message: "Yes Father, I am in heaven, an eternal place, but don't talk to me about a Saviour. Jesus was a good man, but not the Saviour. . . . This is a wonderful place of joy and love. Jesus was a wonderful, enlightened spiritual teacher. He's here with the other cosmic masters."

After a series of these visits Bishop Pike was instructed to go to

Jerusalem to meet his son in the Judean desert. He and his wife entered the Judean desert, where they wandered in the hills, searching for Jimmy. The bishop became dehydrated. His wife ran for help, but it was too late. Bishop Pike died in the desert, looking for his dead son. He should have known better. The biblical counsel on death was clear, but he ignored it.

Spiritualism is both dangerous and deadly. According to Scripture, the dead do not appear to the living. Is spiritualism all a hoax? Is it some grand delusion? Is it make-believe? I am certain a lot of spiritualism is mere fraud and trickery by get-rich-quick hucksters. But it is much more. Although the devil cannot raise the dead, he can certainly impersonate them. His evil angels can masquerade as dead loved ones. Their appearance and voices may seem very real. The apostle Paul observes in 2 Corinthians 11:14: "And no wonder! For Satan himself transforms himself into an angel of light."

Satan attempts to counterfeit the hope of the resurrection by offering us our loved ones now in a spirit form. The Scriptures offer not some spirit being, but the real presence of our loved ones at the resurrection. Cling to the resurrection hope. Grasp it by faith. God offers us something much, much better than some disembodied spirit. He offers us reunion with our loved ones in the glorious resurrection morning.

April 11

THE BLESSED HOPE, A BETTER HOPE

For the law made nothing perfect; on the other hand, there is the bringing in of a better hope, through which we draw near to God. Heb. 7:19.

One beautiful summer day a father and his 9-year-old daughter were swimming together in the ocean. They had been splashing in the waves for a while when suddenly the tide began to go out with considerable force. It quickly took the little girl some distance away. Her father couldn't reach her. She'd need help if she was to get back to the shore.

Fortunately, instead of panicking, the father called out, "Float and swim quietly; don't be afraid. I'll be back to get you." Then he hurried away to find a boat.

When the father got back to the spot with a boat and some rescuers, his heart sank. His daughter wasn't there. She'd been swept far out to sea. A few minutes seemed like hours. But when they finally reached her, the girl was floating around calmly as her father had instructed.

When asked later how she had managed to remain so calm all alone far from shore, she answered, "I just did what Dad told me to do. I knew he'd come back, and I wasn't afraid."

The courageous little girl's hope had kept her alive. It enabled her to survive and be rescued.

Hope builds our spirits. It encourages our hearts, lifting us from what is to what will be. Someone has said, "You can live days without food, hours without water, minutes without air, but only seconds without hope." Hope is what our hearts crave.

Deep within our hearts we ask, "Is there any hope left? Hope for our worried, weary, war-torn planet? Hope for our confused, chaotic children? Hope for our polluted, overpopulated earth? Hope for our fear-driven, famine-stricken world?"

The hope of our Lord's return buoys us up on the sea of this world's uncertainty. Paul talks about "hope in God" amid life's uncertainties (Acts 24:15). He declares, "Hope does not disappoint [us]" (Rom. 5:5).

He affirms that we are "saved in this hope" (Rom. 8:24). Colossians 1:5 speaks of the "hope which is laid up for you." Our great hope is the second coming of our Lord (see 1 Thess. 4:13). In Titus 2:13 the coming of Jesus is called "the blessed hope." In Hebrews 7:19 Jesus' sacrifice on the cross gives us the "better hope" of eternal life.

The blessed hope is a better hope, better than anything this world has to offer. Rejoice today, for the blessed hope is yours. Jesus is coming soon to take you home.

April 12

FEARLESS FAITH

These all died in faith, not having received the promises, but having seen them afar off were assured of them, embraced them and confessed that they were strangers and pilgrims on the earth. Heb. 11:13.

Faith looks beyond what is, to what will be. Faith grasps the hand of God in every trial. Consider the faith of Henri Arnaud and his band of Waldensians. The Waldensians were a small group of faithful Bible-believing Christians who dared to be different. They refused to accept the decrees of the state-sponsored church in place of the Word of God. For them, the commands of God were more important than the traditions of people. The state church responded with an army to destroy them.

One spring morning high on a mountain, the Waldensians heard shouting far below as Colonel DePerot and his troops made ready for attack. "My lads, we shall sleep up there tonight," the colonel boasted. He invited the villagers to a public hanging to take place the next day. "Come and see the end of the Waldensians," he proclaimed.

High atop the peak, Waldensian leader Henri Arnaud opened his Bible and read to his company from Psalm 124:2, 3: "If it had not been the Lord who was on our side, when men rose up against us, then they would have swallowed us alive."

DePerot and his 4,000 troops started up the mountain. All went well until the best climbers were ready to reach for the timbers of the mountain fort. At that point Arnaud's men hailed a volley of stones down upon them. The troops fell back. Colonel DePerot was wounded and had to ask for refuge in the Waldensian fort. The Waldensians graciously gave him a safe place to sleep for the night—up on the mountain as he had predicted, but certainly not under the conditions he had expected.

The next night DePerot's soldiers surrounded the fort, but the Waldensians slipped silently away through a dense fog.

Far out of reach on the heights above walked the Waldensians. The soldiers cursed, "Heaven seems to take special interest in preserving these people." But it was not always so. At last came the day when 250 Waldensians were trapped in a cave by soldiers. A fire was built at the opening, and as smoke filled the cave the Waldensians sang praises to God until their last breath. Along with thousands of others the Waldensians died rather than compromise their integrity. They accepted martyrdom rather than surrender their faith. The witness of these faithful martyrs calls us to loyalty. Their testimony calls us to an unwavering commitment to God.

God is calling this generation to a deeper commitment. He is calling us to an uncompromising faith, to a steadfast loyalty to His Word. Are there areas of compromise in your personal life? Have your values been shaped by the culture around you? Are there some things you feel uncomfortable doing but not uncomfortable enough to stop doing them?

The stalwart faith of the Waldensians echoes down the corridors of time. The unshakable faith of these heroes of yesterday speaks to our hearts. Today, why not determine again, by God's grace, to be faithful until He comes?

TESTIFYING IN TRIALS

But before all these things, they will lay their hands on you and persecute you, delivering you up to the synagogues and prisons. You will be brought before kings and rulers for my name's sake. But it will turn out for you as an occasion for testimony. Luke 21:12, 13.

God often uses our greatest trials to accomplish the most good. They are often our testimony of faith. This was certainly true during the past centuries. One remarkable interrogation comes to us from an ecclesiastical courtroom in sixteenth-century London. Bishop Bonner quizzed a young man named Thomas Hawkes, who stood condemned as a heretic.

"Do you believe," the bishop asked indignantly, "that there remaineth in the blessed sacrament of the altar . . . the very body and blood of Christ?"

Hawkes answered simply, "I do believe as Christ hath taught me."

This didn't satisfy the bishop. He wanted to know exactly what his prisoner thought Christ meant by the words "Take, eat; this is My body" (Mark 14:22).

Hawkes admitted he didn't agree with the current church doctrine, called transubstantiation, that the bread and wine actually became the literal body and blood of Jesus. He pointed out that none of the apostles had ever taught it. He explained that the bread and unfermented wine symbolized Christ's broken body and spilled blood.

This further angered the bishop. "Ah, sir! You will have no more than the Scripture teaches?"

That was precisely Thomas Hawkes's position. He wanted to be taught from the Word of God. Earlier this young man had been taunted for having "nothing but your pretty little God's book."

Hawkes replied, "And is not that sufficient for my salvation?"

Bonner shot back, "Yes, it is sufficient for our salvation, but not for our instructions." For that, Hawkes was condemned to death.

His faith was one worth dying for. His belief in Scripture was solid. He was unmoved by the bishop's taunts. Hawkes accepted the wise man's admonition as his own: "Buy the truth, and do not sell it, also wisdom and instruction and understanding" (Prov. 23:23).

Scripture speaks to us in the twenty-first century. It calls us to allegiance. The truth appeals to us to follow it. Truth may be compromised, but it cannot be changed. It can be neglected, but it cannot be ignored forever. It can be rejected, but it will judge us at last. The only safe path is to accept the truth, believe the truth, and follow the truth.

FAITH IN THE FLAMES

Above all, taking the shield of faith with which you will be able to quench all the fiery darts of the wicked one. Eph. 6:16.

During the Reformation God raised up men and women with different gifts to lead out in a powerful spiritual reformation.

Three university men took leads in spreading the reform. A brilliant young scholar named Nicholas Ridley began to write about the need to return to the gospel.

His colleague Hugh Latimer, a man of bold demeanor and frank tongue, became a powerful preacher who spread the Reformation from the pulpit.

Another university friend, Thomas Cranmer, became an able church leader, eventually carrying out reform in the Church of England as the archbishop of Canterbury.

The scholar, the preacher, and the administrator worked hard to free their church from superstition and dead tradition. But all that came to a standstill when Queen Mary ascended the throne. Suddenly these Reformers became heretics, traitors, outcasts. Each was condemned to death and executed in Oxford, England.

But that is not what makes the Oxford martyrs so unique. Hundreds of others died for their faith during the reign of Bloody Mary. What distinguishes these three individuals is how they died.

On the night before he was to be burned, Nicholas Ridley invited friends to his prison cell for a supper party. They found him dressed in his finest clothes, looking quite upbeat. It was a celebration, he told them: "Tomorrow I must be married." Ridley was not thinking of the horrible death that awaited him, but of his final union with Christ.

When Thomas Cranmer was tied to the stake and felt the flames begin to leap toward him, he held his right hand down into the fire. It was that hand with which, in a moment of weakness, he had signed his well-known recantation. But now he held it there until it turned black, then cried out, "Lord Jesus, receive my spirit."

After Hugh Latimer had been tied to the stake and the wood began to burn, he leaned over to a companion and said, "We shall this day light such a candle, by God's grace, in England, as I trust shall never be put out."

These men met their barbaric deaths with extraordinary calm and steadfastness. They have become justly famous for making such a courageous stand for their faith. Their faith looked beyond the flames. The fires of persecution could not consume it. It leaped from the ashes, ascending with the white trail of smoke in the crimson sky to the very throne of God.

Godly faith is unquenchable. All the fires of hell cannot destroy it. Let God fill your heart with that kind of faith today. Let the faith of Jesus flow from God's throne into you right now.

April 15

THE INCREDIBLE POWER OF INFLUENCE

For none of us lives to himself, and no one dies to himself. Rom. 14:7.

On a hot, humid August morning in 1965 I boarded a Brazilian airliner to fly from Manaus, the old rubber-boom capital deep within the Brazilian jungle, to Belém at the mouth of the Tocantins River. Little did I realize that an experience on the plane that day would remain etched in my brain forever. It lingers in my consciousness, influencing my actions even today.

Buckling my seat belt to prepare for a quiet flight, I glanced up and noticed an Indian holy man walking down the aisle of the plane. His long white robe, flowing shoulder-length hair, and full beard attracted my attention. I was even more surprised when he took his seat beside me. His warm brown eyes and gentle smile put me at ease instantly.

During the flight we discussed our philosophies of life. Of course, I shared the "good news" about my best friend Jesus. I told of His inexhaustible mercy, His limitless love, His infinite power. I told of His creation, His salvation, His friendship, His priesthood, and His soon coming.

At the end of the two-hour flight, to my utter surprise, this Indian holy man placed his hand upon my shoulder and, with his face only a few inches from mine, spoke in distinct, deliberate tones. He hadn't said much during our flight. He let me do most of the talking. Now it was his turn.

"Son," he declared, "everyone we ever meet in life has influence upon us. There are no chance meetings. No life is an accident. We all influence one another for eternal life or for death. Thank you, young man, for influencing me for the nobler principles of the heavenly kingdom today." Then he turned and walked away.

I have thought of that chance encounter often. He was right. There are no chance meetings. Our words and actions have an incredibly powerful influence on other people. Every encounter for the Savior is an opportunity to share the Father's love. Some of Christ's most life-changing moments resulted from unexpected meetings. They were not planned "witnessing events." They were divine encounters in the daily routine of life. Jesus' meetings with Nicodemus, the Samaritan woman, Zacchaeus, the thief on the cross, and the Roman centurion were all spontaneous opportunities. Each morning Jesus made Himself available to the Holy Spirit's leading.

Today you can be an influence for good on someone around you. You can share God's love with someone who needs you. Someone needs your hopeful words today. Someone needs your encouragement today. Make yourself available to the Spirit, and look for an unexpected encounter with one of God's needy children today.

April 16

A REAL HOPE

Blessed be the God and Father of our Lord Jesus Christ, who according to His abundant mercy has begotten us again to a living hope through the resurrection of Jesus Christ from the dead, to an inheritance incorruptible and undefiled and that does not fade away, reserved in heaven for you. 1 Peter 1:3, 4.

During a trip to Russia for meetings in Moscow's Olympic Stadium, I met a woman I'll call Tanya. Years before, her parents emigrated to China and became wealthy in the tea business. Eventually deciding to return to the Soviet Union, they established their tea business in Kazakhstan.

Just as their business was beginning to flourish, Stalin began his purges of the wealthy elite. When Tanya was 17, her father was taken out of the house by the secret police and shot through the head. During the Second World War her brother, sister, and husband were killed. She lost everyone closest to her within a two-year span.

Tanya struggled with depression. She came from an Orthodox Jewish background, but had little interest in religion. She had done rather well for herself, advancing in educational and diplomatic circles, yet she always sensed that something was missing. She could never come to terms with all the suffering her family had experienced. She couldn't accept the terrible finality of their cruel deaths.

Someone on the street handed Tanya a brochure advertising a Christian evangelistic effort. She attended the meetings and accepted Christ.

Tanya was much happier as a believer, but there was still something she couldn't quite grasp. Why would a loving God permit so much suffering? What really happens when you die? Not all the pieces in the puzzle seemed to fit together.

One day as she passed the Moscow Olympic Stadium, she saw a large sign proclaiming "The Bible Way to New Life." She decided to investigate the meetings.

Tanya attended each evening, including the night I spoke on the subject of Jesus' soon return. After the meeting she came up to me and said, "Pastor, I was deeply moved tonight." She began showing me old photographs of her family and telling me about their tragic deaths.

Her face beamed as she exclaimed, "Now I can look forward to seeing them again." She wasn't brokenhearted any longer. Tanya looked forward to the ultimate reunion of the redeemed at the second coming of Christ.

Death is not the end. The grave is not a long night without a morning. One day soon Jesus will break through the clouds. Lightning will flash across the heavens. The earth will shake. The sleeping saints will arise together. With them, in glorious immortal bodies, we will meet Christ in the air. Have you lost some loved one through death? A husband or a wife? A son or a daughter? A father or a mother? A friend or a close working associate? If you have, deep within you know the real hope that the coming of our Lord brings. There is nothing like it.

April 17

DEMONIC DECEPTION

As the cloud disappears and vanishes away, so he who goes down to the grave does not come up. He shall never return to his house, nor shall his place know him anymore. Job 7:9, 10.

Shortly after I preached about death at a series of evangelistic meetings in the Philippines, a typhoon ripped through the city of Legazpi. One of the individuals who attended the meetings was a Filipino army officer who listened attentively to what the Bible teaches about death.

That night he was awakened about midnight by the roaring of the wind. The shutters of his house flapped wildly against the clapboard. The wind howled through cracks around his windows. The rain pounded noisily on the tin roof. As this Filipino officer opened his eyes, he saw a beautiful form above his bed. He was astonished. It appeared to be his wife!

Her skin was an unblemished olive color. Her hair was long, flowing, and black. Her magnificent brown eyes looked clear and appealing. He was convinced it was his wife, but not as she'd been at age 60. This was his wife returned as she had been at 35.

She reached out to him and said in a voice he couldn't mistake, "Darling, I've missed you. I long to embrace you."

Even as he longed to reach out and hold her, he remembered the Bible lecture on death. He remembered that the Bible says, "As the cloud disappears and vanishes away, so he who goes down to the grave does not come up. He shall never return to his house, nor shall his place know him anymore" (Job 7:9, 10). He recollected a verse from Revelation that says, "For they are spirits of demons, performing signs" (Rev. 16:14). He recalled 2 Corinthians 11:14: "Satan himself transforms himself into an angel of light."

He was convinced that no matter how much this being looked like his wife, no matter how much she sounded like his wife, this form above his bed was *not* her. So he looked up and said, "In the name of Jesus Christ, be gone. Be gone, in Jesus' name!"

And when that Filipino military officer told me the story the next day, he said, "Right before my eyes that form disappeared."

The Bible is extremely clear. The dead cannot communicate with the living. Any voice that breaks death's silence is not the voice of God. It is the voice of a demon masquerading as a dead loved one. Isn't it just like the devil to take advantage of people at the moment of their deepest grief? Isn't it just like the devil to capture the affections of family members by impersonating the very person these loved ones are grieving for? The devil is a liar (see John 8:44).

The devil uses psychics, spiritualists, and fortune tellers to support his claims. The straightforward teaching of God's Word is clear: "The dead know nothing" (Eccl. 9:5).

Embrace the biblical teaching, and you will be saved a thousand perils.

April 18

COMING HOME

It was right that we should make merry and be glad, for your brother was dead and is alive again, and was lost and is found. Luke 15:32.

Turning off his Honda 750, Chad paused a moment. Conflicting thoughts raced through his head as he stood in the church parking lot. He hadn't been to church for a while, and he was already 15 minutes late. What would people think when he walked in dressed in a T-shirt and faded blue jeans? Would they disapprove of his long hair?

Yet something drove him on, compelling him to keep going. Deep inside, his heart ached and something was missing. Somehow he felt this was his day to "come home." A voice within seemed to urge, "Chad, just do it."

Entering the sanctuary as quietly as possible, he hoped to slip into the last row unnoticed, but it was packed. As he moved down the aisle, it seemed as if every row were jammed. The congregation quietly sang, "'Softly and tenderly Jesus is calling, calling for you and for me.'" Heads turned. Chad felt that everyone was staring at him.

Nervously he made a quick decision. *I guess I'll just sit in the aisle,* he thought to himself. He sat there a moment feeling as if dozens of eyes were boring into his back. Then he heard footsteps behind him. The church's head elder approached. *Oh, no! He'll probably throw me out,* Chad thought. But to his utter amazement the older gentleman sat on the floor beside him, gently touched him on the shoulder, and simply said, "Glad you're here, boy." Placing a hymnal in Chad's hands, the elder added, "It's number 287."

Kind words, a caring gesture, a moving sermon, an invitation to dinner, and Chad knew he had come home.

The Bible describes the church in a variety of ways. The church is called "the body of Christ," "the bride of Christ," "the little flock," "the remnant of God," and "the pillar and ground of the truth." My favorite picture of the church comes from the Old Testament. God instructed the Israelites to designate six cities strategically scattered throughout the land as cities of refuge. If anyone committed a crime, they could flee to these cities of refuge until their case was fully heard. In the city of refuge they were welcomed. Whatever they had done, they were given a fair hearing. In the cities of refuge they were protected and safe. The church is God's city of refuge in a hostile world. It is God's haven of love, acceptance, and forgiveness.

Bruised, battered, broken, beaten up people will come through the doors of your church this week. Open your arms and hearts to receive them. If you have been bloodied on life's highway, there is still a place of refuge for you.

April 19

WHY INSURANCE COMPANIES ARE WRONG

The field is the world, the good seeds are the sons of the kingdom, but the tares are the sons of the wicked one. The enemy who sowed them is the devil, the harvest is the end of the age, and the reapers are the angels. Matt. 13:38, 39.

An incident in Lake Worth, Florida, a few years back will focus our thought on the source of evil in the universe. A man made a claim to his insurance company based on an unfortunate accident in which he'd been shocked by a high-powered electrical line. The insurance company refused to pay, on the grounds that the incident was an "act of God." The courts agreed.

The man then responded creatively. He filed a suit against "God and Company," implicating 55 Christian churches in his city. During the court proceedings one minister spoke out, saying, "I believe the expression 'an act of God' is wrongly used. God was not responsible for this accident. It should be called 'an act of Satan.'"

According to the Bible, this member of the clergy was absolutely correct, and the insurance company wrong! Two opposing forces exist in the universe, one good and one evil, the powers of heaven and the powers of hell. As the author of love and order, God is in no way responsible for any evil on Planet Earth. Evil is Satan's domain. Hate, suffering, guilt, shame, pain, remorse—all are the fault of the grand usurper.

The question is often asked: "If God is so good, why is the world so bad? Why do innocent people suffer?" We suffer for a variety of reasons. Sometimes we bring disaster upon ourselves by our own poor choices. The teenager who parties all night and gets into an accident on the way home, driving 95 mph, may blame God, but God is in no way responsible. The promiscuous young adult who contracts a sexually transmitted disease suffers the consequences of their own choices.

At times we suffer because of the choices of others. The victims of countless wars have suffered at the hands of selfish, ruthless leaders. Abused children suffer at the hands of perverted adults. God does not always intervene. He allows evil to run its course. He does not take away our power of choice, even if we make wrong choices that harm other people. God values freedom. Lucifer made a tragic choice in heaven, but God allowed him to make it. The same was true of Adam and Eve in Eden. Beyond every wrong and harmful choice is the mastermind of evil, Lucifer.

When the choice of another causes one of God's children to suffer, He is always there, comforting, encouraging, sustaining, inspiring, strengthening. We can be absolutely sure that He will never let us go. His love bridges the widest gaps in order to save us. Now, here is something to rejoice about.

A LION TAMER IN TOWN

My God sent His angel and shut the lions' mouths, so that they have not hurt me, because I was found innocent before Him; and also, O King, I have done no wrong before you. Dan. 6:22.

One cold winter day toward the end of World War II, a woman walked out of what had seemed even worse than a lions' den. She was leaving the Ravensbrück concentration camp, where countless human beings had been systematically starved and worked to death. As the heavy iron gates closed behind her Corrie ten Boom could hardly believe that she was alive—and free.

Corrie had been arrested by the Nazis for hiding Jews in her home in Holland. She and her family believed in a God who gives refuge to all, and they committed themselves to this dangerous work.

This quiet matron in her 50s had not imagined she could survive the horrors of a labor camp. But God had sustained her during the ordeal. Corrie saw many women brutalized at Ravensbrück. Many perished, including her dear sister Betsie. But many of those women died with the name of Jesus on their lips because of the witness of those two sisters. "Those women," Corrie wrote, "were well worth all our suffering."

Finally, as a result of what turned out to be a clerical error, Corrie was released. One week later all the women her age at Ravensbrück were gassed.

As she walked out of this lions' den, Corrie had learned something invaluable. Around the world she gave this testimony: "There is no place on earth so dark, so deep, that God's love is not deeper still."

God's love penetrates prison camps and lions' dens. Wherever God's people are, He is there. The old hymn states it well: "Just when I need Him, Jesus is near, just when I falter, just when I fear; ready to help me, ready to cheer, just when I need Him most." The God who sent His angel to shut the lions' mouths for Daniel is steadfast forever. Are lions roaring in your ears today? The lions of doubt and discouragement may loom in your pathway. You may feel like you will be consumed by the lions of anger and resentment. The lions of lust and sensual allurement may appear about to eat you up. But God still shuts lions' mouths and delivers from their dens.

When the devil "walks about like a roaring lion, seeking whom he may devour" (1 Peter 5:8), God still tames lions. He did it for Daniel, and He will do it for you. Rejoice; there is a lion tamer in town.

THE REALITY OF THE RESURRECTION

Do not marvel at this; for the hour is coming in which all who are in the graves will hear His voice and come forth—those who have done good, to the resurrection of life, and those who have done evil, to the resurrection of condemnation. John 5:28, 29.

In a little English cemetery stands a remarkable tombstone. Etched into the marble is an angel who reaches down with a key in one hand toward a lock. The angel is shading his eyes with the other hand, looking up. Carved into the base of the stone is the inscription "Till He Comes."

What the sculptor intended we should see, through the angel's eyes, is the glory of God at Christ's coming. When Jesus comes again, the tombs will be unlocked. Believers will rise to everlasting life.

Death is not the end. The tomb is not an eternal coffin. For Bible-believing Christians death is a brief rest until the coming of our Lord.

The Bible describes death as a sleep 53 times. When Jesus described Lazarus' death to His closest disciples, He simply stated, "Our friend Lazarus sleeps, but I go that I may wake him up" (John 11:11). Jesus miraculously raised Lazarus to demonstrate His power over the grave. We need not fear death. Our loving Lord marks the grave of every believer.

One day our Lord will descend. The sky will be brightened with His glory. He will burst through the heavens. Just like He called Lazarus by name centuries ago, He will call our loved ones by name. Their graves will open, and they too will come forth. But there will be a significant difference. When Lazarus was resurrected, he did not receive a glorious immortal body. He was resurrected to bear witness to our Lord's power, but he died again. When our loved ones are resurrected, they will be resurrected with glorious immortal bodies, never to die again.

New life will pulsate through their veins. They will rise with all the vigor and vitality of youth. They will be perfectly, completely whole. And we who are still alive will also be changed in an instant to receive our glorious immortal body.

What a hope. What a promise. May the reality of the resurrection encourage your heart today.

April 22

THE RESURRECTION HOPE

Behold, I tell you a mystery: We shall not all sleep, but we shall all be changed—in a moment, in the twinkling of an eye, at the last trumpet. For the trumpet will sound, and the dead will be raised incorruptible, and we shall be changed. 1 Cor. 15:51, 52.

The resurrection hope first became real to me at the time of my own grandmother's death. Grandmother had been a heavy smoker and developed lung cancer. My mother experienced a great deal of anguish as she watched her mother waste away from 130 to 85 pounds.

Added to the pain of seeing her physical agony was another burden. Mom couldn't get the thought out of her mind that her mother might have to endure further suffering of an unknown duration in purgatory. It seemed too much to bear. Before Grandmother's funeral, my dad approached Mother very gently and asked, "May I share with you what the Bible has to say about the state of the dead?"

Dad was a Seventh-day Adventist and had studied the subject at some length. My mother was a Catholic Christian. Dad never argued with my mother about her beliefs. But now he felt the time was right; Mother desperately needed and wanted hope. She was distraught about the question of what awaited her mother beyond the grave.

The biblical answer Dad gave proved quite surprising. He opened the Scriptures to the book of Ecclesiastes, and there from the Bible he read this hope: "The living know that they will die; but the dead know nothing" (Eccl. 9:5).

And then he read verse 10: "Whatever your hand finds to do, do it with your might; for there is no work or device or knowledge or wisdom in the grave where you are going."

As Dad shared these Bible texts Mother felt as though a great weight had been lifted from her mind. He went on to explain that the dead who have been faithful to Jesus are, as the Bible says, "asleep in Christ" (1 Cor. 15:18). Mother realized that her mother was simply asleep, not suffering in a fiery state called purgatory. She would be safe—not conscious, not suffering, just resting.

My father's words of comfort to my mother in her hour of grief deeply impressed me. As he quoted the clear teaching of God's Word I found something solid to build my faith on.

The horrific fear of death no longer gripped me. As a committed Christian I felt the resurrection hope burn brightly in my soul. No family is exempt from the touch of death. The good news is that Jesus has the keys to the grave (see Rev. 1:18). On that glorious Resurrection morning long ago He burst the bonds of the tomb. All the powers of hell could not hold Him in the grave. He lives, and because He lives, as the familiar gospel song says, you and I "can face tomorrow." Death's hold has been broken. Jesus has risen. Death is a conquered foe. By faith, believe it today and let your heart rejoice.

April 23

PRAYER WORKS

We give thanks to . . . God . . . praying always for you. . . . For this reason we also, since the day we heard it, do not cease to pray for you, and to ask that you may be filled with the knowledge of His will in all wisdom and spiritual understanding. Col. 1:3-9.

On an April day in 1912 the famed *Titanic* sped toward New York. No one knew it would be the *Titanic*'s only journey. When the huge ship hit an iceberg with its engines going at full throttle, it ripped a large, gaping hole in its hull.

The massive liner slowly began to sink beneath the waves. Then in an instant it was gone. More than 1,500 people died that fateful night.

One story that has deeply impressed me is that of a little-known man by the name of Colonel Archibald Gracie. Colonel Gracie's wife couldn't sleep the night that the *Titanic* went down. Thousands of miles from the location of the tragedy in the North Atlantic, she anxiously awaited her husband's arrival from Liverpool, England. A strange sense of foreboding gripped her.

Early in the morning she awoke to pray. Little did she know that the *Titanic* had collided with an iceberg. Her husband had leaped overboard into the icy waters of the Atlantic and was struggling for his life. A strange peace came over Mrs. Gracie. Later she commented, "It was as if the arms of God encircled me. I climbed back into bed and fell asleep."

That hour, Colonel Gracie thought, *This is it; life is over.* Just when he could hold on no longer, a lifeboat appeared out of nowhere. Desperately he grasped the side of the boat. Strong arms pulled him aboard.

God does answer prayer. It is thrilling for a husband to know that his wife is praying for him. Blessed is the man whose wife knows God and prays for him. Blessed is the woman whose husband knows God and prays for her. Blessed are those young people whose parents know God and pray for them.

Intercessory prayer is biblical. Confined to a Roman prison, the apostle Paul assured the Philippians of his prayers with the words "Always in every prayer of mine making request for you all with joy" (Phil. 1:4). He told the Colossians, "[I] do not cease to pray for you" (Col. 1:9).

Paul believed his prayers made a difference. He was convinced that there is power in prayer. Ellen White certainly believed in the power of intercession. She urged God's people to pray more, writing, "We do not value the power and efficacy of prayer as we should. Prayer and faith will do what no power on earth can accomplish" (*The Ministry of Healing,* p. 509).

If you don't have a prayer list, why not start one today? Write down your petitions. List specific people. Seek God and ask Him to answer your heartfelt prayers of faith. Watch what He does. You will be amazed.

April 24

CONCEALED OR REVEALED

But if you do not do so, then take note, you have sinned against the Lord; and be sure your sin will find you out. Num. 32:23.

A young man stormed into police headquarters. Someone had broken into his home and had gotten away with several valuable items. He had caught a glimpse of the burglar and demanded that the police do something about it.

The officer in charge led him over to a stack of mug-shot books. He helped the man look through the pictures of people with criminal records.

Suddenly the officer said, "Wait a minute." He slapped his hand down on the page and took a careful look at a photo in the mug-shot book, then at the man's face, then back again at the photo. "That's you!" the officer exclaimed. "And it says there is an outstanding warrant for your arrest!"

The outraged homeowner, who had stomped into the police station demanding justice, ended up unwittingly identifying himself as a wanted criminal!

Most criminals cannot hide forever. Sooner or later they are caught, their crimes exposed. It's rare to commit major crimes repeatedly and not get caught. With God it is not only rare; it is impossible. Sooner or later every one of our sins will be exposed. The apostle Paul speaks the truth when he categorically states, "And there is no creature hidden from His sight, but all things are naked and open to the eyes of Him to whom we must give account" (Heb. 4:13).

In the light of God's all-knowing presence, every sin is exposed. We can't conceal it. Since God already knows our secret sins, He urges us to openly confess them now. When we confess them to Him, He will cover them in the day of judgment. David prayed, "Blessed is he whose transgression is forgiven, whose sin is covered" (Ps. 32:1).

The choice is plain. Either we hide our sins now and have them exposed before the universe to condemn us in the day of judgment, or we openly confess our sins now and have Jesus cover them in the day of judgment. The reality is that no one can hide their sins forever. One day they will be exposed. A loving God whose heart is filled with mercy and forgiveness invites us to come to Him with all the guilt of sin now. The choice is ours.

April 25

GOOD DEEDS PAY

The soul who sins shall die. The son shall not bear the guilt of the father, nor the father bear the guilt of the son. The righteousness of the righteous shall be upon himself, and the wickedness of the wicked shall be upon himself. Eze. 18:20.

All the guy was trying to do was rob a bank. And all the little old lady was trying to do was a good deed.

She saw this young man park his car by Citizens National Bank in Whittier, California, and rush inside. Then she noticed that he had left the keys in the ignition switch. So she grabbed the keys and trailed him into the bank, where she found him talking with a teller.

"Young man," she scolded, "you're going to get your car stolen if you don't stop leaving your keys."

The man had just told the teller he had a gun and wanted a lot of money. But the kindly old woman kept on scolding him. He stared at her and finally gave up. Snatching the keys, he dashed out of the bank and drove away!

Wouldn't it be nice if all our crime problems could be solved so neatly? Wouldn't it be great if good deeds could overwhelm the bad ones?

Although this story is rather unique, it does illustrate a vital point. Good deeds make a difference. The wise man states: "Do not withhold good from those to whom it is due, when it is in the power of your hand to do so" (Prov. 3:27). When Dr. Luke describes Jesus in the book of Acts, he declares, "[He] went about doing good." How would you like these words to be the epitaph on your tombstone? I would surely like to be remembered this way: "Mark Finley, a man who went about doing good."

Jesus unselfishly lived to do good to others. He blessed everything He touched. He broke the bread and fed 5,000 on the hillsides of Galilee. He touched blind eyes; He unstopped deaf ears. He caused the dumb to speak and the lame to walk. Everyplace He went, the Master did good. His words were words of hope, words of encouragement, words of cheer.

Here is a worthy motto to live life by: "I will do all the good I can, to all the people I can, in every way I can." You can make a difference in your world today. God calls us not just to go about, but to go about doing good. He calls us to bless others in our journey through life. What would you like to be remembered for? I can't think of many descriptions better than "a committed Christian, deeply in love with Jesus, who went about doing good."

April 26

SIN IS STILL SIN

The law of the Lord is perfect, converting the soul; the testimony of the Lord is sure, making wise the simple; the statutes of the Lord are right, rejoicing the heart; the commandment of the Lord is pure, enlightening the eyes. Ps. 19:7, 8.

University professor Christina Sommers wrote an article titled "Ethics Without Virtue." Sommers criticized how ethics and values are taught in American colleges. She suggested that there is much debate on complicated social issues, in which one opinion seems about as good as another, but almost no instruction on personal decency, responsibility, and honor.

One of Sommers' colleagues, who also taught ethics, didn't like this interpretation at all. She insisted that social injustice was what really mattered.

But then at the end of the semester this professor walked into Sommers' office carrying a stack of exams.

"What's wrong?" Sommers asked.

Her colleague answered mournfully, "They cheated on their social justice take-home finals. They plagiarized!"

These students had copied material from other sources in order to get an A in ethics! Now Sommers' colleague was eager to find teaching material on personal morality, on taking the law to heart.

Sommers reports that she meets a "surprising number of young people who think there is no right or wrong, that moral choices depend on how you feel."

Right and wrong are more than a matter of our personal opinion. We do not define right and wrong. God does.

The Ten Commandments are God's objective, absolute standard of morality. They define sin. As the apostle John so clearly states, "Whoever commits sin also commits lawlessness, and sin is lawlessness" (1 John 3:4). To break God's law is to violate the eternal principles of His government.

We can rationalize and make excuses, but disobedience is still sin.

Some people justify having an affair outside marriage. They claim, "This is my private thing." Others defend stealing in the workplace as "getting my just due." Still others see nothing wrong with character assassination, otherwise known as plain old gossip. But breaking God's law is still sin. God still has a standard. Through His power He invites us to live obedient lives. God does not conform His law to our personal standards. By His grace He invites us to conform to His.

April 27

SURVIVING DEPRESSION, PART 1

And He said to me, "My grace is sufficient for you, for My strength is made perfect in weakness." Therefore most gladly I will rather boast in my infirmities, that the power of Christ may rest upon me. 2 Cor. 12:9.

Charles Spurgeon, the great Victorian preacher, suffered from periods of deep depression. Once he told a friend that "there are dungeons beneath the castle of despair."

But Spurgeon kept drinking in God's perspective. The basic good news of God's grace and redemption was real for him.

One day as he rode home after a heavy day's work he began to feel extremely weary and depressed. All kinds of people would pour out their troubles to him, but he had few who could listen to his own. Spurgeon felt the old dungeon beckoning again.

But then a text came and rescued him. The words "My grace is sufficient for you" (2 Cor. 12:9) ran through his mind. Once home, Spurgeon looked up the verse in the original Greek. Now this bit of good news hit him even more forcefully. God seemed to talk directly to him: "My grace is sufficient for *you.*"

Spurgeon found himself replying out loud, "I should think it is, Lord." And he burst out laughing. Suddenly he had acquired that merry heart that does good like a medicine. Spurgeon recalled, "I never understood what the holy laughter of Abraham was till then. It seemed to make unbelief so absurd."

"O brethren," Spurgeon wrote his friends, "be great believers. Little faith will bring your souls to heaven, but great faith will bring heaven to your souls."

Spurgeon discovered a great eternal truth. Heaven is not simply a piece of geography; it is living life in God's presence. Although as

Christians we eagerly anticipate the final reward, a land where there is no suffering, tears, want, disease, or death, there is another dimension to heaven that is often overlooked. When the Pharisees quizzed Jesus about the kingdom of God, He succinctly stated, "For indeed, the kingdom of God is within you" (Luke 17:21).

When Christ enters our life through His Spirit, the kingdom of God reigns in our hearts. God's Spirit heals our hurts. God's Spirit dries our tears. God's Spirit gives us new hope. With Spurgeon, we discover that God's grace is sufficient. Even in life's most trying circumstances, wherever Jesus is, that is heaven for us. Rejoice today, with Christ filling your life. The kingdom of God is within you.

April 28

SURVIVING DEPRESSION, PART 2

So all bore witness to Him, and marveled at the gracious words which proceeded out of His mouth. Luke 4:22.

During his period of depression writer William Styron found great help from a friend who simply called every day to ask, "How are you doing?"

Styron says, "Because he had been through this just a few months before, his support was very, very valuable. It was a kind of insistence, of leaning on me and saying, 'Look, this is going to be OK. You're going to recover. Everybody recovers.' "

Styron believes this consistent encouragement was even more important for him than medical intervention. And he says it was important even when he couldn't believe those words of encouragement. In some mysterious way they touched his heart.

It's not great words of wisdom that people need to hear in depression. It is just simple words of care and concern. The fact that we are there makes all the difference.

Jesus modeled encouragement throughout His ministry. When a Samaritan woman approached Jacob's well at noon, the Savior sensed something drastically wrong. Noon is the hottest time of the day. The blazing Palestinian sun is almost unbearable. Most people attempt to find some relief by quietly resting in the cool of their homes. The normal time for drawing water is the much cooler early morning hours. This poor woman, so riddled with guilt, came alone at noon to avoid the scorn of the townswomen who knew of her adulterous affairs. She came hopelessly discouraged, yet Jesus spoke words of encouragement to her. He spoke of a "living water" that could quench the intense thirsting of her soul.

Jesus is an encourager. To a questioning scribe, He replied, "You are not far from the kingdom of God" (Mark 12:34). Think of the thrill of excitement that must have flooded this man's soul. No, not far from the kingdom of God. To a hesitating, self-deprecating Canaanite woman, Jesus responded, "O woman, great is your faith!" (Matt. 15:28). Amazing, but that's what the Master said.

Lift up your head. Let joy fill your heart. Jesus speaks words of encouragement to you today. And Jesus wants you to be an encourager. William Styron found great help when a friend encouraged him. Your friends are counting on you. Don't let them down.

April 29

SURVIVING DEPRESSION, PART 3

Be anxious for nothing, but in everything by prayer and supplication, with thanksgiving, let your requests be made known to God. Phil. 4:6.

No matter what our circumstances, we always have a choice. We can focus on either things we don't like or the things we do. What we look at can make an enormous difference.

A young wife named Sandra walked into her pastor's office one day and poured out a long and painful story. She just couldn't do anything to please her husband, Joe. Each day she dreaded the moment he'd come home from work. Joe seemed to treat her with contempt.

Sandra was an attractive, bright woman, but her sense of rejection had turned her into a depressed, tense wife.

The pastor decided to meet with Sandra's husband. Joe was amazed to learn that he was contributing to his wife's depression. He didn't understand how well his wife could read his attitude.

Fortunately, the pastor had a specific suggestion. "Joe," he said, "I'd like you to select 10 positive qualities in your wife and thank God for them. Thank God twice a day, in the morning and on the way home from work."

That didn't seem terribly difficult. And since his marriage was deteriorating, Joe agreed. He began thanking God for the things he liked about Sandra. He focused on what attracted him instead of what bothered him.

Before long, Sandra started changing before his eyes. She became more cheerful and affectionate. Joe continued to be thankful, and

Sandra grew in self-respect and motivation. She broke out of the walls of her depression.

A little gratitude goes a long way. Focusing on positive qualities makes them expand.

The words we speak to the people around us have incredible power. Listen to these amazing passages from the book of Proverbs:

"Anxiety in the heart of man causes depression, but a good word makes it glad" (Prov. 12:25).

"A man has joy by the answer of his mouth; and a word spoken in due season, how good it is!" (Prov. 15:23).

"A word fitly spoken is like apples of gold in settings of silver" (Prov. 25:11).

When people around us are down, our words have incredible power to lift them up. Think about what you are thankful for in the people around you today. Express your appreciation to them. Encourage them with hope. Consciously share how much they mean to you.

Your words can change your environment. Try it and see.

April 30

SURVIVING DEPRESSION, PART 4

I will bless the Lord at all times; His praise shall continually be in my mouth. Ps. 34:1.

Since the fall of the Soviet Union I have gathered stories of faith in the face of terrible persecution. One pastor shivering alone in a dark isolation cell wrote, "During those long periods of solitary confinement my heart enjoyed the presence of God. Like the apostle Paul, I would spend hours singing hymns. God never forsook me, not in my darkest, hardest hours. The promises of our Lord Jesus Christ work in all of life."

I read of another pastor crammed into a prison cell with 70 hardened criminals. On Easter Sunday this pastor requested the privilege of singing a hymn for his fellow prisoners.

Everyone quieted down. The man began to sing songs of praise. He kept singing for an hour. No one moved. Their eyes were all turned toward him. He sang praise to God for another hour.

There is unusual spiritual power in praise. Praise lifts our spirits. Praise energizes our entire being. Praise revitalizes our spiritual life. Scripture links praise and rejoicing together. "Therefore my heart greatly rejoices, and with my song I will praise Him" (Ps. 28:7). Ellen White observes, "Nothing tends more to promote health of body and of soul than does a spirit of gratitude and praise" (*The Ministry of Healing,* p. 251).

She continues, "It is a law of nature that our thoughts and feelings are encouraged and strengthened as we give them utterance. While words express thoughts, it is also true that thoughts follow words. If we would give more expression to our faith, rejoice more in the blessings that we know we have—the great mercy and love of God—we should have more faith and greater joy" (*ibid.,* pp. 251-253).

Our words not only reveal our inner character; they shape it. Let your mouth be filled with praise. Let your lips express thanks to God for His goodness. Watch how praise pulverizes your discouraging feelings. Praise is one of God's mighty weapons to overcome the enemy. Praise is a weapon we cannot afford to be without.

COPING WITH JOB BURNOUT, PART 1

For thus says the Lord God, the Holy One of Israel: "In returning and rest you shall be saved; in quietness and confidence shall be your strength." Isa. 30:15.

Mr. Jacobsen knew that his job as manager of a thriving company demanded much of him. He knew that he was a very driven individual who rarely got enough rest. But he seemed to like it that way. He loved his job.

And there was always one more program to promote, one more conflict among staff members to resolve, one more sales goal to meet. Something always pushed him on.

In fact, Mr. Jacobsen wore his chest pains, sleepless nights, and jam-packed schedule like merit badges. He was almost proud of them. They symbolized his dedication to his job.

But finally one day shooting pains in his chest forced him to visit the doctor. After the examination the physician asked, "Have you been under a lot of pressure lately?"

The manager answered a little sarcastically, "Pressure! Is there life without it?"

But then the doctor made a shocking prescription. "I don't know what you do, but I recommend that you start looking for another job."

That woke Mr. Jacobsen up in a hurry. He might have to quit the company! Something was indeed wrong. He realized he was 29 years old—and right on the edge of a heart attack.

For many people, it's not easy to stop on the road to job burnout. Sometimes it takes a shocking announcement at the doctor's office. Sometimes we don't stop until the damage has already been done.

There are times in our lives when God calls us to reevaluate our priorities. There are times when His Spirit calls us to reflection. Life tends to speed on. It tends to be over before we realize it. Without periods of reflection, we rush through life, racing from one thing to another without much thought.

Meditation doesn't just happen in life; it must be planned. Do you feel hurried? Do you feel the current forcing you downstream at a frantic pace? Do you see some dangerous, jagged rocks in the swelled river ahead? Here is some biblical counsel that may be helpful:

"It is good that one should hope and wait quietly for the salvation of the Lord" (Lam. 3:26).

"Rest in the Lord, and wait patiently for Him" (Ps. 37:7).

"When I remember You on my bed, I meditate on You in the night watches" (Ps. 63:6).

God's counsel is clear. Don't let life simply fly by. Pause. Reflect. Meditate. Rest. Wait patiently on Him. Evaluate your priorities. Take a deep breath, and let the God of all eternity give you a new perspective today.

May 2

COPING WITH JOB BURNOUT, PART 2

Now then, we are ambassadors for Christ, as though God were pleading through us: we implore you on Christ's behalf, be reconciled to God. 2 Cor. 5:20.

Mark Ritchie works in one of the most stressful environments imaginable. He's a commodities trader at the Chicago Board of Trade, the world's largest futures and options exchange. In this world, fortunes can be won or lost in split seconds. Hundreds of men and women keep their eyes on towering electronic quote boards while they wave their arms wildly, yelling and flashing hand signals. Like fans at a playoff game, they don't let up in their intensity until the closing bell.

Ritchie has worked in this pressure-filled world for many years. He built his trading company, CRT, into what the *Wall Street Journal* called "the envy of the industry." But something keeps Ritchie from being overwhelmed by the constant demands of the exchange. Something keeps him peaceful in the middle of all the frantic activity. And that is his rock-solid sense of values.

Ritchie is a committed Christian who wants to take Christ's values right into the frenzied world of the exchange. In fact, his biggest passion is to help the poor become independent entrepreneurs. That's one place he invests his profits. His development agency, called Ceretech, tries to link people with the right technology. About 120 women in the slums of Nairobi now produce knitted materials profitably because of simple foot-powered machines Ritchie supplies.

Ritchie is not immune to the risks of commodities trading. He once lost $200,000 in the gold market in one day. Pressure is no stranger to him, but there's something bigger in his life than just what the commodities numbers say at the end of the day. His greatest joy is in using his resources to help others. And it's more important for him to spend time helping his wife, Nancy, with their five children than to make a killing on the market.

If Ritchie suddenly realized he had only five minutes to live, he wouldn't have to rush to the phone to send a message to neglected loved ones. He wouldn't suddenly realize that he's missed out on the most important things in life. He would know that he had made the right kind of investment.

Researchers in the field of stress-related burnout have discovered that people with a sense of unselfish purpose live far better, in coping with stress, than people motivated solely by power, position, or their pocketbook. When our jobs stress us out, it's sometimes necessary to ask, Why do I do what I do? Is it merely for the money? Is it because of the strokes I get from others around me when I do a good job? Is it the sense of power I feel in controlling others? Or is there another motive, a deeper, nobler motive, the sense that God has given me talents that I am using for Him?

Whatever we do, we are first and foremost ambassadors for Christ. This new paradigm brings a new dimension to life. Job stress is put in the context of a much, much larger picture. Let Christ give you this new perspective today.

May 3

HEALED IN BROKENNESS

And whoever falls on this stone will be broken; but on whomever it falls, it will grind him to powder. Matt. 21:44.

In spite of its continual conflict, Israel is an inspiring place. The old city of Jerusalem, torn apart by religious strife, holds a special place in my heart. I am always blessed when I visit.

One day I visited a small Seventh-day Adventist church in the heart of Jerusalem. I joined about 60 or 70 people for worship.

Together we celebrated the Lord's Supper. Before partaking of the bread and grape juice, we conducted a foot-washing service.

These Adventist believers followed the example of Christ, who washed His disciples' feet before the Last Supper. The church divided into groups of two. They filled basins with water and draped towels over their shoulders.

An Arab man from Bethlehem approached a Jewish man. Both were believers in Christ. The Arab man knelt and requested permission to wash his Jewish brother's feet.

A Jewish woman knelt down before a Christian Arab from Jericho to wash her feet and dry them with a towel. All over the church, generations of animosity melted away in this service of humility.

Afterward the groups of two prayed together, asking God's blessing in each other's lives.

It was a powerful experience. The peace of Christ made a difference. Instead of tearing one another apart, they were allowing Christ to heal their hurt. Instead of throwing rocks, they were allowing the Rock of Ages to break their hard hearts. They had fallen upon the Rock, Christ Jesus, and were broken.

It takes a certain amount of brokenness to really forgive someone who has wounded you. Sometimes we must be broken before we can ever be made whole. Christ's body was broken on the cross so we could be healed. But there is more. Unless our hearts are broken at the cross, we cannot receive the healing. Jesus uses this analogy of brokenness to describe conversion. He says, "And whoever falls on this stone will be broken; but on whomever it falls, it will grind him to powder" (Matt. 21:44).

Let Christ break your heart with His love. Allow Him to break your heart with His mercy and forgiveness. Allow Him to break away all hardness, resentment, and bitterness. It takes a great deal of brokenness for a Jew to wash an Arab's feet. It also takes a great deal of brokenness to forgive the people who have wronged us today. But brokenness is the pathway to healing.

May 4

FORGIVEN AS WE FORGIVE

And forgive us our sins, for we also forgive everyone who is indebted to us. Luke 11:4.

I've seen Christ's peace at work among families torn apart by deep hurt. I've seen Christ heal the bitterness. I've watched as people estranged for years have reconciled.

I'll never forget the man in Brazil who came to one of our It Is Written spiritual weekends. He came with bitterness in his heart toward his brother. Twenty-five years earlier they had parted ways, and had not spoken since. They ferociously argued over a loan the younger brother requested. The older brother refused to give it. A prolonged conflict ensued. At the It Is Written meetings the younger brother quite unexpectedly found his anger melting, replaced by the peace of Christ.

Then, to his astonishment, he spotted his brother sitting across the aisle. That night a wonderful reconciliation occurred. There were tears and embraces. Twenty-five years of animosity disappeared. The peace and love of Christ shone through the bitter darkness that had separated these two brothers for a quarter of a century.

Here is the single thought that made a difference in this embittered brother's heart. Whatever my brother has done to me, I have done worse to Christ. Whatever injustice I have suffered, Christ has suffered worse at my hands.

If Christ, whom I have treated so badly, forgives me so freely, I must forgive my brother as freely. There is nothing my brother has done to me as bad as my sins against Christ.

I watched as the two men, so long estranged, embraced at last. I witnessed their expressions of deep sorrow over the way they had treated each other. I listened to their testimonies of apology. To forgive someone who has wronged you and doesn't deserve it is a quality of godliness.

The spirit of forgiveness is the Spirit of Christ. Whether it is a little mistake someone has made or a huge injustice, our forgiving Lord invites you to be a channel of His forgiveness today. He invites you to be a channel of His loving forgiveness to people around you.

May 5

GIVE YOUR ANGER TO GOD

He who is slow to anger is better than the mighty, and he who rules his spirit than he who takes a city. Prov. 16:32.

We get control of our anger by giving it up to God. An inner-city kid named Ben can teach us how.

Ben grew up in a Detroit ghetto, a place where anger flows freely in the streets, where getting even with anyone who disrespects you is a way of life.

By the time Ben reached high school, he had developed quite a temper. As he listened to the radio one afternoon his buddy yelled, "You call that music?" and flipped the dial to another station. Ben shot back, "It's better than what you like!" and grabbed for the dial.

His buddy resisted, and in that instant a blind anger took hold of Ben. He grabbed the camping knife that he carried in his back pocket, snapped it open, and lunged at his friend's belly. The blade hit his friend's ROTC belt buckle with such force that it snapped and dropped to the ground.

Ben stared down at the broken blade, and his knees just about gave way. He had almost *killed* someone. He'd almost killed a good friend. Over what?

This incident forced Ben to face his anger head-on. He had to do something about it. He could not handle his temper alone. Ben prayed, "Lord, You have to take this temper from me. If You don't, I'll never be free from it. You can change me."

Back home, Ben locked himself in a bathroom and began reading the book of Proverbs. He read many texts that spoke pointedly about uncontrolled anger and where it leads. The words seemed written just for him. This verse impressed him the most: "He who is slow to anger is better than the mighty, and he who rules his spirit than he who takes a city" (Prov. 16:32).

"The discretion of a man makes him slow to anger, and his glory is to overlook a transgression" (Prov. 19:11). We become angry when we magnify the errors of others. We become obsessed with what another has done to us. Their actions control us.

This is what happened to Ben. He knew he had to deal with it. Proverbs provided the key. He agreed with the wise man that "wrath is cruel and anger a torrent" (Prov. 27:4), and "he who is slow to anger allays contention" (Prov. 15:18).

These words gave Ben hope, something to aim at. He made a commitment to read the Scriptures each day and gave himself and his problem wholeheartedly to God. A sense of peace replaced Ben's anguish and panic. As he walked out of that room he felt God had changed him.

God dealt decisively with this young man's uncontrolled anger. The hands that had once lunged with a knife became the disciplined, skilled hands of a surgeon. Ben Carson became one of America's most respected pediatric neurosurgeons.

God can deal with your anger too, but only if you give it to Him. Is there any anger in your heart? Why not give it to God as you pray today.

May 6

REBUILT LIVES

The Spirit of the Lord God is upon me, because the Lord has anointed Me to preach good tidings to the poor; He has sent Me to heal the brokenhearted, to proclaim liberty to the captives, and the opening of the prison to those who are bound. Isa. 61:1.

The extraordinary resilience of children continues to astound psychologists who study traumatized families. Children can endure neglect and abuse and still bounce back, still love, still hope.

Sarah Moskovitz wrote a remarkable book called *Love Despite Hate: Child Survivors of the Holocaust and Their Adult Lives.* In it she tells the stories of 24 persons she interviewed who had been liberated from Nazi concentration camps as children. It's difficult to imagine a more horrible surrounding for one's childhood.

Sarah Moskovitz wrote, "The prediction for child survivors was that they would all grow up to be antisocial, severely damaged people. Actually, most are communally involved, strongly religious, and live their lives in a deep spiritual plane." Somehow these kids found spiritual values in the midst of the horrors of war and death.

The power of the Christ who heals "the brokenhearted" and opens the "prison to those who are bound" is far greater than the liabilities of our early childhood influences. Secular humanists see heredity and environment as the prime shapers of our destiny. As Christians we do not deny the influence of heredity and environment, or ignore the effect of early childhood influences. We understand the significance of parenting styles. But we also believe that the greatest influence on character is the dynamic life-changing power of the gospel. There are well-adjusted adults who have had horrible childhoods. The power of Christ in their life has made the difference.

Paul wrote, "If anyone is in Christ, he is a new creation" (2 Cor. 5:17). In Christ, God makes a new creation out of us. In Christ, the power of grace is greater than faulty genetics. In Christ, the influence of the heavenly Father is greater than any earthly father's grip. Grasp His love today. Let it deliver you from the dark prison that has bound you for so long.

May 7

CHOSEN BY GOD

For the eyes of the Lord run to and fro throughout the whole earth, to show Himself strong on behalf of those whose heart is loyal to Him. 2 Chron. 16:9.

Geeta Lall was raised in India. Orphaned at a young age, she was brought up by a retired college professor, a staunch Baptist who regularly took her to Sunday school.

Through the miraculous providence of God, a Sabbath-keeping Adventist book salesperson began renting a room in their home. Eventually this bookseller married Geeta's cousin. When the Hindu-Muslim war broke out in 1946, Geeta stayed with her cousin during school vacation periods. She describes her experience in her own words:

"One day an Adventist pastor visited my cousin's home. During this pastor's visit I was asked to serve him a fruit drink instead of the customary tea. I wondered about this. My cousin explained the reason, adding that Adventists refrain from drinking tea or alcoholic beverages, eating pork, and smoking.

"I was curious. Edging into the living room, I began asking the pastor questions about the Adventist faith. During our conversation he mentioned the seventh day as being the hallowed and true Sabbath day. I told him, 'No way. It may have been in the Old Testament, but when Christ came to die for us, He changed the day to Sunday, the day He rose from the dead.'

"The pastor was quiet. Finally he said, 'If you can find a text in the New Testament stating that Christ changed the day of rest, I will become a Baptist.' However, if I could not find such a text, I would have to take Bible studies from him. I hastily added that I would become an Adventist if I could not find a text showing that Christ changed the seventh-day Sabbath to Sunday!

"Needless to say, I could not find such a text, although I hunted through the Bible diligently for hours. Moreover, I was surprised to find that Christ Himself went to the synagogue on Sabbath.

"Bible studies followed, and I was baptized in April 1946 and joined the Calcutta Adventist Church. In June I joined students bound for Spicer Memorial College, where I spent the next six years in study. Amid war and turmoil, gloom and loneliness, God plucked me out of a city of 6 million."

The eyes of the Lord do run through the earth. God sees. God knows. God seeks His honest-hearted children. He sends His Spirit to impress our hearts. He arranges circumstances in our lives to lead us to seek Him. He brings other committed Christians into contact with us to share His love. When we need encouragement, He is there. When we need strength, He is there. When we need hope, He is there. When we need inspiration, He is there. What a God He is!

May 8

PATRICK: A CHAMPION FOR GOD

And you will seek Me and find Me, when you search for Me with all your heart. Jer. 29:13.

Seized in the quietness of his country village, Patrick was beaten and dragged to a waiting ship. He gained consciousness in time to recognize that he was being transported to Ireland as a slave. After serving there a short time, he discovered a way to escape. He fled to Gaul, where he heard the preaching of Christ's gospel. He accepted it and was baptized. Sensing a responsibility to preach the gospel in the land of his enslavement, he set sail for Ireland. Here he preached moving biblical sermons that led multitudes to the foot of the cross. Even the royal "high kings" of Ireland were impressed by his deeply spiritual preaching.

Eventually the king's son, Conall, along with thousands of others, was baptized by Patrick. Conall's great-grandson, Columba, was in line for the throne through the royal heritage of his mother, Eithne. Columba accepted the Bible message preached by Patrick. In fact, it is likely that he went so far as to give up his throne for the cause of Christ. Along with Patrick, he upheld the Bible as the only foundation of faith. He placed strong emphasis on the necessity of loving obedience to the Ten Commandments, which he called "Christ's Law."

The Spirit of God wrought mightily through Columba. He founded a Christian school and missionary center on the small island of Iona, just off the British coast, in approximately A.D. 563. It is probable that he personally hand-copied the New Testament at least 300 times, as well as large portions of the Old Testament.

According to Dr. Leslie Hardinge in his outstanding work, *The Celtic Church in Britain,* one of the distinguishing characteristics of the Celts was a sacred regard for the biblical Sabbath.

God's champions, Patrick and Columba—one a runaway slave, and the other the heir to a throne—kept the light of God's truth burning in Ireland and Scotland during the Dark Ages.

God has men and women in every age who stand faithful to His truth, regardless of the consequences. There are those in our day who give up what the "world offers" for the cause of Christ. Their hearts burn with one desire: to serve their Master. They have been charmed by another lover. The world's enticements are not attractive. They are "steadfast in the faith." They are surrendered, committed, dedicated people of faith. They are God's heroes—His true champions. He invites each one of us to join this royal line.

May 9

WALDENSIAN WITNESS

But Daniel purposed in his heart that he would not defile himself with the portion of the king's delicacies, nor with the wine which he drank; therefore he requested of the chief of the eunuchs that he might not defile himself. Dan. 1:8.

In his book *Truth or Propaganda* my late friend and colleague, Pastor George Vandeman, of our *It Is Written* television program, tells this fascinating story:

A number of years ago a pastor led a group of young people on a guided tour of the Waldensian valleys of the Piedmont region of Italy. One evening they were singing around the campfire and telling mission stories.

Some of the Waldensian people drifted in and stood listening in the darkness. Their hearts were touched as they listened to the testimonies of those young people and heard them singing about the second coming of Christ.

When the songs and stories were over, a Waldensian elder stepped into the light of the campfire and said, "You must carry on! We, the Waldensian people, have a proud heritage behind us. We are proud of the history of our people as they have fought to preserve the light of truth high upon these mountainsides and up and down these valleys. . . . This is our great heritage of the past. But we really do not have any future. We have given up the teachings we once believed in. The sad thing is, we are not moving forward with courage to face the future. *You must carry on!*"

The cry of the centuries comes ringing down the corridors of time, echoing in our ears this very moment. Someone must carry on. Someone must carry the torch of truth. Someone must faithfully preserve the truth Christ died for. Someone must stand guard till He comes.

God is looking for people to stand like Daniel, who purposed in his heart to serve God. To purpose means to decide, to choose, or to determine. The heart is the biblical seat of decision. Daniel chose not to violate his conscience. He determined not to displease God in any area of his life. Compromise is the road to spiritual disaster. Daniel held the torch of truth high. He uncompromisingly stood for right.

God honored Daniel's faithfulness. Kings and empires rose and fell, but Daniel stood firm. His witness echoes throughout the centuries. Hold the torch of truth high. The words of that old Waldensian elder ring in our ears in this generation. "You must carry on." We dare not fail now.

May 10

SLOW DOWN

Blessed is the man who does this, and the son of man who lays hold on it; who keeps from defiling the Sabbath, and keeps his hand from doing any evil. Isa. 56:2.

A story is told about the biologist Thomas Huxley's arriving late in a city where he had to deliver a lecture. He jumped into a cab and yelled up at the driver, "Top speed!"

The cabby obediently cracked his whip, and the vehicle bumped along the streets at a wild clip. The frazzled Huxley settled into his seat for a second, greatly relieved, and then sat up with a jolt. He called up, "Hear, hear, do you know where I want to go?"

"No, your honor," the cabby replied, "but I'm driving as fast as I can."

A lot of people are in motion these days. They're always going somewhere fast. They are in a rush but are not really certain where they are going. A frenzied panic moves them, but they are not really certain why. They push themselves to the limit to achieve success, then wonder, "What really is success?" God has an answer.

The Sabbath calls us to reflect on life's important values. It reminds us of our roots. It speaks to us of a Creator God who cares for us intimately. Amid the hectic pace of twenty-first-century living, the Sabbath calls us to reevaluate our priorities.

When Egypt's pharaoh pushed the children of Israel beyond their limits in a massive building program, Moses led them back to Sabbath-keeping. Infuriated, Pharaoh made this charge: "Look, the people of the land are many now, and you make them rest from their labor" (Ex. 5:5). The word "rest" in this passage can also be translated "Keep the Sabbath." Moses knew the children of Israel could easily lose their perspective. He knew their burdens could easily obscure their view of God. He invited them to slow down and enjoy Sabbath rest.

Reevaluate your priorities. Reconnect with your Creator. Return to your roots. The Lord of the Sabbath still beckons us, in the dizzying pace of our time, to rediscover eternal values. Without this pause to reflect and worship we easily lose our perspective. With it our lives stay in focus.

May 11

TO LIVE IS CHRIST

For to me, to live is Christ, and to die is gain. Phil. 1:21.

Like Paul, John Huss based his life on total commitment to his Lord. Condemned to the stake, Huss endured what was called "the ceremony of degradation." Church dignitaries at the scene publicly stripped away his identity as a priest and a Christian.

First, the cup of Communion was taken from his hands, and the dignitaries denounced Huss. He responded by saying, "I hope to drink from the cup in the kingdom of God."

Next, the officials removed his garments one by one, pronouncing in each instance the appropriate curse. Huss replied that he was quite willing to suffer shame for the name of the Lord.

Finally, a tall paper crown was placed on his head. On it was a picture of three devils fighting for possession of a soul and the inscription "This is an arch-heretic." The bishops intoned a final curse: "We commit your soul to the devil!"

John Huss calmly replied, "And I commit it to the most merciful Lord Jesus Christ."

This courageous man was saying in effect, "You can take everything away from me. You can degrade me publicly, but you can't take away the most precious thing in life, my relationship with the Lord Jesus Christ."

John Huss echoed the words of Paul centuries earlier. Imprisoned in Rome, Paul penned the book of Philippians. Many Bible scholars have termed Philippians the "Epistle of Joy." Paul lost his freedom, yet his heart rejoiced. His reputation was maligned, but his heart was filled with joy. He was about to lose his life, yet his heart was glad. Jubilantly he wrote, "For to me, to live is Christ" (Phil. 1:21).

Paul continued, "But what things were gain to me, these I have counted loss for Christ. Yet indeed I also count all things loss for the excellence of the knowledge of Christ Jesus my Lord, for whom I have suffered the loss of all things, and count them as rubbish, that I might gain Christ" (Phil. 3:7, 8).

If you are stripped of everything and still have Christ, He is enough. You may be stripped of your health, your money, your job, your possessions, and even your family. Your heart may be broken. You may be crushed with grief, yet somehow Christ sustains you through it all. He gives you the strength to persevere. The apostle Paul and the great reformer John Huss found that Christ was enough in life's greatest trials. You can find that He is enough as well.

May 12

JUDGED BY WORKS

And I saw the dead, small and great, standing before God, and books were opened. And another book was opened, which is the Book of Life. And the dead were judged according to their works, by the things which were written in the books. Rev. 20:12.

On May 25, 1979, John Spenkelink, a 30-year-old drifter convicted of murder, was put to death in the electric chair in Florida. The U.S. Supreme Court refused to delay his death. Spenkelink was the first person to be executed in the United States since Gary Gilmore had demanded to face the firing squad in 1977.

It is difficult to describe the tension in a courtroom when a jury is about to announce its verdict. When all the evidence has been presented and the case has been carefully reviewed, the head juror faces a room full of people waiting eagerly for the jury's decision.

The judge asks, "What is your verdict?" All creation seems to hold its breath for one eternal moment. Two words—"not guilty"—can bring a collective sigh of relief to much of the courtroom, flooding the defendant with joy, releasing his loved ones from the clutches of despair.

But in John Spenkelink's case no such relief ever came. "Guilty" was the only word pronounced. With that single word his life on earth was cut short.

One word or two words. A simple pronouncement either way. We all face one of the two verdicts.

In any trial the jury weighs the evidence carefully. Every shred of evidence is meticulously examined.

In the divine drama of destiny in God's heavenly courtroom, as heaven's records are opened, countless numbers of heavenly beings examine the evidence. God reveals His incredible love. He has attempted to save every human being. He has gone to any length to redeem us. There is nothing He would not do for our salvation. Heaven's judgment reveals how we have responded to God's wooing. Although salvation is by faith alone, our works reveal the genuineness of our faith. A faith that is not manifested in good works is not the real thing. It is not faith at all. It is presumption. The apostle James states it plainly: "Do you want to know, O foolish man, that faith without works is dead?" (James 2:20). Our works matter. Where there are no genuine works, there is no genuine faith.

Today let your faith be revealed in an obedient life. In God's final judgment all shame and pretense will be stripped away. Only biblical faith revealed in good works will last.

May 13

GOD'S LAW A MIRROR

But be doers of the word, and not hearers only, deceiving yourselves. For if anyone is a hearer of the word and not a doer, he is like a man observing his natural face in a mirror; for he observes himself, goes away, and immediately forgets what kind of man he was. James 1:22-24.

Arthur Bietz tells of an African princess whose subjects extolled her great beauty and comeliness. However, her self-esteem was shattered one day when a trader passing through her village sold her a mirror. Horrified by the reflection of her own ugliness, she smashed the mirror!

Like a mirror God's law reveals exactly who we are. As we peer into the reflective glass we may be horrified as was the princess with what we see.

Destroying or ignoring the law will not change our condition. The imperfections will remain.

A casual look at God's law may leave us feeling complacent. In our smugness we might feel we are doing quite well. Jesus reveals obedience to the law as a matter of the heart. Here are some examples Jesus gave.

Breaking the sixth commandment, "You shall not murder" (Ex. 20:13), deals with much more than the physical act of killing. All uncontrolled anger, resentment, and bitterness is a violation of the commandment.

Breaking the seventh commandment is much more than the physical act of adultery. The lustful glance precedes the adulterous act. Anyone who allows their mind to be filled with sexual acts, nudity, pornography, or lustful affairs outside marriage—whether these are experienced vicariously through videos, movies, television, or in reality—is violating the seventh commandment.

In the light of God's law we all are sinners. Our only hope is God's grace. Our self-righteous pride or our smug complacency can never save us. Only God's grace can redeem us. Without it we are hopelessly lost. Right now praise Him for His grace, for it is enough. Determine by His grace to obey His law.

May 14

DIFFICULTIES WITH A PURPOSE

For as the sufferings of Christ abound in us, so our consolation also abounds through Christ. 2 Cor. 1:5.

On one of his many journeys through the Himalayas the Indian evangelist Sundhar Singh discovered a Tibetan preacher whom the people treated with superstitious reverence. He proclaimed Christ without fear of reprisal, even though other preachers were violently persecuted. The preacher told Singh his story.

He'd once been secretary to a Buddhist priest, but met a Christian from India. Eventually he declared himself a follower of Jesus. He first confessed his faith to his own master, the Buddhist priest.

Within a few days the preacher was sentenced to death. In front of the temple walls men bound a wet yak skin around him and sewed it up tight. They left him out in the scorching sunshine, where the contracting skin would crush him to death.

He did not die quickly enough, so red-hot skewers were thrust through the yak skin into his body. Later they tore off the skin and dragged him through the streets to a refuse dump outside of town. After further abuse the preacher was dropped on a dunghill. His body showed no signs of life. The crowds left, and the vultures gathered.

But he was still alive. Somehow he managed to crawl away and recover. Instead of fleeing for his life he marched right back into the village and began preaching about Christ! He could still testify about his faith, and he could speak of a great God who had come close. The people now listened in awe.

God sometimes allows us to go through very difficult experiences to give real credibility to our witness. When we experience hardship, we have an opportunity to build a stronger faith. Rather than destroying faith, difficult life experiences make our faith believable to those who observe our steadfast allegiance to God. The apostle Paul, who suffered so much, declares that God "comforts us in all our tribulation, that we may be able to comfort those who are in any trouble, with the comfort with which we ourselves are comforted by God" (2 Cor. 1:4).

We comfort because we are comforted. We comfort others in the difficult times of their lives because God has comforted us in our trying times. Open your heart to receive God's comfort. You will need it to comfort someone else whom God brings into your life this week.

May 15

TROUBLES

He shall deliver you in six troubles, yes, in seven no evil shall touch you. Job 5:19.

The story is told of a grieving woman in China who visited a holy man and asked him to help her get over her intense sorrow. He told her to get a mustard seed from a home that had never known loss or sadness, for that would banish her grief.

The next day the woman visited from home to home in her city to make inquiries, but she could find no family that had not experienced some kind of tragedy. The more people she talked to, the more she began to feel a kinship with them. Finally this woman understood the holy man's point. When you see the sorrow of others, your own sorrow seems much smaller.

Recently I interviewed Melodie Homer for one of our *It Is Written* television programs. Melodie's husband, Leroy, was the copilot on United Airlines Flight 93, which crashed on September 11, 2001. Melodie's life changed in an instant.

Melodie deeply impressed me. Her faith lifted my own spirits. Her courage in the face of her sorrow inspired me. Her firm hold on Christ in the light of her personal tragedy brought hope to my own heart. My own difficulties seemed smaller. If God could sustain Melodie through her unbearable grief, certainly He would sustain me.

Shortly after Melodie's interview aired, I received an e-mail from Cameroon, West Africa. The writer had never viewed *It Is Written* prior to Melodie's interview, but the program touched him. He wrote, "Her story was certainly an inspiration to me, and made my relatively small problems seem like a grain of sand in God's hand."

No matter how great or small our sorrows, God is fully capable of handling them. We are not alone in sorrow, for others are experiencing deep tragedy at this very moment. Job's testimony is still true today. "He shall deliver you in six troubles, yes, in seven no evil shall touch you" (Job 5:19).

Seven is a perfect number indicating completeness. Rejoice; God's deliverance from sorrow is complete. Rejoice; God's healing grace is complete.

May 16

FREE INDEED

And you shall know the truth, and the truth shall make you free. John 8:32.

Before Abraham Lincoln's Emancipation Proclamation, a slave named Joe was shoved on the auction block. Bitter and resentful, he muttered, "I won't work! I won't work!" But a wealthy landowner purchased him anyway. He led Joe to the carriage, and they drove out of town to the plantation.

There by a lake stood a little bungalow with curtains, flowers, and a cobblestone walkway. The new master stopped the carriage. Turning to Joe, he smiled. "Here's your new home. You don't have to work for it. I have bought you to set you free." For a moment Joe sat stunned. Then his eyes filled with tears. Overwhelmed, he exclaimed, "Master, I'll serve you forever."

Christ has purchased us to set us free. In Christ we are free from sin's slavery. In Christ we are liberated from sin's bondage. As Christians we may sin, but we are no longer controlled by sin. We have a new power in our lives. The power of God's grace.

As the apostle Paul states, "For sin shall not have dominion over you, for you are not under law but under grace" (Rom. 6:14). The word *dominion* means "lordship." Sin is no longer our lord; Jesus is.

Ellen White wrote, "It is not the work of the gospel to weaken the claims of God's holy law but to bring men up where they can keep its precepts" (*Faith and Works*, p. 52).

The gospel lifts us up. It brings us to where God wants us to be. In Christ we are free. Best of all, our obedience springs from a heart filled with love and appreciation for our Master. Once we truly appreciate His immense sacrifice, we can only serve and praise Him. The freedom we enjoy in Christ is not a freedom to continue in sin. It is the freedom to live a life liberated from sin's chains. Why not rejoice right now that in Christ you are truly free?

May 17

ENDURING FAITH

I am the resurrection and the life. He who believes in me, though he may die, he shall live. John 11:25.

About 100 years ago two lawyers crossed the state of Kansas by train. One was a Christian, the other an agnostic. Time seemed to drag; for the most part they were wasting it in small talk.

The agnostic lawyer turned to his Christian friend and said, "Lew, we're wasting our time. Why don't we talk about the great themes? Is the Bible inspired? Is Christ divine?"

As the miles went by, the skeptic seemed to be winning the arguments. The Christian lawyer became increasingly embarrassed as he failed to give adequate answers to his friend.

The skeptic pressed his advantage: "Lew, why aren't you a Buddhist or a Muslim or a follower of Confucius? Aren't all religions good and equal? Aren't you a Christian simply because of a geographical accident, because you were born in a Christian country?"

The Christian was completely nonplussed by these direct questions.

The questions raised that day by skeptic Robert Ingersoll must be answered. They won't disappear simply by ignoring them. Nor can we hide our heads in the sand and pretend they do not exist.

Let your mind travel back over the centuries. It is early in the second century. A Roman arena is filled to capacity. More than 80,000 people are on their feet, screaming at the top of their lungs. Lions are tearing Christians apart limb by limb. What gave these early Christians such death-defying faith? Why were they willing to die rather than to renounce their belief in this Christ?

For one reason only. They believed Jesus was more than a good man, more than an ethical teacher or a moral philosopher. They believed Jesus was the divine Son of God. They accepted Jesus' words to Martha: "I am the resurrection and the life. He who believes in me, though he may die, he shall live" (John 11:25).

Based on the Old Testament prophecies of Jesus' birthplace (Micah 5:2), His parentage (Gen. 49:10), His virgin birth (Isa. 7:14), His ministry (Isa. 61:1-3), and His death (Ps. 22; Isa. 53), these early believers established a bedrock faith. They were willing to die rather than surrender their belief in Him. They had the absolute confidence that Jesus' offer of eternal life was real.

We can have that same confidence. He was their Messiah and He is ours, too. His offer of eternal life is real, and that offer can keep us through any storm.

May 18

GOD'S ETERNAL WORD

The grass withers, the flower fades, but the word of our God stands forever. Isa. 40:8.

In the nineteenth century some historians claimed that the ancient city of Babylon was built by Queen Semiramis. Yet in Scripture, the Babylonian king Nebuchadnezzar boastfully claimed, "Is not this great Babylon, that I have built for a royal dwelling by my mighty power and for the honor of my majesty?" (Dan. 4:30).

In 1899 Robert Koldewey began excavating the old ruins of Babylon, unearthing tens of thousands of kiln-baked bricks, all bearing the stamp of King Nebuchadnezzar and all taken from the walls and temples of the city! Among the finds was a cuneiform tablet recounting Nebuchadnezzar's achievements. On that tablet Nebuchadnezzar remarks, "O Babylon! The delight of mine eyes. The excellency of my kingdom. May it last forever!"

The East India House Inscription, now in London, devotes six columns of Babylonian writing to a description of the huge building projects of Nebuchadnezzar. The spade again confirmed the accuracy of God's Word.

Another issue that added fuel to critics' fire was the absence of the name Belshazzar as a ruler of Babylon. Although this ancient king was referred to in Scripture, secular records provided no evidence of his reign. Yet if you visit the British Museum today, you will find a cylinder proving that Belshazzar ruled jointly in Babylon, as the Bible says.

Some amazing prophecies give credibility to the scriptural account. One of the most remarkable is Isaiah's prediction regarding King Cyrus of Persia and his subsequent attack on the mighty city of Babylon. The name of the man who would lead the armies against Babylon was prophesied 150 years before his birth. Isaiah wrote, "Thus says the Lord to His anointed, to Cyrus, whose right hand I have held—to subdue nations before him and loose the armor of kings, to open before him the double doors, so that the gates will not be shut" (Isa. 45:1). These prophecies were exactly fulfilled. Cyrus diverted the Euphrates River. He marched his troops down the dry riverbed that ran through the city of Babylon. He found the inner gates open exactly as predicted.

Were the prophecies of the Bible fulfilled? Indeed they were! In the Persian Hall of the British Museum stands the Cyrus Cylinder, found in the ruins of Babylon. On this clay cylinder Cyrus tells of his conquest of the ancient city. The stones indeed cry out.

We can have confidence in God's Book. Through the ages it has stood the test of time. There is no other book like it in the world. It transcends time and culture. Take time with this inspirational masterpiece. Let God's voice speak to you through the pages of Scripture. Let the Holy Spirit, who inspired God's Word, inspire you as you read it.

May 19

STRENGTH IN WEAKNESS

Therefore I take pleasure in infirmities, in reproaches, in needs, in persecutions, in distresses, for Christ's sake. For when I am weak, then I am strong. 2 Cor. 12:10.

A devoted Christian, Dave Dravecky entrusted his life to God every morning. If you are a baseball fan, you probably know what happened to the former pitcher for the San Francisco Giants. When a cancerous tumor in his arm threatened to cut short his career, Dave did not demand to be healed. Instead, he committed himself to God's will, and his quiet faith was a witness to millions.

God worked a miracle for Dave Dravecky. Although his cancer operation required the removal of muscle that he used for pitching, against all odds he came back to play again. Thousands of San Francisco fans cheered wildly when he took the mound again at Candlestick Park. Incredibly, he even won the game.

Dave Dravecky was back! But the comeback miracle lasted less than a week. Dave was playing in Montreal, winning the game, when suddenly, as he pitched, his arm broke. He collapsed in a heap at the foot of the mound. The whole crowd heard that awful snap of the bone.

As they carried Dave off the field he quietly affirmed his faith in God. That faith did not waver during long months of uncertainty. Finally doctors determined that they had no choice but to amputate his arm, and they did.

Did Dave become bitter when God did not heal him, leaving him with a lifelong handicap?

Not at all. Secular sports writers around the country marveled at his faith, solid as a rock. May I suggest that it took more faith for Dave Dravecky to maintain his trust in the God who apparently failed him than it would have taken for him to demand healing? I believe God displayed a miracle greater than physical healing in the amazing display of Dave's contented commitment.

The apostle Paul experienced this rock-solid faith. He too suffered from an incurable physical affliction. Three times he asked God to miraculously heal him. God's response was plain. "My grace is sufficient for you, for My strength is made perfect in weakness" (2 Cor. 12:9). Paul's answer is remarkable: "I will rather boast in my infirmities. . . . I take pleasure . . . in distresses, for Christ's sake. For when I am weak, then I am strong" (verses 9, 10).

There is a sense that we are the strongest spiritually when we are at our weakest point. God is near, and by faith we reach out and grasp His hand. Our faith reassures us that He will never let us go. Like Dave Dravecky and the apostle Paul, God invites us to hang on to Him today with the hand of faith.

May 20

A PROMISE OF PROTECTION

He shall cover you with His feathers, and under His wings you shall take refuge. Ps. 91:4.

The story is told of an Australian logger who built a simple cabin at the edge of a forest. One day, returning home from work, he was stunned and heartbroken to find his home reduced to a heap of smoldering ruins. All that remained were a few pieces of charred lumber and some blackened metal. Walking out to where his old chicken coop had stood, the man discovered only a mound of ashes and some burned wire. Aimlessly he shuffled through the debris. Then, as he glanced down at his feet, his eyes caught a curious sight, a mound of charred feathers. He kicked it over. Four fuzzy baby chicks scrambled out, miraculously protected by the wings of a loving mother.

In the most beautiful and meaningful language of Scripture God describes what He longs to do for every one of His children on earth when the plagues fall. "He shall cover you with His feathers, and under His wings you shall take refuge" (Ps. 91:4).

Only in eternity will we really understand God's protecting power. I am convinced that my life could have been snuffed out numerous times if it were not for God's protection. God protects us in ways we cannot know until the day we meet Him face to face.

Ellen White wrote, "The omnipotent power of the Holy Spirit is the defense of every contrite soul. Not one that in penitence and faith has claimed His protection will Christ permit to pass under the enemy's power" (*The Desire of Ages,* p. 490).

This promise is for us. In Christ we are secure. In Christ we are safe. In Christ all fear is banished. "The Saviour is by the side of His tempted and tried ones. With Him there can be no such thing as failure, loss, impossibility, or defeat; we can do all things through Him who strengthens us" *(ibid.).*

When you are assaulted by the enemy, fix your mind on your almighty deliverer. He has never failed one dependent, trusting soul, and He certainly will not fail you. He is our refuge, our serenity, our divine protector. In Him we are safe today, tomorrow, and forever.

May 21

THE MEANING OF TRIAL

Before I was afflicted I went astray, but now I keep Your word. You are good and do good. Ps. 119:67.

A busy editor developed serious trouble with his eyes. The long hours of tediously poring over detailed manuscripts had severely strained them. Thinking he might need a custom-fitted pair of glasses, he visited an eye specialist. The specialist told him his real need was not new glasses, but rest for his eyes. The editor explained to the specialist that this was impossible, for his work required him to sit all day bent over a desk, reading and writing.

The specialist asked the editor where he lived. He replied that he lived within sight of a high ridge on the majestic Pyrenees Mountains in France. "Go home and do your work as usual," the specialist said, "but every hour, leave your desk, go out on your porch, and look at the mountains. The faraway look will rest your eyes after the long strain of reading manuscripts and proof sheets."

Sometimes we too need the faraway look. It is possible to become so overwhelmed with the difficulties we face each day that we become discouraged. Life becomes a real grind. Our trials and obstacles overwhelm us. We ask why, if God is leading, life is so filled with challenges.

Here is a key to relating to trials. Every trial we experience is an opportunity to seek God for a solution. It is an opportunity to pause and take the "faraway look."

"The path of sincerity and integrity is not a path free from obstruction, but in every difficulty we are to see a call to prayer" (*The Desire of Ages*, p. 667).

Difficulties are doorways to God. Obstacles are opportunities to know God better. Trials are teaching tools to reveal faults we were previously unaware of. "Trials and obstacles are the Lord's chosen methods of discipline and His appointed conditions of success" (*The Ministry of Healing*, p. 471).

We can testify with the psalmist David, "Before I was afflicted I went astray, but now I keep Your word. You are good, and do good" (Ps. 119:67).

Even in trials, difficulties, and afflictions God is good. Take the faraway look. In Him all of our troubles are placed in perspective. In Him we see life clearly.

May 22

LEAVING A LEGACY

And He who sent Me is with Me. The Father has not left Me alone, for I always do those things that please Him. John 8:29.

Oswald Glait repeatedly risked his life for the Sabbath truth. Authorities captured him in 1545 while he was on an evangelistic mission in central Europe. He spent a year and six weeks in jail, until awakened at midnight by the thunderous footsteps of soldiers marching down the hall. The mercenaries bound him hand and foot, dragged him through the city, and cast him into the Danube. They little realized that the truth he gave his life for, like ripples created by a rock thrown into a pond, would rapidly spread throughout central Europe.

Oswald took the long view of life, looking beyond his immediate circumstances. He knew his influence would continue beyond his death. He had confidence that the truth he died for would eventually triumph.

Most people live for the immediacy of the moment. They are concerned with the present. Their concern is with what happens to them now. They are absorbed in self-interest.

Great men and women of faith through the centuries viewed life from a different perspective. Pleasing God absorbed their attention. Living for Christ consumed them. Faithfulness to His truth meant everything to them. With the apostle Paul they proclaimed, "I press toward the goal for the prize of the upward call of God in Christ Jesus" (Phil. 3:14).

What kind of legacy will you leave for those whose lives touch yours? Is it a legacy of compromise or of commitment? a legacy of complacency or consecration? The witness of Oswald Glait echoes down the corridors of time, calling us to commitment today. It calls us to deeper dedication, to "stand for the right though the heavens fall." Our Lord asks us not only to be willing to die for Him, but also to live for Him now and forever.

May 23

GETHSEMANE: CRISIS IN A GARDEN

He went a little farther and fell on His face, and prayed, saying, O My Father, if it is possible, let this cup pass from Me; nevertheless, not as I will, but as You will. Matt. 26:39.

Medical literature indicates that it is possible, under the stress of excessive terror or extreme exhaustion, for a person to sweat drops of blood. In fact, the French skeptic Voltaire, in his essay on the civil wars of France, described a scene in which a man sweat blood.

Almost two years after the St. Bartholomew's Day Massacre, King Charles IX was attacked by a strange malady for which doctors could find no cure. His blood oozed out, forcing its way through the pores of his skin. As Voltaire described it, "this was the result of excessive fear, of violent struggle within and the divine vengeance of God against sin."

There was a night when our Savior sweat great drops of blood. The destiny of the world was at stake. The issues were huge. Jesus was confronted with the most difficult choice of His life—either return to heaven, assuring His salvation, or face the cross as a condemned sinner, assuring ours.

Ellen White writes, "The awful moment had come—that moment which was to decide the destiny of the world. The fate of humanity trembled in the balance. Christ might even now refuse to drink the cup apportioned to guilty man. It was not yet too late. He might wipe the bloody sweat from His brow, and leave man to perish in his iniquity. . . .Will the innocent suffer the consequences of the course of sin, to save the guilty? The words fall tremblingly from the pale lips of Jesus, 'O My Father, if this cup may not pass away from Me, except I drink it, Thy will be done' " (*The Desire of Ages,* p. 690).

Three times Jesus uttered this prayer of commitment. He could not bear the thought of our being lost. The blood that oozed from His brow that awful night foreshadowed the blood that would flow from His hands, feet, and side. It is redeeming blood, the blood of His sacrifice. It is salvation's blood shed for you and me, the life of God poured out on the cross at infinite price. All we can do is fall on our knees and say, "Thank You,

Jesus! Thank You that You were willing to pour out Your blood so that we could experience an outpouring of Your grace."

May 24

REDEEMED BY THE BLOOD OF THE LAMB

And from Jesus Christ, the faithful witness, the firstborn from the dead, and the ruler over the kings of the earth. To Him who loved us and washed us from our sins in His own blood. Rev. 1:5.

In the early-morning light Eliud walks through the encampment of Israel, leading a small pure-white lamb. Eliud is headed to the tabernacle to slit this animal's throat. A splinter in his memory drives him there, a sin that's been gnawing at his bones. He has to make it right.

At the entrance to the outer court of the tabernacle Eliud waits with others who have also brought their sin offerings. He watches as the priests perform their ancient ritual. And then it's his turn.

Eliud kneels beside the lamb and places one hand around its neck. A priest approaches. Eliud places his other hand on the lamb's head and confesses his sin. He tries not to look in the animal's trusting eyes.

Quickly its head is lifted. A swift flash of the knife, and dark blood spurts out on the ground. The lamb kicks once and falls limp. Priestly assistants take the carcass toward the large altar. They drain the blood into a trench at its base, then place the slain animal on the grating, flames beginning to consume it.

This spotless sacrifice points to a divine forgiveness. That grace is as real to Eliud as the blood that still stains his hands.

God's grace is free, but sin is costly. It cost the death of God's own Son. Every Old Testament sacrifice foreshadowed Christ's death. Without the death of the slain lamb there was no forgiveness.

Don't misunderstand. The blood of a million sacrifices could not possibly atone for our sins. Only the blood of the eternal sacrifice could. Scripture is absolutely clear: "The wages of sin is death" (Rom. 6:23). Sin is ugly. It destroys everything it touches. To remind His people of the horrifying, deadly nature of sin, God instructed them to offer sacrifices. "Without shedding of blood there is no remission" (Heb. 9:22).

It takes the life of God, freely sacrificed on Calvary, to atone for our sins. Every animal sacrificed pointed forward to Calvary. Here is the best news ever. Jesus Christ, the divine Son of God, offered His life on Calvary. He died the death we deserve. He paid sin's price. Like Eliud, we too can come—not to the Old Testament sanctuary, but to the cross.

As we come to Calvary in our imagination, confessing our sins, our guilt is transferred to the spotless Lamb of God. We are free! Sin's penalty is paid. Praise God, we are redeemed.

May 25

COME DOWN FROM YOUR PILLAR

I am the light of the world. John 8:12.

Throughout history some have distorted the character of God in the name of Christianity. An Egyptian peasant named Anthony was regarded as a saint for living nearly 90 years alone in the desert.

Simon Stylites took the denial of the body to new heights. Living alone out in the desert wasn't enough. He built a platform 60 feet in the air and lived there for 30 years, dressed in animal skins.

A hermit named Makarios of Alexandria also became legendary. During one fast he remained in a corner of his cell without speaking or moving for 40 days.

The idea that a Christian is to have no contact with the world lest he or she become contaminated by its evil is a perversion of Christianity. It is a misunderstanding of the mission of Christ, who plunged into the snake pit of this world to save us from the venom of its sin. Jesus earnestly petitioned the Father in these words: "I do not pray that You should take them out of the world, but that You should keep them from the evil one" (John 17:15).

Someone has said the Christian is like a boat in the water. It is all right for the boat to be in the water as long as there is no water in the boat. It is all right for the Christian to be in the world as long as there is no world in the Christian. It is God's will for Christians to transform their world. We are to be like "light" and "salt," impacting the world around us.

God calls us to light up the darkness, to positively flavor our environment. He calls us to be world shapers, not shaped by the world. Filled with the Spirit of Christ, motivated by His love, leap into your world today and make a difference.

Don't climb up onto your sanctimonious pillar like Simon Stylites and watch the world march into the lake of fire. Climb down from the heights. Get involved with the people around you. Share Christ's love and grace with them, and watch God work a miracle in their lives.

GOOD GOD, BAD WORLD

And war broke out in heaven: Michael and his angels fought with the dragon; and the dragon and his angels fought. Rev. 12:7.

In 1981 Harold S. Kushner wrote a book that promised to answer a question asked from the time of Job to the present. *When Bad Things Happen to Good People* instantly catapulted to best-seller fame.

Kushner's answer to the universal question of suffering, however, was limited by his own narrow idea of God. Beginning with a denial of God's power in the creation of this world, Kushner went on to reject the literal accounts of miraculous Old Testament occurrences. Bad things happen to good people, he concluded, because the God who set this universe in motion is powerless to intervene in natural laws.

The Bible presents a much different picture. God is certainly not powerless. He is all-powerful, but for the present He chooses to limit His power. There are two forces in the universe, good and evil. When the disciples asked Jesus where the tares came from in the parable of the field, Jesus responded, "An enemy has done this" (Matt. 13:28).

A rebel angel rebelled against the government of God millennia ago (Isa. 14:12-14). The Bible calls him the devil, Satan, the serpent, the dragon, Lucifer, and the evil one. This egotistical maniac is consumed with controlling the universe. His supreme desire is to take God's throne. The devil is behind all sickness, suffering, and sorrow in our world.

In His infinite wisdom God allows the great controversy between good and evil to play out before the universe. He permits Satan a certain amount of freedom. He allows human beings to make choices that sometimes cause suffering to themselves or others. Why do bad things happen to good people? The answer is plain. We are in the middle of a cosmic struggle between good and evil.

A teenage boy was dying. His strength was spent, his body weakened by the ravages of disease. He sensed that he had only a few more days to live. One night as his father made that long vigil by his bedside, the boy looked up through tear-stained eyes and asked, "Dad, why me? Where is God in all of this?"

Dad hesitated, cleared his throat, and thoughtfully responded, "Son, we are in a war. Christ and Satan are fighting a vicious battle. In any war there are casualties. Some soldiers die. The most important thing is to be a faithful soldier. Son, be a good soldier for your Lord, because Jesus is going to win. One day the war will be over."

"I will, Dad, I will," the boy replied.

The good news is that Christ entered the battlefield. He met Satan head-on. He won the war on a bloody cross. In Christ victory is certain. One day the war will be over.

May 27

WHERE IS GOD WHEN INNOCENT PEOPLE SUFFER?

Yea, though I walk through the valley of the shadow of death, I will fear no evil; for You are with me; Your rod and Your staff, they comfort me. Ps. 23:4.

How can we relate to tragedies in our lives? Where is God when innocent people suffer? How can we make sense out of life's hard knocks?

I believe there is a way. The Bible presents an incredibly encouraging picture of God. This view of God gives us courage in times of overwhelming crisis, hope in times of despair, and peace in times of sorrow.

The world we live in is the battleground between intense hatred and incredible love. Good and evil are locked in mortal combat. An all-wise God does not always step in to prevent the results of evil. He does not yet eradicate all suffering.

God values freedom. He allows men and women to make choices, even if those choices are terribly wrong. His only option would be to remove their freedom of choice altogether. Then they would become mere human machines—robots. God allows evil to run its course, but He is always there in the midst of human suffering.

He weeps with the grieving and suffers with those in pain. He sustains, strengthens, and supports. He encourages the brokenhearted and embraces the bruised.

The well-known twenty-third psalm declares, "Yea, though I walk through the valley of the shadow of death, I will fear no evil; for You are with me." Psalm 46:1 adds, "God is our refuge and strength, a very present help in trouble." In the midst of our personal pain and grief God is there. Beyond the tears and heartache and sorrow of it all, we may hear Him saying, "I will heal your broken heart and bind up your wounds. I am there in your deepest times of need."

"The eternal God is your refuge, and underneath are the everlasting arms; He will thrust out the enemy from before you" (Deut. 33:27). "I have become as a wonder to many, but You are my strong refuge. Let my mouth be filled with Your praise and with Your glory all the day" (Ps. 71:7, 8).

Let your heart be filled with praise. Rejoice! God is there. He has not promised we would never be touched by the world's evil, but He has promised to be with us when we are. God has not promised His children would never suffer, but He has promised to be with them when they do. There is something much greater than the absence of pain. It is the presence of God in our pain.

Whatever you go through today, accept His promise: "Lo, I am with you always" (Matt. 28:20).

May 28

OPEN MY EYES

The Lord opens the eyes of the blind. Ps. 146:8.

One evening in 1849 British teenager J. Hudson Taylor knelt by his bed and prayed for a deeper consecration to God. Before rising from his knees, Hudson discovered the purpose of his life. He would go to China for Christ. God had called him.

From that day everything Hudson Taylor did related to this great mission. Missionary agencies tried to discourage him. His health was not good. He had no formal religious preparation. He did not have enough money for the necessary medical training. But the main obstacle was people's indifference to China. The needs of China's millions were a blind spot for most Christians. China was so remote, so intangible.

But not for Hudson Taylor. He wrote to his sister, "I have a stronger desire than ever to go to China. That land is ever in my thoughts. Poor neglected China! Scarcely anyone cares about it."

Hudson Taylor continued pleading with mission boards until finally one agency shipped him off to the land of his dreams. Taylor established China Inland Mission, working in remote areas where no foreigner had ever dared to go. His was the first of the interdenominational "faith" missions that led the way in world evangelism in the nineteenth century.

Hudson Taylor played a key part in the birth of the modern missionary movement. He opened many eyes that had been blinded to the needs of millions living and dying without the gospel. How did Hudson Taylor see so distinctly when everyone else had a blind spot? I think we find the answer in his early development. As a youth Hudson learned to respond to God in small things. His conscience became sensitive through practice.

When God's voice suggested that he give his last half-crown coin to a needy family, he gave it. When God suggested that he speak to a cynical coworker about Christ, Hudson spoke. And wonderful things happened as a result.

Hudson felt more keenly and saw more clearly than his contemporaries because he allowed God to enlighten him step by step.

Are there blind spots in your life? Are there things that keep you from hearing the voice of God? Are there obstacles you may not see that keep you from being everything God wants you to be? Why not pray this simple prayer: "Lord, open my eyes so I can see—really see—my sin and Your cleansing grace. Help me to see any blind spots or defects in my character. Give me a willing heart to surrender all these blind spots to You. In Jesus' name, amen."

May 29

ONE IN CHRIST

But now in Christ Jesus you who once were far off have been brought near by the blood of Christ. Eph. 2:13.

Stepping off a plane in Pune in central India felt like wading into a giant sauna. The temperature was 115 degrees in the shade. Gentle breezes blew, and within seconds beads of sweat stood out on my forehead and began running down my face.

My host and ministerial colleague, John Wilmot, met me at the airport. As we traveled together we entered a Hindu village. John said to me, "Mark, I held an evangelistic series here, and I want you to meet a woman who came to my meetings. She was a Hindu and became a Christian. The light of Christ shines in her face."

We drove along a narrow dirt road to a small thatched-roofed, mud-walled hut. It was probably six feet wide and eight feet long.

An older woman greeted us. Deep lines etched her face, and her hair flowed long at her back. Her eyes drew me, dark eyes that just sparkled. We could not speak the same language, but I knew she was a sister in Christ.

She gestured to me to come in. Bending low, I entered her home on my hands and knees, crawling into her little hut. A flickering light illuminated the darkness. I could see the mat on the floor, and in the dim light I also saw something on the wall: a picture of Jesus.

As we sat there unable to communicate with words, she kept motioning with a smile toward the picture on the wall. The face of Christ and the beauty of His glory reflected in her face, testifying to our kinship in Jesus.

Christ breaks barriers of race and ethnicity, of conflict and jealousy, of position and power. The harsh abrasiveness that characterizes so much of today's interaction is mellowed in Him. Christ bridges the power struggles and turf protecting that alienate people from each other. He eradicates the criticism and gossip that so destroy relationships.

In Christ we are part of one family, forgiven so that we can be forgiving. The closer we get to Christ, the closer we get to one another. When we are drawn to Him, we are drawn to one another.

Reach out to the people around you with the same love that Christ reached out to you with. Embrace the people around you as Christ embraced you. In Him we are one united family.

May 30

DON'T MISS THE INVITATION

The Lord is not slack concerning His promise, as some count slackness, but is longsuffering toward us, not willing that any should perish but that all should come to repentance. 2 Peter 3:9.

An American general named Taylor met destiny one day when he confronted an army three times the size of his own. General Santa Anna's Mexican forces threatened to destroy his troops. Though vastly outnumbered, Taylor managed to outmaneuver his adversary and win a decisive victory at the Battle of Buena Vista.

He became a national hero. After he retired to his home near Baton Rouge, all kinds of people wrote him congratulatory letters. Taylor appreciated the correspondence at first, but soon it was just more than he could handle. Many of the letters had insufficient postage and started piling up at the post office.

Finally General Taylor decided to decline any more mail. The local postmaster had it all sent to the dead-letter office in Washington.

That would have been the end of the story and the end of Taylor's career except for the chance visit of an old friend. This man offhandedly asked if he'd received a very important letter from Philadelphia.

The general hadn't received a lot of mail lately, but his friend persuaded Taylor to contact the dead-letter office to try to get it back. He did.

That's how General Zachary Taylor finally received an invitation to a certain political convention in Philadelphia, where he was nominated for presidential candidacy. Taylor became the twelfth president of the United States of America, yet he almost missed the call.

The most amazing invitation ever given is our Lord's invitation to live together with Him for eternity. It is possible to miss it. I am convinced that more people will *neglect* salvation than reject it. The Epistle to the Hebrews agrees. "How shall we escape if we neglect so great a salvation?" (Heb. 2:3).

Salvation can be neglected. There is much more to salvation than our initial response to Christ's call. Every day He invites us to follow Him. Every day He sends His Spirit to our hearts and urges us to serve Him. The same choice we exercised to respond to the claims of His love initially, He invites us to exercise each day.

Why not tell Him again today, "Lord, I accept Your invitation; today I am Yours"?

May 31

THE GOD WHO INTERVENES

The nations were angry, and Your wrath has come, and the time of the dead, that they should be judged, and that You should reward Your servants the prophets and the saints, and those who fear Your name, small and great, and should destroy those who destroy the earth. Rev. 11:18.

You may not be aware of how close we have come to nuclear war in recent decades. Anytime the heads of the Russian Federation or the United States travel, they are accompanied by an aide carrying a briefcase of electronic controls. The Americans call it the nuclear football. It's essentially the ignition key that turns on all-out nuclear war.

The former Soviet Union has three operational sets of such devices. The Russian president has one that can be used only in conjunction with another set controlled by the defense minister. A third briefcase is usually guarded by the defense ministry and can replace either of the other two.

But something happened after the aborted 1991 coup in Moscow. Western intelligence lost sight of the third briefcase. No one could figure out where it had gone. Did one of the Communist coup plotters have it? Officials were forced to think about the grave possibilities of some maniac launching a nuclear war. Fortunately, after some hours of anguish this third set of controls turned up in the Russian defense ministry.

Never before has the human race had the capacity to destroy itself. The devastating effects of the Chernobyl nuclear reactor disaster are a grim reminder of the potential destruction of a major nuclear blast.

Today it is possible to kill millions of people with the simple pushing of a few nuclear control buttons. Will this world be reduced to a spinning globe of ash? Will we experience the nightmare of a nuclear winter?

God's Word gives us hope. Our Lord will intervene. He will destroy the destroyers. Help is on the way. The future is bright with the promises of God. This world is not in human hands; it is in God's hands. Our destiny will be determined by our divine deliverer.

The greatest event of the ages is just around the corner. Our Lord has promised to return at a time such as this. He has much better plans for our world than destruction by some nuclear disaster. A new world is coming. Now, that's something to sing about! "Lift up the trumpet, and loud let it ring: Jesus is coming again!"

THE HAPPINESS FORMULA

If you know these things, blessed are you if you do them. John 13:17.

Mike had no use for any laws. He especially resented all the rules that governed driving. "Rules are for sissies and grannies," he told himself.

Mike sped everywhere he went. He was lucky—seldom getting a ticket more than once a year. And he often beat those tickets in court.

Then one day after a couple of drinks at a bar, Mike set out in a great hurry to nowhere in particular. He whizzed through a school zone at 45 miles an hour.

A little girl was just then crossing the street. Six-year-old Jennifer arced through the air, leaving her shoes behind on the pavement.

For days her life hung in the balance at a county hospital. Night after night her parents kept up a desperate prayer vigil. Jennifer survived, but her recovery was slow and painful.

Mike would never again look at traffic laws in the same way. He realized they weren't just silly rules; they protected people. If he'd obeyed them, they could have protected a child from a great deal of pain and terror.

God's law is similar. He has given it for one basic reason—our protection. The Ten Commandments were not written by some killjoy God whose motive is to keep us from being happy. God's law does not restrict our happiness; it frees us to enjoy life to the fullest. Obedience is the doorway to happiness.

"Great peace have those who love Your law, and nothing causes them to stumble" (Ps. 119:165).

"But happy is he who keeps the law" (Prov. 29:18).

"If you know these things, blessed are you if you do them" (John 13:17).

Happiness comes from knowing and doing God's will. God's law is not some galling millstone around our necks; it is a stepping-stone, a pathway to genuine, lasting, forever happiness. The God who made us knows much better than we do how to make us happy. Of that we can be certain.

WORLD CHANGERS

That you may become blameless and harmless, children of God without fault in the midst of a crooked and perverse generation, among whom you shine as lights in the world. Phil. 2:15.

In a moving speech to key leaders of the Communist Party, Karl Marx once enthusiastically exclaimed, "The purpose of philosophy is to interpret the world. The purpose of Communism is to change the world." The church and Communism clashed for 70 years on precisely this point: They were both out to change the world, and their methods were diametrically opposed. Make no mistake about it: the church's purpose is to change its world radically.

The purpose of the church is not to compromise with the world; it is to change it. It is not to conform to the world; it is to transform it. The purpose of the church is not to join in the world's perversions, but to be instrumental in its conversion. The church is the arena of God's grace. Its members are to shine "in the midst of a crooked and perverse generation" (Phil. 2:15). Ellen White's book *The Acts of the Apostles* begins with the words "The church is God's appointed agency for the salvation of men. It was organized for service, and its mission is to carry the gospel to the world" (p. 9). She continues: "The church is the repository of the riches of the grace of Christ; and through the church will eventually be made manifest, even to 'the principalities and powers in heavenly places,' the final and full display of the love of God" *(ibid.)*.

The church is to be a force in the world, not a mere dead form. The only way that can happen is if each member is transformed by God's grace.

What really is the church? The church is not merely a corporate institution, although the church is organized for a mission. The church is not some bureaucratic structure. The church is a body of converted Christians saved by grace, committed to His will, with a mission to the world. The church is God's people redeemed to serve, meeting needs everywhere in Jesus' name. The church is administrators, pastors, laypeople, youth, children, you, and me sharing His love, proclaiming His truth to everyone everywhere. The church is us—all of us.

The church can never be what God wants it to be until I become what God wants me to be. An evangelist once said, "The world has yet to see what God can do by our will and through the man who is totally consecrated to Him. By His grace I will be that man."

Is this your decision today? Will you be that man, that woman, that boy, that girl? By God's grace you can be.

THE BANANA PRINCIPLE

So then, my beloved brethren, let every man be swift to hear, slow to speak, slow to wrath. James 1:19.

A woman once came to me and told me that she had learned to use the "banana principle" with her teenage daughter.

I wondered, "What on earth is the 'banana principle'?"

She explained. She'd noticed that her daughter often clammed up when they got into a discussion. The girl just wouldn't share what was really on her heart.

One day the woman got a banana from the kitchen, sat beside her daughter, and asked a question. While the girl answered, the mother very deliberately peeled the banana and took a bite. After she chewed the piece, she asked another question and took another bite. And so it went, through the evening. She found that her daughter opened up about a lot of things.

What had happened? The mother had made sure she listened after she asked a question. She didn't rush in with a comment or criticism while her daughter was answering. She just listened and chewed, and chewed and listened.

The "banana principle" simply means take time to listen. Ask, and then listen carefully.

Jesus was a master at asking questions and patiently listening to the answers people gave. Jesus focused on others. Most people focus on themselves. To them, listening is simply a pause. They can hardly wait for the other person to stop talking so they can say what is on their minds. They are more interested in unloading their thoughts than really hearing the answer.

Here is a vital principle. You can't learn what is in another individual's mind if you do all the talking. The essence of Christianity is concern for others. Love allows other people the freedom to share their inmost thoughts and feelings. To love another is to genuinely care. The apostle John wrote, "Beloved, let us love one another, for love is of God; and everyone who loves is born of God and knows God" (1 John 4:7).

You cannot love me if you do not know me. And you cannot know me if you don't take the time to listen to my heart. So grab a banana. Peel it. Ask a question and take a bite. Then listen with your heart as well as with your ears.

SURROUND EVIL WITH GOOD

So he [Elisha] answered, "Do not fear, for those who are with us are more than those who are with them." 2 Kings 6:16.

During the Revolutionary War a lone American soldier came upon a small party of Hessians in the woods foraging for food. The Hessians were professional mercenaries hired by the British. The American soldier noticed that they'd laid aside their weapons. Moving noiselessly over the forest floor, he gathered up their arms and then, pointing his musket at the men, commanded them to halt. They were shocked into submission. Making loud threats, the American soldier managed to drive them back to camp. His entrance caused a great deal of amazement, and several officers brought him before General Washington himself.

"How did you round up these enemy troops single-handedly?" Washington asked.

The soldier scratched his head a moment and replied, "Well, General, I surrounded them."

When Syrian forces surrounded Elisha, he recognized that God had already surrounded the enemy army. With God even one is a majority. There is no evil foe greater than our God. Through Him we can win our greatest battles. Here is a strange paradox. You do not win over evil by battling against evil. The more you battle, the more powerless you feel. The only way to win is to concentrate on God's power. You win over evil by surrounding it with good. "For the weapons of our warfare are not carnal but mighty in God for pulling down strongholds, casting down arguments and every high thing that exalts itself against the knowledge of God, bringing every thought into captivity to the obedience of Christ" (2 Cor. 10:4, 5).

The apostle Paul appeals to us to be "mighty in God." He urges us to bring "every thought into captivity to the obedience of Christ." We overcome evil through the spiritual weapons of prayer, faith, and the Word. We surround evil with the promises of God, appealing to the mighty powers from on high to rescue us from the clutches of the enemy.

Today, through the unfailing power of the Almighty, victory is ours. The enemy attacking you is surrounded by heaven's forces. Whatever foe you are facing, God is mightier, stronger, and more powerful. Rest in His arms in faith today.

CLOAKED IN HUMANITY

Therefore, in all things He had to be made like His brethren, that He might be a merciful and faithful High Priest in things pertaining to God, to make propitiation for the sins of the people. Heb. 2:17.

Apollo spacecraft crew member James Irwin found himself awed and humbled before God as he walked on the moon. About a year after his moon mission he retired from the Air Force and launched the interdenominational Christian High Flight Foundation, an organization dedicated to sharing the good news that "God walking on earth is more important than men walking on the moon."

Captain Irwin is right. The greatest news in history is Jesus Christ's becoming a man, dwelling in human flesh, dying on our behalf, and rising from the dead. Since Jesus became one of us, He understands us. "In taking our nature, the Saviour has bound Himself to humanity by a tie that is never to be broken" (*The Desire of Ages*, p. 25).

He "was in all points tempted as we are, yet without sin" (Heb. 4:15).

I wondered how this could possibly be true. Does Jesus really understand how a woman feels when her husband has an affair with someone else? He was never married. How could He possibly understand divorce? Does Jesus really understand the craving of a drug addict? Can Jesus really identify with the feeling of a young couple who have just lost a baby in childbirth? These thoughts raced through my mind until I discovered this eternal principle. It is possible to experience the same emotions without going through the exact same experience.

Jesus understands rejection and betrayal because He was rejected by His disciple Judas. Jesus understands physical pain because He suffered so intensely on the cross. Jesus understands our greatest cravings because He fasted for 40 days in the wilderness. We can experience no physical craving greater than what Jesus experienced in the wilderness. There is no emotional pain any greater than what Jesus endured.

In every area of life, physical, mental, emotional, or spiritual, Satan unleashed his fiercest attacks on Jesus. Satan tempted Jesus in every area we are tempted in, with much greater ferocity. Satan does not need to use all of his power on us, but he did use all of it on Jesus. There is no area we can be tempted in that Jesus does not understand.

Take your temptations to Christ. Come to Him with all of your struggles and spiritual battles. He understands. He will deliver. You can be sure of it.

THE SABBATHKEEPING PRIEST

For assuredly, I say to you, till heaven and earth pass away, one jot or one tittle will by no means pass from the law till all is fulfilled. Matt. 5:18.

Andrew Fisher, a onetime Catholic priest, thought carefully about his decision to worship on Saturday. He argued that the Sabbath commandment was not a part of the ceremonial law, because it was instituted at Creation, before the sacrificial system was in place. Quoting Matthew 5:17, 18, he showed that Jesus refused to remove one iota from the law. With James 2:10-12 he demonstrated that the disciples didn't change the Sabbath. He boldly pointed to the Catholic Church as the source of the apostasy. Sunday worship, he suggested, was the direct fulfillment of the Papacy's changing the set "times and laws" as predicted in Daniel 7:25. Fisher lost his life because of his stand. In 1529 Fisher and his wife were sentenced to death.

There are some things worth dying for. King Solomon, the wisest man who ever lived, said, "Buy the truth, and do not sell it" (Prov. 23:23).

Fisher and his wife had moral courage. They had spiritual backbone.

Some people will not stand for much of anything. They go with the flow, marching to the tune of the crowd, unwilling to be different from the majority. But then there are the Josephs, the Daniels, and the Pauls. "The greatest want of the world is the want of men—men who will not be bought or sold, men who in their inmost souls are true and honest, men who do not fear to call sin by its right name, men whose conscience is as true to duty as the needle to the pole, men who will stand for the right though the heavens fall" (*Education,* p. 57).

Fisher and his wife made a fundamental decision. They would do right because it was right, and leave the results with God. Their life motto was "Truth is worth following." Truth is still truth, whether the majority believes it or not. Truth is truth, whether it is popular or not. Truth is truth, whether some people accept it or not.

Will you stand with the faithful men and women of God down through the ages? Will you commit your life to doing right, whatever the cost? Will you live by principle, whatever the results? Will you determine to follow truth at any cost and leave the results with God?

THE HEART SPECIALIST

For unto us a Child is born, unto us a Son is given; and the government will be upon His shoulder. And His name will be called Wonderful, Counselor, Mighty God, Everlasting Father, Prince of Peace. Isa. 9:6.

In Sydney, Australia, a self-employed repair wizard developed a unique advertising sign to attract customers. It said simply, "Everything mended here . . . except broken hearts."

But this repairer's exception is our Lord's specialty.

Jesus specializes in putting broken lives back together. Isaiah, the prophet, jubilantly shouts, "Unto us a Child is born, unto us a Son is given" (Isa. 9:6). Jesus is ours. Isaiah's passage lists five names of Jesus. He is *wonderful.* He is a wonderful Savior, Redeemer, and Lord. His love, grace, mercy, and forgiveness are wonderful.

He is a *counselor.* He listens sympathetically to our needs. He gently guides us at life's crossroads. He gives us wisdom for our decisions. He is concerned about meeting our needs. His ear is bent low to listen to our concerns. He is never too busy to listen.

He is the *mighty God.* He has never lost a battle with the enemy. He has met Satan and defeated him. Demons flee at His presence. He breaks the chains that bind us. He delivers us from the bondage of enslaving habits. He renews our minds and transforms our attitudes.

He is also the *everlasting Father.* He is eternal. He is dependable. We can count on Him. He is always there. He will never let us down. From eternity in the past to eternity in the present, He is reliable. He is the loving Father some people never had.

Jesus is also the *Prince of Peace.* He brings peace to troubled hearts. He brings calm to troubled minds. He brings order to chaotic lives. What a heart specialist indeed. Heaven has given us a wonderful Savior, an understanding Counselor, an all-powerful God, a reliable everlasting Father, and a comforting Prince of Peace.

Let your spirits rejoice in His incredible care for you today.

KNOWING AND DOING

Therefore whoever hears these sayings of Mine, and does them, I will liken him to a wise man who built his house on the rock. Matt. 7:24.

On July 11, 1804, the vice president of the United States, Aaron Burr, challenged Alexander Hamilton to a duel. The two men had developed quite a bitter rivalry. It was political and it was personal.

Hamilton accepted the challenge. The two men met at Weehawken, New Jersey, overlooking the Hudson River.

Aaron Burr fired a bullet that cut through his rival's liver and spine. After 30 hours of agony Hamilton died.

Interestingly enough, dueling had already been declared illegal in New York. Even offering or receiving a challenge to duel was against the law.

Alexander Hamilton himself had helped in the effort to pass this ban on dueling. He'd argued for it. He'd helped put it on the books. But that law hadn't become a big enough principle in his own life.

It is one thing to know right, another thing to do it. The law Alexander Hamilton fought for was not a law he applied to his own life. There was a difference between his beliefs and his actions. This is true of many people. They believe one way but live another. Their inner convictions do not find expression in their lifestyle. Why? What is the difference between belief and action?

The difference lies in understanding the life-changing power of a divinely empowered will. Here are two remarkable statements. "Strength of character consists of two things—power of will and power of self-control" (*Counsels to Parents, Teachers, and Students,* p. 222). "You can make yourself what you choose" (*Testimonies,* vol. 2, p. 565).

When we make a positive choice to place our lives under God's control, He will empower our wills to do right. Although our wills may be weak when we place them on the side of right, our Lord empowers us to do right.

God has given us the power of choice. Our choice united with God's power is invincible. Not only does God impress us to make right choices; He empowers us when we do make right choices, and He sustains those choices. He invites us to place our wills on the side of right. When we do, He works miracles in our lives.

Will you choose in every area of your life to serve Him today?

A LETTER FROM A FRIEND

Be still, and know that I am God. Ps. 46:10.

Have you ever felt unusually lonely? I remember one time when I had deep feelings of loneliness, the summer of 1965. I had just completed my freshman year at Atlantic Union College, in a rural New England town about 45 miles west of Boston, Massachusetts. The college administration had chosen me to spend the summer as a student missionary in Brazil. I had never traveled out of the United States.

I flew to São Paulo, Brazil, and then to Belém, Brazil, on the Amazon River. From there I joined a medical missionary team on a launch called the *Luzerio VI.* Our launch traveled up the Amazon. We were out of touch with civilization for about a month.

I often longed for home during those long summer days and evenings. I thought about my parents, but most of all I thought about a young woman I was dating. I longed to return to the mission headquarters just to get a letter from her. Without telephones, e-mails, faxes, or other means of communication, letters were my only tie to home. They lifted my spirits. They let me know that somebody at home loved me and cared for me.

Letters can make a profound difference. Letters inspired by God can make an even more profound difference. The remarkable bond that developed between Teenie and me through those letters led eventually to our marriage.

There is someone who loves you very much, who cares deeply, who is thinking about you constantly. He has sent you a series of letters inspired by His Spirit. Every page of Scripture reveals His love.

It must be extremely disappointing to Him that we are often too busy to spend time reading His love letters. Busyness is the enemy of spirituality, a spiritual cancer that saps the vital energy of the soul. You cannot rush spirituality. You cannot sprint through the presence of God. The words of the Psalmist echo in our ears: "Be still, and know that I am God" (Ps. 46:10).

Someone who loves you dearly has written you a precious collection of letters. Why not spend time reading them today?

THERE IS STILL RIGHT AND WRONG

There is a way that seems right to a man, but its end is the way of death. Prov. 14:12.

Abraham Lincoln faced a grave crisis. The issue of slavery had dogged America for decades. The Constitution had stepped sideways around it. The Missouri Compromise of 1820 had preserved a sort of equilibrium between free and slave states, but the issue could not be swept under the carpet forever. Now Southern states looked ready to secede. They argued that their entire economy, their whole way of life, depended on slave labor.

Lincoln wanted more than anything else to preserve the Union. He was a reconciler, a bridge builder. He did everything he could to prevent his country from being torn apart. "United we stand, divided we fall," a watchword of the American Revolution, was Lincoln's motto.

But Lincoln saw another principle at stake, what he called the "monstrous injustice of slavery." He once said, "If slavery is not wrong, nothing is wrong. I cannot remember when I did not so think, and feel."

To Lincoln, human beings owning other human beings just wasn't right. No matter how many people thought it was OK, or how much the country's economy was tied to it, or what people threatened to do if slavery ended, it still was wrong.

On January 1, 1863, Abraham Lincoln finally issued the Emancipation Proclamation, a symbolic declaration that paved the way for true freedom. Lincoln faced the crisis, and he made a stand. With that proclamation America took a giant step toward truly becoming the land of the free.

Are there things that you believe so deeply that you are willing to take a stand for them? Many people believe there is no right and no wrong. Everything is a moral blur on their spiritual radar screen. They define right and wrong as a matter of individual preference.

We are living at a time similar to the days of the judges, when everyone "did what was right in his own eyes" (Judges 21:25). It is a time similar to Isaiah's, when everyone turned "to his own way" (Isa. 53:6). Solomon's words speak with increasing relevance to this generation: "There is a way that seems right to a man, but its end is the way of death" (Prov. 14:12).

That way is our own way. Right and wrong are not a matter of individual concern; they are a matter of God's will. Lincoln took a stand for right, contrary to the will of the majority. God invites us to do the very same thing. He urges us to take a stand based on the principles of His Word and to stick by it.

June 11

IS YOUR CONSCIENCE A SAFE GUIDE?

This being so, I myself always strive to have a conscience without offense toward God and men. Acts 24:16.

A university student and I recently discussed moral issues. His comment is typical of others I have heard.

When I asked how he defined the difference between right and wrong, he replied, "I let my conscience be my guide. If I don't feel something is wrong, I know I am safe. I listen to my convictions."

This statement has some truth in it. I empathize some. It is certainly true that God's Spirit convicts us of right and wrong. If we are in touch with God, the still small voice of the Spirit will guide us. But let's look a little deeper.

Is conscience alone a safe guide? What is conscience? Our conscience is the voice within us that prompts us to duty. It is the inner voice that convicts of sin. It is the inner sense of awareness of right and wrong. God has given us a conscience as an inner moral radar system. Our consciences do not operate in a vacuum. They are influenced by what we put into our minds. They are shaped by our environment, by our choices, and by the suggestions of others. The Bible talks about a good conscience (Acts 23:1), a conscience of faith (1 Tim. 1:5), a pure conscience (1 Tim. 3:9), and a purged conscience (Heb. 9:14). It also describes a defiled conscience (1 Cor. 8:7), a weak conscience (1 Cor. 8:12), a seared conscience (1 Tim. 4:2), and an evil conscience (Heb. 10:22).

This leads us back to our question: "Is the conscience a safe guide?" Yes and no. If the conscience is shaped by God's Word, sensitive to the Holy Spirit, conditioned by right choices, and influenced by godly counsel, it can be trusted. But if the conscience is defiled by disobedience, seared by sin, influenced by compromising Christians, and conditioned by faulty choices, it is unreliable.

God's Word stands above our conscience. God's law stands outside our conscience. God's will is not shaped by our conscience—our conscience must be shaped by God's will.

Open your heart to the Spirit, and allow Him to shape your conscience. Fill your mind with His Word, and let it mold your conscience. Let your life be guided by a sanctified conscience today.

BEARING ONE ANOTHER'S BURDENS

Bear one another's burdens, and so fulfill the law of Christ. Gal. 6:2.

If you visit Boys Town, founded by Father Flanagan near Omaha, Nebraska, you'll find an interesting statue at the entrance.

It depicts two boys whom the priest once encountered. A brightly smiling boy carries on his back a younger child who can't walk.

The priest asked the older one if he ever tired of carrying his companion around. The boy's reply is the statue's unforgettable inscription: "He ain't heavy; he's my brother."

The essence of Christianity is love, expressed in encouraging words, kind deeds, and caring actions. Love always reveals itself in action. The apostle John wrote, "By this we know love, because He laid down His life for us. And we also ought to lay down our lives for the brethren" (1 John 3:16). Jesus revealed His love on the cross. Every drop of blood speaks to us of a love that goes to the limit.

In light of His love, we lay down our lives in love by pouring them out in sacrifice for others. We too give ourselves away at the cross. We give ourselves not only to Jesus in sacrifice, but to the larger Christian community in service. "The strongest argument in favor of the gospel is a loving and lovable Christian" (*The Ministry of Healing,* p. 470). "Love can no more exist without revealing itself in outward acts than fire can be kept alive without fuel" (*Testimonies,* vol. 1, p. 695).

"Duty has a twin sister, love" (*Testimonies,* vol. 4, p. 62).

Love without action or duty is mere sentimentalism. Duty without love is drudgery. It is rigid legalism. The love of Christ overflowing from our hearts reaches out in kind acts to people around us. Our greatest joy comes from blessing others. Bearing their burdens is not a galling yoke; it is a welcome opportunity to serve. It is a glorious privilege to minister, walking in the footsteps of the one who "did not come to be served, but to serve" (Matt. 20:28).

Join with the homeless lad at Boys Town in saying, "He ain't heavy; he's my brother."

COME AS YOU ARE

All that the Father gives Me will come to Me, and the one who comes to Me I will by no means cast out. John 6:37.

Television stations in Barcelona aired spots in which unemployed individuals could talk about their qualifications for potential jobs. A man named Bernardino got on and really moved viewers with his story of hardship and hunger. People called with all kinds of job offers and even cash contributions. Bernardino made arrangements to collect the money.

But as he was leaving the studio he was greeted by the police. They recognized Bernardino as an infamous burglar named El Niño, wanted for stealing thousands of dollars' worth of jewelry.

Many people looking for God can relate to Bernardino's story. They want God's help, of course, but at the same time they're afraid that they'll be exposed. Their inner guilt keeps them away from God. They view God as a police officer waiting to arrest them. They picture God as a judge ready to sentence them. They want to "clean themselves up," then come to God. Their sinfulness keeps them from approaching Him.

Steps to Christ, page 31, declares: "If you see your sinfulness, do not wait to make yourself better. How many there are who think they are not good enough to come to Christ. Do you expect to become better through your own efforts? . . . We must not wait for stronger persuasions, for better opportunities, or for holier tempers. We can do nothing of ourselves. We must come to Christ just as we are."

Christ's arms are open to receive the guilty. If we were not sinners, we would have no need of Jesus. He renounces pride, arrogance, and self-righteousness. He lovingly reassures us with the words "The one who comes to Me I will by no means cast out" (John 6:37).

He invites us to come with our guilt-ridden lives, anxieties and fears, worries and stresses, failures and weaknesses—to come with the heavy burden of sin and lay it all at His feet. He will embrace us with His arms of love and set us on the right path again.

THOMAS JEFFERSON AND OUR DUTY TO GOD

Who gave Himself for us, that He might redeem us from every lawless deed and purify for Himself His own special people, zealous for good works. Titus 2:14.

The Thomas Jefferson Memorial is quite an imposing monument. Walking between its classic columns, one is humbled by the vision of a man who worked so hard to make America truly democratic.

"All men . . . are endowed by their Creator with certain unalienable rights," he wrote. These are words that changed history.

There on those memorial walls we find words from Thomas Jefferson that are a little less familiar.

"I tremble for my country when I reflect that God is just."

A simple statement. But it speaks volumes about this man's perspective and his worldview. Jefferson had a strong sense of God's justice and our moral obligation to a holy God. He was not an orthodox Christian, in part because he had seen so much misuse of religion by people calling themselves Christians. But he and the other founding fathers shared a profound awareness of our moral duty to God.

Jefferson called the moral system of Jesus "the most perfect and sublime that has ever been taught." He admired Christ most of all because "He pushed his scrutinies into the heart of man, erected his tribunal in the region of his thoughts, and purified the waters at the fountainhead."

The gospel provides redemption from both sin's guilt and power. Christ longs to purify us within. Jesus urges us to "purify your hearts" (James 4:8). Peter encourages those who "have purified your souls in obeying the truth through the Spirit" (1 Peter 1:22). The aged apostle John says of those waiting for the return of our Lord, "Everyone who has this hope in Him purifies himself, just as He is pure" (1 John 3:3).

A merciful God forgives us. A just, all-powerful God longs to purify us. When John urges us to purify ourselves, he is not encouraging self-centered introspection or self-righteous purification. He is talking about an attitude, an honest repentance or godly sorrow for sin, that allows God to do His work in us. He is the "refiner's fire." He is the one who will "purify the sons of Levi, and purge them as gold and silver, that they may offer to the Lord an offering in righteousness." God won't do it without us, and we certainly cannot do it without Him. A loving God graciously invites us to come to Him to receive mercy. A just, righteous God graciously invites us to come to Him to receive cleansing.

IN GOD'S HANDS

He who has the Son has life; he who does not have the Son of God does not have life. 1 John 5:12.

I met Peter in Gdansk, Poland. His mother was a committed Christian who prayed for her son daily. When I visited Gdansk to hold an evangelistic series in the Lenin Theater in 1987, the boy's mom pleaded, "Pastor, pray for my boy."

A few weeks later I learned that Peter had brain cancer. The only human solution was an operation. The physicians removed the tumor, but didn't get all of it. The tumor continued to grow. Radiation treatments seemed to have little effect.

Peter began listening to my taped series of evangelistic sermons. The Holy Spirit convicted him. He opened his heart to Jesus. The hope of heaven became real. He sensed that he was a son of God.

In a few months Peter lost 60 pounds. During the last weeks of his life he didn't eat. Down to 84 pounds, he continuously vomited. On a cool October morning his mother called the church and asked me to come immediately. Peter was dying.

I knelt before him, a basin in my hands, catching the vomit. His skin was a sallow color. His eyes rolled around in his head. His very breath smelled of death. Peter's dying wish was for me to baptize him.

I explained that it would be impossible to baptize him by immersion in his condition. His weak state made transporting him to the church impossible. A lake or river was totally out of the question. I gave him the assurance that Christ accepted him. Still, he urged me to baptize him. It was his final wish. He wanted the sense that all of his sins were washed away.

My heart was touched. I encouraged his mother to fill the bathtub with warm water. Peter stripped to the waist. I carried him in my arms to the bathroom. We knelt there on the floor as I prayed. The presence of God surrounded us. It was one of those eternal moments in which I felt as if I could reach out and touch God. After prayer I lowered Peter into the bathtub, into the "watery grave" of baptism. As I lifted him out of the tub a smile spread over his face as he said, "I am Christ's. Eternity is before me, and death no longer frightens me, because my destiny is heaven."

Our loving Lord allowed Peter to live peacefully for another month.

Peter had the assurance of eternal life. Do you have that assurance today? God wants to give it to you right now. The apostle John declares that eternal life is a gift Jesus offers to each one of us now. "These things I have written to you who believe in the name of the Son of God, that you may know that you have eternal life" (1 John 5:13).

If Christ is living in your heart today, you have eternal life. Grasp that reality. Rejoice in that assurance. Hold on to that hope today. It is as sure as the other promises of God.

June 16

THE THANKFUL HEART

Let us come before His presence with thanksgiving. Ps. 95:2.

An attitude of thankfulness will go a long way toward reducing stress and keeping you well. We can learn to develop this thankful attitude when misfortune comes as well as when things run smoothly.

One day many years ago, bandits robbed an English preacher traveling to a neighboring town. That evening he made this entry in his journal:

"I was robbed today, yet I am thankful.
I am thankful first that, although they took all
I had, they really didn't take much.
I am thankful that, although they took my purse,
they did not take my life.
Lastly, I am thankful that it was I who was robbed and not I who robbed!"

Learn to give thanks continually. Paul's Epistles give us this divine prescription: "In everything give thanks; for this is the will of God in Christ Jesus for you" (1 Thess. 5:18).

"Let the peace of God rule in your hearts, . . . and be thankful" (Col. 3:15). "With thanksgiving, let your requests be made known to God" (Phil. 4:6). The courts of heaven sing, "Blessing and glory and wisdom, thanksgiving and honor and power and might, be to our God forever and ever. Amen" (Rev. 7:12).

Thanksgiving is the natural expression of a converted heart. When our lives are filled with complaining, we testify that God has dealt with us harshly. The spirit of complaint casts a reflection on God. It reflects an inner root of bitterness. Where there is murmuring, there is heart trouble.

On the other hand, a thankful heart accepts life's joys and sorrows alike. The spirit of complaint occurs when life doesn't go our way or we don't get exactly what we want. "Let us not be always thinking of our wants and never of the benefits we receive. We do not pray any too much, but we are too sparing of giving thanks. We are the constant recipients of God's mercies" (*Steps to Christ,* p. 103).

A thankful heart can be cultivated. Think of something you are thankful for today. Express it to a family member, a friend, or a coworker. Make a list of seven things you are thankful for. Praise God for the blessings He has given you. Let's have thanksgiving every day of the year.

June 17

PEACE IN THE MIDST OF THE STORM

Evening and morning and at noon I will pray, and cry aloud, and He shall hear my voice. He has redeemed my soul in peace from the battle that was against me, for there were many against me. Ps. 55:17, 18.

On February 3, 1943, a torpedo struck the S.S. *Dorchester* in the North Atlantic. Filled with American soldiers, the transport ship took on water rapidly and began listing to starboard. Chaos reigned on board. The radio had been knocked out. Men rushed around on the ragged edge of panic. Many had run up from the hold without life jackets. Overcrowded lifeboats capsized; rafts drifted away before anyone could reach them. Survivors testified that there seemed only one little island of order in all the confusion—the spot where four chaplains stood, on the steeply sloping starboard side.

George Lansing Fox, a pastor from Chicago; Alexander David Goode, a rabbi from New York City; Clark Poling, a minister from Schenectady, New York; and John Washington, a priest from New Jersey, calmly guided men to their boat stations. They distributed life jackets from a storage locker and then helped men frozen with fear over the side.

One survivor recalls hearing the noise of hundreds of men crying, pleading, praying, and swearing. But through it all, the chaplains spoke words of courage and confidence. "Their voices were the only thing that kept me going," he said.

When the supply of life jackets was gone, the four chaplains gave away their own. One of the last men to leave the ship's flooding deck looked back and saw the chaplains still standing firm. Their arms linked, they braced against the slanting deck. Across the waves their voices still sounded, praying in Latin, Hebrew, and English. As one sailor put it: "It was the finest thing I have ever seen, or hope to see, this side of heaven."

There is only one thing that gave these four chaplains the ability to remain calm in the midst of these chaotic circumstances. God's peace filled their hearts. The Hebrew word for peace is "shalom." The root word for shalom means "completeness." When your mind is at peace, you are complete.

No destructive anxieties tear you apart. No devastating fears destroy your joy. No paralyzing worries uproot your happiness. In every circumstance God offers us His gift of peace. "A man at peace with God and his fellow men cannot be made miserable. . . . The heart in harmony with God is lifted above the annoyances and trials of this life" (*Testimonies,* vol. 5, p. 488). Isaiah's promises ring true in the twenty-first century. "You will keep him in perfect peace, whose mind is stayed on You, because he trusts in You" (Isa. 26:3).

What a gift! His peace can be yours today.

June 18

SOLVING PROBLEMS GOD'S WAY

Moreover if your brother sins against you, go and tell him his fault between you and him alone. If he hears you, you have gained your brother. Matt. 18:15.

A steady stream of gripes poured into Dean Morgan's office. He had his work cut out for him. Every troublemaker on campus seemed to have found his way to his dormitory. Constant complaining buzzed through the halls. Nobody could get along. Dean Morgan just couldn't solve all the problems.

But as he read Matthew one day, a verse jumped out at him. Jesus said, "If your brother sins against you, go and tell him his fault between you and him alone. If he hears you, you have gained your brother" (Matt. 18:15).

Dean Morgan decided to do something. He wanted to see what would happen if his residents actually acted on these words of Christ.

He called everyone together and laid down a new rule. From then on, before anyone came to him with a complaint, they would have to go and talk to the person they were complaining about. They must first talk about the problem directly, in private, with the person who had offended them.

Dean Morgan watched to see what would happen. At first he feared all this "going to your brother" might result in a lot of confrontations. Instead, he began to notice that the dorm was much quieter than usual. No one pounded on his door with a complaint.

Dean Morgan discovered that the students were putting the words of Christ into practice, with wonderful results. All kinds of problems and conflicts were quickly resolved.

The students in that infamous dorm kept on *acting* on the Word of Christ, and they kept on seeing good results. By school year's end the dormitory had become a model for the rest of the school. The worst place on campus had become the best.

I have seen this principle at work in my own ministry for 35 years. When it is followed, hearts are healed, barriers are broken down, and conflicts are resolved. Determine never to discuss someone else's negative behavior without first approaching them. Go in a spirit of Christian love. Share the problem humbly. Give God a chance to work. Problems that you thought were huge may evaporate when the other individual has a chance to explain.

Commit yourself to solving interpersonal relationship problems God's way, and watch what happens.

June 19

SPIRITUAL STRENGTH IN A SIBERIAN PRISON

Blessed is the man whose strength is in You. . . . They go from strength to strength. Ps. 84:5, 7.

Pastor Mikhail Azaroz's faith landed him in a Siberian prison camp.

Among the men crowded together in his cell was a bloodthirsty giant named Yura. He and his criminal gang spent much of their time terrorizing other prisoners. They never touched Pastor Mikhail, but the shrieks and groans of the victims were heartrending.

As the pastor began to pray about this a verse in Luke came to mind. "I give you the authority to trample . . . over all the power of the enemy" (Luke 10:19).

Mikhail felt that God was directing him to do something. That night when Yura began shouting his usual order, "I want to see blood!" the pastor took hold of his arm and said, "Yura, the Scriptures say, don't do to others what you don't want them to do to you."

All eyes froze on the scene. Yura pulled his arm away and barked, "I don't want to hurt you, old man. Go sit on your bunk."

But the pastor persisted. "Let's make a deal. You give me just one hour to talk, and I'll tell you about my past."

Yura thought for a moment. He knew that Mikhail always told the truth. Turning to his gang members, he asked, "Should we let him talk?"

They shrugged. Yura said, "Go ahead!"

So the pastor started talking. He told them about his faith and about the persecution that believers had to endure. He talked for an hour. Then two hours. Then three hours. By then the guards had come to turn off all the lights.

Amazingly enough, Yura wanted to hear more. Mikhail promised to continue the next evening. And that's what he did night after night, telling these men about Jesus. The savagery in that cell ended.

This lone Christian pastor had proved that even in the gulag God is stronger than brutality. He's bigger than the wild beast within human hearts.

God changed the entire prison environment through the Christian witness of one individual. That's not surprising. God changed the course of history through Moses. God changed Babylon through Daniel. God changed Persia through Esther. God changed Rome through Paul. God can change your family, your workplace, your school, your neighborhood, your apartment complex—through you.

One man, one woman, one young person—plus God—equals a majority.

June 20

DEFLATING OUR FEARS

Do not fear, little flock, for it is your Father's good pleasure to give you the kingdom. Luke 12:32.

Patricia had always been a people person, happily wrapped up in her family, mothering her three daughters through the ups and downs of adolescence. But now they had all married and moved away, and her husband was increasingly gone on business.

She found herself sitting alone night after night, wondering what purpose she had anymore. Fear nagged her as she tried to go to sleep in an empty house.

Patricia realized that if she didn't get a hold on her fears, they would inflate out of control. She had to have something else on which to fasten her mind. She turned to God. She asked God to give her some clear purpose that she could cling to, even in an empty house. And God answered.

She realized that she could either become a complaining, nervous woman focused on her loneliness, or she could accept her situation and reach out cheerfully toward others.

Patricia focused her attention on such promises as "For I know the thoughts that I think toward you, says the Lord, thoughts of peace and not of evil, to give you a future and a hope" (Jer. 29:11).

What a promise! God deflates our fears by assuring us of the new future He is building for us. No matter what our circumstances, God has planned a positive future. Our Lord says, "Do not fear, little flock, for it is your Father's good pleasure to give you the kingdom" (Luke 12:32). "Be strong, do not fear!" (Isa. 35:4).

Patricia found a way out of her fears by fastening her thoughts on the purpose she felt God was giving her. She looked on His call as the focal point of her thoughts. She found an alternative to dwelling on the loneliness and the danger.

Patricia looked to God, the strong tower, to give her a sense of purpose. She was no longer just a passive victim, a sitting duck for fear to prey on.

Patricia accepted the reality that God was stronger than her fears. "Unbelieving fear will be swept away before living faith" (*Testimonies to Ministers,* p. 226).

Fear imagines the worst. Faith sees God's best. Faith trusts God to work out His best plans for our lives. When fear seizes your mind, let faith take away your fear. Focus your mind on God's powerful promises, and live in hope.

June 21

A TIME TO WAKE UP

Set your mind on things above, not on things on the earth. Col. 3:2.

The Scottish philosopher and economist Adam Smith sometimes got so lost in thought that he forgot where he was.

One Sunday morning he wandered out into his garden wearing only a nightgown. Soon he became totally engrossed in working out some obscure theoretical problem. Smith strolled out of his yard and onto the street. He actually walked 12 miles to a neighboring town, completely oblivious to everything around him.

But the loud ringing of church bells in the town reached some level of his consciousness. He made his way into the church and took his place in a pew, still pondering. Regular churchgoers were astonished to see the philosopher in their midst, clad only in his white nightgown.

Adam Smith had become so engrossed in his thoughts that he lost sight of reality.

Although we smile at the absent-minded philosopher walking into church in his nightgown, is it possible that we too can become so preoccupied with our lives that we miss out on eternal reality? The apostle Paul states, "And . . . knowing the time, that now it is high time to awake out of sleep; for now our salvation is nearer than when we first believed" (Rom. 13:11).

Since "Satan is playing the game of life for [our souls]" (*Testimonies,* vol. 6, p. 148), he attempts to keep our minds entranced with the things of this world. In the light of eternity, it is now time to wake up to his deceptions. Satan's strategy is to occupy us with present things so that eternity has little place in our thinking, to fill our heads with the earthly so that there is no room for the heavenly.

God's response is "Set your mind on things above, not on things on the earth" (Col. 3:2).

The battle between Christ and Satan is waged in our minds. Today, invite Jesus to take control of your thoughts. Invite Him to reign supreme in your mind. Take time to allow His Spirit to shape your thoughts, and you will win the battle for your mind.

June 22

THE HOUND OF HEAVEN

Where can I go from Your Spirit? Oh where can I flee from Your presence? If I ascend into heaven, You are there; if I make my bed in hell, behold, You are there. Ps. 139:7, 8.

A few years ago I conducted an evangelistic series in a Holiday Inn in Brockton, Massachusetts. One evening, after preaching a sermon entitled "How to Discover Bible Truth," I extended a call to people who desired to accept Jesus, follow truth, and look forward to baptism. A young woman in her late 20s responded. She slowly unfolded her story.

This was her first night at our meetings. Previously she had learned about the Bible while living in Canada. She studied Scripture with an Adventist pastor, accepted Jesus, and began attending an Adventist church.

Her husband became very upset. Hoping to distract his wife, he suggested a short vacation to attend his brother's wedding—in Brockton, Massachusetts.

Reaching Brockton, they attempted to find a room at several motels. Finally they found a room available at the Holiday Inn—where they discovered our meetings.

"We can't get away!" the husband exclaimed. "We have run right into this Bible business again!"

You can't get away from God. Francis Thompson wrote a poem about the "hound of heaven" to describe God's relentless love. Like a hound on a hunt, God is relentless in His search for us. The psalmist echoes it in the words "Where can I go from Your Spirit? Or where can I flee from Your presence? If I ascend into heaven, You are there; if I make my bed in hell, behold, You are there. If I take the wings of the morning, and dwell in the uttermost parts of the sea, even there Your hand shall lead me" (Ps. 139:7-10).

The story of the Bible is not so much our seeking God, as it is God's seeking us. When Adam and Eve sinned in Eden, God sought them there.

In tender loving tones He called, "Where are you?" (Gen. 3:9).

When Elijah fled to a cave, disappointed and discouraged, God followed him once again, asking, "What are you doing here, Elijah?" (1 Kings 19:9).

After he denied Jesus, Peter wanted to get away from it all. He fled to Galilee and went fishing. Jesus, after His resurrection, followed him and asked, "Simon, son of Jonah, do you love Me more than these?" (John 21:15).

What a God. He won't let us get away. When we are running from Him, He is running toward us.

Today, praise Him for His relentless love.

June 23

PRAYER: A TWO-WAY CONVERSATION

But his delight is in the law of the Lord, and in His law he meditates day and night. Ps. 1:2.

Jeremy Levin's world turned upside down when he was captured by Shiite Muslims and held hostage in Lebanon's Bekaa Valley. The Beirut bureau chief for CNN, Levin felt isolated, helpless, and afraid. The only time he saw another human being was when his captors escorted him to the bathroom once a day. Crouched in the corner of a windowless room hour after hour, month after month, Jeremy desperately needed to talk. But he feared that if he talked with himself, he would go crazy. So he considered the idea of talking to God.

At first this made him feel uncomfortable. Although he was the grandson of a rabbi, Jeremy had decided, long before, that he could believe only in concrete things, things he could touch and feel. He had rejected his religious heritage.

But with so little to touch and feel in that lonely cell, Jeremy eventually reached out to God and began talking. Soon he realized that he was having a meaningful two-way conversation.

Prayer is much more than a monologue. As we quietly meditate, opening our hearts to God, He speaks. His Spirit impresses our hearts. In the rush of twenty-first-century living, it is difficult to hear His voice. His voice is drowned out in the clutter of our daily lives. The psalmist describes the righteous person as one who daily meditates on God's law (Ps. 1:2), as one who meditates on God's works (Ps. 77:12), and as one who meditates on God in the night watches (Ps. 63:6).

Christian meditation, as part of a meaningful prayer life, is dramatically different from Eastern mysticism. Christian meditation is not an attempt to clear the mind; it is an attempt to fill the mind. It is focused. Meditating on God's love, God's law, God's works, God's goodness, God's generosity, we are filled with thoughts of Him. In those quiet moments He comes preciously close.

"The relations between God and each soul are as distinct and full as though there were not another soul upon the earth to share His watchcare, not another soul for whom He gave His beloved Son" (*Steps to Christ*, p. 100).

Meditation provides the setting for God to speak. It is the atmosphere in which God quietly impresses our souls. In the stillness we can hear His voice. Why not develop this devotional habit this week? Take your Bible, and find some quiet place early in the morning or later in the evening. Begin with the first psalm. Read a little, asking God to speak to you through His Word. Listen for His voice. You may need to follow the devotional pattern for a few days to get used to it, but soon you will sense the personal presence of God. Once you do, you will find yourself drawn to these devotional moments again and again.

June 24

BUSYNESS, THE ENEMY OF GODLINESS

While your servant was busy here and there, he was gone. 1 Kings 20:40.

Syrian king Ben-Hadad approached Israel with thousands of troops. The vast Aramean army dwarfed Israel's, yet God's prophet promised total victory over the enemy. With God's assurance, Israel overwhelmed their enemy on the battlefield—yet King Ahab settled for a truce, letting Ben-Hadad live.

As a rebuke, the prophet told King Ahab the story of a servant assigned to guard a prisoner of war. The servant got so busy that he forgot his task, although his life depended on it. The prisoner slipped out of his hands.

The prophet's point was clear. Total victory was attainable, but Ahab let it slip through his fingers. Could this parable apply to us? Have we too made a truce with evil?

Victory is within our grasp, but we are just too busy to seize it. Triumph is certain, but we are too busy to claim God's promises. We are too busy to study the Bible . . . too busy to pray . . . too busy to meditate upon Scripture.

Does your spiritual life need revitalizing? In the frantic pace of a rushed life, here are three suggestions for personal spiritual renewal.

1. Use the Bible as subject matter for prayer. There are 10 chapters on

the death of Christ in Scripture. There are two in the Old Testament: Psalm 22 and Isaiah 53. There are eight more in the New Testament: Matthew 26 and 27; Mark 14 and 15; Luke 22 and 23; and John 18 and 19. On your knees, open the Bible. Read one verse at a time. Pray about what you are reading.

2. Rediscover God's precious promises. According to Adventist pioneer J. N. Loughborough, there are more than 3,500 promises in the Bible. Purchase one of the many books of Bible promises. Read a few promises a day, and claim them by faith.

3. Slowly read through the Gospels or the Epistles of Paul. Write a one-line summary of each chapter.

As you spend time with God in His Word your spiritual life will be energized. The sword of the Spirit will slay the dragon of busyness in your life.

June 25

THE SABBATH: A SPIRITUAL HOME

There remains therefore a rest for the people of God. For he who has entered His rest has himself also ceased from his work, as God did from His. Heb. 4:9, 10.

Kurt, a young Danish man, sat in his Copenhagen apartment looking through a stack of old newspapers. As he glanced over the headlines he realized he was looking for much more than just news. That old familiar feeling of restlessness was back again, and he couldn't shake it off.

Kurt was a handsome man of 28, with jet-black hair and a stocky build. He had been raised in an affluent family. He had a good education and was now working at a well-paying job in computers. But he knew, now more than ever, that something important was missing in his life.

Suddenly Kurt stopped his rather aimless look through the newspapers. Something caught his eye—a lecture titled "How to Have Peace of Mind."

"This is exactly what I need, what I've been looking for," Kurt told himself.

But then he noticed the date. The presentation had taken place two weeks before. Kurt berated himself for not looking at the newspaper earlier. Still, he decided to go to the theater where the lecture had been scheduled and see if he could somehow find out more information.

When Kurt arrived at the theater, he found the lecture series was continuing.

I met Kurt that evening in Copenhagen while greeting guests at the door after my presentation on the Bible Sabbath.

Kurt pulled me aside and said, "This is the first Christian meeting I have ever attended. I heard the call of God to my heart. I sense God is inviting me into His rest. I have been restless all my life, like a kid separated from home and always thinking about going back. Well, Pastor Mark, to me the Sabbath is a doorway home."

The Sabbath *is* a doorway home. It takes us back to our roots. It allows us to connect with our past. It brings us all the way to Eden's garden, a perfect world, and a loving Creator.

In Sabbath rest we discover wholeness. Our hearts are one with our Maker. Our minds are at peace with our Redeemer. We rest in the care of our Creator, the righteousness of our Redeemer, the interest of our Intercessor, and the love of our returning Lord.

The Sabbath meets that inner longing for home. In those sacred, precious hours we find true soul rest.

June 26

WHAT A SAVIOR

But when the kindness and the love of God our Savior toward man appeared, not by works of righteousness which we have done, but according to His mercy He saved us, through the washing of regeneration and renewing of the Holy Spirit. Titus 3:4, 5.

Good Friday, April 17, 1987. Debbie Williams and a half-dozen friends jumped out of an airplane at 12,000 feet in the clear skies near Phoenix, Arizona. A few seconds into her free fall, Debbie went into a corkscrew, a fast dive to catch up with four others below her. But she miscalculated her descent and slammed into another diver. The 50-mph impact knocked Debbie unconscious. She bounced away, limp as a rag doll.

Debbie plummeted toward earth with her parachute unopened and no way to open it. Blood covering her face, she hurtled past her instructor and jump master, Gregory Robertson. Immediately Gregory forced his body into a "no-lift" dive, head tucked into his chest, toes pointed, and arms flat to his sides. Quickly he was diving at 180 mph. But when he looked, Debbie still seemed to be falling away from him.

Gregory kept going, trying to dive faster and faster. As the horizon came up to meet him he maneuvered his shoulders ever so slightly to guide his decent toward the unconscious young woman. And then he was there beside her, looking for all the world like Superman without a cape. Gregory reached out and grabbed Debbie's reserve cord. Yanking it hard, he quickly moved away. Her chute opened, and she began drifting slowly toward the ground.

At 2,000 feet, only 12 seconds from impact, Gregory opened his own chute. Debbie and her instructor both survived. Though Debbie would recover fully from her injuries, she would remain always grateful to the one who had miraculously snatched her from a fatal impact.

Someone has snatched us from certain death. We too were quickly heading for disaster when Jesus rescued us at the cross. Sin's curse condemned us to eternal loss. We were headed for the grave, the lake of fire, the second death, and eternal banishment from God's presence. But then a Savior appeared. The New Testament describes Jesus as Savior 24 times. Mary exults, "My soul magnifies the Lord, and my spirit has rejoiced in God my Savior" (Luke 1:46, 47).

The angels sing, "For there is born to you this day in the city of David a Savior, who is Christ the Lord" (Luke 2:11). The Samaritan woman exclaims, "This is indeed the Christ, the Savior of the world" (John 4:42). Peter declares, "Him God has exalted to His right hand to be Prince and Savior" (Acts 5:31). The apostle Paul is amazed at "the kindness and the love of God our Savior toward man" (Titus 3:4).

Of all the terms used to describe Jesus, Savior is the most precious. He is not only the world's Savior; He is your Savior and mine. Through my Savior I am accepted. I am redeemed. I am a child of God. I am part of the royal family of heaven. What a Savior! He is all I need for salvation. When I have Him, I have enough.

June 27

THE GOD OF THE UNEXPECTED

Now on the first day of the week, very early in the morning, they, and certain other women with them, came to the tomb bringing the spices which they had prepared. But they found the stone rolled away from the tomb. Luke 24:1, 2.

It started like any other day. The sun rose. The birds sang, roosters crowed, and donkeys brayed. People awoke, stretched, yawned, stirred, and breakfasted on hard crusted bread and dried fish.

The two Marys quickly hastened toward Jesus' burial place to perform a common task. It wasn't hope that led the women to the tomb that Sunday morning; it was duty and devotion. They expected nothing in return. After all, what could a dead man offer? The last time they saw Jesus' body, it was bruised, battered, and bloodied.

Mary knew this task needed to be done. Jesus' body had to be prepared for burial. Peter didn't offer to do it. Andrew didn't volunteer. John didn't step forward. Cleansed lepers, healed sufferers, forgiven sinners, didn't offer their support. The two Marys decided to do it. No selfish motive prompted them. They were not giving to get. They were giving to give.

There are times we too are expected to love, expecting nothing in return. There are times we are called to give to people who will never say thanks. There are times when God asks us to forgive people who will never forgive us. We are sometimes called to come early and stay late when no one else notices. There are times when we do a task simply because it needs to be done.

God saw their tears that morning. He knew their commitment. He honored their faithful service. And the God of the unexpected did something amazing. In the course of a very common day the two Marys met our resurrected Lord.

Joy filled their hearts. Their Lord was alive! As they sprinted from the empty tomb to tell the disciples, Jesus met them and encouraged them to "rejoice." He was risen (Matt. 28:9).

Pause for a moment, and grasp the impact of this thought. Two women in the daily rounds of ordinary duties came face to face with the living Lord. What a God of unexpected blessings! You can meet Him today. You can meet Him in the routine activities of your life. You can meet Him while you are going about your daily duties.

When we serve for service's sake, desiring nothing in return, our hearts will be strangely warmed, and we too shall meet Him. Today, look for His unexpected blessings in your life. He is there with His hand open with blessings for you.

June 28

GOD STILL MOVES STONES

And behold, there was a great earthquake; for an angel of the Lord descended from heaven, and came and rolled back the stone from the door, and sat on it. Matt. 28:2.

Imagine a church board meeting the Saturday night before the Resurrection. Mary speaks to the small group of Christ's followers assembled in the upper room. "Early tomorrow morning we are going to the tomb to anoint Christ's body."

Peter speaks up, "Anoint the body? Don't be foolish. It's dangerous.

There are Roman soldiers in the streets. Tensions are high." Thomas speaks, "Anoint the body? It is impossible. Who is going to roll away the stone?" The board's consensus: the mission is just too dangerous. Roman soldiers are guarding the tomb. The stone weighs hundreds of pounds. How are two frail women ever going to roll it away?

The two Marys don't have all the answers, but they do have plenty of faith. Early the next morning, while Jerusalem sleeps, they hasten to the tomb. Surprise of all surprises, the stone is rolled away.

God is a God of the unexpected. Donkeys talk. Water flows from a rock. Manna falls from heaven. Ravens bring food. Water turns to wine. Peter finds a coin in a fish's mouth.

When we "walk by faith, not by sight" (2 Cor. 5:7), God will overturn stones for us. Stones of difficulty. Stones of doubt, discouragement, and despair. He is the God of impossible possibilities. "With men this is impossible, but with God all things are possible" (Matt. 19:26).

"Faith is the living power that . . . plants its banner in the heart of the enemy's camp" (*Sons and Daughters of God,* p. 202). "Faith lightens every burden, relieves every weariness" (*Prophets and Kings,* p. 175). "Obstacles that are piled by Satan across your path . . . shall disappear before the demand of faith" (*The Desire of Ages,* p. 431).

By faith grasp God's hand and watch Him move the stones in your life. By faith believe His promises and expect His miracles. By faith trust Him in every circumstance and watch what He will do in your life.

June 29

HEROES OF FAITH: ABRAHAM

As for Me, behold, My covenant is with you, and you shall be a father of many nations. Gen. 17:4.

The single hallmark of Abraham's experience is his steadfast faith in the will of God.

This is certainly not to imply that Abraham never questioned. His life was marked with failure. The Old Testament reveals his human lack of trust. Sometimes he was impatient. Sometimes he was deceitful, but his faith was constantly growing. Throughout his life experience he developed an unwavering trust in God.

God summoned Abraham to leave his home in Ur of the Chaldees. God selected this patriarch as a special recipient of His blessings. Abraham was given his first great test of faith when he was 75 years old. God promised that he would become the father of a great nation, but only if he passed the test of faith by heading for the unknown land of Canaan, 400 miles south. God promised, "I will bless those who bless you . . . and in you all the families of the earth shall be blessed" (Gen. 12:3).

Abraham believed God and stepped out in faith. His faith must have been unusually strong, because when God called, he packed his family belongings and left. Yet Abraham's faith was not complete. When a famine swept through Canaan, he did not wait for the Lord to provide for him; he fled to fertile Egypt in search of food. There he resorted to lying, claiming that Sarah, his wife, was his sister. He did not object when she was taken to Pharaoh's household. Only God's intervention prevented Sarah from becoming one of the Egyptian ruler's wives.

Abraham's faith was tested again as he waited longer and longer for a child. Again he failed the test by conceiving a child with Sarah's maid, Hagar. With great guilt he repented, and Sarah at last bore Isaac.

Abraham's final test of faith came at the climax of his life story. God commanded him to offer Isaac as a sacrifice. The old man followed God's instructions. He woke his son. He cut the wood. He climbed Mount Moriah and erected the altar. He even lifted the knife. As the old man prepared to slay his faithful, obedient son, God cried out, "Do not lay your hand on the lad, or do anything to him; for now I know that you fear God" (Gen. 22:12). God Himself provided a ram for sacrifice. Faith conquered.

God led Abraham to the same test again and again. Each test challenged his faith, and at each test his faith deepened. God is daily leading us to the "test of faith." Each day He appeals to us to trust Him more. When we fail the test of faith like Abraham once did, He prepares another one. He will never give up on us. He strengthens us for each test until that day we pass the final test and can go home with Him.

June 30

HEROES OF FAITH: PETER

They immediately left their nets and followed Him. Mark 1:18.

There are days like no other—days of testing, days of decision, days when we face a crossroads and take a path that forever changes us. Peter had one of those days.

Peter and his companions had just completed a luckless night of fishing. Weary and despondent, they pulled their boat onto the Galilean shore. Silently they washed their nets. What do you say when you have fished all night and caught nothing? There is certainly nothing to brag about.

Jesus requested permission to use Peter's boat as His platform to preach. He asked Peter to put out a little from shore. There Jesus sat and taught. When Jesus concluded His discourse, He encouraged Peter to sail out into deeper water and let down their nets again. Although Peter resisted at first, he finally agreed. He responded to Christ's invitation with these words: "Master, we have toiled all night and caught nothing; nevertheless at Your word I will let down the net" (Luke 5:5).

The nets immediately began pulling furiously with a huge catch of fish. Peter was astonished. He realized this was more than good luck. He sensed that he was in the presence of the Divine One, whom all nature obeyed. His immediate response was one of unworthiness. He fell down at Jesus' knee, saying, "Depart from me, for I am a sinful man" (Luke 5:8). But Jesus would never depart. Peter realized his own sinfulness. Peter sensed his own weakness. Jesus saw in him incredible potential. He saw one whom He could mold into a powerful preacher of His grace.

Jesus responded, "Do not be afraid. From now on you will catch men" (Luke 5:10). Peter left everything to follow Christ.

Although he stumbled, revealing his weakness, Peter became the leader of a religious revolution. More than 3,000 were baptized on the day of Pentecost when the Holy Spirit worked through his sermon. Along with the apostle Paul, Peter had the greatest impact on the Christian church.

That day by the sea changed Peter's life permanently. He was never the same again. Today can be a day of decision for you too. Jesus sees in us incredible potential. He looks beyond our faults and weaknesses. He sees what we can accomplish through His Spirit. "There is no limit to the usefulness of one who, by putting self aside, makes room for the working of the Holy Spirit upon his heart, and lives a life wholly consecrated to God" (*The Desire of Ages,* pp. 250, 251).

If you are a committed Christian, God wants to lead you deeper today. He wants to give you that "something more." If you have never fully committed your life to Christ, He wants to lead you on an adventure in faith that will amaze you.

HEROES OF FAITH: JOSEPH

You meant evil against me; but God meant it for good. Gen. 50:20.

One strong piece of evidence for the Bible's inspiration is its honesty. Scripture does not cover up the conflicts or faults of its heroes.

Joseph grew up in a tense family atmosphere of jealousy and discord. The first time Joseph is mentioned after his birth, he brings a "bad report" (Gen. 37:2) to his father about his brothers. Adding fuel to the sibling rivalry were Joseph's tales of dreams of prominence over his brothers, with each one bowing before him. Angry and resentful, the brothers hatched a plot to murder Joseph. After throwing Joseph into an empty cistern, they sold him into slavery.

Joseph's lot had gone from bad to worse. Purchased by Potiphar, the young Hebrew slave distinguished himself through his hard work. Quickly he gained Potiphar's trust and respect. When Potiphar's wife made improper advances toward Joseph, he cried out, "How then can I do this great wickedness, and sin against God?" (Gen. 39:9).

Joseph's commitment to right landed him in an Egyptian dungeon. But though he was isolated, alone, and imprisoned in a foreign land, Joseph did not lose his faith.

While in prison, Joseph ministered to Pharaoh's chief butler, interpreting one of his dreams. When the butler was released from prison, he forgot about Joseph . . . until Pharaoh had a strange dream. The butler knew exactly whom to call upon.

Joseph told Pharaoh that interpreting dreams was beyond his power as a human, but God could reveal the meaning. He added, "God will give Pharaoh an answer of peace" (Gen. 41:16). When Pharaoh shared the mysterious details, Joseph revealed the God-given meaning. Recognizing the significance of Joseph's interpretation, Pharaoh quickly appointed him a ruler in Egypt, second only to himself.

The story of Joseph is replete with lessons for us today. Joseph grew through adversity to be virtuous and wise. His trials did not make him bitter, they made him better. His trials taught him to trust. Joseph was able to reconcile the discord between his brothers that had scarred his family.

Like Joseph, one man or woman of faith can change the world. God and one other individual are a majority. God can take the most hopeless of circumstances and use them for the glory of His name and the blessing of humanity. Let Him do that in your world today.

HEROES OF FAITH: MOSES

By faith he forsook Egypt, not fearing the wrath of the king; for he endured as seeing Him who is invisible. Heb. 11:27.

Moses is the preeminent figure in the Old Testament. Naturally shy and humble, he sought obscurity. But when the Lord called him to rescue the Israelites from Egyptian bondage, this man of faith revealed the courage, tenacity, and moral convictions of a true hero. Although Moses would reveal great flaws more than once, he was the great spiritual leader of his people.

Moses barely survived infancy. Threatened by the growing number of Israelites in Egypt, the pharaoh issued a decree to kill all male Hebrews under 2 years old. Moses' mother hid her child. She placed him in an "ark of bulrushes" and "laid it in the reeds by the river's bank" (Ex. 2:3). Miraculously, the pharaoh's daughter discovered the crying baby. Moses' sister, Miriam, watching the child from a distance, offered her mother's assistance in raising Moses.

Moses' mother raised him his first 12 years. He was then educated in the pharaoh's royal school. We might reasonably assume Moses was given the best possible education in reading, writing, history, geography, political science, management, leadership, weapons, and horsemanship—lessons he used well when he later led the Israelites out of Egyptian bondage.

God turned the curse of Pharaoh's death decree into a blessing. God used the very decree Pharaoh issued to *destroy* Israel to educate Moses to *deliver* Israel. A decree of death brought life. God used an instrument of slavery to establish freedom. God brought victory out of defeat through one faithful, humble, godly man.

God turns curses into blessings. He took the cross, an instrument of cruelty, suffering, and death, and turned it into salvation. Jesus delivers us from the curse of death. All Satan can throw against Him, Jesus turns into blessing.

Moses prefigures Christ. In the New Testament, Jesus is the Moses of His people. He is the deliverer. He is the mighty conqueror. He is the one who will lead us to victory. Whatever trials you are facing today, Jesus is still the mighty deliverer. He still turns curses into blessings. He still turns defeats into victories. He still delivers us from bondage. He still causes us to triumph.

HEROES OF FAITH: JOSHUA

Be strong and of good courage; do not be afraid, nor be dismayed, for the Lord your God is with you wherever you go. Joshua 1:9.

A remarkable stone carving stands in the garden of the Israeli Parliament in Jerusalem. Aaron and Hur support Moses' arms as Joshua leads the Israeli armies to victory at Rephidim in the plains below.

The name Joshua means "Yahweh saves." God would fight his battles. Joshua is a model of faithful obedience. He was the only person permitted to ascend Mount Sinai with Moses at the giving of the Law (Ex. 24:13). He was chosen by Moses from the tribe of Ephraim to spy out the promised land (Num. 13:17). Upon their return, Joshua and his companion Caleb were the only spies who urged the people to trust that God would deliver Canaan into their hands.

As Moses led Israel through the Red Sea, Joshua led the people across the Jordan River on dry land. Joshua experienced the powerful hand of God at Jericho as its walls collapsed. Joshua continued to take one Canaanite city after another. "All these kings and their land Joshua took at one time, because the Lord God of Israel fought for Israel" (Joshua 10:42).

Joshua was faithful, and God fought his battles. When we are faithful and trust and obey and depend, God fights and triumphs and overcomes and defeats the satanic forces that battle against us.

The battle is His, not ours. Just as the Israelites fought fierce fights with their enemies, we too struggle daily with evil forces. We "do not wrestle against flesh and blood, but against principalities, against powers, against the rulers of darkness" (Eph. 6:12). But in His power victory is certain. Like Joshua, we too can be "strong and of good courage," for the Lord our God is with us.

July 4

HEROES OF FAITH: DANIEL

Daniel purposed in his heart that he would not defile himself. Dan. 1:8.

Daniel's story spans two world empires. It begins when the Babylonian king Nebuchadnezzar took Jewish captives from Jerusalem into exile in 605 B.C. It extends through the days of Cyrus in the Persian Empire. Daniel's life demonstrates that faithfulness to God can bring success, even under the most adverse circumstances.

As a captive in a foreign land, Daniel determined in his late teens to be true to God. Ushered into the luxurious banquet hall of the Babylonian king, he refused to worship the king's idols, drink the king's wine, or eat the king's unclean delicacies. Yet he did it with such grace that he eventually won the hearts of his captors.

Daniel's spiritual integrity continued throughout his life. When he was in his mid-80s, he faced perhaps his greatest test. Conniving coworkers schemed against him. They slyly influenced the king to pass a decree forbidding worship of any god except himself for 30 days. Obviously Daniel could not comply. The price for disobedience was high.

The prophet did not make his decision based on the consequences of his actions. He made it based on faithfulness to God's Word. Had he considered the consequences, death in the lions' den, he might have yielded. Being torn apart limb by limb by ferocious bloodthirsty lions is not a very pleasant thought. Anytime the consequences of a decision become the driving force in making a decision, we are likely to yield.

One of the most successful coaches in the history of professional football was Vince Lombardi, of the Green Bay Packers. A reporter asked why they gave so much of themselves each Sunday. He queried, "Why is your team notably different? Why do you leave everything out on the field?" The players responded, "We are not playing for the crowd in the stands or the millions in the television audience. We aren't overly concerned about what the news media says. We are playing for one thing: 'the coach's eyes.' When we review the film Monday mornings, we want to know we have satisfied Coach Lombardi."

Daniel did not play to the crowd. He lived to please his heavenly Father. He played for the "Father's eyes."

When the final films of life are shown, living life to please God is what will truly count. The great heroes of faith all lived for a purpose. They stood above the masses. They viewed life from a different perspective. They did not live to please themselves or the crowd. The prime purpose of their life was to please God. In making this fundamental decision, Daniel lived a centered life. God's formula for true peace and lasting success is still the same today.

HEROES OF FAITH: DAVID

The Lord does not see as man sees; for man looks at the outward appearance, but the Lord looks at the heart. 1 Sam. 16:7.

The news electrified all of Israel. It was one of the most amazing archaeological finds of modern times. Archaeologists had unearthed a stone fragment with a reference to King David. For the first time an extrabiblical source confirmed the reign of Israel's most renowned king.

David's name appears more than 1,000 times in the Old and New Testaments, more than any other biblical character. David was a shepherd, soldier, warrior, musician, poet, composer, author, king, and empire builder. He not only changed the history of Israel in his own time, but left his mark on the nation for all times. David took a weak, struggling nation and made it into a powerful empire.

David rose to prominence at a unique time. The kingdoms of Assyria and Egypt were in decline. David used his military experience to rally Israel's forces. He organized strong, well-trained armies and expanded them into a powerful fighting machine. Under his leadership the nation's borders were expanded, taxes were reduced, and prosperity flourished. Under David's reign Jerusalem was founded as the nation's religious and political capital.

David's psalms reveal his intense devotion to God. At times David soars into the heights of ecstasy. At others he is in the dungeon of despair. Sometimes the psalms reveal him as forgiven, while in others he feels God's heavy hand of condemnation. There are times when David forgives his enemies, and times when he wants to crush them.

When Nathan the prophet confronted David about his adulterous affair with Bethsheba, David cried out, "Have mercy upon me, O God, according to your lovingkindness; according to the multitudes of your tender mercies, blot out my transgressions" (Ps. 51:1).

Three great spiritual truths stand out in David's life. First, he is painfully honest. He is certainly not a hypocrite. He candidly shares his feelings. He is open in expressing his doubts, faults, and emotions. Second, he has a heart for God. In the changing circumstances of life he longs to please God. Third, David believes that God is always there. He has a sense of God's presence.

God speaks again in our day. He invites us to express our emotions honestly to Him. He encourages us to bare our souls to Him, seeking to know Him. We can never shock Him. He urges us to believe He is always there—for He is!

In the conflicting emotions inside us and the changing circumstances around us, He is a constant. We can count on it.

July 6

HEROES OF FAITH: ESTHER

I will go to the king, which is against the law; and if I perish, I perish! Esther 4:16.

Have you ever grieved over your background? Have you wished your early childhood was different? Have you felt you were born with three strikes against you? Esther certainly could have. She was orphaned at an early age and brought up by her cousin Mordecai. His family had been taken captive years earlier by the Babylonians after the fall of Jerusalem in 586 B.C.

Esther never knew her real parents. She was a Jew in a foreign land, brought up in a hostile environment as part of the despised minority. When Vashti, the wife of the Persian king Ahasuerus, embarrassed him, Esther was one of the many young women brought into the harem and put in the custody of the king's eunuch. A corrupt palace lifestyle in the ancient world was hardly conducive to Esther's faith.

Mordecai kept his eye on her, even in the king's palace. He urged her to keep her ethnic background hidden. For a year Esther was trained in the life of the harem. When she finally made her appearance before the king, he "loved Esther more than all the other women, and she obtained grace and favor in his sight more than all the virgins" (Esther 2:17). Enamored with her beauty, poise, and character, Ahasuerus immediately appointed her as his new queen.

What was God's strategy in all of this? Why was Esther exalted to such a key position? Haman, one of the king's princes, hatched a plan to destroy Mordecai and the Jews. Every Jew was to be slaughtered

Mordecai overheard rumors of the plot. He appealed to Esther to speak out. "If you remain completely silent at this time," he said, "relief and deliverance will arise for the Jews from another place, but you and your father's house will perish. Yet who knows whether you have come to the kingdom for such a time as this?" (Esther 4:14).

Esther met the challenge, and God responded. Thanks to her courageous attitude, God's people were delivered.

In the divine drama of destiny, God has placed you in the world for a time such as this. We did not choose to live in the beginning of the twenty-first century. This is God's doing. Like Esther, we have been called to the kingdom for a time such as this.

God calls us to faithfulness. No matter what our backgrounds, He wants us to be loyal to Him. Esther made a powerful difference in her world. We can make a difference in ours today.

Take on today with courage. You are God's man, God's woman, God's youth, destined to live at this time, this day, to make a difference for Him.

July 7

HEROES OF FAITH: JOHN

Now there was leaning on Jesus' bosom one of His disciples, whom Jesus loved. John 13:23.

John and his brother James, the sons of Zebedee, were the first disciples Jesus called. Common fishers, there was nothing particularly special about their upbringing or family background. The only notable thing about their characters was that Jesus referred to them as "Sons of Thunder" (Mark 3:17).

Jesus saw something good in this hot-tempered John. The Master looked beyond the surface deep within his soul. He saw not what he was but what he could become, refined and enabled by His grace.

Jesus believed in John, and John responded. Christ delights to take apparently hopeless material and make it an object of His grace. John became one of the most loving, caring disciples. Part of Christ's inner circle, he was with Jesus on the Mount of Transfiguration, in Gethsemane, and at the cross. Just after Mary Magdalene reported that Jesus' tomb was empty, John ran to the tomb with Peter and believed.

John's Gospel presents a firsthand account of the Savior's life. With his pen dipped in love, he wrote the Epistles we know as First, Second, and Third John. Toward the end of his life Emperor Domitian exiled him on the Isle of Patmos for his faith.

Jesus changed John from an impatient firebrand, ready to explode at each slight, to a gentle, loving man. John wrote, "Beloved, if God so loved us, we also ought to love one another" (1 John 4:11). John believed that the essence of all Christianity was love. Christ's love flowed from his heart to the people around him—even his enemies.

John's story shows us an eternal truth. When you spend time with Jesus, you become like Him. When you accept what Jesus declares you to be, you become what He sees you are. Thank God, He sees the good in us today, and if we let Him, He will make us into the kind of person He wants us to be.

Jesus looks beyond the surface. He sees the potential deep within every life. Today you can become what God already knows you are.

July 8

HEROES OF FAITH: PAUL

When it pleased God . . . to reveal His Son in me, that I might preach Him among the Gentiles. Gal. 1:15, 16.

After Jesus Himself, the apostle Paul was the most powerful and most influential voice in the Christian church. Paul was born in an ultraconservative Jewish family in the Greek city of Tarsus, in the southern section of Asia Minor. Growing up in two worlds, Greek and Jewish, uniquely prepared Paul for his later work of proclaiming the gospel.

As Paul told an assembly of Pharisees and Sadducees, "I am a Pharisee, the son of a Pharisee" (Acts 23:6). The Pharisees were the strictest of all Jews and fierce persecutors of Christians. They were militant in the protection of Jewish orthodoxy.

About A.D. 35, just five years after Jesus' crucifixion, Paul journeyed to Damascus with letters from the high priest, declaring that Christians were criminals worthy of death. He was probably about 30 years old at the time. God chose that moment to change the entire course of Paul's life. The Lord appeared to him in a vision, declaring, "Saul, Saul, why are you persecuting Me?" (Acts 9:14).

Blinded by the glorious light, prostrate on the ground, Paul could only ask, "Who are You, Lord?" A voice came from heaven: "I am Jesus, whom you are persecuting" (verse 5).

Paul was never the same again. Meeting Jesus transformed his life. He committed his entire life to proclaiming the Christ he loved.

The apostle Paul was compelled to share his faith as widely as possible. He centered his efforts on the major cities of Asia Minor. He traveled the Mediterranean world from his hometown in Tarsus throughout Syria, Arabia, Greece, and Turkey. His first missionary journey, beginning in Antioch, took him on a 1,200-mile trek preaching the Word. His next journeys took him yet farther. On these frequent journeys he was stoned, beaten with rods, imprisoned, shipwrecked, hunted by wild beasts, robbed, and left for dead. But he kept witnessing for his Lord (2 Cor. 11:24-27).

Paul's faith made a difference. His commitment to Jesus transformed his life. To Paul, faith was an active, dynamic, living reality that led him to share the Christ he loved with everyone he met.

Does your faith make a difference in your life? Is it the transforming power that influences everything you do? Is the living Christ the center of your life as He was Paul's?

Today, let the living, loving, life-transforming Christ be the center of your life too.

July 9

HEROES OF FAITH: MARY

Mary kept all these things and pondered them in her own heart. Luke 2:19.

God chose Mary for a special assignment. He called her to bear the Messiah. God sent the angel Gabriel to appear to her with the words "Rejoice, highly favored one. . . . You have found favor with God. And behold, you will conceive in your womb and bring forth a Son, and shall call His name Jesus" (Luke 1:28-31).

The sudden news confused Mary. How could this be? Although she was engaged to Joseph, she was still a virgin—how could she now bear a son? "The Holy Spirit will come upon you," Gabriel said, "and the power of the Highest will overshadow you" (verse 35).

Mary's heartfelt response is genuine. "Let it be to me according to your word," she said (verse 38). Although the Gospel narrative does not say a great deal about Mary, it tells us enough to reveal her incredible strength of character. She was sincere, honest, tenderhearted, pure, obedient, and filled with compassion. She was profoundly perceptive. Although most likely in her midteens, she understood the magnitude of God's call.

Mary acknowledged her "lowly state," exalted by blessings which all generations would recognize. She accepted the eternal truth that God had "scattered the proud" and "put down the mighty" while He "exalted the lowly" and "filled the hungry with good things" (verses 48-53).

Peaks and valleys marked Mary's life. They begin with Joseph threatening to leave her when he learns she's pregnant. They continue with a wearying journey from Nazareth to Bethlehem. They include using a feed trough for a newborn's bed. Her emotions turn to fear at Herod's threats to kill all Jewish males under 2 years old. With Joseph and the newborn she hastens into Egypt.

It is at Mary's knee that Jesus learns the songs of Zion and the promises of the prophets. From her He learns submission and trust, prayer and obedience.

She smiles when He takes His first step, and she weeps when they spike

His feet to a wooden bar. Throughout His life she believes in Him. She never walks away.

God's assignments are not always easy or popular. There are highs and lows, joys and sorrows. As He called Mary, God calls us to be faithful as well. He calls us to stay by Jesus' side now and forever, through all eternity.

July 10

A REMINDER TO REMEMBER

You are worthy, O Lord, to receive glory and honor and power; for You created all things, and by Your will they exist and were created. Rev. 4:11.

Our world desperately needs the reassuring message of Creation. For this God gave us the Sabbath. In the mid-1800s, as the theory of evolution took root in the intellectual world, God sent a message of incredible hope. It is found in Revelation 14:6, 7:

"Then I saw another angel flying in the midst of heaven, having the everlasting gospel to preach to those who dwell on the earth—to every nation, tribe, tongue, and people—saying with a loud voice, 'Fear God and give glory to Him, for the hour of His judgment has come; and worship Him who made heaven and earth, the sea and springs of water.' "

God's last-day message calls all humanity back to worshiping Him as the Creator of heaven and earth. The basis of all worship is the fact that God created us. John the revelator succinctly states it in these words:

"You are worthy, O Lord, to receive glory and honor and power; for You created all things, and by Your will they exist and were created" (Rev. 4:11).

He is worthy precisely because He has created. If God has not created us, if we merely evolved and life is a cosmic accident, there is no reason to worship.

God has given the Sabbath as an eternal symbol of His creative power and authority. It is a weekly reminder that we are not our own. He created us. Life cannot exist apart from Him. "In Him we live and move and have our being" (Acts 17:28).

When Joy was 4 years old, her baby brother was born. Joy began to ask her parents for some time alone with the new baby. They worried that like some 4-year-olds she might be jealous and shake or hit the baby, so they said no.

Over time, though, since Joy showed no signs of jealously, they decided to let Joy have her private conference with "Baby." Elated, Joy went into the baby's room and shut the door, but it opened a crack, enough for her curious parents to peek in and listen. They saw Joy walk quietly up to her baby brother, put her face close to his, and say, "Baby, tell me what God feels like. I am starting to forget."

The truth is that we all tend to forget. That's why God says "remember." The Sabbath is a weekly reminder of what God is like, calling us to a new relationship with Him.

The Sabbath calls us to communion with our Creator. It calls us to marvel in our Maker. To enjoy the eternal. To hope in the heavenly. When it is so easy to forget, the Sabbath is a reminder to remember what God is really like.

July 11

AN ADVANCE ON ETERNITY

It shall come to pass that from one New Moon to another, and from one Sabbath to another, all flesh shall come to worship before Me, says the Lord. Isa. 66:23.

R*eader's Digest* featured an article on the late Harvey Penick. Its opening lines caught my eye: "For 90-year-old golf pro Harvey Penick, success has come late." His first golf book, *Harvey Penick's Little Red Book,* sold more than 1 million copies. His publisher believes the book is one of the best-selling sports books of all time. The story of how the book came to be published is fascinating.

Harvey Penick certainly didn't write it for money. In the 1920s Penick bought a red spiral notebook and began jotting down his personal observations regarding golf. For nearly 70 years he never showed the book to anyone besides his son. In 1991 Penick shared it with a local writer and asked the man if he thought it was worth publishing. The elated writer contacted publishing giant Simon and Schuster. The next evening the publishers agreed to a $90,000 advance.

The jubilant writer passed the news on to Penick's wife. When the writer saw Penick later in the evening, the old man seemed troubled. With all of his medical bills, Penick said, there was no way he could advance Simon and Schuster that much money to publish his book. The writer had to explain that Penick would be the one to receive the money.

In the Sabbath, God has given us an "advance" on eternity. Every Sabbath heaven touches earth. As the Jewish author Abraham Heschel so aptly put it, the Sabbath is a "palace in time." The Sabbath calls us from the things of time to the things of eternity. It calls us to enter into His heavenly rest, to experience a foretaste of heaven today. It calls us to a relationship with our Creator that will continue throughout eternity. The Sabbath is an advance on eternity. There is much more coming, but in the Sabbath we have the first installment.

Is it possible that in the busyness of life, we are too exhausted on Sabbath to renew our relationship with God? Is it possible that in the stress of life Sabbath is a day of superficial worship rather than intimate fellowship? Is it possible that God is calling us to something deeper, something broader, something higher, something larger than we have ever experienced before?

God longs for us to see a new depth of meaning in the Sabbath. He yearns for us to experience a genuine heart revival. Do you hear Him speaking to your heart today?

"Come to Me, all you who labor and are heavy laden, and I will give you rest" (Matt. 11:28).

Like Harvey Penick, we have been given an advance. Not $90,000 from Simon and Schuster, but an advance on eternity by a loving heavenly Father in a Sabbath filled with eternity's blessings.

July 12

CONQUER YOUR MOUNTAIN

Now therefore, give me this mountain of which the Lord spoke in that day. Joshua 14:12.

Todd Huston is a remarkable young man. Todd set the world record for climbing the highest peak in all 50 of the United States. The previous record was 101 days. Todd shattered that record single-handedly by completing his 50 climbs in 66 days, 22 hours, and 47 minutes.

His toughest climb was Mount McKinley in Alaska. Mount McKinley rises out of the Alaskan range to a majestic elevation of more than 20,000 feet, the highest point in North America. Its jagged peak lies just 3.5 degrees south of the Arctic Circle. The mountain is perpetually covered in a shroud of snow and ice. Climbers who have attempted the ascent know that the mountain's moods are capricious and unforgiving.

One of Todd's biggest tests came when he met a group of climbers on their way down from Mt. McKinley. "What's it like up there today?" Todd asked. One of the men shook his head. "Bad storms and high winds. We were locked in at Denali Pass for three days."

Todd Huston had to make a choice. Was he going to try it? Was he going to take on this tremendous obstacle with only one leg? You see, Todd had lost his leg in a waterskiing accident when he was only 14 years old.

Todd's faith and courage led him on.

Some time ago I interviewed Todd on *It Is Written* television. I asked him how he was able to climb the mountains he climbed, not just physical ones but mountains of discouragement and disillusionment as well. Todd's answer was right to the point.

"If you are going to look at your affliction or your injury and focus on that, you are going to live around it," he said. "But, if you focus on the Lord, He is just going to get you through it."

At 85 years of age Caleb refused to give into the doubters around him. He urged the Israelites to take the promised land. "Now therefore, give me this mountain," he cried out (Joshua 14:12). "Bring on the giants. Show me the walled cities. The Lord and I will conquer them."

Ellen White wrote, "The unbelieving had seen their fears fulfilled. Notwithstanding God's promise, they had declared it was impossible to inherit Canaan, and they did not possess it. But those who trusted in God, looking not so much to the difficulties to be encountered as to the strength of their Almighty Helper, entered the goodly land" (*Patriarchs and Prophets,* p. 513).

With God, you too can conquer the mountains before you. With Caleb and Joshua, cry out today, "O God, give me this mountain," and move on in faith.

July 13

STILL STANDING TALL

Watch, stand fast in the faith, be brave, be strong. 1 Cor. 16:13.

Nikita Khrushchev, premier of the former Soviet Union, gave a major address on the state of Soviet affairs before the Supreme Soviet in Moscow. His speech broke new ground as it openly addressed the savage excesses of the Stalin era. As Khrushchev spoke, someone from the audience sent up an embarrassing note. "Premier Khrushchev, what were you doing when Stalin committed all these atrocities?"

Khrushchev angrily shouted, "Who sent up this note?"

Not a person stirred.

"I will give him one minute to stand up," Khrushchev pronounced.

The seconds ticked off. Still no one moved.

"All right, I will tell you what I was doing," Khrushchev said. "I was doing exactly what the writer of this note was doing—exactly nothing! I was afraid to be counted."

Afraid to be counted. Afraid to take a stand. Afraid to stand tall. It seems to me that if there ever was a time in the history of the world when God was calling us to stand tall, it's today.

Every great hero of faith has been willing to take a stand. Moses took a stand against Pharaoh's armies. Elijah stood against the prophets of Baal. Paul took a stand against rigid legalism. John took a stand against emperor worship, and Jesus took the most courageous stand of all on a bloody cross.

Love always demands commitment. Its cost is a heart totally surrendered to the Master, the willingness to take a stand. If we are not willing to stand for what is right, we will fall for what is wrong. If we do not have the courage of our convictions to stand for principles of conscience, our hearts will be calloused by compromise. Like Pilate, Judas, and King Agrippa, our souls will be barren.

There is a better way. Through the grace of Christ, stand by the convictions of your conscience. You will be glad you did.

July 14

GOD'S STRANGE ACT

That He may do His work, His awesome work, and bring to pass His act, His unusual act. Isa. 28:21.

The book *Bitter Harvest* tells of a grain company employee in Michigan who mistook a deadly poison for a vitamin supplement, and mixed it with the grain.

The poisonous grain contaminated cattle, chickens, and pigs on many farms. Farmers had no choice but to isolate the contaminated animals, kill them, and burn the bodies to prevent the contamination from spreading. They knew that if they didn't destroy their animals, it would jeopardize the entire Michigan cattle industry.

God is "not willing any should perish" (2 Peter 3:9). It is His will that "all [humanity] be saved and come to the knowledge of the truth" (1 Tim. 2:4). But there are some that even God cannot save. They have chosen sin rather than righteousness, rebellion rather than obedience, self-centeredness rather than loving service. If God risked bringing them to heaven, they would infect it with the sin virus all over again. If God did not act to eradicate sin, its malignant effect would eventually destroy the entire universe.

God offers pardon for our past sins and power to live the Christian life in the present. His grace provides forgiveness when we have failed and strength to keep us from repeating the same failures again and again.

In the final analysis God must act. He must rid the universe of sin. "Our God is a consuming fire" (Heb. 12:29). A holy God must eventually consume sin. Sin and sinners will be consumed, turned to ashes (Mal. 4:1-3; 2 Thess. 2:8; Ps. 37:20).

Today God gives us a choice—for Him to consume sin in us through the fiery presence of His Holy Spirit, or to be consumed with our sin at the fiery presence of His soon return. A loving God weeps as sinners are destroyed.

The destruction of the wicked is an unusual and strange act, but it is unavoidable if the universe is going to be secure forever. Will you allow Jesus to do His cleansing work in your heart today? Will you allow the fire of His presence to purify you within?

July 15

OUR CHOICE DETERMINES OUR DESTINY

I have set before you life and death, blessing and cursing; therefore choose life. Deut. 30:19.

Robert Ingersoll, one of the best-known infidels of the past century, was born into the home of a minister. After hearing his father preach on the fires of hell, Ingersoll said, "If God is like that, if God would burn millions and trillions of people, men, women, children, and babies, I don't believe He exists. I believe He is a figment of human imagination."

Ingersoll concluded that a God who would torment people for millions of years must not be a loving God. Further, he decided that such a God must not really exist.

And Ingersoll was right. A vengeful God who delights to inflict and delight in such suffering doesn't exist.

My mind could never worship a God who would torment people in hell for millions and millions of years. Could you picture a heaven in which the redeemed viewed people suffering in hell? One popular religious writer claimed that if the fires of hell were extinguished and the lost ceased suffering, one of the chief delights of the redeemed would be over. In other words, he asserted that one of the joys in heaven is to watch the wicked suffer. What a travesty. What a distorted picture of God.

The Bible's picture of God is dramatically different. God's love will not allow Him to torment sinners for the ceaseless ages of eternity. His justice will not allow Him to overlook their sin. Sin is combustible material in the presence of a Holy God. God leaves sinners to their own choices. Unshielded by His loving protection, they are destroyed in the flames of His holiness.

The deepest agony of hell is the mental torture of knowing they are banished from the presence of God forever. God offers life. They have chosen death. The words of the ancient prophet resound through the centuries, "I call heaven and earth as witnesses today against you, that I have set before you life and death, blessing and cursing; therefore choose life, that both you and your descendants may live" (Deut. 30:19).

Salvation is a choice. Eternal loss is a choice. Ultimately every one of us will get what we have eternally chosen.

Today the God of heaven appeals to each one of us to choose life.

July 16

SEEING THROUGH GOD'S EYES

I say to you who hear: Love your enemies, do good to those who hate you. Luke 6:27.

Rodney Roberson could tell it was going to be a bad night. Working at a homeless shelter to pay his way through the seminary, he'd grown accustomed to challenging situations, but this night looked particularly difficult. Rain splattered the cold ground outside. Soon all the shelter's cots and sleeping mats were taken, but street people kept coming. Arguments broke out. People cursed angrily. Some began to fight over sleeping mats.

In the midst of this tension, a large man named José stumbled in and threw down his sleeping mat. Managing to yank off his boots, he collapsed in a drunken stupor. The stench from José's feet quickly filled the air. People nearby insisted that Rodney do something about it.

The obvious solution was to persuade José to take a shower, but Rodney could not rouse him. José was breathing, but he seemed dead to the world. Rodney and two coworkers discussed hauling José to the shower, but he weighed more than 200 pounds.

Some of the street people demanded that Rodney drag José back out to the sidewalk. But others howled in protest. It seemed that for anyone to win, someone had to lose.

But then Rodney got an idea—why not bring the shower to José? He found a wash basin and some lemon-scented dishwashing liquid. Kneeling by the drunken man, he began to peel off his filthy socks. The stench almost overwhelmed him.

But for several minutes Rodney scrubbed José's feet with a soapy washcloth. He carefully dried them with a towel. Suddenly he noticed he was surrounded by people. Rodney stood up warily and looked around.

Everyone was grinning at him—even those who'd complained the loudest. In fact, people he'd never seen smile before were grinning. Men and women of all races.

A quiet hush had fallen over the place. There would be no more shouting or threats that night. People with sleeping mats gave to someone without one. The conflict was over. It had been washed away by someone who didn't need to take sides, someone who didn't need to score points, someone willing to be, like Jesus, chief among them by becoming a servant.

One act of kindness can change an entire office. One act of unselfish love can change a family. One act of caring can change a classroom. Kindness breaks down barriers. Kindness leaps over walls. Kindness builds bridges. Dr. Luke spoke of our heavenly Father as the one who is "kind to the unthankful and evil" (Luke 6:35). God Himself models kindness for us in all of His actions. He invites us to be kind to those around us today.

July 17

EVERY WIND OF DOCTRINE, PART 1: GOD STILL GUIDES HIS CHURCH

I will build My church, and the gates of Hades shall not prevail against it. Matt. 16:18.

The Methodists of Swanquarter, North Carolina, were deeply committed to building a church to worship their God. The only piece of property they could afford was a marshy low spot in an undesirable part of town. Having no choice, they secured the deed and the land and went to work. Soon their labor of love was completed—a small white structure propped up on brick pilings.

On Sunday, September 16, 1876, they joyously dedicated the new house for God. Three days later a terrible storm burst upon the town. All night long and into the next day the wind raged as floodwaters rose.

Finally the storm subsided. The townspeople ventured out of their homes. To their utter amazement, the little white church was floating down the street. It floated down Oyster Creek Road. It floated down Main Street through Swanquarter, and then made a mysterious right turn. It stopped exactly on the property the townspeople originally wanted to purchase but the owner wouldn't sell. The owner, believing that this was the hand of God, hastily offered the property.

Today this church is called "Providence," placed there by the hand of God. The winds blew, the hurricane gale-force breezes swirled, but the church survived.

God's hand is still upon His church. All the hurricanes from hell cannot destroy it.

Our Lord promised that His church would survive. "And I also say to you that you are Peter, and on this rock"—Peter's statement that Jesus was the Messiah—"I will build My church, and the gates of Hades shall not prevail against it" (Matt. 16:18).

God's church will survive. The winds of lawlessness and fanaticism will blow; the dust storms of doubt will stir up clouds of confusion; the gentle zephyrs of Laodiceanism will put thousands of God's people to sleep; but His church will survive. "Every wind of doctrine" will blow (Eph. 4:14), but "nothing else in this world is as dear to God as His church" (*Testimonies,* vol. 6, p. 42).

God's church will not be disorganized or broken up (*Selected Messages,* book 2, pp. 68, 69). Christ and His church will not only survive—they will triumph.

July 18

EVERY WIND OF DOCTRINE, PART 2: THE WHIRLWIND OF LAWLESSNESS

Behold, disaster shall go forth from nation to nation. And a great whirlwind shall be raised up from the furthest parts of the earth. Jer. 25:32.

Dr. Shervert Frazier served as director for the National Institutes of Health. His book *Psychotrends* expressed concerns about the escalating violence in our society. Dr. Frazier described what he called a "co-violent society," one that "celebrates mayhem while simultaneously condemning it." It ends up making violence seem amoral and inevitable.

In other words, the 6:00 news shows us a tragic picture of a child sprawled on the street in a drive-by shooting. Then the 8:00 movie shows us a hero mowing down or blowing up the bad guys in some new spectacular, heart-stopping way. And that's entertainment!

We live in a world in which different values compete for our loyalty and attention. A major U.S. magazine recently described the United States as "America the violent." Another article stated that 23,700 people were murdered in our country in a recent year. The average 18-year-old has witnessed 200,000 violent acts on television, including 40,000 murders.

There are two significant issues here. First, violence begets violence. Our minds are shaped by the things we put into them. Ellen White wrote that "the character of our spirituality is determined by the food given to the mind" (*Testimonies,* vol. 8, p. 169). Violence has entered our homes. Don't be deceived—our minds are not rocks that violence runs off of like water, with little or no effect. Our minds are like sponges, absorbing our life experiences.

Something dies within us when our minds are stimulated by the media's synthetic violence. We become anesthetized to the suffering of others, reaping a spiritual callousness in our own souls.

There is a second issue here. God's Word predicts that Jesus will return at a time of unprecedented crime and violence. The psalmist asserts, "It is time for You to act, O Lord, for they have regarded Your law as void" (Ps. 119:126).

Jesus adds these telling words: "Because lawlessness will abound, the love of many will grow cold. But he who endures to the end shall be saved" (Matt. 24:12, 13).

The whirlwind of lawlessness devastating our society indicates that the coming of our Lord is near. In this crisis hour Jesus invites us to live committed, obedient lives. Anchored in Christ, the hurricane of lawlessness cannot move us.

July 19

EVERY WIND OF DOCTRINE, PART 3: THE ICY WIND OF FORMALISM

These people draw near to Me with their mouth, and honor Me with their lips, but their heart is far from Me. Matt. 15:8.

Jesus uttered His most scathing rebukes against the formalism of the Pharisees. He called them "whitewashed tombs . . . full of dead men's bones" (Matt. 23:27). He said they were "hypocrites," merely playacting (Matt. 15:7). He claimed they were "without understanding" (verse 16). Rigid formalism plagued God's people in the first century, and it plagues us now.

Ellen White wrote, "The evil of formal worship cannot be too strongly depicted" (*Testimonies,* vol. 9, p. 143). "We do not obtain a hundredth of the blessing we should obtain from assembling together to worship God" (*Testimonies,* vol. 6, p. 362).

Formalism focuses on the external rather than on the heart. It places supreme importance on rituals, ceremonies, forms, and tradition that overshadow the worship of the heart and spirit. When the icy wind of formalism blows through our lives, we emphasize the outer without the inner. External behavior replaces heart conversion. There is conformity without transformation, duty without devotion, obligation without obsession. Formal Christians may be patently proper, but they are not passionately possessed with the Spirit of Christ.

Jesus offers something better than the cold formalism that places dreary drudgery and oppressive obligation before joyful, worshiping hearts. Jesus offers us the indwelling of the Spirit. Jesus invites us to much more than "a form of godliness but denying its power" (2 Tim. 3:5). He offers us Himself.

I long for the winds of the Spirit to blow through our churches. I long for "a revival of true godliness among us [which] is the greatest and most urgent of all our needs" (*Selected Messages,* book 1, p. 121). We cannot expect a genuine revival without earnest prayer and heartfelt Bible study. The Spirit dwells in our heart through the Word. All great, genuine revivals throughout history have been Word-based.

Many people turn to new forms of worship as answers to formalism. While these may create a temporary euphoria, they are of no value if we do not worship with our hearts. The issue is not so much the form of worship as it is the heart of the worshiper. God invites us to come to worship with our hearts overflowing in a new appreciation for Him through His Word. When our own hearts are broken over our personal failures, Christ will fill them with His forgiveness. Out of the joy of a forgiven heart we will overflow with praise for our Redeemer. Daily His truths will become more precious.

With Jeremiah we will say, "Your words were found, and I ate them, and Your word was to me the joy and rejoicing of my heart" (Jer. 15:16).

EVERY WIND OF DOCTRINE, PART 4: THE BURNING WIND OF FANATICISM

The time will come when they will not endure sound doctrine, but according to their own desires, because they have itching ears, they will heap up for themselves teachers; and they will turn their ears away from the truth, and be turned aside to fables. 2 Tim. 4:3.

Fanaticism may take many forms. In Moses' day fanatics danced around the golden calf. They were certainly enthusiastic. They were definitely fervent. But they were in rebellion against God.

Fanatics tend to believe they have a direct line to God. Their independent judgment becomes supreme. They justify their behavior based on what they believe is God's will for them. Their own minds become the essence of their religion.

Some fanatics make up their own rules. They tend to be wary of any church organization.

In 1985 an epidemic of divorce broke out among the members of Seattle's Community Chapel. In one year some two dozen couples divorced or began proceedings. The reason wasn't hard to find. Men and women, usually not spouses, were supposed to experience a deeper level of spiritual love with one another. They made these connections by spending a lot of time together, and especially by dancing together in church. Expressions of affection with someone else's spouse led to the breakup of many homes.

Their pastor believed he had a direct line to God, which gave him "a truth never given to man before." The congregation didn't wake up until many families had broken apart.

Biblical faith is always Word-centered. Any worship experience that shifts emphasis from the authority of God's Word to the supremacy of personal feelings can lead to fanaticism. Biblical faith is always part of a community of believers. When someone claims to have new light, beware. When someone claims to have a direct line to God, no matter how sincere they are, beware.

Biblical faith believes in the triumph of God's church. Fanatics often believe and teach that God's church is corrupt or in a state of apostasy. Ellen White wrote, "Some have advanced the thought that, as we near the close of time, every child of God will act independently of any religious organization. But I have been instructed by the Lord that in this work there is no such thing as every man's being independent" (*Testimonies*, vol. 9, p. 258).

We are told, "The church may appear as about to fall, but it does not fall. It remains, while the sinners in Zion will be sifted out" (*Selected Messages,* book 2, p. 380).

For as "enfeebled and defective" as it may be, God's church is still the object of His supreme regard (*The Acts of the Apostles,* p. 12).

Here is one thing the fanatics will never tell you. Stay with the church, because by God's grace it will triumph at the end.

July 21

EVERY WIND OF DOCTRINE, PART 5: THE DEADLY BREEZES OF HERESY

Be diligent to present yourself approved to God, a worker who does not need to be ashamed, rightly dividing the word of truth. 2 Tim. 2:15.

Bioterrorism poses a new threat to American society. Deaths from anthrax spores, sent via the mail service, showed us our vulnerability to a disease we'd scarcely imagined. What if some terrorist poisoned our water or food supply? What if some deranged maniac hijacked a crop duster and sprayed a jammed stadium? Airborne pestilence has the capacity to take tens of thousands of lives.

Heresy brings similar destruction. When the pestilence-laden breezes of heresy blow through the church, many of God's people develop deadly spiritual disease.

The church has always faced heresy. Paul warned young Timothy about a certain "Hymenaeus and Philetus" who overthrew the faith of some (2 Tim. 2:17). He admonished the church at Galatians, "O foolish Galatians! Who has bewitched you that you should not obey the truth?" (Gal. 3:1). Paul was concerned about Judaizers who were entering the church, claiming that salvation came by obedience to the laws of Judaism, not by faith in Christ alone. Many were deceived and lost their souls as the result of these heresies.

In His masterful sermon on last-day signs, Jesus declares, "Take heed that no one deceives you. For many will come in My name, saying, 'I am the Christ,' and will deceive many" (Matt. 24:4, 5). Ellen White wrote, "The days are fast approaching when there will be great perplexity and confusion. Satan, clothed in angel robes, will deceive, if possible, the very elect. There will be gods many and lords many. Every wind of doctrine will be blowing" (*Testimonies,* vol. 5, p. 80).

How can we keep from being deceived by the master deceiver? Here are three principles God has given us:

1. Love the truth. Jesus said, "If anyone wills to do [God's] will, he shall know concerning the doctrine, whether it is from God or whether I speak on My own authority" (John 7:17). Commit your heart to doing God's will.

2. Know the truth. Jesus said, "You shall know the truth, and the truth shall make you free" (John 8:32). Knowing the truth liberates you from the deceptions of Satan.

3. Share the truth. When Jesus invited His disciples to "follow Me" (Matt. 4:19), He knew that following His will and sharing His truth would strengthen their own faith. Here is God's serum to vaccinate you against heresy. Love the truth, know the truth, share the truth, and you will remain strong in the truth.

July 22

EVERY WIND OF DOCTRINE, PART 6: DUST STORMS OF DOUBT

O you of little faith, why did you doubt? Matt. 14:31.

Dust storms can be deadly, blocking our vision. As I have driven across the dry Texas plains into a dust storm, sometimes the only smart thing to do was to pull off to the side of the road.

One of Satan's deceptions is his dust storms of doubt. Satan used doubt in the garden with Eve. He asked, "Has God indeed said, 'You shall not eat of every tree in the garden'?" (Gen. 3:1). Satan's question was intended to create doubt. His tactics are the same today. If he can deceive us into doubting God's love, questioning God's truth, or becoming skeptical of God's church organization, he knows we are on the road to spiritual disaster.

The hallmark of twenty-first century thought is open-mindedness. Certainly there is a time for investigation, questions, and an open mind. There is also a time for closed-mindedness. I know God loves me. I know His Word is true. I have accepted His message of the Bible Sabbath. I believe His church will triumph. On these great eternal truths I am closed-minded. I do not have to wake up each morning wondering whether God loves me; I don't have to question my convictions daily.

When Dr. Luke wrote to Theophilus, he longed for him to "know the certainty of those things in which you were instructed" (Luke 1:4). Some issues must be settled in our hearts.

If we fill our mind with doubt, we will become uncertain. If we fill our minds with questions, we will become skeptical. Not every question will be answered this side of eternity. The chief question is Do I have enough evidence to believe? Once that question is answered there comes a point where I close my mind to doubts.

Ellen White had a remarkable experience with D. M. Canright. Pastor Canright left the Seventh-day Adventist Church. He wrote to Mrs. White about his doubts. She wrote back, "I refused to hear it. The breath of doubt, of complaint and unbelief, is contagious; if I make my mind a channel for the filthy stream, the turbid, defiling water proceeding from Satan's fountain, some suggestion may linger in my mind, polluting it. If his suggestions have had such power on you as to lead you to sell your birthright for a mess of pottage—the friendship of the Lord's enemies—I want not to hear anything of your doubts, and I hope you will be guarded, lest you contaminate other minds; for the very atmosphere surrounding a man who dares to make the statements you have made is a poisonous miasma" (*Selected Messages,* book 2, p. 166).

The devil's dust storms of doubt can lead only to eternal ruin. Fill your mind with God's Word. Saturate your soul with God's truth. Settle it in your heart. God loves you. His truth will win in the end.

July 23

EVERY WIND OF DOCTRINE, PART 7: THE GENTLE ZEPHYRS OF LAODICEANISM

Behold, I stand at the door and knock. If anyone hears My voice and opens the door, I will come in to him and dine with him, and he with Me. Rev. 3:20.

The seas were rough on the apostle Paul's voyage to Rome. Sailing was dangerous. Paul urged the captain to winter in a place called Fair Havens.

The rest of the crew were nervous, and urged the captain to sail on. Dr. Luke wrote, "When the south wind blew softly, supposing that they had obtained their desire, putting out to sea, they sailed close by Crete" (Acts 27:13). A gentle warm wind called a zephyr blew. The captain and crew were lulled to sleep. They felt safe. They believed they were capable of handling any storm.

The gentle breezes soon turned to fierce gale winds. The winds whipped the waves into fury. Only the providence of God saved the boat.

Gentle warm breezes make you sleepy. Likewise, Laodicea is a state of spiritual lethargy, of perceived spirituality. Laodicea believes all is well with its spiritual experience.

Some time ago I visited Laodicea in south-central Turkey. Laodicea was a prosperous commercial center in John's day. Its population was far more than 100,000 people. Its banking business was the envy of the Roman world. When an earthquake destroyed part of the city in the middle of the first century, the proud Laodiceans refused Roman assistance. They wanted to rebuild the city themselves.

Laodicea was a center for fashion, specializing in the production of woolen goods. Laodicea also was a medical center, producing a medical salve for the ears and eyes. The proud inhabitants of Laodicea had everything they needed. They were convinced that no city could rival theirs.

John the revelator's message to the church at Laodicea speaks with relevance to God's church today. His message speaks to spiritual pride, humbling the heart. God says, "You say, 'I am rich, have become wealthy, and have need of nothing'—and do not know that you are wretched, miserable, poor, blind, and naked" (Rev. 3:17).

Living for self is the essence of Laodiceanism. Ellen White wrote that "Love of self excludes the love of Christ. Those who live for self are ranged under the head of the Laodicean church" (*The Seventh-day Adventist Bible Commentary*, vol. 7, p. 962).

God longs for each one of us to have a new vital experience with Him. He longs to have spiritual fellowship with us. He says, "I stand at the door and knock. If anyone hears My voice and opens the door, I will come in and dine with him" (verse 20). The door is our ego, our pride, our self-centeredness. The door is doing things our own way, in our own strength. Our Lord longs to fill our hearts, guide our thoughts, and mold our minds.

Don't allow yourself to be lulled into a spiritual slumber. Christ in the center of our hearts, lives, and all we are is the only answer to the dull religion of Laodiceanism.

HEAVEN'S BLESSINGS WRAPPED IN A SINGLE PACKAGE

He who did not spare His own Son, but delivered Him up for us all, how shall He not with Him also freely give us all things? Rom. 8:32.

Comedian Billy Crystal was in Manhattan shooting a movie on his daughter Lindsay's eleventh birthday. He called her in Los Angeles and apologized about his work schedule—but promised that a package would be delivered soon. Lindsay was disappointed, but she thanked him for the coming present.

Later that same day a most unusual package arrived at her front door: a six-foot-high cardboard carton. Lindsay ripped it apart on the spot, and out stepped Dad! He'd flown from New York to Los Angeles right after phoning her.

Lindsay hugged and hugged her father, crying, "Pinch me, pinch me." She couldn't believe this unusual gift was real.

Billy Crystal's own father died of a heart attack when Billy was 15. He says, "I've missed 25 birthdays with my father. I won't let that happen to my girls."

Crystal gave his daughter the most valuable gift he could possibly give—himself. Heaven has given us its most precious gift in Jesus. He gave Himself to us.

In giving Himself, Jesus lavishes all of heaven's blessing upon us. This thought so overwhelmed the apostle Paul with joy that he exclaimed, "He who did not spare His own Son, but delivered Him up for us all, how shall He not with Him also freely give us all things?" (Rom. 8:32).

When the Father gave the Son, He gave the whole package. All of heaven's blessings are ours. Think of it—God freely gives us forgiveness, pardon, power, strength, wisdom, provisions for our daily needs, security, assurance, self-esteem, and on and on and on. It is all ours in Christ. Heaven's blessings have no end. For "God has a heaven full of blessings for those who will cooperate with Him" (*Christ's Object Lessons,* p. 145). "Whatever blessings the Lord may give, He has an infinite supply beyond, an inexhaustible store from which we may draw" (*Testimonies,* vol. 5, p. 71).

Christ provides all of life's good things. In Him there is nothing lacking. Every breath we take is a gift from God. The food we eat comes from heaven's abundance. The love and affection we experience in our earthly relations flows from the heart of God through His Son. Today we can rejoice because all of heaven's blessings are wrapped in the single package of Jesus.

PULL THE RIP CORD OF FAITH

I am the vine, you are the branches. He who abides in Me, and I in him, bears much fruit: for without Me you can do nothing. John 15:5.

Sandy's friends craned their necks up at the blue sky and caught her tiny figure hurling itself out of the plane. This was her first time to jump without a line, and this time Sandy was going to pull the rip cord herself.

Her friends far below counted with her—one one thousand, two one thousand, three one thousand. But the parachute didn't open. Nothing was happening. They waited as Sandy fell farther and farther. Why didn't she pull the rip cord? If something was wrong, what about her reserve chute?

Tragically, this young woman plummeted all the way to the ground and died instantly. When the ground crew rushed to the site, they noticed her parachute still folded neatly in the pack on her back. What had happened?

Then they saw the cloth of her jumpsuit torn away on the right side of her chest. It seemed as if she'd been desperately clawing at it. In fact, she'd dug through her clothing and actually lacerated her flesh with her fingers. The terrible truth dawned on them. Her rip cord was on her *left* side! In a moment of panic she had forgotten and kept pulling and yanking and clawing at the rip cord on the right, but it wasn't there.

Is it possible that we are frantically pulling on a rip cord that isn't there? Any time we trust in our own strength to overcome temptation we are pulling on a cord that isn't there. Any time we trust our own power to overcome the enemy we are diving for disaster. It wasn't that Sandy didn't put forth any effort—she was frantic. She tried as hard as she could. Her problem was that her effort was misplaced.

The Scriptures make two counterbalancing statements. The first says, "I can do nothing." The second says, "I can do all things." Jesus said, "Without Me you can do nothing" (John 15:5). Without Him all of our best efforts are in vain. Without Him we are powerless. Without Him all of our best efforts are doomed to failure. "Human effort avails nothing without divine power" (*Prophets and Kings*, p. 487).

The apostle pulls the right rip cord when he triumphantly declares, "I can do all things through Christ who strengthens me" (Phil. 4:13). Through Jesus the weak become strong. In His strength and power we are overcomers. Our Lord has never lost a battle with the enemy. He is not about to begin now. Grasp His power. Fight in His strength. Yield to His grace. Pull the rip cord of faith.

THE GLAD REUNION

Then we who are alive and remain shall be caught up together with them in the clouds to meet the Lord in the air. And thus we shall always be with the Lord. 1 Thess. 4:17.

Returning one morning from a short walk, I heard my home phone ringing. I hurried up the driveway to answer it. The unfamiliar female voice on the other end of the line seemed extremely upset. "Are you Pastor Mark Finley?" the woman asked. I affirmed that I was, and she continued. "I am the nurse at Dr. Adams' office in Trenton, Georgia. Do you know a teenager by the name of Jenny?"

"Yes; is something wrong?"

"I'm afraid so, Pastor," she answered. "Jenny was baby-sitting for the Jarod family. The baby's parents were not home. The baby suffocated in the crib." The nurse paused. "Pastor, can you drive to Trenton immediately? Can you find Jenny and give her some comfort? And Pastor, can you . . . can you tell the baby's parents that he is dead?"

I sped around the curves between Wildwood and Trenton, thoughts swirling inside my head. Should I contact Jenny or the baby's parents first? I decided to head for the home of the baby's parents.

As I pulled into the driveway, I noticed two little boys playing with toy cars and trucks in the dirt. The younger one looked up, his face somber, and said, "Mister, the baby's dead." Obviously the parents knew by now as well.

I entered the home and found the mother huddled on the couch beside her husband. He had an arm around her shoulders, but she was crying uncontrollably. Her sobs wrenched my heart. I couldn't imagine what it would be like to go through this horror.

I walked over to where the young mother sat and put my hand on her shoulder. Through her tears and sobs she looked up and said, "Pastor, thank you for coming."

For a few moments I said nothing at all. And then simply, "Ma'am, I can't possibly understand your pain. I can't possibly understand the heartache and the sorrow you're going through. I've not lost one of my children. But there *is* One who can understand. His Son died. He willingly left the glory of heaven to die on the cross so the death of our loved ones would not be forever.

"The grave could not hold Him. He burst the bonds of that tomb. He was resurrected from the dead, and He lives. Because Christ lives today, your boy can live again too. Jesus understands your heartache. He knows your sorrow. There is a day coming when the living, all-powerful Christ will descend the corridors of the sky, and life will be new again. The righteous dead will be resurrected, and the righteous living will be caught up to meet Him in the air."

I could see, through her tears, that a new hope dawned in that grieving mother's heart. The coming of our Lord is the only hope we have of seeing our dead loved ones again. It is the only hope we have of being reunited with our families forever. It is a solid hope. A real hope. It is a hope we can count on now and forever.

July 27

BRINGING GLORY TO GOD IN TRIAL

Count it all joy when you fall into various trials, knowing that the testing of your faith produces patience. James 1:2.

Young Claude de Praet spent five long days in prison before he learned the charges against him. Finally, on the morning of the sixth day, the jailer opened Claude's cell and escorted him to the interrogation room. Three judges sat solemnly in high-backed chairs. A clerk waited with pen and paper to take down the prisoner's statement. The court bailiff began the questioning.

Claude was on trial for one reason and one reason alone. His beliefs were different from those of the state church. He accepted the authority of the Bible rather than the authority of the church. He believed salvation came through Jesus Christ, not through the church's sacraments.

This interrogation occurred in 1556, in the city of Ghent, in what is now Belgium. We discover something amazing about this man's faith in the letters he managed to send out of the prison. Speaking of his trial, he wrote, "My heart kindled within me with joy to the Lord, my God, so that all my troubles and anxiety were drawn from me as dust I swept from the street."

What made such a difference? Strangely enough, it was the jailer's coming to his cell and ushering him before his accusers. It was the start of the interrogations. His ordeal was just beginning. So why was he so happy? Because finally he would get a chance to testify for his faith, and could bear witness to what God had done in his life. Come what may, his adversaries would know what Jesus meant to him.

He wrote, "I sat down with good cheer, my heart lifted up to the Lord, my God, forgetful of myself and the things that are in this world."

Every trial is an opportunity to testify of God's goodness. Even non-

Christians are cheerful when things are going well in their lives. If the only time we are cheerful is when everything is going well, our testimony is no better than that of a non-Christian. But if we rejoice at God's goodness in our trials, we give a positive testimony to a Lord who sustains us even in life's difficult moments.

Claude de Praet saw his courtroom trial as an opportunity to share Christ. Are you going through some challenging trial today? A trial with your family or your friends or your health? Perhaps you have a trial in interpersonal relationships, or a trial on your job. If you are, ask yourself "How can I be a witness to the people around me in this trial? How can Christ be glorified in this problem? How can I use this experience to bring honor to Christ's name?"

If we approach every one of life's challenges from the perspective of bringing glory to God, our trials will become doorways to unique witnessing opportunities.

May the prayer of each of our hearts be "Lord, teach me to see in every trial an opportunity to bring glory to Your name."

July 28

PRIDE, A SPIRITUAL CANCER

By pride comes nothing but strife. Prov. 13:10.

It happened in a Boston suburb in August 1973. You may recall the story of presidential adviser Chuck Colson and his unexpected encounter with God. He had gone to visit a friend named Tom Phillips. He didn't know that this corporate executive had just experienced a conversion. Sitting in Phillips' elegant living room, Colson began to complain about how unfairly the press was treating him. The Watergate affair was starting to blow up.

After Colson ran out of his explanations, Phillips said gently, "If only you had believed in the rightness of your cause, none of this would have been necessary." Leaning forward, he said, "You had to try to destroy your enemies. You had to destroy them because you couldn't trust in yourselves."

Colson began to wipe the sweat from his forehead. It seemed unbearably hot in the room.

Colson tried to explain to his friend that in politics you just have to do certain things to survive. Phillips asked if he could read a few words from a book by C. S. Lewis called *Mere Christianity*. Colson leaned back in his chair, still feeling defensive.

Phillips read something that cut deep into Colson's heart. "It is Pride which has been the chief cause of misery in every nation and every family since the world began. . . . Pride always means enmity. . . . Pride is spiritual cancer; it eats up the very possibility of love . . ." As Phillips read, Colson saw scenes from his whole life flash before him. He saw how he'd become arrogant. How step by step he'd cut himself off from love.

Later that night, on his drive home, it all came over him. He began weeping uncontrollably. Finally he dropped his defenses. He saw the terrible emptiness behind his mask of self-assurance. Colson said the first real prayer of his life. Reaching out to God, he gave himself to the God of love. Later this man who had been so trapped in his pride found great joy in ministering to inmates in prisons.

Pride is one of the worst prisons of all. Solomon puts it this way: "Pride goes before destruction, and a haughty spirit before a fall" (Prov. 16:18). "A man's pride will bring him low, but the humble in spirit will retain honor" (Prov. 29:23).

Pride is a feeling of smug satisfaction and superiority. It exaggerates its own achievements while downplaying the accomplishments of others.

God invites us to come humbly to Him, recognizing all of our abilities, all of our opportunities, all of our talents that come from Him. With Charles Colson we discover life's true meaning in humble submission to the God who made us.

July 29

THE HEALING POWER OF FORGIVENESS

If You, Lord, should mark iniquities, O Lord, who could stand? But there is forgiveness with You. Ps. 130:3.

When Hitler's forces mistakenly released Corrie ten Boom from the Ravensbrück prison camp, she was one of the few who got out alive. After the war she set up a home in Holland for former prisoners of the war. She said that the difference between those who suffered mental breakdowns and those who recovered from their horrific experiences was their ability to forgive. Those who could not forgive, who bore bitterness and resentment, were often mentally unbalanced for the rest of their lives.

Corrie took the message of God's forgiveness and brought God's love to the bombed-out cities and devastated people of Germany. One night she spoke in Munich. After eloquently describing God's forgiveness to hundreds of eager listeners, she noticed one man in the crowd. After the service, he approached her. He was a stocky man, five feet ten inches, with deeply set eyes and a square face. She immediately recognized him as one of the cruelest guards in Ravensbrück.

Now this man stood before Corrie. He reached out his hand to ask for her forgiveness. As Corrie remembered later: "I wanted to spit in his face. I wanted to reach out and slap him across the face. Every emotion in me cried out for revenge. But I said to myself, I know that unless I forgive him, every ounce of love in me will dry up. I know that bitterness and resentment and unwillingness to forgive will eat out my spiritual heart."

Forgiveness is a choice to release another from your condemnation because Christ has released you from His condemnation. It is treating them as if they had always loved you, because Christ has always loved you.

Contrary to conflicting feelings within, Corrie reached out, grasped the man's hand, and sobbed out, "Brother, I forgive you." She recalled, "When I reached out my hand, I reached out against all the inclinations within me. When I said those words, 'Brother, I forgive you,' immediately a new peace flooded through my life."

Forgiveness is healing. When we forgive another who does not deserve it, we open our hearts to God's healing. Forgiveness is God's remedy for anger, bitterness, and resentment. We are encouraged to "cultivate a forgiving spirit" (*Testimonies,* vol. 3, p. 98) and not to become weary of granting forgiveness for wrongdoing (see *Christ's Object Lessons,* pp. 249, 250).

The forgiving heart is one God can fill with His love. The hardened heart is one resistant to God's love. Today ask God to give you a forgiving heart. Like Corrie ten Boom, reach out to those who have wronged you saying, "Brother, Sister, I forgive you."

July 30

SURRENDER AND TRUST

Behold, God is my salvation; I will trust and not be afraid. Isa. 12:2.

In one of the most magnificent passages in all of Scripture, Jesus powerfully states the essence of the Christian life. Mark 14:36 tells us, "And he said, Abba, Father, all things are possible unto thee; take away this cup from me: nevertheless not what I will, but what thou wilt" (KJV).

Abba is a word a young child used to address their father, an everyday family word that indicates childlike trustful obedience. Even when He did not understand, Jesus called His Father "Daddy." Confronted with the cross, faced with darkness and despair, tempted to mistrust, He called His Father "Daddy."

Life may be cruel, but God isn't.

Life may not be fair, but God is!

Trust doesn't mean that I understand what is happening, or that I accept it. Trust doesn't mean that I like what is happening or that it is fair. It doesn't mean that the experiences are just or even that I deserve them. Trust doesn't mean that I believe God caused what I am going through.

- Trust means that I understand God loves me, and He is going to bring me triumphant through this experience.
- Trust means that in spite of what is happening, I still have confidence in God.
- Trust means that I rest in His care and love, even though I don't understand.
- Trust means that I believe He desires me no harm. He is my friend.

"[God] will never disappoint those who put their trust in Him" (*Testimonies,* vol. 9, p. 213). So I surrender in absolute confidence. With the prophet Isaiah I proclaim, "I will trust and not be afraid." With the hymnist I sing, "Trust and obey, for there's no other way to be happy in Jesus, but to trust and obey."

July 31

IT IS FINISHED, PART 1

Thus the heavens and the earth, and all the host of them, were finished. Gen. 2:1.

Christmas Eve, 1968. It had been a long, difficult year for America. In January of 1968 North Korea captured the U.S.S. *Pueblo.* In February and March U.S. casualties in Vietnam skyrocketed. Public sentiment against the war hit at an all-time high. Springtime brought the assassinations of Martin Luther King, Jr., and Robert F. Kennedy. Summer brought no relief as the Vietnam peace talks dragged on and antiwar protests intensified. No doubt about it, 1968 was a year we would just as soon forget.

But on Christmas Eve a beacon of hope shone through the darkness. The thrill of accomplishment inspired us. For the first time in history men were orbiting the moon. And they were Americans! We could hardly believe our eyes as television relayed the dramatic pictures of the moon's surface. Astronauts Frank Borman, James Lovell, and William Anders sent their Christmas greetings. In a magnificent Christmas Eve moment, our astronauts read from a centuries-old book those familiar words in Genesis 1:1: "In the beginning God created the heaven and the earth" (KJV).

Orbiting the moon, looking back at Earth from a perspective of nearly

250,000 miles away, the astronauts reminded us all that life is not a cosmic accident. "In the beginning God created the heaven and the earth."

There is deep meaning, practical significance, and lasting truth in these words. Let's consider this Creation scene a little more carefully.

When God completed Creation week, He crowned it by creating Adam and Eve. He joyfully exclaimed to the whole universe, "It is done."

Genesis 2:1 describes the scene this way: "Thus the heavens and the earth, and all the host of them, were finished." The words "It is finished" at Creation speak of something God did. Creation is the work of God. We did not evolve. We did not create ourselves. The words "It is finished" speak of a Creator who finished His creation and a Creator who cares for the things He has made. You never again need fear that you are of little value.

God says, "I have completed the intricate design of your being. I have fashioned the complexity of the beating heart, the life-giving cell, the electrical/chemical particles of the brain, and the intricacy of your personality. I have made you. I have created you. To undervalue yourself is an insult to the one who made you."

In light of our Creator's love we never again need to feel unknown, unwanted, uncared for, unvalued, unloved. When God declared, "It is finished" on Creation morning, He declared a love so complete that it would forever banish feelings of alienation, abandonment, and aloneness. With the apostle Paul we can proclaim, "Now, therefore, you are no longer strangers and foreigners, but fellow citizens with the saints and members of the household of God" (Eph. 2:19).

God created us. He loves us. We are not cosmic orphans. We are children of the household of God. And that's plenty of reason to rejoice.

IT IS FINISHED, PART 2

He said, "It is finished!" And bowing His head, He gave up His spirit. John 19:30.

Jesus' dying words were "It is finished!" What did He mean? What was finished?

Guilt was finished. In Jesus there is "now no condemnation" (Rom. 8:1). He who "knew no sin [became] sin for us" (2 Cor. 5:21). All of our guilt was nailed to the cross in the body of Christ. Sin's bondage was broken. It was finished. Jesus was "obedient to the point of death" (Phil. 2:8). At the cross Jesus demonstrated that the power of grace is greater than the power of sin. Satan's fiercest temptations could not deter His commitment to our salvation. The cross offers freedom from the slavery of sin. Grace frees us, and sin is no longer our master. It is finished.

At the cross fear is finished. Never again do we need to fear death. Sin's war has been paid. Christ turned the tomb into a tunnel. In the face of death, the cross offers hope. For Jesus the cross was not the end. Even in death Jesus is victorious. The glorious resurrection morning reveals that He has power over the grave.

At the cross all misapprehension about the character of God is finished. The cross reveals a loving Father's heart. It shows the lengths God will go to save us. It answers Satan's charges that God is unjust.

Romanian schoolchildren learn a delightful legend that marvelously reveals the meaning of the cross.

A Romanian nobleman lived in a palatial estate. He had extensive land holdings, fields, cattle, horses, sheep, goats, and many servants. A peasant owned a single cabin with a few sheep and goats next to the wealthy man's property. The greedy wealthy landlord bribed some townspeople to drive the poor man's animals onto his land at night. He then claimed that the poor man was irresponsible and needed to forfeit all of his belongings.

A trial was held in the town square. Trumped-up charges were brought against the poor peasant. The peasant lost everything he had. All the town mocked him. The nobleman spit on him. The poor peasant wandered through the countryside a penniless beggar.

One day the poor peasant met the king, who was visiting towns throughout his kingdom. The peasant explained the situation to the king. The king kindly listened, then gave the peasant two large bags of gold—worth much more than he had lost.

In front of the whole town the king bent down and kissed the peasant on both cheeks. As the king kissed the poor beggar he said, "Tell everyone, where the evil man spit on you, the king kissed you. I have now kissed away your shame."

At the cross the King of the universe gave us much more than we ever lost. He placed the treasure of His own love in our hands. When Jesus shouted, "It is finished!" He kissed away our shame. We are children of the kingdom, accepted in the beloved, kissed on both cheeks by the King of the universe.

August 2

IT IS FINISHED, PART 3

And He said to me, "It is done! I am the Alpha and the Omega, the Beginning and the End." Rev. 21:6.

Loneliness, pain, injustice, and death are the results of living in a sinful world. God's immortal words spoken in Revelation 21:6, "It is done!" speak of an eternal end to everything that disrupts our happiness.

One day loneliness will be gone forever. Every one of us longs to be loved unconditionally, to be accepted no matter what we have done in the past. Revelation 21:3 tells us that one day we will be with God. We were made for Him. He will fill the empty loneliness of our lives. "Behold, the tabernacle of God is with men, and He will dwell with them, and they shall be His people. God Himself will be with them and be their God." When our Lord says "It is done!" loneliness will be gone forever. We will live in intimate fellowship with Him through all eternity.

God's final words also banished pain forever. For "there shall be no more pain" (verse 4). At cancer wards across the country, patients have had their bodies weakened through multiple surgeries, chemotherapy, and radiation therapy. They have lost their hair, their weight, and their strength, and some have lost their will to live. God gives us the ability to hope again. The words "It is done!" are His promise that one day He will give us new bodies that will pulsate with life and joy and health. He will take us to a land where there is no sickness, suffering, or sorrow.

His words "It is done!" speak of a God who will "make all things new" (verse 5). This life is filled with injustice and unfairness. But one day the King of righteousness will reign. Christ will sit upon His heavenly throne. In eternity the heavenly society will be fair and just and right. Justice may not always be found on earth, but it will be found in heaven. It may not always be meted out by humans, but it will be given to us freely by God. When you have been treated unfairly, look beyond the hurt to God's new society, when He will reign in righteousness.

God's final pronouncement "It is done!" shouts that death is done forever. Have you lost a loved one through death? Does the grief seem too much to bear alone? One day death will be a thing of the past. God's glorious tomorrow will put an end to death forever. It will be gone, finished, over. In that glorious resurrection morning "death is swallowed up in victory" (1 Cor. 15:54). Through our tears of loss of a loved one, we can cling to God's promise. One day death will be banished forever.

In one final triumphant note, Heaven's divine announcement is decreed, "It is finished!" The war is over. Hunger, horror, and heartache are over. Disease, disaster, and death are over. Poverty, pain, and pestilence are over. Sickness, sorrow, and suffering are over. Tears, terror, and turmoil are finished. IT IS DONE! Righteousness reigns forever.

August 3

NO CONDEMNATION

There is therefore now no condemnation to those who are in Christ Jesus, who do not walk according to the flesh, but according to the Spirit. Rom. 8:1.

His skeleton lay beside a makeshift shelter on the beach, near the pounding surf of the mid-Atlantic. He'd tried to survive alone on a desolate island called Ascension. Beside the man was a journal that told one of the most remarkable stories in seafaring history.

Some terrible crime had caused the authorities to abandon him on this desolate island with only a cask of water, a hatchet, a teakettle, a trap, and a few other items. Soon there was no water to be found anywhere. The man was reduced to drinking the blood of the turtles he killed with his hatchet, and then to drinking seawater, even though this was deadly. His last journal entry reads, "I am becoming a moving skeleton; my strength is entirely decayed; I cannot write much longer."

This anonymous seaman endured great physical suffering during his grueling struggle to survive. But a much greater pain stood out, something repeated throughout his journal—his consuming guilt.

He wrote mournfully, "Night is an emblem of my crimes, and each clear day reviews my punishment." Later he exclaimed in the journal, "What pangs, alas, do wretched mortals feel who headstrongly tread the giddy maze of life and leave the beauteous paths of righteousness."

There's nothing in this world quite as isolating as guilt. The punishment this nameless prisoner received would be considered cruel and unusual today. But it gives us a picture of one of our deepest problems—guilt, inescapable guilt.

In recent years pop psychology has tried its best to rid us of this chronic problem. We have been assured we are no worse than the next person. Well-meaning people have done their best to sweep guilt right off the horizon. But there is a major problem here. Guilt doesn't go away, no matter how much we try to massage the psyche.

One of the principal reasons is this: We keep trying to deal with the symptoms instead of the root problem. We want to anesthetize those unpleasant feelings instead of facing or dealing with their sources.

Jesus pointed out our basic problem to a Pharisee named Nicodemus. He said, "Light has come into the world, and men loved darkness rather than light, because their deeds were evil. For everyone practicing evil hates the light and does not come to the light, lest his deeds should be exposed" (John 3:19, 20).

Some people will be lost because they turned away from the light. They are afraid of being exposed. Guilt can never be solved until we acknowledge that we have sinned. Guilt is not to be swept under the carpet. It is a sign pointing us to the cure. People have a chronic problem with guilt only if they keep ignoring it.

The purpose of guilt is to lead us to the one who takes away the sins of the world (John 1:29). It is to lead us to the Savior, who delivers us from condemnation. Today, let the guilt of your heart lead you to the Savior of your soul. Don't deny it. Acknowledge it and flee to Him.

August 4

TO BE LIKE HIM

Beloved, now we are the children of God; and it has not yet been revealed what we shall be, but we know that when He is revealed, we shall be like Him, for we shall see Him as He is. 1 John 3:2.

In 1739 the town of Kingswood, England, was considered a religious wasteland. Respectable clergy had more or less given up on the place. It was a town of miners, men who spent the daylight hours underground, hardened by poverty and ignorance. They'd never been inside a church and had never heard the voice of a preacher.

But one day a man stood in the Kingswood commons and began to speak to about 200 of them. His name was John Wesley. The doors of the established churches had been closed to him. He could preach only in the open air.

The miners began to listen. Somehow John Wesley's proclamation of the gospel penetrated decades of deprivation. Tears began to stream down blackened faces.

More and more miners and their families gathered. Soon 10,000 were packed on the grass of the common, and a spiritual revolution in England began.

John Wesley's spiritual revolution was one of the most remarkable movements in the history of the Christian church. But here's something you might not know about him. John Wesley preached with a fiery urgency because he believed the coming of the Lord was near. As an ardent student of the prophecies of Daniel and Revelation, Wesley preached a message of repentance. He called people to holiness. In the light of his belief in the coming of Christ, he appealed for total commitment.

The message of the soon return of our Lord is not only a message of hope; it is a call to holiness. It's an earnest appeal for God to do a deep work in our hearts. The message of the Second Advent urges us to make a total surrender to Christ as Lord. As one writer so ably put it, "If He doesn't reign as Lord of all, He doesn't reign as Lord at all." The Savior who died for us longs to be the Lord in us.

"The ideal of Christian character is Christlikeness" (*The Desire of Ages*, p. 311). The words of an old hymn speak powerfully to our hearts today:

"Earthly pleasures vainly call me; I would be like Jesus;
Nothing worldly shall enthrall me; I would be like Jesus.
Be like Jesus, this my song, in the home and in the throng;
Be like Jesus, all day long! I would be like Jesus."

August 5

MORE THAN A HOSTAGE

The apostles said to the Lord, "Increase our faith." Luke 17:5.

They had endured years of imprisonment, isolation, and even outright brutality. But the faces that emerged from "somewhere in Lebanon" didn't quite fit the part. They didn't seem broken by their long ordeal as hostages. Their broad smiles and easy laughter spoke of something entirely different.

When Terry Anderson, the last American hostage in Lebanon, was finally freed in December 1991, he and his companions were at last able to tell their harrowing story. The picture that emerged made it difficult to see how any of them had survived with their sanity intact. They told of airless, windowless cells, barely larger than a grave. Of extremes of heat in the day and cold at night, of the same clothes year after year. They told of filthy blindfolds that infected their eyes, of steel chains unlocked only once a day for a 10-minute toilet visit to a hole in the ground. Of just enough food to keep body and soul together, usually eaten alone in the dark.

Almost all the hostages were beaten, some so severely that they were permanently injured. Terry Anderson recalls hearing a hostage with pneumonia in the next cell, choking to death on his own fluids.

What sustained Terry Anderson through 2,455 days of captivity? He said it was the Bible and a picture of his newborn daughter, whom he had never seen, that got him through. In captivity he rediscovered his faith.

French hostage Roger Auque made a similar discovery. After his release he said simply, "Before, I didn't believe in God, and now I do."

Hostage Benjamin Weir looked up in his cell one day and noticed three bare wires hanging from the ceiling. For some reason those wires suggested to him the extended fingers of God in one of Michelangelo's paintings in the Sistine Chapel. Weir recalls, "That became to me a representation of the sustaining, purposeful hand of God."

Faith blossomed in those dark cells in Lebanon. Lonely people found the strength to survive. The secret behind their survival and their good spirits, when released, was what the hostages called their "Church of the Locked Door." They conducted regular Christian services, using bits of bread to celebrate Communion. They kept their faith alive, and faith kept them alive.

For "faith lightens every burden, it relieves every weariness" (*Prophets and Kings,* p. 175). "Faith is the spiritual hand that touches infinity" (*Testimonies,* vol. 6, p. 467).

Let your faith soar into the heavens and energize your soul today.

August 6

END-TIME PROPHECY REVEALS GOD'S CHARACTER

Behold I am coming quickly! Hold fast what you have, that no one may take your crown. Rev. 3:11.

The books of Daniel and Revelation reveal a panoramic view of the future. Their prophecies clearly reveal events soon to break upon our world. The central theme of these two end-time books is God's character. Daniel and Revelation give us a magnificent picture of God. He is the God who gives His children "knowledge and skill in all literature and wisdom" (Dan. 1:17). He delivers His people out of the hands of angry kings and fiery furnaces, and powerfully shuts the mouths of lions to keep His servants safe. He is the God whose dominion is an everlasting dominion, whose kingdom is from generation to generation, whose promises are always fulfilled, and whose ways are always just (Dan. 4:34, 37; 7:13, 14).

Revelation pictures him as the God who cares about an aged, exiled old man named John on a lonely isle. He sends an angel with a message of encouragement. What is this God like? Listen to His invitation to come sit with Him on His throne (Rev. 3:21). Listen to the spontaneous love and worship that leaps from the lips of beings who already have spent eons with Him: "Blessing and honor and glory and power be to Him who sits on the throne, and to the Lamb, forever and ever" (Rev. 5:13).

What kind of God would see to it that among the reeling of the earth, the flashes of lightning, and the roar of thunder, a resurrected little girl is carried to the arms of her mother? What kind of God begins His unopposed reign by wiping all tears from our eyes?

Jesus is the conqueror, but He gives us the crown. Jesus fought the battle for us, but He places the symbol of victory in our hands.

Upon the heads of the overcomers Jesus places the crown of glory. For each there is a crown bearing his own name (Rev. 2:10) and the inscription "Holiness to the Lord" (see *The Great Controversy*, p. 646).

Can you get excited about serving a God like that? Do you look forward with eagerness to the wonderful day when those nail-pierced hands will place a crown upon your head? I can hardly wait for the day my Savior will say, "Come, you blessed of My Father, inherit the kingdom prepared for you from the foundation of the world" (Matt. 25:34).

August 7

PEACE IN THE STORMS OF LIFE

Then He arose and rebuked the wind, and said to the sea, "Peace, be still!" Mark 4:39.

Exhausted, Jesus fell asleep in the stern of the boat. But suddenly the wind began to blow across the Galilean sea, whipping the waves into a fury. The sky darkened as lightning flashed and thunder crashed. The boat tossed and turned on the sea like a cork on the waves. Jesus' strong-armed Galilean disciples, men of the sea who often piloted their boats in storms, had never encountered a storm like this.

Though seafarers, the disciples felt like little children. They thought, *There is no way through this, no way around this.* Shivering in the cold, their muscles burning, as they tried to row against the storm, but they were taken farther and farther out into the sea. The disciples were certain they were going to lose their lives.

And then they refocused their attention. They looked away from the storm to Him. For there was one aboard their boat who could help. Didn't He care? Their souls cried out, "Master, don't You care when it looks like we are going down, when there is nothing secure around us, when there's nothing we can have confidence in? When all of our human genius, all of our human strength has failed, don't You care?"

Mark 4:39 says, "Then He arose and rebuked the wind, and said, 'Peace, be still!' And the wind ceased and there was a great calm. But He said to them, 'Why are you so fearful?' "

The only reason to be fearful in the storm is if you're rowing your own boat, focused on the storm. The more you look at the waves and dark clouds, listen to the thunder, and see the lightning, the more fearful your heart becomes. Ellen White wrote, "Living faith in the Redeemer will smooth the sea of life, and will deliver us from danger in the way that He knows to be best" (*The Desire of Ages,* p. 336).

If there was ever a time to readjust our priorities, it's now. If there ever was a time to refocus our vision, to know that our hearts are one with God, and to know that Jesus is aboard our boat, it's now.

August 8

A LIFE BUILT ON THE WORD

Whoever hears these sayings of Mine, and does them, I will liken him to a wise man who built his house on the rock. Matt. 7:24.

Satan has specially reserved the greatest temptations for the generation living at the time of the end. This need not trouble us, for the greatest outpouring of Heaven's power to sustain His people will come at the end as well.

Matthew 7:24-27 describes two groups of people. One group makes it through their time of trial. The other group collapses. "Whoever hears these sayings of Mine, and does them, I will liken him to a wise man who built his house on the rock: and the rain descended, the floods came, and the winds blew and beat on that house; and it did not fall, for it was founded on the rock. But everyone who hears these sayings of Mine, and does not do them, will be like a foolish man who built his house on the sand: and the rain descended, the floods came, and the winds blew and beat on the house; and it fell. And great was its fall."

Two houses—one built on the sand, the other on the rock. Two houses go through the same storm, yet one survives while the other collapses. Ellen White wrote, "Self is but shifting sand. If you build upon human theories and inventions, your house will fall. By the winds of temptation, the tempests of trial, it will be swept away. But these principles that [Jesus has] given will endure. Receive [Him]; build on [His] words" (*The Desire of Ages*, p. 314).

In the last days Satan will unleash fierce winds of temptation. Any attempt to build spirituality on formalism or religious rituals will end in disaster. Any spiritual life centered on human attempts to overcome temptation will collapse like a house built on sand.

The spiritual house that will survive is one built upon the solid rock, Jesus Christ. In our passage for today, Jesus says, "Whoever hears these sayings of mine, and does them, I will liken him to a wise man" (verse 24). To build a spiritual life on Christ is to build a life of trust in His Word. A life built on the Word of God will survive the winds of temptation. As we open God's Word, the same Holy Spirit who inspired the Word applies its principles to our hearts.

Finding time for God's Word is one of the great challenges in our fast-paced society. Any life not built upon the Word will be swept away when the storms of temptation come. The Word solidifies our faith. The Word is our rock, our foundation, the anchor of our faith. Determine today to spend time with God in His Word and build on the solid rock.

August 9

BY EVERY WORD

Lay aside all filthiness and overflow of wickedness, and receive with meekness the implanted word, which is able to save your souls. James 1:21.

When Bobby was 5 years old, his mother began to notice something wrong. He was losing weight. His appetite was poor, and he seemed to consistently run a low-grade fever. After a series of medical tests, the results indicated any mother's worst fear—cancer. Immediately Bobby began a series of treatments. The chemotherapy left him unusually weak and sick.

At the end of 12 months of treatment Bobby's cancer appeared to be in remission. At one of Bobby's medical checkups, his physician, Dr. Brown, needed to perform a very painful test. A needle would be inserted at the base of Bobby's skull to draw spinal fluid. The fluid would then be sent in for laboratory tests.

Dr. Brown looked at little Bobby and said, "Bobby, I know this is going to be painful." Bobby replied, "It's OK, Dr. Brown. I have begun to grow a little hair. Are you going to have to shave all my head?"

"No, just that little patch in the back. Bobby, do I need to have my nurse hold your hand while we insert the needle in the back of your neck? I know it's going to be painful."

"Doctor, if I can say the twenty-third psalm, I'll be all right. Is it OK, Dr. Brown, if I say the twenty-third psalm?"

"Bobby," Dr. Brown said, "if you want to say the twenty-third psalm when we put that needle in the back of your neck, go ahead."

As the doctor worked, Bobby recited, "'The Lord is my shepherd; I shall not want. He makes me to lie down in green pastures; He leads me beside the still waters. He restores my soul . . .'"

Bobby looked up and smiled. "Dr. Brown, it didn't hurt very much." And then he said, "Dr. Brown, have you ever memorized the twenty-third psalm?"

"Well, yes, Bobby," Dr. Brown said. "I did when I was a child."

"Dr. Brown," said Bobby, "I said it for you—could you say it for me?"

Later Dr. Brown wrote, "I noticed that all my colleagues began to scatter. They were afraid they were going to be asked to say it next! I began, and sort of fumbled through it, drawing back in my memory. Then Bobby said, 'You know, it would be good if all of you learned the twenty-third psalm, because when you memorize the Bible, Jesus tells you inside your heart that He is being strong for you when you can't be strong for yourself.'"

God is being strong for you when you can't be strong for yourself! The Word of God strengthens you. The Word of God gives you power in your life. When the winds of temptation come, "it is written, 'Man shall not live by bread alone, but by every word that proceeds from the mouth of God'" (Matt. 4:4).

Let God's Word strengthen your heart today.

August 10

WHEN GOD SAYS YES!

[I] do not cease to give thanks for you, making mention of you in my prayers. Eph. 1:16.

The unfolding drama captured the world's attention. Millions sat glued to their television screens, watching CNN's coverage of the live events.

Hard-line Communists had placed Mikhail Gorbachev

under house arrest in the Crimea. Boris Yeltsin was barricaded in the Russian White House. The coup leaders met in the Kremlin to plan to crush the resistance. A return to Communism seemed likely.

A group of committed Adventist Christians defied the curfew. Leaving their apartments, they quickly made their way to a rented facility to pray. The "intercessors" prayed through the night. They followed Paul's instructions, "I exhort . . . that supplications, prayers, intercessions, and giving of thanks be made for all men, for kings and all who are in authority" (1 Tim. 2:1, 2).

The date, August 21, 1991. A crowd estimated at 15,000-20,000 packed Moscow's streets around the Russian White House in support of democracy.

Military leaders refused to obey their commanding officers. KGB officers with their crack Alpha troops refused to advance. For 14 long hours the coup leaders seemed paralyzed. This vital time delay enabled thousands of Moscow's resisters to gain even more courage. Defying the curfew, they flooded the streets. When a ragtag band of dissident army officers, KGB military, and police finally advanced at 2:00 a.m. the resistance from the people was so strong that the raid absolutely failed. The coup leaders, sensing their defeat, attempted to leave the country as quickly as possible.

Intercessory prayer is powerful. It changes the destiny of nations. It alters the course of history. It radically transforms the way things happen.

God's promise is still true: "If My people . . . will humble themselves, and pray and seek My face, and turn from their wicked ways, then I will hear from heaven, and . . . heal their land" (2 Chron. 7:14).

Prayer opens the door for God to work mighty miracles. Prayer unites us with the all-powerful Creator of the universe. Prayer unlocks Heaven's resources. Illness cannot confine it. Adversity cannot chain it. Poverty does not hinder it.

You don't need an educational degree to pray. You don't need to know how to read to pray. All you have to do to pray is pray.

Will you accept God's invitation to become a mighty prayer warrior?

SAVED TO SERVE

In His love and in His pity He redeemed them. And He bore them; and He carried them all the days of old. Isa. 63:9.

As the speaker/director of It Is Written's international television ministry, I spend nearly 200 days a year traveling. Preaching appointments, evangelistic meetings, and television taping sessions keep me away from home a great deal. My wife and I spend a lot of time in hotel rooms. Here is a family secret. I am notorious for losing the key to my hotel room. It seems I have difficulty keeping track of those incredibly thin plastic card-like keys. I don't know how I lose them but I sure know I spend a lot of time looking for them, and sometimes I give up in despair.

There is one thing for certain: Human beings are a lot more valuable than some hotel room key, and Jesus never gives up in despair. I can replace my hotel room key, but Jesus can never replace us.

The essence of Christianity is summarized in these words: "The Son of Man has come to seek and to save that which was lost" (Luke 19:10).

Jesus was passionate about saving others! The heart of true Christianity is a loving ministry to others. The essence of the Christian faith is participating in Christ's mission of saving lost people. Following Jesus means following Him in a redemptive mission to reach people with His love.

Some people have a strange idea about Christianity. They believe Christianity is giving up bad things so they can be saved. They don't smoke or drink, they don't wear this or that, and they think this is the essence of religion. Don't misunderstand. Jesus does invite us to full surrender, but was there anything evil in heaven? How much bad was there in heaven that Jesus gave up? What did Jesus surrender? He surrendered some very good things: the worship of the Father, the adoration of the angels, the praise of cherubim and seraphim.

Christianity is not giving up bad things so *I* can be saved. It is giving up good things so *others* can be saved. Christianity does not focus on my attempting to save myself. It focuses on my giving my life to save others, participating in Jesus' mission.

Jesus was centered on other people. The essence of Christianity is a heart filled with Christ's love, passionate about serving others. We best represent Christ in loving, compassionate ministry. When we are filled with His love, we too long to share it with others. Chained by His love, men and women are born into the kingdom of God. Indeed, this is life's greatest joy. We are saved to serve, saved to bless, saved to meet the needs of others in Jesus' name.

August 12

LASTING PLEASURE

You will show me the path of life; in Your presence is fullness of joy; at Your right hand are pleasures forevermore. Ps. 16:11.

Researchers at a prestigious Eastern university researched motivating factors in monkeys. Choosing a male monkey for the experiment, they placed him in a cage and began a process of carefully recorded observations. They observed the monkey's eating, sleeping, and mating patterns. They watched how this monkey cared for his young.

They then hooked an electrode to the monkey's brain, which when stimulated could give the monkey a sensation of pleasure. The researcher taught the monkey how to push the pleasure button. The monkey now had the key to happiness—a pleasure button.

The monkey soon became obsessed with pleasure, ignoring his young, his food, and even his mate. The highest goal for the monkey was pleasure, stimulating the nerve endings, doing what made him feel good. Finally he knocked himself out having fun. The excessive stimulation killed the monkey.

Sin is an awful lot like the monkey's pleasure button. It does produce an illusion of pleasure. If it didn't, nobody would do it. The problem is that the pleasure is not only short-lived; it is destructive.

Moses chose rather "to suffer affliction with the people of God than to enjoy the passing pleasures of sin" (Heb. 11:25). Sin's pleasures pass quickly, leaving us empty. When the bubble bursts, discouragement floods the soul. Fortunately, Jesus' joy is eternal. God's deep, inner joy lasts. The psalmist called God his "exceeding joy" (Ps. 43:4). Isaiah testifies that God will give us the "oil of joy for mourning" (Isa. 61:3). Jeremiah called God's Word "the joy and rejoicing of my heart" (Jer. 15:16). Jesus says that His joy remains in us (John 15:11). Paul prays that his readers will be filled with "all joy and peace in believing" (Rom. 15:13). James says we can even "count it all joy" when we have trials (James 1:2).

When our Lord returns, He will say, "Well done, good and faithful servant; you were faithful over a few things, I will make you ruler over many things. Enter into the joy of your lord" (Matt. 25:21).

Our Lord offers much more than a temporary, short-lived, illusionary pleasure. He offers the deep, lasting joy of His presence now and through all eternity. One thing is certain—there is no joy like this joy anywhere.

August 13

SAFELY HOME

Being confident of this very thing, that He who has begun a good work in you will complete it until the day of Jesus Christ. Phil. 1:6.

I grew up on the coast of Long Island Sound in Connecticut. I remember the long, hot, sticky days of summer, especially the Sundays. Sundays Dad took us boating from Spicers Marina in Groton, Connecticut, along the New England coast.

Mom, Dad, my sisters, and I packed into our 16-foot boat. Dad faithfully obeyed the "No Wake" signs, guiding our little craft past cabin cruisers, yachts, and New England whalers.

Once we hit the open sea, Dad opened up and gunned the engine. Here he was master of the sea, leaving the stress of his machine shop behind.

Hair flying, salt breezes biting our faces, yelling, screaming as we hit the waves, we listened to Dad shout, "Ah, this is life! Ain't this something, kids?"

One day Dad and I fished off the New England coast. Fog began to settle in. The breeze picked up as storm clouds threatened on the horizon. For almost an hour we fought the elements. The waves shoved us toward rocks. I can still picture Dad, rain pouring off his weather-beaten face. Dad knew the sea well—there was nothing for me to fear. I had complete confidence that my dad would get me home safely. My eyes were not on the storm—they were on Dad.

In the storms of your life, refocus your vision. The book of Hebrews urges us to look "unto Jesus, the author and finisher of our faith" (Heb. 12:2).

God tells us in Isaiah, "Look to Me and be saved, all you ends of the earth! For I am God, and there is no other" (Isa. 45:22). Someone has said, "When we look around us, our trouble grows; when we look to God our trouble goes." Ellen White wrote, "'Looking unto Jesus' is ever to be our motto" (*Testimonies*, vol. 7, p. 94).

Life is filled with problems and challenges. Looking to God turns our troubles into opportunities for Him to work. We place our confidence not in our ability but in His. When a storm on Long Island Sound almost sank my family's small boat, I knew I could never get us safely home, but I was sure Dad could.

Today place your confidence in a loving heavenly Father. Whatever your circumstances, He will get you home.

RECEIVING BY GIVING

It is more blessed to give than to receive. Acts 20:35.

When I was a boy we sometimes played a simple game with a ball. One person stood on one side of the house, another person on the other. The first person attempted to throw the ball over the house. The second tried to catch it! In the beginning my arm was too weak to throw the ball high enough. The ball would go up to the top of the roof and roll back. It went up and back, up and back, up and back.

Some people's Christian experience is like that—up and down, up and down. They attempt to pray, they study the Bible regularly, but it seems there is no life to their Christian experience.

Is it possible to attend church consistently, feasting on a spiritual banquet each week, and still die of a spiritual heart attack? Without a clear focus on service, our spiritual arteries become clogged. For this reason Jesus said, "It is more blessed to give than to receive" (Acts 20:35).

In giving we are blessed. As we share with others what Jesus has done for us, our own spiritual experience is strengthened. The more we give away our faith, the more our faith grows. It grows when we share it.

Ellen White wrote, "If you will go to work as Christ designs that His disciples shall, and win souls for Him, you will feel the need of a deeper experience and a greater knowledge in divine things, and will hunger and thirst after righteousness. You will plead with God, and your faith will be strengthened, and your soul will drink deeper drafts at the well of salvation" (*Steps to Christ,* p. 80). "Those who would be overcomers must be drawn out of themselves; and the only thing which will accomplish this great work is to become intensely interested in the salvation of others" (*Fundamentals of Christian Education,* p. 207).

If you want a growing Christian experience, share your faith. Make a prayer list. Begin praying for your family members, neighbors, or work associates who don't know Christ. Share truth-filled literature with people God leads into your life. The Lord may lead you to open your home for a small group Bible study. He may open the door for you to give Bible studies to a close friend. The Lord may even lead you to conduct your own evangelistic series.

However God leads you, be sensitive to His leading. You will be utterly amazed at how you grow spiritually by getting involved in sharing your faith. When we witness to others, the soul we save may very well be our own, for it is always "more blessed to give than to receive."

August 15

DEFLATING OUR FEARS

There is no fear in love; but perfect love casts out fear, because fear involves torment. But he who fears has not been made perfect in love. 1 John 4:18.

I want to tell you about one man who discovered that God's love breaks through our worst fears.

Al Kasha told his friends that he had to be alone in order to be creative. What they didn't know was that he had to be alone in order to survive. Crowds terrified him. Out in a restaurant or at a supermarket he'd start to hyperventilate, his heart would palpitate, and his hands would perspire. The panic attacks would send him rushing home.

Al had become agoraphobic, afraid to go out anywhere, a prisoner in his own home.

It all started after he made it big as a songwriter, with 13 gold albums and two Academy Awards. Wrote Al, "I had created a life based on doing and having and achieving to the point that I had a nervous breakdown."

Al began systematically constricting his life. One morning when he was at a particularly low point, Al flipped on the TV. A minister quoted the Bible verse "Perfect love casts out fear" (1 John 4:8). Those words went straight to Al's heart. He listened intently as the minister talked about God's kind of acceptance.

Al Kasha began weeping and crying out to God. As he prayed he heard a voice say, "I love you, and you are My son."

Strengthened by God's love, he was finally able to respond positively to his overwhelming fears. Al's compressed life expanded within the security of God's presence.

Fear often results from feeling out of control. We are afraid of the unknown, about what might happen. But when we open our hearts to God's love, He gradually dissolves our fears.

There is security in God's love. We are not in control, but He is. There is a sense that He loves us and desires only our best. Ellen White wrote, "His love is as far above all other love as the heavens are above the earth. He watches over His children with a love that is measureless and everlasting" (*The Ministry of Healing*, p. 482). His "measureless and everlasting" love gives us complete confidence that our lives are in His hands.

You can trust in His love today. You can rest in His love right now. Be assured that His love will indeed cast out all fear.

THE GOD OF SURPRISES

With men this is impossible, but with God all things are possible. Matt. 19:26.

The Resurrection story speaks of the God of the unexpected. The empty tomb speaks of the God of unexpected blessings. He is the God of possible impossibilities, or, to state it another way, God makes the impossible possible.

Picture this scene: As the sun rises over Jerusalem, painting the horizon in fiery crimson, the two Marys quickly hasten to the place of Jesus' burial to perform a very common task. It isn't hope that leads the women through the quiet cobblestone streets that Sunday morning. It is duty. Naked devotion. They are going to the tomb to give, expecting nothing in return. The last time they saw Jesus' body, it was broken, bruised, battered, and bloodied. There was no pulse or heartbeat. His lifeless body was cold and still. The two Marys were simply doing a task that needed to be done with no thought of receiving anything in return. We, too, are called to give, expecting no thanks. We are kind for kindness sake. We serve for service sake. There are times when we do a task simply because it needs to be done. When we do, God notices. He knows our commitment. He sees our faithful service.

As the two Marys approached the tomb, God was about to do something amazing. He is the God of unexpected surprises. The stone was rolled away. The tomb was empty. Christ had risen. In the course of doing their duty, they were the first to see the empty tomb. They were the first to witness the miracle of the Resurrection. They were the first to bear witness of the resurrected Christ.

When we do our duty, God surprises us. When we unselfishly do what needs to be done because it needs to be done, God amazes us. He moves the stones in our way. He opens doors of opportunity. He works unexpected miracles. Most miracles occur when we least expect them. They take place when honest-hearted people of faith commit themselves to follow the living Christ at all costs. When they do, the God of the unexpected miraculously works to roll away the stones. Look for His unexpected blessings in your life today.

THY WILL BE DONE

O My Father, . . . not as I will, but as You will. Matt. 26:39.

One central truth makes anything we have to fear bearable: God is our loving heavenly Father. This may be hard to grasp for those whose earthly fathers were harsh, abusive, or nonexistent. But rightly understood, it is the core of Scripture.

A loving father's hand will never cause His children needless pain or a needless tear. Trials surround us and heartaches rip us apart, but the Father's love is constant.

Jesus accepted the constancy of a Father's love in His greatest night of trial. In the midst of Gethsemane's sorrow He cried out, "Father, Thy will be done." Jesus accepted that His Father always planned the best. He could give up His plans and accept the Father's, because He trusted a heart of divine love. This is not to say that all of life's sorrow, suffering, and sickness is good. It is to say "God is always good."

Life may not be fair, but God is. When, like Jesus, we don't understand, we can trust. Through it all we can say "Thy will be done." How we say it makes all the difference. There are four ways to say it.

First, I can say it in hopeless submission, as one so overpowered that it seems useless to fight. For example, in the grip of terminal illness I can say "Thy will be done," and say it in hopeless resignation.

Second, I can say it as one who has been battered into submission. The pressures of life have become too great. This is the call of one who is defeated because the enemy is too powerful—like a defeated army general who says, "Here's my sword; your will be done."

Third, I can say it as one who is utterly frustrated, who sees their dreams broken and smashed. The words may be of regret, of bitter anger.

Or I can say it with the confidence of perfect trust. This is how Jesus said it. He was speaking to one who was His Father—to one who held His hand, one who had His everlasting arms beneath. He was submitting to a love that would not let Him go. He was absolutely resigned to the Father's will because in the long run He knew it was best.

We can submit to that same love today. It didn't let Jesus go, and it won't let us go either. We can say, "Thy will be done," because we know His will is always best.

THE DEPTH OF GOD'S LOVE

Oh, love the Lord, all you His saints! Ps. 31:23.

In one of the most profound passages in the New Testament, Paul states, "For He [God] made Him [Christ] who knew no sin to be sin for us, that we might become the righteousness of God in Him" (2 Cor. 5:21).

God made Christ to be sin for us. Did Jesus ever sin? Did He ever think an evil thought or commit a sinful act? Certainly not!

But He who knew no sin *became* sin. What does this mean? It means that Jesus was accused and condemned for sins *we* committed. How is this possible? Only through love.

We don't need a theological definition of the cross as much as we need to understand its practical realities. Our great need is to experience its transforming power. Understanding what Jesus really suffered helps us comprehend its deeper message. As Paul wrote, "Christ has redeemed us from the curse of the law, having become a curse for us (for it is written, 'Cursed is everyone who hangs on a tree' ") (Gal. 3:13).

Christ has redeemed us from the curse of the law. What is the curse of the law? Death. Is it the first death—or the second death? The first death is the death the entire human race dies as the result of the corporate sin of humanity. When Adam and Even sinned, this world was plunged into death and separated from God, the source of life.

If the death of Christ on the cross is for only our physical death, we have no salvation. Sin also necessitates the second death, which is banishment forever from the presence of God.

For us, Jesus was willing to be banished from the presence of God forever. He was willing to bear all of sin's horrible guilt and condemnation for us (Heb. 2:9). "The Saviour could not see through the portals of the tomb. . . . He feared that sin was so offensive to God that Their separation was to be eternal" (*The Desire of Ages*, p. 753). It is this incredible love that breaks our hearts. It changes our lives. The thought that Jesus would be lonely in heaven without us is overwhelming. The thought that He would rather be lost than have us miss heaven is the most amazing in all of the universe. There is nothing like it in any religion in the world except Christianity. No other religion has an unselfish, loving God who gives His own life to redeem His people.

All we can do is sing with the angels, "Worthy is the Lamb who was slain" (Rev. 5:12). All we can do is fall at His feet and worship Him.

JOY IN THE MORNING

Weeping may endure for a night, but joy comes in the morning. Ps. 30:5.

It was Friday—dark, dark Friday. They nailed Him to the cross on Friday and put a crown of thorns on His head—on Friday. They put a spear wound in His side—on Friday. Judas betrayed Him. Peter denied Him. The disciples forsook Him. The Jews rejected Him, and the Romans crucified Him.

The sun veiled its face. The earth quaked and the heavens roared. It was Friday—dark, dark Friday.

We all have our dark Fridays, days when nothing seems to go right. But for Jesus and for us, Resurrection morning was coming. Beyond the rejection, the betrayal, and the despair, Resurrection morning was on its way. Beyond the agony, the blood, and the tears, a glorious new day would dawn.

The sun rose on Resurrection morning. The birds sang, and the Father spoke, "Son, Your Father calls You."

Legions of Roman soldiers could not hold Him down now. In the brightness of heaven's angels, they fell over like dead men. The stone sealing the entrance rolled away like a pebble as the Son of God burst the bonds of the tomb. The shackles of death could not hold Him.

There is hope in despair. There is joy in the morning. Although there are dark, dark Fridays, the Resurrection points us to a glorious new day. Our Lord says, "Behold, I will do a new thing" (Isa. 43:19).

Whatever experience you are going through right now, there is hope. The resurrected Christ wants to do a "new thing" in your life. You may be going through despair. You may be experiencing some deep sorrow. You may face the diagnosis of a malignant tumor. You may have financial or marital difficulty. Your burdens may be so heavy it is difficult for you to bear them. You may even be ready to give up. The resurrected Christ knows. He understands. He is alive and from heaven's sanctuary sends you a message of encouragement today.

Christ speaks in tenderest tones, "I understand. I will strengthen you. Hang on. A better day is coming."

"Weeping may endure for a night, but joy comes in the morning" (Ps. 30:5).

JESUS' HOMECOMING

While they watched, He was taken up, and a cloud received Him out of their sight. Acts 1:9.

A human being steps off a mountain and goes down. The Son of God steps off a mountain and goes up. The Creator is not bound by the laws of His creation. He is going home. Soon He is out of sight of earth and in sight of heaven. As He ascends still higher, He is met by tens of thousands of angelic beings. The Bible actually records the chorus the heavenly choir sang as they greeted their returning Lord. David pictures the scene in Psalm 24.

The angels divide into two groups. One group sings the melody, asking a question, and the other sings a harmonious response. The combined voices of countless angels reverberate throughout all heaven: "Lift up your heads, O you gates! And be lifted up, you everlasting doors! And the King of glory shall come in" (verse 7).

Listen as one group of angels asks in song, "Who is this King of glory?" And another group responds, "The Lord strong and mighty, the Lord mighty in battle" (verse 8). They do not ask "Who is this King of glory?" because they don't know. They want to sing praises to His name. The joyous song echoes and reechoes through the chambers of heaven.

The gates of heaven swing open. Surrounded by the rapturous singing of tens of thousands of adoring angels, Jesus Christ enters into the glorious splendor of heaven. His Father stands before Him with arms wide open. In that magnificent moment, Father and Son are reunited. As they approach one another, in the ecstasy of eternity, a hush falls over heaven. Seraphim and cherubim are silent. The angels prepare to lift their voices again in a rapturous song of praise. But Jesus raises His hands and waves them back. He stands silent before His Father for a moment.

Jesus stands and lifts His nail-scarred hands and says, "Father, I want those whom You have given Me to be with Me where I am. I cannot accept Your warm embrace or the praise of the angels until I know that because of Calvary's cross, because of My sacrifice, My followers on earth will be here with Me someday." The Father replies, "Son, the sacrifice is accepted."

The angels sing anew: "Worthy is the Lamb that was slain" (Rev. 5:12; see *The Desire of Ages*, pp. 833-835).

If Jesus would not accept His Father's embrace until He knew that I could be there, if He loves me that much, I want to be there! I don't want to miss the glorious reunion Jesus is longing for.

Is this the burning desire of your heart too?

August 21

WHAT ARE WE WORTH?

Since you were precious in My sight, you have been honored, and I have loved you. Isa. 43:4.

Jesus reveals God's estimate of human worth in the timeless story of the good shepherd. Once we understand God's estimate of human value, the illusion of low self-worth is burst like a balloon in a carnival shooting range.

"So He spoke this parable to them, saying, 'What man of you, having a hundred sheep, if he loses one of them, does not leave the ninety-nine in the wilderness, and go after the one which is lost until he finds it? And when he has found it, he lays it on his shoulders, rejoicing. And when he comes home, he calls together his friends and neighbors, saying to them, "Rejoice with me, for I have found my sheep which was lost!"'" (Luke 15:3-6).

The Eastern shepherd cares deeply about the sheep. He's willing to leave the comfort and convenience of home to traverse desert sands and to hasten through narrow, rocky ravines with blistered feet, bruised knees, and bloody hands to find the one lost sheep. He climbs over rocks, slides down steep crevices, and wanders through thorns and briars with one thing on his mind—finding the sheep that was lost.

George Adam Smith gives us this picture of the Eastern shepherd:

"On some high moor across which at night the hyenas howl, when you meet him, sleepless, far-sighted, weather-beaten, leaning on his staff and looking out over his scattered sheep, every one of them on his heart, you understand why the shepherd of Judea sprang to the front in his people's history" (William Barclay, *Luke*, p. 207).

This parable tells us three things about Jesus. First, the shepherd was concerned about each individual sheep. Second, he carefully observed that one was missing. And finally, he was willing to go make any personal sacrifice to get his sheep back. What a picture of God! No wonder God likens Himself to an Eastern shepherd. As God looks at the human race, He doesn't see masses of humanity clawing at one another for living space. He sees individuals, each precious in His sight. We are more than skin covering bones—we are the unique creation of God.

The prophet Isaiah encourages us with these words of God: "I am the Lord your God, the Holy One of Israel, your Savior. . . . Since you were precious in My sight, you have been honored, and I have loved you" (Isa. 43:3, 4).

Precious, honorable, and loved! These are God's thoughts toward us. This is how God describes us. We matter to Him. He cares. Now, *that* is something to rejoice about today.

YOU ARE VALUABLE

Who loved me and gave Himself for me. Gal. 2:20.

Picture Jesus in your mind right now, with His hands outstretched. Imagine the cruel, rusty, blunted nails driven through His tender flesh. Imagine the nerves and tendons stretched out tightly on the cross. Imagine the fiery pain that shoots up His arms and the back of His legs as He is suspended between heaven and earth. Imagine the crown of thorns jammed upon His head and the thick blood spurting from His temples and running down His beard. Look into His eyes filled with agony. Listen to His cry of woe. Hear His statements of grief. Feel the pain that shoots through His whole body.

Yet His physical suffering, painful as it was, constitutes only a fraction of His real suffering. The world's guilt, which He bears, shuts Him out from His loving Father. He is judged as a sinner—forsaken, condemned, and accused. On the cross, He is alone. He feels His very soul being torn apart. Separated from His Father, He hangs in agony. Why does He suffer so?

He experiences the pain that sinners will feel at the end of time when totally separated from God. He feels what it would be like to be lost. In those agonizing hours on the cross, He absorbs in Himself all of sin's shame, all of sin's degradation.

At this dark moment Jesus does not see Himself coming through the portals of the tomb. He sees only the blackness of the grave and the horrors of death. But He is willing to experience it all for you and me. Calvary shouts to us, "You are valuable! You are Mine by creation. I have made you. I have fashioned you. You are Mine by redemption. You are more than skin covering bones."

Calvary reveals the immensity of God's love. I like the way the poet puts it:

"Souls of men! why will ye scatter
Like a crowd of frightened sheep?
Foolish hearts, why will ye wander
From a love so true and deep?
Was there ever kindest shepherd
Half so gentle, half so sweet,
As the Saviour who would have us
Come and gather us round his feet? . . .
For the love of God is broader
Than the measure of man's mind.

And the heart of the Eternal,
Is most wonderfully kind."

—Frederick William Faber, 1862

His warm heart of love breaks my cold heart of stone, and I kneel before Him in praise.

August 23

HE KNOWS MY NAME

He counts the number of the stars; He calls them all by name. Ps. 147:4.

If God knows the names of each of the billions of stars, He certainly has not forgotten ours. Have you ever felt lonely? Have you ever felt that no one in the world understood what you were going through at the moment?

Hagar served as a maidservant in Abraham's household. God had promised Abraham many offspring, but his wife, Sarah, was barren and old. Sarah decided she'd help God out of a jam, so she offered Hagar to her husband, and the girl became pregnant.

But the barren wife became more and more jealous of her pregnant servant. Finally Sarah mistreated her so badly that Hagar was forced to flee.

Hagar found herself on the desert road between Kadesh and Bered. She was utterly alone and had no place to go—and she was pregnant. In that sandy wasteland she was nothing. She was a slave with no one to work for, a prospective mother with no family, an Egyptian in wild Canaan.

Finally exhaustion broke through the emotions driving her on. Hagar stopped by a spring to rest. In this moment of total despair and isolation, someone called her by name: "Hagar, servant of Sarah."

Who knew her out there in that wasteland? And who cared? An angel of the Lord did. He asked where she was going. She replied, "I'm running—"

Then God, through this angel, gave Hagar the same kind of promise He'd given her master. He said, "I'll make your descendants too numerous to count." Her baby would be a boy, to be named Ishmael, meaning "God hears."

So Hagar found the strength to survive. She returned to Abraham and Sarah, had her son, and became the mother of the Arab nations. Now, Hagar knew that God wasn't just up in the stars over Abraham; He was down in the desert by her side. And she now called Him "The God who sees me." She knew He'd come close. He'd called her by name.

That's what makes the God of the Bible so special, particularly for lonely people. He calls us by name. He doesn't issue computer-generated form letters. He doesn't just shout from mountaintops. He calls out our name—even in the desert of isolation.

God knows our name. He understands everything about us. And here is some incredibly good news. The one who knows us best loves us most.

August 24

HOW OFTEN SHALL I FORGIVE?

Lord, how often shall my brother sin against me, and I forgive him? Up to seven times? Matt. 18:21.

I think we'll be indebted to Peter through all eternity. Peter speaks for us all. There is something about his humanness that I really like. I can identify with his experience. You probably can too. Peter is no isolated saint sitting in some monastery praying all day. In the rub of life, he speaks his mind. He frankly lets you know where he stands. At times he is impulsive and outspoken. But he's always honest.

One day Peter came to Jesus and asked an important question. "Master," he said, "if my brother sins against me, how often shall I forgive him?" Before waiting for Jesus' answer, Peter went ahead and answered his own question: "Seven times?" (Matt. 18:21). To Peter seven was an extravagant figure. He assumed Jesus would applaud him for his willingness to forgive.

The rabbis had a saying: "If a person sins against you once, forgive him. If he sins against you twice, forgive him. If he sins against you three times, forgive him. If he sins against you four times, repay him for his sin." They thought that three times was enough to forgive anybody. After that, mercy was exhausted. Justice demanded retribution.

The first-century rabbi Hanna wrote, "He who forgives his neighbor must not do so beyond three times." Rabbinical law required justice after the third offense.

Peter thought that to forgive a brother seven times was akin to Godlike perfection. He took forgiveness far beyond the limited Pharisaic idea. Seven is more than double the number of times the rabbis were willing to forgive. Seven is the number of perfection.

Imagine Peter's astonishment when Jesus said, "I do not say to you, up to seven times, but up to seventy times seven" (verse 22). How could anyone forgive someone who wronged them a whopping 490 times? Our loving heavenly Father did. He mercifully bore with the Jews for centuries, extending His mercy again and again and again. He sent them prophet after prophet, messenger after messenger. Then He sent His own Son, and they crucified Him. Patiently He offered forgiveness, yet continually Israel rebelled.

Jesus wanted Peter to understand this vital truth, and He longs for us to understand it too: Forgiveness is not measured by the number of times someone wrongs you. Forgiveness is rooted in God's very nature. It is an attitude of mercy. It holds no grudges. It harbors no resentment. It forgives because forgiveness is the right thing to do. It is Godlike.

Has someone wronged you, wounding you deeply? In Jesus' name do the Christlike thing. Forgive them today.

August 25

THE SMITTEN FACE

Then they spat in His face and beat Him; and others struck Him with the palms of their hands. Matt. 26:67.

It seems incomprehensible that vile human beings would treat the Son of God with such disrespect. Think of it—they actually spit on the face of the Son of God, the one worshiped by ten thousand times ten thousand angels. The face of the one who existed with the Father from all eternity and joined Him in hanging the worlds in space.

The Bible says, "They spat in His face and beat Him; and others struck Him with the palms of their hands" (Matt. 26:67).

Who is this whom they strike? Who is this who suffers so? Who is this who endures such agony? Who is this with the blackened eyes and the bloody face? It is Jesus, the divine Son of God. Puny human beings, created by the living God, approached the Creator and struck Him in the face. Cursing and swearing, they mocked Him.

In a sense I was there, and so were you. All humanity was there that night in the shadows in Pilate's courtyard. We slapped Him in the face, because every departure from right and every deed of cruelty brings sorrow to His heart.

When I know better and I willingly turn my back on Him today, I bring grief to Him. When I know better and I am dishonest, when I know better and I openly lie, when I know better and I lose my temper and get angry, when I know better and lustful thoughts dominate my mind, I rebel against Him still. I bring Him heartache. The one who loves me so, the one who endured the suffering on the cross so I wouldn't have to suffer eternally, suffers still when I rebel against Him.

So in the shadows I come to that cross and say, "O Lord, I lay down my weapons of warfare. I surrender everything I have and everything I am to You. I want to bring joy to Your heart today. Here at the cross I give myself away."

August 26

A CALLOUS HEART BROKEN

The centurion and those with him . . . feared greatly, saying, Truly this was the Son of God! Matt. 27:54.

It was a violent age, in a violent land, among a violent people—and he was a violent man. The Roman centurion was a hard-hearted, callous, rough fighter, a soldier of fortune always on guard for the unexpected ambush. He was truly an unlikely prospect for the kingdom of God. As superintendent of executions, his heart was hardened.

Friday morning he received orders to carry out the execution. His only thoughts: *Let's be on with it—let's be done with it!*

"Move over, you weeping women!" he shouted. "You, there! Get back!"

The Scripture calls him a centurion, the commander of 100 soldiers. He was amazed that Jesus offered no resistance. Christ's suffering only revealed His kingly glory.

The centurion was a hardened military man. He was schooled to win. There is a little of the centurion in us all. At times we defensively fight to protect our little kingdoms. Conflicting opinions become battlegrounds between people. But there was something different about Jesus.

Something about Jesus attracted his attention. Jesus' look of pain gave way to serene trust. Each time He moved His head on the rough cross, the wooden bar pressed the thorns more deeply into His forehead, but He uttered no word of complaint. The nails tore ever-widening, gaping holes in His hands and feet, yet no curses flowed from His lips.

The centurion listened as the Savior prayed, "Father, forgive them" (Luke 23:34). As he beheld the drama unfolding before him something pulled him out of himself. He was being drawn to this man.

The centurion may have recalled Pilate's judgment hall. Jesus was mighty in weakness. His cross was His throne. His crown of thorns was His diadem of glory.

There at the cross the centurion exclaimed, "Truly this was the Son of God."

Even the centurion was changed by the power of God. Jesus took that cruel, callous, unfeeling Roman officer, and changed him into another man.

A *callous* man became a *converted* man. A *hard-hearted* man became a *tender, sensitive* man.

Jesus is still in the business of transforming calloused hearts. His love still conquers our pride. Why not allow Him to do it for you today?

August 27

SATAN'S RETIREMENT SALE

O you of little faith, why did you doubt? Matt. 14:31.

I would like you to attend an imaginary auction with me. Here is the scene. Satan has just announced his retirement to his evil angels. To raise adequate retirement money, he decides to auction off the formulas for various sinful behaviors.

The auction proceeds all morning and long into the afternoon. Satan shouts, "I have the formula for lying. What do you bid for it? Here is the special formula for dishonesty. What will you give me? Castles, palaces, country estates? When we overthrow the world and reign, what will you give me for the formula for greed or pride? What? Yes, what is your bid?"

Each formula is stored in a special golden jar surrounded by a hazy mist. Soon all the jars are sold . . . except one. The evil angels shout, "You must sell that one, too! We'll give our richest palaces in exchange for it."

"No," Satan replies. "This one formula is used for professed Christians. It works almost every time. When they are under its spell, they have no defense against sin."

"At least tell us what it is," the evil angels persist.

"It is doubt," Satan responds. "This formula deceives Christians into doubting God's love. It's my most powerful weapon. I will never sell this formula, because if I can get Christians to live in a world of uncertainty and doubt, I can lead them to commit any other sin. When they lack assurance, they are vulnerable."

Satan repeatedly used this formula on Jesus in the wilderness. He would preface his challenges to Christ with "If You are the Son of God . . ."

"Is it really true," he was implying, "that You are God's Son? Look at You, Jesus. You are haggard, worn, and hungry. Your emaciated form and filthy, ragged garments betray You. You certainly cannot be the Son of God."

Doubt was Satan's strategy then, and it is his strategy now. "Satan is ready to steal away the blessed assurances of God. He desires to take every glimmer of hope and every ray of light from the soul; but you must not permit him to do this" (*Steps to Christ*, p. 53).

Daily fill your mind with thoughts of God's love. Think, *God loves me, and I am His child. He doesn't want me to be lost. He will never let me go.*

God is speaking directly to me when He says in Jeremiah 31:3, "I have loved you with an everlasting love." And I will stake my life on it.

MUCH MORE JESUS

When they had lifted up their eyes, they saw no one but Jesus only. Matt. 17: 8.

Eliza Hewitt knew what it was like to experience tragedy. Her career as a public school teacher ended when an unruly student struck her with a heavy blackboard slate. Eliza suffered a severe spinal cord injury and was never able to teach again.

While recovering from her injury, she turned to the promises of God that had been fulfilled in Jesus Christ. She was amazed at how accurately Old Testament prophecy pointed forward to the Messiah. In her distress she discovered a vital new relationship with Jesus. Overcome with emotion, she penned this well-known gospel song:

"More about Jesus I would know,
More of His grace to others show;
More of His saving fullness see,
More of His love who died for me.
More, more about Jesus, more, more about Jesus . . ."

Whatever we know about Jesus, there is always much more to know. Whatever experience we have with Jesus, there is always much more to experience. The apostle Paul regularly used the expression "much more." He seems to be filled with wonder when he says, "Much more then, having now been justified by His blood, we shall be saved from wrath through Him" (Rom. 5:9). He continues, "Much more, having been reconciled, we shall be saved by His life" (Rom. 5:10).

In verse 15 he exclaims, "Much more the grace of God . . . abounded to many." Paul uses the expression "much more" at least 10 times in his writings. For him there is always much more grace, much more forgiveness, much more pardon, much more righteousness, much more of Jesus.

Jesus' love is infinite. The "unsearchable riches of Christ" speak (Eph. 3:8). The "pearl of great price" speaks (Matt. 13:46). The "treasure hidden in a field" speaks (verse 44). They invite us to search His Word, to discover the "much more" He has to offer. His gems do not lie on the surface. "Deep calls unto deep" (Ps. 42:7).

God is calling each of us to a relationship with Jesus that goes beyond the surface. The deeps of God are calling us to much more, much, much more of His grace than we can imagine.

MUCH MORE GRACE

He gives more grace. James 4:6.

Our security in Christ is not based on our performance or behavior. We don't gain security through doing good things. If we base our security on our works, we will constantly wonder if we have done enough. Our security comes from what Christ has done for us—the life He lived; the death He died.

And once we accept our security in Christ, He helps us to grow in Him as well. As we surrender our will to Him He begins in us the work of developing a Christlike character, and what He begins, He finishes! He is the "author and finisher of our faith" (Heb. 12:2).

Suppose I am in the first grade at elementary school. Each student in the school has different learning abilities and problem-solving skills, but if we faithfully do the lessons the teacher assigns, in time we will graduate. Likewise, if I faithfully accept the lessons my heavenly Father assigns me, I will grow in knowledge and character. He will see to it that I "graduate."

A seasoned old preacher once stated it well when he said, "You're 'once saved, always saved,' *if* you *stay saved.*"

My son is just as much my son when he makes mistakes as when he doesn't. Of course, he can choose to separate himself from the family. He has the right to change his name. He is free to leave home at any time. But he will always remain my son. He has the assurance that I will not angrily throw him out of the home simply because he has failed.

God does not cast off Christians when they fail. When we fail, God leads us to deep repentance. But failure does not make us less dear to the heart of God. Failure does not disqualify us for God's grace—it is our very failure that *qualifies* us for His grace! God's grace is *reserved* for failures, for sinners, for those of us who are weak.

"If in our ignorance we make missteps, the Savior does not forsake us. . . . Satan may come to you with the cruel suggestion, 'Yours is a hopeless case. You are irredeemable.' But there is hope for you in Christ. . . . When sin struggles for the mastery in the heart, when guilt oppresses the soul and burdens the conscience, when unbelief clouds the mind, remember that Christ's grace is sufficient to subdue sin and banish the darkness" (*The Ministry of Healing,* pp. 249, 250).

His grace is greater than our sin. In Him there is always much more grace than we will ever need. Heaven's supply never runs out.

MUCH MORE LOVE

Love never fails. 1 Cor. 13:8.

In 1985 my wife and I and our three children, Debbie, Rebecca, and Mark, Jr., moved from Chicago, Illinois, to St. Albans, England. There I served as ministerial secretary for the Trans-European Division of Seventh-day Adventists.

When we moved to England, my wife and I found driving on the left-hand side of the road difficult. And the first few times out on the road, the English roundabouts nearly scared us to death.

One day, getting up her courage, my wife drove alone to Watford, a small city not far from our home. It was just before Christmas, and the streets were absolutely packed with shoppers. Our son, Mark, about 7 at the time, got lost. My wife panicked. For 15 minutes she searched, calling frantically. Quickly she organized groups of passers-by to form a search party.

Who was putting more effort into the search, my wife or my boy? Did she idly say, "Look, son, you pulled your hand out of mine. You wandered away from me. You are lost, and I hope you find your way back. If you do, fine, and if you don't, that's your problem." Not at all! Nothing else mattered except finding our son.

I am convinced that God wants to find us more than we want to find Him.

Romans 8:30 joyfully proclaims the good news: "Moreover whom He predestined, these He also called." Not only has God predesigned a plan to save you, He actively calls you to accept that plan. God is the good Samaritan who comes seeking us as we lie bruised and bleeding on the highway of life. He cradles us in His arms, whispers encouragement in our ears, and, at infinite expense to Himself, takes us to the inn of safety (see Luke 10).

Yes, God is a seeking God. In Christ He has taken the initiative.

There is only one thing our wonderful Lord does not have unless we give it to Him—our love. He is lonely for our affection. He is seeking you today. He longs for you much more than you could possibly know. There was a joyous reunion that day on the streets of Watford, England, when my wife eventually found our son, and there will be a joyous reunion one day when we fall into the arms of the one who has been searching for us all along.

MUCH MORE TRUTH

His truth shall be your shield. Ps. 91:4.

Cult leaders tend to distort truth. Their interpretation of truth becomes the standard for their followers.

David Koresh made up his own rules. He claimed that as a type of King David, he had the right to take the wives of his followers. People accepted this man's bizarre beliefs as truth.

Jim Jones made up his own rules. He claimed that mass suicide was the way to get ready for the apocalypse. Jones's followers drank poisoned Kool-Aid and became victims of lawlessness.

Members of the Heaven's Gate cult became victims in the same way. They accepted their leader's teachings about a comet rescue as absolute truth—and killed themselves.

All cults are based on human wisdom, not God's truth. The antichrist principle exalts human reasoning above divine revelation. Satan works to distort truth, but God works to make it plain. Satan works to confuse people, but God works to instruct them. Satan delights in darkness, but God delights in light.

"The path of the just is like the shining sun, that shines ever brighter unto the perfect day" (Prov. 4:18). The more we walk with Jesus, the clearer His truth becomes. His word is "a lamp to [our] feet and a light to [our] path" (Ps. 119:105).

The Holy Spirit is eager to reveal God's light and truth to our hearts. His light dispels darkness. His truth overwhelms error. His truth is the antidote to deception.

Ellen White wrote, "None but those who fortified their mind with the truths of the Bible will stand through the last great conflict" (*The Great Controversy,* pp. 593, 594).

We have not seen the last David Koresh-, Jim Jones-, or Heaven's Gate-style cult. More leaders and groups like these will arise. The good news is that God's truth is stronger than error. As we daily fill our minds with His Word, we have a mighty shield of defense against the devil's fiery darts of deception. Truth is God's protective wall of defense against the enemy. God's smooth stones of truth slay the Goliaths of error. Fill your mind with truth and watch the giants fall.

MUCH MORE GLORIOUS

I will meditate on the glorious splendor of Your majesty, and on Your wondrous works. Men shall speak of the might of Your awesome acts, and I will declare Your greatness. Ps. 145:5, 6.

The story is told of Marco Polo, the Italian explorer who returned home from China after spending more than 20 years in the Orient. His incredible tales made his friends fear he'd gone crazy.

He said that he had traveled to a city full of silver and gold. That he had seen black stones that burned (they hadn't heard of coal). That he'd seen cloth that refused to catch fire when thrown into the flames (they hadn't heard of asbestos). He talked of huge serpents, 10 paces long, with jaws wide enough to swallow a man (they hadn't seen a crocodile). He told of nuts the size of a man's head (they had never seen coconuts).

Most of his countrymen just laughed at such stories. Years later, as Marco Polo lay dying, a devout man at his bedside urged him to recant all the tall tales he'd told. Marco refused. "It's true," he declared, "every bit of it, and the half has not been told."

The Bible writers could say the same about Jesus: the half has not been told.

He is the Alpha and the Omega, the beginning and the end. He is the way, the truth, and the life. He is the Good Shepherd, the Lion of the tribe of Judah, and the slain Lamb. He is the Rock of Ages, the Bright and Morning Star, the Pearl of Great Price, and the Rose of Sharon. He is the Bread of Life, the Living Water, and the Sun of righteousness.

Jesus opens blind eyes, unstops deaf ears, and heals withered arms. He makes the mute sing and the lame walk. He changes lives, and He is resurrected from the dead. He ascended to heaven, and He is coming again.

The entire Bible testifies of this glorious Christ (John 5:39). Whatever is said about Him, there is much more to say. A million biographies wouldn't tell a fraction of His story. The most magnificent symphony can't begin to tell of His glory. The world's greatest musicians can't write a song to describe His magnificence. The most gifted artist can't portray His splendor.

Throughout all eternity we will learn more of His glorious majesty. For the half has not been told. The good news is that right now we can keep drinking from heaven's fountain and learn to know Him more and more—much more.

September 2

MUCH MORE HOPE

But if we hope for what we do not see, we eagerly wait for it with perseverance. Rom. 8:25.

He was one of the world's most remarkable communicators. Accomplished in 14 languages, he shared his faith with Turks, Hindus, Armenians, and Syrians. He testified before sheiks, shahs, kings, queens, and American presidents.

Joseph Wolff was a Bavarian who traveled to London, where he studied the Bible in depth with several evangelical friends. He became convinced that the blessed hope of the return of Christ was the ultimate solution to humanity's problems. He became the first great herald of the second coming of Jesus in modern times. Wolff, along with other preachers of the Second Advent, led a significant portion of the world into an amazing spiritual awakening.

Joseph Wolff really believed the return of our Lord was near. The Advent hope changed his life. He did not merely preach it or teach it or say it—he believed it deep within the fabric of his being. This one great hope drove him to cross continents in his missionary endeavors. It propelled him beyond the cold, traditional religion of his day.

He found something much better—a genuine spiritual power in the hope of our Lord's return. This hope led him to repentance and sorrow for anything that might keep him from being prepared to meet his Lord. He devoted himself to deeper Bible study and prayer lest he not understand God's last-day truths. Joseph Wolff traveled more widely than almost any European of his day. He held discussions with Bedouins near Cairo; he proclaimed the gospel to Turks in Alexandria; he testified to Arab chieftains after being captured by bandits; and he studied the Scriptures with Jewish rabbis throughout the Middle East.

He was once sold as a slave, and was condemned to death three times. He was a devoted scholar who was able to penetrate Islam with the gospel. He was fluent in Hebrew and proclaimed the message of the coming Messiah to the Jews as well.

Does the blessed hope make a difference in your life? Do you live any differently because of your belief in the second coming of Jesus? If you knew that Jesus was coming tomorrow, would you do anything differently?

Down through the corridors of time the witness of one life speaks. Be passionate about the coming of the Lord. Let the hope and joy of His soon return fill your soul. The King is at the door, and that really should make a difference in how we live.

HEALTH IS NOT A MATTER OF CHOICE

Present your bodies a living sacrifice, holy, acceptable to God, which is your reasonable service. Rom. 12:1.

In his book *Proof Positive,* Dr. Neil Nedley tells a fascinating story of how to combat disease and achieve optimum health. Dr. Nedley was giving a treadmill test to a patient he suspected had coronary heart disease. Harold, the patient, looked up and said, "Doctor, I really don't think it matters how I check out on the test today. We each have a time we are going to die; that time is set, and there is nothing we can do about it."

Harold believed that God determines if you live or die. When God calls your number, it's up. There is nothing you can do about it. Harold's thoughts are not unique. Many people believe health is a matter of chance. It's like rolling the dice.

An abundance of scientific evidence proves this theory totally false. It fails to take into account how our own personal lifestyle choices affect our health. Research clearly demonstrates the relationship between faulty living habits and increased disease.

I am convinced that God wants to build our health up and the devil wants to destroy it. The apostle John stated God's desire for us this way: "Beloved, I pray that you may prosper in all things and be in health, just as your soul prospers" (3 John 2). Ellen White wrote, "The health should be as sacredly guarded as the character" (*Child Guidance,* p. 343).

Jesus is the restorer. His New Testament miracles clearly reveal His longing to keep us in good health. Satan is a deceiver and destroyer. He carefully plans to destroy our health. The evil one deceives people into defiling their bodies and thinking it makes little difference to their spiritual health. They accept the temporary pleasure of some physical indulgence—drugs, alcohol, tobacco, junk food, or sexual immorality—and in the process destroy both their bodies and their souls. The relationship between the mind and the body is so intimate that any physical habit that affects the body also affects the mind.

God desires that we be healthy, but not simply because He wants us to live a fuller, longer, more abundant, disease-free life. He certainly wants that, but health is not an end in itself. Health is not some super goal to be achieved so I can say I am healthy. One purpose of a healthy body is to have a clear mind so we can know God better, so our minds can comprehend His will and hear His voice. Another is so we can serve others more effectively. God longs for us to live healthful, productive lives, knowing Him and joyfully ministering to others. Our health is a priority with God, and He desires that it become a priority with us, too.

September 4

COMPELLING CONSCIENCE

Elijah came to all the people, and said, "How long will you falter between two opinions? If the Lord is God, follow Him." 1 Kings 18:21.

Dr. Stanley Milgram conducted experiments to discover just how far a person will go in causing pain to another individual. His experiments contain significant lessons for those of us living at the end of time.

The experiments were conducted some years ago at Yale University. Advertisements asked for 500 male volunteers, who were placed in pairs.

The two men were told that they were participating in a study on the effects of punishment on learning. One was to be the teacher and the other the learner. Participants were allowed to draw to see which role each would play.

The drawing was rigged. The actor always played the role of the learner. The teacher and learner were in separate rooms, but the teacher could observe that the learner was hooked up to what seemed to be an electrode. The teacher was instructed to administer an electric shock to the learner whenever he made a mistake and to increase the voltage with each new mistake.

In reality, the actor received no shocks at all, but pretended to endure greater and greater pain as part of the experiment. When the voltage was raised to 75 volts, he would act as if he had been mildly hurt. At 120 volts he would begin to complain, and at 150 volts he would demand that the experiment stop. If the "teacher" continued to administer shocks, at 285 volts the actor would let out agonizing screams.

Many "teachers" would begin to protest when they realized they were injuring another person. They would be ordered to go on. Many of them would continue giving shocks up to the highest levels.

You may think that anybody in his or her right mind wouldn't even give the first shock, but the truth is that almost two thirds of the participants were willing to go to almost any length when commanded to do so. Many went all the way up to 450 volts, no matter how hard the victim begged to be released.

The volunteers were interviewed afterward and asked why they had continued giving the shocks. Almost invariably the answer was the same—because they had been ordered to do it. Many believed that what they were doing was very wrong, but they didn't have the courage to refuse to continue. By the time the experiment was over, they had justified their conduct on the basis that they were simply following orders.

Following orders can be dangerous if they are not God's orders. Listening to the voice of another can be dangerous if it is not God's voice. Anytime we surrender our conviction of right to another person we are in danger of losing our own soul. We risk compromising our integrity anytime our values are shaped by another against our own convictions of conscience.

The words of the prophet Elijah thunder in our ears at this crisis hour of earth's history: "How long will you falter between two opinions? If the Lord is God, follow Him." There is really only one choice. Listen to God's voice and follow it.

September 5

UNMASKING THE DECEIVER

When he speaks a lie, he speaks from his own resources, for he is a liar and the father of it. John 8:44.

In the 1820s the Indian state of Kolhapur was terrorized by a vicious band of thieves. The raja, or ruler, of Kolhapur seemed unable to stop them. This was the era of powerful maharajas who wore exquisite silks and surrounded themselves with gold and gems. The raja had plenty of resources at his disposal, so he increased the size of his personal army. He handpicked guards to surround himself and his valuables. But the band of thieves kept breaking into his treasury and plundering the countryside.

The raja's word was law in the land, and sometimes he would thunder in rage, "These devils must be stopped! I want their leader caught, and I want him killed, and I want him now!" But no one ever did catch the infamous villain. The band went right on stealing and killing for the rest of the raja's life. And that's because the raja of Kolhapur had become a kind of Jekyll and Hyde. By day he was the protective sovereign, calling for law and order. By night he led that band of cutthroat robbers. He plundered his own kingdom and enriched himself.

What an apt description of the father of all lies. Satan is a deceiver. Millennia ago, in the courts of heaven, he spoke with gracious, tender tones, deceiving the angels. He disguised his true purpose, veiling his selfishness under the pretense of doing good. Satan used the same strategy with Eve in Eden. Once again he disguised his true motives. He has used the same tactics generation after generation, disguising evil as good.

Truth shines its searchlight on his evil intents. David prayed, "Let Your lovingkindness and Your truth continually preserve me" (Ps. 40:11). The Holy Spirit is called "The Spirit of truth" (John 16:13). When we study God's Word with a sincere heart, the Holy Spirit impresses its truths upon our minds.

The only way to be kept from Satan's deadly deceptions is to be sensitive to the Spirit's leading. God invites us to submit our minds to His Word and our hearts to doing His will, and to surrender to the guidance of the Holy Spirit. Then, and only then, will we be secure.

September 6

SATAN'S FINAL STRATEGY

"Man of God, there is death in the pot!" And they could not eat it. 2 Kings 4:40.

The early-autumn sun cast its first faint rays across Lake Michigan, beautifully silhouetting the sleeping city of Chicago. The glow of that soft dawning light cast an aura of peace. No one suspected that soon a grisly real-life drama would take place that would stun a whole nation.

Twelve-year-old Mary Kellerman awoke unusually early, complaining of a sore throat and runny nose. Her parents gave her one Extra-Strength capsule and encouraged her to rest. At 7:00 a.m. they found Mary dying on the bathroom floor.

Before the week ended, seven Chicago area residents had died after consuming Tylenol. More would follow.

No one had suspected the medication wasn't safe. No one dreamed that someone, somewhere, somehow had tampered with some capsules, lacing them with cyanide, a poison so deadly it kills within minutes.

This Tylenol tragedy made us all aware of how vulnerable we really are. No one wanted to be deceived by some madman's hoax. We realized as never before that some deceptions are terribly fatal. But how could we know the facts? How could we be safe?

Pharmaceutical companies rushed tamperproof containers onto the market and desperately tried to reassure consumers.

With the forces of evil gaining momentum in the last days of human history, is there any way to tamperproof our lives? Where are we to find protection today?

A significant step is to understand the nature of the poison, the nature of the threat. For centuries a worldwide hoax has deceived millions. A fallen angel has adulterated the truth with the poisonous fallacy that obedience is unnecessary or unimportant. The issue is God's authority. Satan's real motive is found in the expression "I will exalt my throne."

A throne implies rulership. It indicates kingly authority. Lucifer wanted to usurp the authority that belongs only to God. That's why he incited discontent among the angels. Submission to God had become distasteful to him. Satan maintains that the law of God is optional, that we don't have to submit to it. That's what has poisoned so much of our world today. The only solution is a heart submitted completely to God's authority. A mind surrendered totally to God's will, a heart in which Jesus Christ rules supremely. God's ways are indeed best.

As the old gospel hymn says: "Trust and obey, for there's no other way."

September 7

SONGS OF EXPERIENCE, PART 1

The Lord is my strength and song, and He has become my salvation; He is my God, and I will praise Him. Ex. 15:2.

Doom seemed certain. Defeat appeared inevitable. Mountains loomed large on either side. The Red Sea was before them. The Egyptian army breathed down hard upon the Israelites. The fleeing Israelites were quite certain their lives were finished.

Imagine their surprise when the Red Sea opened before them. Imagine their absolute astonishment when after they passed through the sandy passageway, walls of water crashed down upon their enemies, killing them instantly. Safely on the other side of the sea, Moses and all of the children of Israel sang a marvelous song of deliverance.

It was a song of Israel's unique experience. It told of Egypt's defeat. "I will sing to the Lord, for He has triumphed gloriously! . . . The Lord is my strength and song. . . . The Lord is a man of war. . . . Pharaoh's chariots and his army He has cast into the sea" (Ex. 15:1-4). The Israelites acknowledged God's greatness. They had experienced His power firsthand, eyewitnesses of a miracle.

In the problems of life, God is a mighty deliverer. In the impossibilities of life, God is our triumphant conqueror. In the impossibilities of life, God opens the way. In the challenges of life, God has a solution. In the dark night of life, God's light still shines. He still opens the "Red Seas" of our lives, too. He still gives us a song to sing. It probably wasn't always easy for Fanny Crosby to believe God still guides in each aspect of our experience. When she was only 6 weeks old, she lost her sight, largely because of a doctor's error.

Although she was blind, God gave her a new vision. He placed a song in her heart—and not just a song, but more than 8,000 of them. Fanny Crosby, the blind hymn writer, saw much more than the people around her saw. In the eyes of her mind she saw God's amazing mercy, forgiveness, care, power, and love. She once wrote, "I have always believed that the good Lord, in His infinite mercy, by this means [my blindness] consecrated me to the work I am still permitted to do."

Her hymns have blessed generations of Christians. One gospel song that sums up Miss Crosby's philosophy of life is "All the Way." The hymn ends gloriously with the refrain "When I wake to life immortal, wing my flight to realms of day, this my song through endless ages, Jesus led me all the way; this my song through endless ages, Jesus led me all the way."

Along with Fanny Crosby and the ancient Israelites you and I can sing, "This my song through endless ages, Jesus led me all the way."

September 8

SONGS OF EXPERIENCE, PART 2

Even from everlasting to everlasting, You are God. Ps. 90:2.

England faced a crisis. The year was 1714. Queen Anne lay dying. She had no heir in immediate succession to take the throne. The nation stood on the brink of political turmoil.

Famed English hymn writer Isaac Watts wondered what the future held. The previous ruling family had imprisoned his father for his views.

Watts turned to the Psalms for comfort. Psalm 90 was one of his favorites. Of all the psalms this one exalts the eternity of God, while it recalls the frailty of all mankind. The psalmist sings, "Lord, You have been our dwelling place in all generations. Before the mountains were brought forth, or ever You had formed the earth and the world, even from everlasting to everlasting, You are God" (Ps. 90:1, 2).

God is eternal. God is all-wise and all-powerful. He stands above time because He is the author of time. He stands outside all history because He is the ultimate arbiter of heaven's history. Though God allows earthly rulers to make decisions, He is the one shaping the destiny of the nations. He is the one in ultimate control. Solomon echoes this thought in the words "The king's heart is in the hand of the Lord, like the rivers of water; He turns it wherever He wishes" (Prov. 21:1). The prophet Daniel adds, "The Most High rules in the kingdom of men, [and] gives it to whomever He will" (Dan. 4:17).

When events seem out of control, God is still in control. When uncertain circumstances trouble our hearts, God says, "Let not your heart be troubled" (John 14:1). He is still in control. Isaac Watts captured this thought well in his beloved hymn "O God, Our Help in Ages Past." Many Christians believe that of all of Isaac Watts's more than 600 hymns, this is his most sublime.

"O God, our help in ages past,
Our hope for years to come,
Our shelter from the stormy blast,
And our eternal home!
Under the shadow of Thy throne,
Still may we dwell secure;
Sufficient is Thine arm alone,
And our defense is sure."

Here is an eternal truth we can count on, something certain, something stable. God is our shelter, our eternal home. In Him our defense is sure. We can have the absolute confidence that God is in control, so we can sleep well and let Him care for the world.

September 9

SONGS OF EXPERIENCE, PART 3

For He is like a refiner's fire. Mal. 3:2.

In Isaac Watts's day the church in England drifted toward a cold formalism. It was fashionable to attend church. Sunday services were often packed. But the business-as-usual Christianity greatly troubled Isaac Watts. The lethargic state of Christianity deeply concerned him. He knew there was only one way complacent Christians could be shaken out of their spiritual stupor. They needed to experience the fire of the Spirit.

With a pen dipped in the ink of urgency, he wrote:

"Come, Holy Spirit, heavenly Dove,
With all Thy quickening powers;
Kindle a flame of sacred love
In these cold hearts of ours."

One stanza often omitted from the powerful song is the fourth:

"Father, we would no longer live
At this poor dying rate;
To Thee our thankful love we give,
For thine to us is great."

Have you felt your love for Jesus growing cold? Only the fire of the Spirit can rekindle the flame. John the Baptist appealed to the formal religionists of his day to come to Jesus, who "will baptize you with the Holy Spirit and fire" (Matt. 3:11). What is the baptism of fire? Throughout the Bible, fire is a symbol of the presence of God. When Moses was fleeing in the wilderness, he met God at the burning bush. The bush burned, but was not consumed. The fire symbolized the presence of God. The glory of God's presence between the cherubim in the Old Testament sanctuary symbolized God's nearness. The pillar of fire guiding Israel by night symbolized God's presence. The fire that fell from heaven igniting the altar Elijah built on Mount Carmel represented God's presence. The tongues of fire that fell upon the disciples on Pentecost again represented God's presence. The baptism of fire represents immersion in the purifying, life-giving presence of God.

Only one thing can give life to a cold Christian experience. It is the warmth of God's presence. In his book *The Coming of the Comforter*, LeRoy E. Froom writes, "We need that cleansing fire to pass over us and through us—to penetrate every fiber of our being, every chamber of our soul. That is what happened at Pentecost. You recall that before Pentecost the disciples were filled with selfish wrangling, striving for supremacy, seeking for position, striving to exalt self. But after Pentecost self was abased, and Christ alone had first place in thought, in action, and in life" (pp. 276, 277).

Is your prayer for God's cleansing fire? Today may Isaac Watts's prayer "Kindle a flame of sacred love in these hearts of ours" be our own.

September 10

SONGS OF EXPERIENCE, PART 4: JUST AS I AM

If anyone thirsts, let him come to Me and drink. John 7:37.

The hymn "Just as I Am" is probably the best-known appeal song in America today. It has been sung at the conclusion of tens of thousands of evangelistic sermons.

George Beverly Shea popularized it as he sang those familiar words "Just as I am, without one plea, but that Thy blood was shed for me, and that Thou bid'st me come to Thee, O Lamb of God, I come, I come" to conclude Billy Graham's evangelistic appeals.

Most Christians are not familiar with the hymn's composer or its background. The story is an inspiring one.

Charlotte Elliott was an unusually gifted young woman, an outstanding portrait artist and a writer of humorous essays. She seemed to have everything going for her. While she was still in her early 30s, she suffered a debilitating illness that left her sickly and depressed. A godly preacher named Caesar Malan visited her. Pastor Malan asked Charlotte if she had peace with God. The question distressed her. She became upset and refused to discuss it.

As she thought about her lack of courtesy and respect for this noted man of God, she felt a tinge of sorrow. In a few days she approached him to apologize. She said she wanted to become a Christian but needed to clean up a few things in her life first. The pastor simply looked her in the eyes and said, "Come as you are." Charlotte surrendered her life to Christ immediately. She opened her heart to His loving acceptance.

Fourteen years later she remembered the words spoken to her by the one who had led her to Christ and composed the hymn "Just as I Am," which has led so many millions to Christ.

There is no other way to come to Jesus than "just as we are." There is no other place to begin than just where we are. And there is no better time than now.

Ellen White states it well: "Jesus loves to have us come to Him just as we are, sinful, helpless, dependent. We may come with all our weakness, our folly, our sinfulness, and fall at His feet in penitence. It is His glory to encircle us in the arms of His love and to bind up our wounds, to cleanse us from all impurity" (*Steps to Christ,* p. 52). "Just as I am, and waiting not to rid my soul of one dark blot, to Thee whose blood can cleanse each spot, O Lamb of God, I come."

Maybe you have never come before. Today is your day to come. Or if you have come before, why not come again right now on your knees into His presence?

SONGS OF EXPERIENCE, PART 5: BE THOU MY VISION

I am my beloved's , and his desire is toward me. S. of Sol. 7:10.

The Song of Solomon is an inspired love song. It speaks of love's commitment. Love is not a sentimental emotion based on physical attraction. It is not a superficial feeling centered on the external. Love is a lasting commitment based on the character of another. Love is a divine attractiveness between two individuals.

Love is passionate about the one loved. Love can never be casual, complacent, or passive. Love is always active, always aggressive, always pursuing.

The lover in Song of Solomon sings, "I found the one I love. I held him and would not let him go" (S. of Sol. 3:4). "My beloved is mine, and I am his" (S. of Sol. 2:16). Genuine, authentic love is a passionate commitment to the one loved. This passion, this commitment, this dedication characterizes all genuine Christianity. Genuine Christianity is not something artificial. It is a real experience with Jesus. It is possible to have the "outer form without inner passion." Today God is calling us to an inner-heart experience with Him.

Between A.D. 500 and 700 the Irish church was synonymous with spiritual fervor. Early Celtic Christians emphasized the presence of God in their lives. Their hymns and poems and prayers reflect their deepening godliness and personal encounters with God. The prayers of these early Celtic Christians reveal the possibility of a love relationship, an actual friendship with God.

"I am bending my knee,
In the eye of the Father who created me,
In the eye of the Son who purchased me,
In the eye of the Spirit who cleansed me,
In friendship and affection."

Linked in love with us, God longs for our affection. He longs for our friendship. He calls us to authentic Christianity. In the words of the old Celtic hymn, "Be Thou my vision, O Lord of my heart; naught be all else to me save that Thou art, Thou my best thought, by day or by night, waking or sleeping, Thy presence my light."

Solomon was right. Love leaves us no other choice than to be passionate about the one we love. We desire Him, and He desires us. We are content with Him, and He is content with us. We are His committed friends now and through all eternity.

SONGS OF EXPERIENCE, PART 6: 'TIS SO SWEET TO TRUST IN JESUS

The Lord is near to those who have a broken heart. Ps. 34:18.

Louisa's life changed in an instant. One moment she was basking in the warm sunshine, listening to the ocean waves crash on a Long Island beach, and the next moment she was horror-struck. She and her husband, along with their 4-year-old daughter, were startled when they heard the frantic cries of a drowning boy. Louisa's husband tried to save him, but the boy pulled him under the water. Both drowned as Louisa and her 4-year-old watched in stunned agony.

Louisa Stead was an immigrant in America. She and her husband had recently come to New York with their daughter, seeking a better life. Now she felt like she was a strange woman in a strange land with no family, friends, or support. She had no one to depend on except the Lord. She and her daughter lived in abject poverty. At times they had very little to eat. One morning she came to the end of her resources, without money or food. After earnestly seeking God, Louisa opened the front door. To her utter surprise, she discovered someone had left food and money on her doorstep. In deep gratitude she wrote this hymn:

"'Tis so sweet to trust in Jesus,
Just to take Him at His word;
Just to rest upon His promise,
Just to know, 'Thus saith the Lord.'
Jesus, Jesus, how I trust Him;
How I've proved Him o'er and o'er!
Jesus, Jesus, precious Jesus!
O for grace to trust Him more!"

The life of trust is sweet. It relieves us of all absorbing anxiety. It delivers us from paralyzing worry. It chases away the depressing darkness that takes the light from our eyes and the joy from our souls. "When in faith we take hold of His strength, He will change, wonderfully change the most hopeless, discouraging outlook. He will do this for the glory of His name" (*Testimonies*, vol. 8, p. 12).

Like Stead, we too can live the sweet life of trust. In the difficult circumstances of our own lives we too can sing, "I'm so glad I learned to trust Thee, Precious Jesus, Savior, Friend; and I know that Thou art with me, wilt be with me till the end."

Whatever the circumstances of your life today, God sees. God knows. God understands. God is holding on to you.

"'Tis so sweet to trust in Jesus."

September 13

SONGS OF EXPERIENCE, PART 7: STAND UP FOR JESUS

Watch, stand fast in the faith, be brave, be strong. 1 Cor. 16:13.

The apostle Paul knew what it meant to stand fast in the faith. He was persecuted, beaten, imprisoned, and stoned. He was shipwrecked and spent day and night fighting for survival. He experienced a physical ailment that he called his "thorn in the flesh." Amid all these trials the apostle wrote, "Three times I pleaded with the Lord to take it away from me. But he said to me, 'My grace is sufficient for you'" (2 Cor. 12:8, 9, NIV).

Paul faced opposition in God's grace. He experienced trial through God's grace. He accepted physical ailments in God's grace. The courageous apostle "stood fast" in God's grace.

Paul appealed to the New Testament Christians to stand fast. It was one of his favorite themes. To the church at Corinth he wrote, "For by faith you stand" (2 Cor. 1:24). To the Ephesians he added, "Stand therefore" (Eph. 6:14). He appealed to the church at Philippi, "Therefore, my beloved and longed-for brethren, my joy and crown, so stand fast in the Lord, beloved" (Phil. 4:1).

In 1858 a Spirit-filled revival swept through the churches of Philadelphia. Every morning and evening, services were held in the churches throughout the city. The Spirit of God moved with great power. A 29-year-old evangelist, Dudly Tyng, was at the center of this revival. He preached to more than 5,000 people. One thousand responded to his appeal for full commitment to Jesus.

Four days after the most powerful sermon of his life, he was fatally injured in an accident. As he lay near death, some of his fellow pastors gathered around him. Pastor Tyng was still thinking of those who had made decisions for Christ when he whispered his last words, "Tell them to stand up for Jesus."

The next Sunday one of those ministers, George Duffield, preached on Ephesians 6:10-14: "Finally, my brethren, be strong in the Lord and in the power of His might. . . . Stand therefore, having girded your waist with truth." At the conclusion of his sermon Pastor Duffield made a moving appeal based on a poem he had just written titled "Stand Up for Jesus."

"Stand up! stand up for Jesus!
Ye soldiers of the cross;
Lift high His royal banner,
It must not suffer loss;
From victory unto victory,
His army shall He lead,
Till every foe is vanquished,
And Christ is Lord indeed."

Hang on! Be steadfast! Don't give up! This is the time to stand up for Jesus.

September 14

WHEN THE ODDS ARE STACKED AGAINST YOU, PART 1

Look at the birds of the air, for they neither sow nor reap nor gather into barns; yet your heavenly Father feeds them. Are you not of more value than they? Matt. 6:26.

Growing up in an urban ghetto, young Ethel didn't seem to have much chance of finding a healthy picture of God—in any place.

This is how Ethel describes her earliest years: "I never was a child, I never was cuddled, liked, or understood by my family. I never felt that I belonged. I was born out of wedlock. Nobody brought me up." Ethel ran wild in the streets as a little girl. She became a leader in a gang and later started hanging around nightclubs.

Ethel also felt drawn to one spot of holy ground: a local church where the congregation sang and the preacher preached with great power and eloquence. She longed more than anything else to get close to God, to sense His presence.

So Ethel began to attend revival services. She began to pray, night after night after the meetings. She prayed earnestly, "Lord, what am I seeking here? What do I want of You? Help me! If nothing happens, I can't come back here anymore!"

That night, this empty young girl found herself filled with a peace she had not imagined existed. She realized that this was exactly what she'd been seeking all her life. Ethel recalled the experience this way: "Love flooded my heart, and I knew that I had found God, and that now and for always I would have an ally, a friend close by to strengthen me and cheer me on."

Ethel Waters went on to become one of America's most beloved gospel singers. For many years she shared her faith in Billy Graham crusades. She always felt that God was very close, watching over her. That reality was expressed in her trademark song, "His Eye Is on the Sparrow."

The song expresses God's watchcare in the well-known line "His eye is on the sparrow, and I know He watches me." When the odds are stacked against you, God is still watching over you. The prophet Zechariah uses one of the Bible's most endearing terms when he says, "He who touches you touches the apple of His eye" (Zech. 2:8). God will not allow anything to touch your life that will not eventually work out for your good and His glory.

If God can take the extreme dysfunctionality of Joseph's family and bring good out of it, He can do it for you. If anyone had the odds stacked against him from childhood, it was Joseph. His own brothers sold him into slavery. He was cast into a pit, then falsely accused and sent to prison, but he ended up in a palace, as prime minister of Egypt. At the end of his life he could say, "You meant evil against me, but God meant it for good" (Gen. 50:20).

You and I and Joseph and Ethel Waters have a special bond. We have something in common. When the odds are stacked against us, God breaks through with a miracle of His grace.

September 15

WHEN THE ODDS ARE STACKED AGAINST YOU, PART 2

As a father pities his children, so the Lord pities those who fear Him. Ps. 103:13.

A Muslim noblewoman once brought her grandson to a Christian hospital in Rawalpindi, Pakistan, for an ear examination. Her name was Bilquis Sheikh. Her husband had left her some years before. Bilquis was well respected in her community. Still, she could not shake a crushing sense of loneliness.

Her physician was Dr. Pia Santiago, a woman of vibrant Christian faith. Dr. Santiago noticed that Bilquis was holding a Bible. Quite curious, she asked, "Madam Sheikh, what are you doing with that Book?"

As it turned out, this stately woman had been studying the Bible and the Koran for some time, earnestly searching for God. It seemed a hard quest indeed. Dr. Santiago shared what God's love meant to her.

The doctor leaned closer, took Bilquis's hand, and quietly said, "Talk to Him as if He were your father." Those words shot through the Muslim woman like electricity. Could it be God was really like a father? *It can't be true,* she thought. *God a loving Father?*

But what if God really was like a father? On the way home, Belquis couldn't get that thought out of her mind. Hours after she went to bed it kept her wide awake. She fondly recalled how her own father would put everything aside to listen to his beloved child. Suppose, just suppose, God was like that?

Finally, sometime after midnight, Bilquis got up and knelt on the rug by her bed, trembling with excitement and uncertainty. Looking up toward heaven, she spoke aloud, "O Father, my Father—Father God!"

Bilquis was not prepared for the surge of confidence that followed. Suddenly she didn't feel alone at all. God was present. This is how she described the experience: "He was so close that I found myself laying my head on His knees like a little girl sitting at her father's feet. For a long time I knelt there, sobbing quietly, floating in His love. I found myself talking with Him . . ."

Nothing in this woman's past had prepared her for such an encounter with a heavenly Father. From what her own religious culture had taught her about God, she could not imagine His meeting her needs as a forsaken woman. But that's exactly what God did. He became father, husband, and brother to her.

When the odds are stacked against you, God is there as a loving Father. He is there to speak words of encouragement. He is there to lift your spirits with hope, to fill that aching void of loneliness. He is there to strengthen you to face tomorrow's journey. He is there to give you all the love your heart needs.

September 16

WHEN THE ODDS ARE STACKED AGAINST YOU, PART 3

I have been crucified with Christ; it is no longer I who live, but Christ lives in me. Gal. 2:20.

Dudley just had too many strikes against him. His father deserted the family when he was 6, and his mom had to go to work in a defense plant. She soon married a man who was prone to fits of rage. Dudley would never forget the loud arguments in the night as he heard the sounds of hitting and his mother's sobs.

Finally Dudley went to live with his grandmother. But she couldn't handle him. In desperation she enrolled him in a military academy. Within a year he was kicked out.

One weekend he wandered over to New Castle Air Base and got his first close-up look at an airplane, a Mustang fighter. Dudley was hypnotized. A former fighter pilot befriended him. Captain James Shotwell seemed to sense how lost and confused the boy was.

They had long talks on the wing of a Mustang. Once when the boy said he wanted to quit school, the captain said, "Dud, you remind me of a blind sparrow. It knows how to fly, but it can't because it can't see. . . . You have all the right tools, Dud. Use them! No matter what you do in this life, you need to develop one thing—a sense of direction!"

One day Dudley received shocking news. James Shotwell had been killed. He'd lost an engine while returning to the air base from a practice mission. Shotwell could have ejected to safety, saving himself, but the plane was going down over a populated area. Shotwell stayed with his plane, steering it away from the houses, until it was too late to bail out.

For the first time Dudley realized how much Captain Shotwell meant to him. Shotwell's words about the blind sparrow kept coming back.

Dudley's negative attitude gave way to a deep faith in God. His entire life was turned around because someone he loved made the ultimate sacrifice. That one courageous act seemed to overshadow Dudley's dysfunctional past. It gave him a new starting point.

Christ's sacrificial death gives us a new starting point. At the cross we can begin again. We are blessed "with every spiritual blessing in the heavenly places in Christ" (Eph. 1:3). We who were "dead in trespasses and sins" are now made alive (Eph. 2:1).

Our identity is in Christ. When He was nailed to the cross all of our dysfunctional past was nailed there. Paul triumphantly declares, "I have been crucified with Christ" (Gal. 2:20).

All your scars, all the mistakes, all the guilt, all the failure is gone in Christ. When the odds are stacked against us, we can begin again at the cross.

WHEN THE ODDS ARE STACKED AGAINST YOU, PART 4

That was the true Light which gives light to every man coming into the world. John 1:9.

Lizzie started out about as low as one can imagine. Crushed by abuse and neglect in childhood, at last she escaped to a life on the streets.

As a child, almost every evening when her father came home from work he forced Lizzie to hold her arms straight out in front of her. Then he flailed away at her with his belt until she cried. He just assumed she had done something wrong that day.

As Lizzie grew older the abuse increased. She was a classic case of a person who had no chance in life, and no chance of a healthy emotional life, because she'd suffered so much abuse so early.

Yet somehow this little girl beat all the odds. Fast-forward a few years, and you find Lizzie transformed into Angel Wallenda, performing before large audiences on the high wire with her husband, Steven.

Steve Wallenda was a member of the most famous family of circus high-wire performers. When he met Lizzie he was immediately captivated by her warm, friendly personality. She'd been through so much and yet seemed so optimistic about everything. Steven came to regard her as a gift that God dropped into his life.

The little girl whom a cruel father had knocked around could now hold her head high and move straight and steady on the high wire. And she could do more.

Angel also demonstrated extraordinary emotional stability. When cancer threatened her career and her life, she didn't fall apart. She fought back and proved to be a source of strength to her husband. When part of her leg had to be amputated, she didn't give up. She fought to do the impossible. Angel became the only person in history to perform on the high wire with an artificial limb!

Steve Wallenda described Angel this way: "She gives, and she gives. That's her nature. It's her beauty. She reminds me of that passage in the Bible—she really does have the 'peace of God, which passes all understanding.'"

Whatever your background, whatever odds are stacked against you, Christ is the true light that lights every person. The light of Christ's love can lift up your life today. The light of Christ's grace can shine out of your face in spite of whatever circumstances you have been through. Christ's light shines most brightly when the darkness is the deepest.

When the odds are stacked against you, let the light of Christ shine through you.

September 18

WHEN THE ODDS ARE STACKED AGAINST YOU, PART 5

And they overcame him by the blood of the Lamb and by the word of their testimony. Rev. 12:11.

Two men confronted each other in a Romanian prison. One was a self-assured, intelligent, tough young lieutenant named Grecu. The other was a committed Christian pastor named Richard Wurmbrand.

Richard was weak and pale. On his face hung the heavy shadows of a man who has endured torture and deprivation.

Grecu sat at a desk with a rubber truncheon in his hand, ready to interrogate Wurmbrand once again. On this morning he shouted, "Your story was lies." Wurmbrand's refusal to give the names of his associates and of his connections with the West infuriated him.

Grecu pushed back his chair and shouted, "Enough! Here's some paper. We know you've been communicating in code with other prisoners. Now we must know exactly what each of them said." The lieutenant cracked the truncheon on his desk. "You have a half hour." He stomped out of the room.

Richard Wurmbrand faced a terrible dilemma as he stared at that white piece of paper. He had to write a confession, yet he didn't want to reveal anything that might endanger his fellow prisoners. Almost anything he said could be twisted and turned into evidence that he was a spy.

Finally this pastor decided to make a confession—of his faith in Jesus Christ.

He wrote these words: "I am a disciple of Christ who has given us love for our enemies. I have never spoken against the Communists. I understand them and pray for their conversion so that they will become my brothers in the faith."

Richard Wurmbrand's testimony had a powerful effect on the atheistic Grecu. Grecu's heart was touched. Richard Wurmbrand's confession of his faith led to a series of discussions on Christianity and life's true meaning. Eventually Grecu yielded to the claims of Christ.

Our testimony of Christ's faithfulness is a powerful witness: "And they overcame him by the blood of the Lamb and by the word of their testimony" (Rev. 12:11).

In every situation, God has placed a positive testimony in our lives to bless others. Whatever your circumstances today, let Christ's love speak through you. Let His testimony touch others through your life. When the odds are stacked against you, let Christ give you a testimony.

September 19

WHEN THE ODDS ARE STACKED AGAINST YOU, PART 6

I am the way, the truth, and the life. John 14:6.

Lin Yutang was a third-generation Chinese Christian. His father served as a Presbyterian minister in a small village. After Lin went through college and began teaching in Peking, he began absorbing the humanist ideas around him.

Lin went on to make quite a name for himself as a scholar and best-selling author. Then one day his Christian wife invited him to go to church with her. They were in New York City at the time. Lin wasn't much interested, but his belief that people could pull themselves up by their own bootstraps had begun to fray around the edges. It had become all too clear to Lin that, despite technological progress, men and women could still behave like savages in the twentieth century.

Lin tagged along with his wife, and they attended a church on Madison Avenue. The minister was quite eloquent in his sermon on eternal life, but the topic didn't much interest Lin.

Yet something he heard that day stuck in his head. *Could there really be something more to life than this secular routine?* The question haunted him and finally compelled him to take a closer look at the Bible. He told himself he was just rereading the Gospels, but soon he found himself staring at God face-to-face in the person of Christ. As he later said, he discovered "the awe-inspiring simplicity and beauty of the teachings of Jesus. No one ever spoke like Jesus."

Lin's picture of God began to change. He was astounded that God, as Jesus revealed Him, was so different from what people had made Him out to be.

The gospel made all the sense in the world to Lin. Now it was materialism that didn't square with reality. He couldn't believe that the world was, as he put it, "only a swirl of blind atoms obeying blind mechanical laws." No, human beings had real moral choices to make. Complacent, frail human beings had to accept or reject the gospel.

Lin Yutang found in Christ and His gospel a complete sufficiency. He put it simply, "Looking back on my life, I know that for 30 years I lived in this world like an orphan. I am an orphan no longer."

At times doubts may crowd into the minds of sincere Christians. Jesus provides certainty in our times of doubt. He reminds us, "I am the way, the truth, and the life" (John 14:6). Jesus clears up our doubts. He does not necessarily answer all our questions, but He gives us Himself. Christianity is not an argument; it is Jesus. When doubts threaten to overwhelm your faith, open the Gospels. Reacquaint yourself with Jesus. Fall in love with Him again.

When the odds are stacked against you, there is still Jesus, and He is enough.

September 20

WHEN THE ODDS ARE STACKED AGAINST YOU, PART 7

He who is in you is greater than he who is in the world. 1 John 4:4.

Lou became quite successful at his investment firm. After his father died he'd started work at a very young age and made his own way in the world. Lou became addicted to the taste of success.

Picking just the right companies, knowing which stock might be undervalued, which markets might be expanding, all gave him a rush. Lou became obsessed with success. He could never get enough.

Lou began to play fast and loose with some company funds. He was determined to have a flashy lifestyle, and nothing was going to get in his way.

Finally Lou's fast track started hitting major road bumps. He started withdrawing money from various company investment funds, a few thousand here and a few thousand there. He disguised these transactions so they would not be traced to him.

But Lou just kept losing money. One day someone at the company exposed his transactions. The boss had to confront him. Lou could either pay back several thousand dollars or face a lawsuit.

At the time, Lou had been seeing a physician for physical problems. The doctor was a Christian who believed that there were spiritual problems behind his patient's physical complaints. They'd talked quite a bit. And now Lou decided to unburden himself to this doctor.

The Christian doctor told Lou about another force in the world, the force of God's love. He talked about the God who gave Himself away at the cross. Lou decided to rebuild his life on new foundations. He didn't want to just react anymore. He wanted to invest in the grace of God.

Lou confessed everything he'd done to his boss. Most important, Lou confessed everything to God. Unable to pay back the money, he was arrested and tried. Lou confessed everything to the judge. Eventually he was given a suspended sentence as a first-time offender.

In the following years Lou would face tough times, cut off from his family, unable to find anyone who would hire him. His success was long gone, but he had found something else that made him much happier.

We may find ourselves in extremely embarrassing situations. Life may crumble around us. But God is a master at pulling us out of tough circumstances. When the odds are stacked against you, remember the God who rebuilt Lou's life can rebuild yours, too. It is still true that "He who is in you is greater than he who is in the world."

September 21

DON'T FORGET TO REMEMBER

Remember the sabbath day, to keep it holy. Ex. 20:8.

Since our world so desperately needs the reassuring message of Creation, God gave us the Sabbath. In the mid-1800's when the evolutionary hypotheses was taking the intellectual world by storm, God sent a message of incredible hope. It is found in Revelation 14:6, 7.

"And I saw another angel fly in the midst of heaven, having the everlasting gospel to preach to them that dwell on the earth, and to every nation, kindred, tongue and people. Saying with a loud voice, 'Fear God and give glory to Him for the hour of His judgement is come. And worship Him that made heaven and earth and the sea and the fountains of water.' "

God's last-day message is one which calls all humanity back to worshiping Him as the Creator of heaven and earth. The basis of all worship is the fact that God created us. Accept evolution and you destroy the very basis for worship.

God is worthy precisely because He has created. If God has not created us, if we merely evolved and life is a cosmic accident based on chance and random selection, there is absolutely no reason to worship.

In an age of evolution, God has given the Sabbath as an eternal symbol of His creative power and authority. The Sabbath is a weekly reminder that we are not our own. Life cannot exist apart from Him. "In Him we live and move and have our being." (Acts 17:28)

The Sabbath calls us back to our roots. It's a link to our family of origin. It is an unbroken connection back through time to our Creator. The Sabbath tells us that we are not just a product of time plus chance. It keeps us focused on the glorious truth that we are children of God. It calls us to an intimate, close relationship with Him.

When Joy was four years old, her baby brother was born. Little Joy began to ask her parents to leave her alone with the new baby. They worried that like some four year olds she might be jealous and shake or hit the baby, so they said no!

Over time though, since Joy wasn't showing signs of jealously, they changed their minds and decided to let Joy have her private conference with "Baby." Elated, Joy went into the baby's room and shut the door. But, it still opened a crack. Her curious parents to peeked in and listened. They saw little Joy walk quietly up to her baby brother, put her face close to his and say, "Baby, tell me what God is like. I am starting to forget."

The truth is we all tend to forget. That's why God says, "remember." The Sabbath is a weekly reminder of what God is like. It calls us to a new relationship with Him. It calls us to communion with our Creator. It calls us to marvel in our Maker. It calls us to enjoy the eternal. It calls us to hope in the heavenly. When it is so easy to forget, the Sabbath is a reminder to remember what God is really like.

September 22

A HEAVENLY VISITOR

Do not be afraid; I am the First and the Last. Rev. 1:17.

In May of 2001 our It Is Written production team visited the island of Patmos, to tape a new series of programs, "Letters From a Lonely Isle."

We arrived on a Friday afternoon. As the sun set, painting the horizon in flaming crimson, as with the stroke of the Master Artist's brush, I sat on the shores of the Aegean Sea reading Revelation. My mind drifted back over the centuries.

Late in the first century, Roman officials banished the apostle John to this barren outcrop, approximately 10 miles long. John was an old man who hardly seemed to pose a threat to the stability of Rome. But Roman officials feared what John had seen and heard. His eyes were still bright with a vision of the most revolutionary figure in history. He was enamored with Jesus.

John had been one of Jesus' closest disciples, and he couldn't stop talking about Him. He couldn't stop talking about Christ's love and grace, even when that meant standing against the cult of emperor worship. John became a threat to the Roman Empire, not because of the armies he commanded, but because of the Christ he proclaimed.

So in his old age John was arrested and sent to this rocky island. Isolated and alone, he was cut off from fellow believers.

As I sat overlooking the sea that night, meditating on Scripture, Jesus came preciously close. I sensed His presence, and how John must have felt when, in exile on that very same island, he received a Visitor.

It wasn't someone his Roman guards allowed him to see—it was Jesus Christ Himself. All the Roman armies in the world could not hold Him back. It was the glorified Christ in a startling vision. Christ's face shone like the sun.

Christ is nearest to His children at the times of their deepest loneliness. Jesus' words to John, "I am the First and the Last" (Rev. 1:17), echo across the centuries. He is the eternal Christ. He is forever present. He is always with us. John did not see Jesus high above His suffering people, watching their grief from a throne. John saw "One like the Son of Man," "in the midst of the seven lampstands" (Rev. 1:13). The lampstands are Christ's church, His people (Rev. 1:20). Wherever they are, He is.

Today you may feel as isolated as John did on Patmos. Jesus Christ is with you as surely as He was with John. Ask the Spirit to open your eyes of faith so you can see Him walking in your life today.

September 23

PRESCRIPTIONS FROM THE DIVINE PHYSICIAN

Write the things which you have seen, and the things which are, and the things which will take place after this. Rev. 1:19.

When Jesus visited John on the island of Patmos, He showed John marvelous things that the apostle would record in the book of Revelation. The Savior chose to reveal His urgent truths for the end time to an exiled, aged apostle. God broke through with a powerful message of truth at one of John's most trying moments. As difficult as it is to understand, God's greatest gifts often come during our greatest challenges. God is a God of surprises. In our sorrows we are often surprised by the joy of His presence.

Jesus gave John special messages to pass along to churches that were close to John's heart, yet which John could no longer personally visit.

The seven churches in Asia Minor are congregations facing a variety of challenges. Some are healthy and growing. Some are in crisis. Some are almost dead.

Each letter is like a prescription, written out by the Great Physician. Jesus is saying, "Here is a divine solution to your spiritual problem." There is no problem without God's remedy. Every message from Jesus ends with the words "To him who overcomes." In other words, whatever your problem, you can overcome it. What encouragement! What hope! Whatever problem we face, our Lord has a divine remedy.

A prescription from the greatest Healer in history was valuable for seven ancient churches in Asia Minor, and it is valuable for us. These messages are especially significant because we face many of the same issues that confronted these churches. They are basic human challenges. Jesus meets each of them with practical, powerful suggestions that are life-transforming.

These are messages that go to the heart. They focus on what is essential. They point us to what works. Jesus is more interested in solving our problems than in condemning us for them. Although the messages to the seven churches honestly portray the particular churches' weaknesses, they focus on God's solutions.

Is there some spiritual fault in your life? Do you sense a character deficiency? God has a solution. You too can overcome. Grasp God's promises. Accept His Word and move forward.

September 24

WHEN OUR FIRST LOVE GROWS COLD

Nevertheless I have this against you, that you have left your first love. Rev. 2:4.

Even today Ephesus wows you. Its well-preserved ruins reveal the glory of a past civilization. Ephesus was once one of the proudest cities in the Roman Empire. It was proud of its great library and theater, and famed Temple of Artemis (or Diana), one of the Seven Wonders of the Ancient World. Ephesus served as the capital of Asia Minor and was a vital trade center.

The great theater at Ephesus could hold 25,000 people, who often packed it for the plays of the classic Greek and Roman writers. Despite the ravages of time the Ephesus theater is one of the best preserved in the world.

Ephesus has a remarkable story to share with us. The apostle Paul preached successfully in Ephesus, leading many of its citizens to accept Christ. In fact, Paul's preaching was so powerful that it threatened the sale of images of Diana, a homegrown Ephesian goddess. An angry mob dragged two of Paul's compatriots to the theater, shouting, "Great is Diana of the Ephesians!" The Ephesians panicked when Paul exalted Jesus Christ above Diana, better known as Artemis.

The Christian church in Ephesus stood firmly for the truth. These early Christians were doctrinally pure. The word Ephesus means "desirable." Ephesus, the first of the seven churches, symbolizing the church in the first century, was characterized by zeal and doctrinal purity. Filled with the Holy Spirit, the believers shared Christ everywhere. The forces of hell were shaken as thousands accepted Christ. Speaking of the rapid growth of Christianity, one Roman writer said, "You are everywhere. You are in our army. You are in our navy. You are in our shops and schools. You are in our homes and prisons. You are even in our senate."

Filled with a love for Christ and armed with His Word, the church proclaimed the Savior's love. But gradually a change came. Jesus said, "Nevertheless, I have this against you, that you have left your first love" (Rev. 2:4).

After some time the first love had cooled. The early Christians were still standing for the truth of God. They had become skilled at exposing anyone who veered from correct doctrine, but they were not acting out of love anymore. They shouted boldly proclaiming their loyalty on the outside, but they were cold and empty on the inside.

God warns us of a similar fate today. We can accumulate a lot of correct knowledge, we can have all the right doctrines, yet still end up empty like a shell. When your heart grows cold and you have lost your first love, here is Jesus' solution: "Remember therefore from where you have fallen" (verse 5).

Remember those feelings of closeness with God in prayer. Remember those precious moments of closeness with the Lord in Bible study. Remember how His love filled your heart. He hasn't changed. He is still the same God who welcomed you into His arms. He is still the same God who won you by His grace. And He can renew your soul again. He can fill you with love again. Will you open your heart to Him right now? Will you allow Him to rekindle the first love in your heart again?

September 25

FAITHFUL UNTIL DEATH

Be faithful until death, and I will give you the crown of life. Rev. 2:10.

Exiled on the island of Patmos, in the Aegean Sea, John was cut off from believers who regarded him as their spiritual father. What perhaps hurt him most was to be cut off from believers going through difficult times, especially Christians in a city called Smyrna.

The word Smyrna means "sweet-smelling savor." Satan attached the church viciously in the second and third centuries. Christians were burned at the stake. They were thrown to lions and martyred in the Colosseum in Rome. Yet Satan's efforts did not halt Christianity's growth. Instead, the church flourished. The number of believers grew. One of the early Church Fathers, Justin Martyr, triumphantly declared, "The blood of the martyrs is the seed of the church." The more the forces of evil persecuted the church, the more it grew. Christ had established His church, and all the powers of hell could not prevail against it.

Domitian, one of Rome's cruelest emperors, ruled from A.D. 81 to A.D. 96. He is portrayed in stone as a colossal, awe-inspiring figure.

In a very real sense, he once towered over the citizens of Smyrna. Domitian tried to terrorize believers into submission. The followers of Christ would not participate in the rites of emperor worship, which good citizenship demanded at the time. The Romans accused them of being disloyal, of undermining Roman law and order.

Jesus had a special message to Christians in Smyrna. He told them, "Do not fear any of those things which you are about to suffer" (Rev. 2:10). I know you are facing tough times, He said. I know you are facing tribulation. I know you are experiencing persecution, but I am with you. "Be faithful until death, and I will give you the crown of life" (Rev. 2:10).

This is not only an incredible promise, it is practical counsel for living a joy-filled life today. What makes the prospect of hard times so difficult? Our imaginations. We think of all the terrible things that could happen. We "what if" ourselves into anxiety, dwelling on worst-case scenarios.

Jesus is telling the Christians in Smyrna, and us, that even if the worst happens to us, even if we die, He will reward our faithfulness with eternal life at the Second Coming. Jesus says, "He who overcomes shall not be hurt by the second death" (verse 11). You will not experience the second death, eternally separated from God. With Christ we are safe and secure. Through Christ we will triumph in even the worst of circumstances. Even if we have to give up our earthly lives, we will be untouched by the second death. We will have a crown of life, eternal life with God in heaven. Now, that's something to praise Him for.

September 26

UNTOUCHED BY THE SECOND DEATH

He who overcomes shall not be hurt by the second death. Rev. 2:11.

Roman guards loomed large over the marketplace of Smyrna. Poseidon, Artemis, and Demeter played a key role in the lives of most Roman citizens. Rome demanded ultimate allegiance to the emperor, and as a gesture of allegiance, each citizen was compelled to burn incense to the gods of Rome.

Christians refused. They believed it idolatry to worship at the shrines of the Roman gods. They often paid for this belief with their lives.

Polycarp was a disciple of the apostle John and elder of the church at Smyrna. One night Roman officials arrested him at a farmhouse outside the city. Christians were being tortured to death in this area, their bodies flayed open for refusing to worship the emperor.

But Polycarp greeted these officials with a shocking cheerfulness. He even invited them to sit down and have a meal. Then he asked to be allowed an hour to pray undisturbed. That done, Polycarp went with the soldiers to the stadium in the city. The huge crowd roared as Polycarp entered.

Led to a large pile of wood, Polycarp received one last chance to renounce Christ. "Swear supreme allegiance to the emperor," the consul declared, "and I will dismiss you. Revile Christ."

Polycarp turned to the consul and replied calmly, "Eighty and six years have I served Him, and He never did me wrong—how can I blaspheme my King that has saved me?"

Throughout his ordeal, witnesses were struck by the look of confidence, and even joy, on this Christian leader's face. It was, they said, "brightened with grace."

Polycarp wasn't just looking at the bloodthirsty pagans in the stadium or at the wood waiting to be set on fire. He was looking beyond, to the horizon. When the official announcement was made that Polycarp had confessed himself a Christian, the crowd cried out, "Let him be burned alive."

Soldiers tied Polycarp's hands behind him, and he lifted up a prayer. Polycarp thanked his Lord for the honor of bearing witness to his faith in this way.

Polycarp's prayer finished, the executioner kindled the fire. The flames quickly engulfed him.

Polycarp had spoken with confidence to the very end. He spoke of the resurrection. He spoke of eternal life. The horror of his trial could not swallow him. He was looking beyond it. He was looking at the far horizon.

God can give us this kind of confidence, this kind of assurance. He can help us look beyond the flames, beyond the shouts of an angry crowd. He can keep us strong to the very end.

September 27

THE LIGHT OF TRUTH STILL SHINES

Let your light so shine before men, that they may see your good works and glorify your Father in heaven. Matt. 5:16.

Traditionally Turkey has been part of the Muslim world, but its government is now quite secular. For some time there has been a fair amount of religious tolerance. Christian churches are permitted by the government, and the light of Jesus still shines.

Izmir is the third-largest city in Turkey; only Istanbul and Ankara, the nation's capital, are larger. It is the site of biblical Smyrna.

One Friday evening I was eating at our hotel in Izmir, preparing for a quiet Sabbath. It was there our Turkish Adventist guide, Melek Jones, introduced me to a man I had never met before. A robust, cheerful Turk greeted me with a warm embrace. Evidently he knew me, though I did not know him.

Erkin was raised a Muslim, as was his wife. They met as students at Istanbul University. After graduation they decided to broaden their horizons by immigrating to the United States. Living in America, they noticed the large number of Christian churches. Regularly they came across Christian radio and television programs.

At this time they knew little of Christianity. The Bible was a foreign book. Jesus was an unknown Jewish teacher. Almost out of curiosity they began to read the Bible. Something inside compelled them to consider the claims of Christ. The still small voice of the Spirit led them to study more.

Erkin encouraged his wife to inquire where she might learn more about the Bible truths they were now discovering. She asked one of her professional Christian colleagues for more information. This working associate was a Seventh-day Adventist. The Vienna, Virginia, Seventh-day Adventist Church just happened to be sponsoring a series of satellite evangelistic meetings known as NET '95, and I just "happened" to be the speaker.

Erkin's wife faithfully attended the entire series. She shared her newfound faith with her husband, and together they studied the Scripture with the pastor of the Vienna church for almost a year. Sensing the claims of Christ, they were both baptized.

A new joy flooded into their lives. They now had a desire to share their faith with their Muslim friends. Through a series of miraculous providences, God led them back to Turkey, to Izmir, ancient Smyrna, the birthplace of Erkin's wife. Today they are mighty witnesses for God. They have been led full circle.

God still leads, reaching His people no matter what their life circumstances. He sees the honest in heart.

The light of truth still shines in Smyrna. God still has His witnesses there. When I visited Erkin's little house church that Sabbath morning, I was struck by the dedication of these Smyrna Christians. Their motto is the same today as it was 2,000 years ago: "Be faithful until death, and I will give you the crown of life" (Rev. 2:10).

September 28

WHEN COMPROMISE CREEPS IN

Repent, or else I will come to you quickly and will fight against them with the sword of My mouth. Rev. 2:16.

It was dry and hot the day our It Is Written production crew lugged our television equipment up the narrow rocky trail leading to Pergamos. The city's location is a fitting symbol for its spiritual condition. Pergamos, like many ancient cities, was built high above the plain. Even the largest armies would have had a difficult time attacking it. The word Pergamos means "exalted."

When Satan could not destroy the church through persecution, he switched methods. The church grew in favor with the Roman state. Eventually over the centuries thousands of pagans became Christians. Constantine, the pagan Roman emperor, accepted Christianity. With this new "exalted" position, changes began to occur in the church. As pagans professed Christianity, they brought pagan practices with them.

The worship of images or idols was introduced into the church. Constantine had a particular fondness for the sun god. *The History of the Christian Church* observes: "Constantine's coins have on one side the letters of the name of Christ and on the other side the figure of Apollo, the sun god, as if he could not dare to relinquish the patronage of the luminary" (p. 184).

Slowly, gradually human dogma was substituted for the truth of God. The simple principle of salvation by faith in Jesus Christ was replaced by a complicated system of salvation through church decrees.

God's call to His people in Pergamos is faithfulness to His Word in the face of compromise. Compromise happens when we persuade ourselves that God's truths are not really that important. It happens when we substitute our human reasoning for God's divine revelation. When we know something is contrary to God's will but we cozy up to it anyway, we compromise. We turn a blind eye.

Turning a blind eye is quite dangerous if you are walking on the edge of a cliff. It matters a great deal if you take a few steps in the wrong direction. I almost learned this lesson the hard way at Pergamos. While taping our program on compromise, we shot a piece near Pergamos's altar of Zeus, called Satan's throne in Revelation 2:13. The altar was huge. The altar's centerpiece was a great platform, nearly 20 feet high and 60 feet long, decorated with a fringe representing the battle of the gods and giants. Today the altar is in extreme disrepair. The splendor of another age is gone. Weeds grow over this large collection of stones.

Against my better judgment, I climbed over the makeshift barrier to the top of the altar of Zeus. As our cameras began to roll, I let out a scream. A large green viper with a diamond-shaped head hissed at me. My heart pounding, I leaped from rock to rock, scrambling off the altar as fast as possible.

The serpent's bite is deadly, and so is Satan's. Compromise is deadly. Going against your conscience can be costly. Take it from me. I almost learned the hard way.

September 29

A SHARP TWO-EDGED SWORD

And to the angel of the church in Pergamos write, "These things says He who has the sharp two-edged sword." Rev. 2:12.

Jesus identifies Himself to the believers at Pergamos as the one who wields a sharp two-edged sword. Sounds like quite a surgical instrument for this doctor of the soul. But what does it really symbolize? The Bible makes it pretty clear. Look at something the apostle Paul tells the believers.

In Ephesians he talks about Christians' spiritual armor. He says, "And take the helmet of salvation, and the sword of the Spirit, which is the word of God" (Eph. 6:17). The sword of the Spirit is the Word of God. The

Spirit penetrates our defenses by the words God utters.

The book of Hebrews makes the picture even more striking. It tells us, "For the word of God is living and powerful, and sharper than any two-edged sword, piercing even to the division of soul and spirit, and of joints and marrow, and is a discerner of the thoughts and intents of the heart" (Heb. 4:12). The Word of God pierces the deepest part of us, uncovering our secret thoughts, laying open our hidden motives.

This is the instrument Christ brings to the people of Pergamos. The medicine He brings to His compromising church at Pergamos and to His compromising people today is the Word of God. Christ wields His Word in battle against those who would undermine faith through compromise. His Word is the remedy for compromise.

We need to take that Word in. We need to allow the Word of God to penetrate deeply into our hearts. We need to build our faith on its clear statements. The Word will show us what is God's truth and what isn't. The Word will show us what steps lead to a healthy relationship with God, and what will lead away from it.

Our feelings won't always guide us reliably. Other people won't always guide us reliably. But the Word of God can keep us going in the right direction.

September 30

THE WHITE STONE

And I will give him a white stone, and on the stone a new name written which no one knows except him who receives it. Rev. 2:17.

Eusebius, an early church historian, tells the story of how the apostle John rescued a man who almost compromised himself over the cliff. The young man had been a bright, earnest Christian when John first met him near Ephesus. The apostle recommended him for leadership, and the young man received pastoral training.

But then he fell in with a group of young troublemakers. One by one he compromised his principles. Finally he plunged into a life of crime as the head of a violent gang of thieves.

When John heard about this young rebel, he summoned a horse and guide. Riding into the country, he was soon taken prisoner by these thieves. John asked to be taken to their captain. As soon as the young man recognized the apostle, he turned to flee, overcome with shame. But, forgetting his age, John set out after him. John called out, "Fear not. You still have hope of life. I will intercede with Christ for you. I will give my life for yours. Stay, believe Christ has sent me."

Finally the young man stopped. Looking miserable, he slowly turned back to the apostle. Then he threw down his sword and fell into John's arms, weeping bitterly. The apostle assured his young friend that pardon was still possible. This captain of thieves fell to his knees.

John spent some time with him, teaching him from the Word of God, building up his faith. Finally he was restored to the church and went on to lead an exemplary Christian life.

This story may be only legend, but it illustrates the early church's sense of God's grace, even for believers who have compromised. It illustrates God's power to cut the cords of compromise and restore us again to a vibrant faith.

There's a wonderful promise in the message to the church at Pergamos. It's a promise for the one who overcomes, the one who turns back from compromise. Jesus says in Revelation 2:17, "I will give him a white stone, and on the stone a new name written."

In ancient times, jurors used white and black stones to signify innocence or guilt. A white stone signified innocence. For Jesus to give us a white stone is to declare that all our past, no matter how dark and painful, is wiped out. We are forgiven.

A white stone was also sometimes given to guests when they departed a friend's home. The host cracked the stone open, keeping one half and handing the other half to the guest. "If any of your loved ones ever pass this way," the host said, "have them bring this stone. I will fetch mine, we'll match the two halves, and they will be welcomed joyfully into my home."

The white stone is God's way of saying "You're not only declared innocent, you're welcomed into My home. You have a place at My table." That's the promise our heavenly Father holds out to us. We may yield to pressure, slide into compromise, or nearly fall off a spiritual cliff, but there is rescue in the Word of God. There is truth in the Word of God that will set us free.

WHEN CORRUPTION INFLUENCES THE CHURCH

But hold fast what you have till I come. Rev. 2:25.

We have been following an ancient letter around the western coast of Turkey, searching for its seven destinations. It was a letter sent by the Great Physician, Jesus Christ, through the apostle John, to seven churches in varying degrees of spiritual health.

We are interested in these seven churches for two specific reasons. First, God has chosen these particular churches to represent the Christian church in its different spiritual phases throughout history. Second, the divine prescription our Lord gave to these churches applies to our spiritual condition, too. We face similar spiritual challenges in our day.

Today we will briefly consider the church at Thyatira. All that is left of this ancient trading center is a pile of stones in the middle of the modern Turkish city of Akhisar. In John's day Thyatira was a thriving community and an important center of trade and industry. The city had gained a measure of notoriety for its powerful guilds of weavers and dyers of wool.

Jesus begins His message to Thyatira with words of encouragement. "I know your deeds," He says, "your love and faith, your service and perseverance, and that you are now doing more than you did at first" (Rev. 2:19, NIV).

Christ appreciates the faith and love of these believers. But the believers in Thyatira will face some tough choices. To keep growing they will be called to stand up for the right. "Nevertheless," Jesus continues, "I have a few things against you, because you allow that woman Jezebel, who calls herself a prophetess, to teach and seduce My servants to commit sexual immorality" (verse 20).

The problem of Thyatira is the problem of spiritual adultery. Adultery is an illicit union, emotional or physical, with a person who is not your true spouse. Adultery speaks of unfaithfulness, the breaking of the sacred vows of commitment. This message is to the ancient church at Thyatira, but it also applies to an entire period in church history known as the Dark Ages. The Christian church symbolized by Thyatira was unfaithful to her true lover, Jesus Christ. She broke her vow of loyalty to her Lord.

The message to the church at Thyatira is a jarring wake-up call to us, an urgent appeal to faithfulness. It is a call to commitment. How do you survive when the spiritual environment around you becomes spiritually destructive?

The answer is to determine by God's grace to be faithful to Christ at all costs. You make whatever decision is necessary to preserve your spiritual experience. If you lose your spiritual health, what do you really have left?

October 2

DEADLY AND FATAL

Indeed I will cast her into a sickbed, and those who commit adultery with her into great tribulation. Rev. 2:22.

The danger Jesus warned the believers at Thyatira about was precisely this. Besieged believers braced themselves to face the external threat of the Roman Empire, but the greatest threat came from within. Believers stood at the walls with their weapons facing the outside, but Jesus told them to look internally. The church is sick, He told them, and not getting any better.

Jesus used the figure of Jezebel, the corrupt queen who led ancient Israel into idolatry, as a symbol of the internal corruption and compromise that plagued Thyatira. "Indeed I will cast her into a sickbed," Jesus said, "and those who commit adultery with her into great tribulation, unless they repent of their deeds. I will kill her children with death, and all the churches shall know that I am He who searches the minds and hearts" (Rev. 2:22, 23).

This may sound like fierce judgment, but remember that Jezebel is a symbolic figure. The Great Physician is trying to make the people of Thyatira aware of a malignancy. The problem is not just a head cold, nor a flu that will be gone in a couple of days.

He's saying, "Look! This is a dangerous illness. You can't just coexist. You can't just live with it. You must deal with the malignancy."

Jesus goes on to say, "But hold fast what you have till I come. And he who overcomes, and keeps My works until the end, to him I will give power over the nations" (verses 25, 26).

The challenge is to hold on to what you have, the faith that you have. How do you do that in a sick environment?

The very beginning of the letter to Thyatira describes Christ: "Who has eyes like a flame of fire, and His feet like fine brass" (verse 18). "Eyes like a flame" suggests someone whose gaze penetrates deeply. It suggests a gaze that burns through the superficial, that pierces the heart.

I believe the Great Physician is telling us to open our eyes. Look at what's going on around us, inside the church. Don't be blinded because it's so familiar. Don't be blinded because you've been looking at how bad it is on the outside.

We see something else in the description of Jesus as well. His feet are like fine brass. This suggests to me that Jesus is capable of firm, decisive steps. Where He treads, the earth trembles.

Sometimes we need to take decisive steps. Sometimes it's time to leave, to separate ourselves from a spiritually destructive situation. We don't want to keep clinging to the familiar until the sickness around us results in death. We don't want to get locked up in the box of what we're accustomed to. We don't want to sacrifice our spiritual lives.

Your heavenly Father is working right now for your spiritual health and healing. He wants to be able to tell you, "I know your works, your love and service and faith."

Don't let any other loyalty get in the way of that relationship with Him. Don't let any false sense of obligation make you stay in a destructive situation. You can follow in the decisive footsteps of the Christ whose feet are like fine brass. You can believe that He will show you a better place, a place of freedom, a place where you can grow.

Commit today to go wherever Christ leads you.

October 3

THE GOD OF NEW BEGINNINGS

Be watchful, and strengthen the things which remain, that are ready to die. Rev. 3:2.

Few cities rivaled Sardis for wealth. Archaeologists have unearthed a large marketplace, suggesting that Sardis, the Lydian capital, was a thriving community. The first coins in history were used in Sardis in 640 B.C., but first-century Christians there seemed to be without means of supporting themselves. Very little existed to nourish them spiritually, so their spiritual life dried up.

What prescription does the Great Physician bring to Sardis? It's a rather simple one—on the surface.

Jesus told Sardis, "Be watchful, and strengthen the things which remain, that are ready to die" (Rev. 3:2). Strengthen what remains.

Christians in Sardis saw opposition on all sides. Have you ever been in that predicament? Have you ever reached a place in your life where your hopes and dreams just died? Perhaps you're feeling that way now. Things happen—divorce, the death of a loved one, the loss of a job. Tragedies strike, and we just feel dead. Our spiritual life drains away. We're ready to give up.

But the Great Physician has a message for us. He says, "Be watchful." Take a good look "Strengthen the things which remain."

You may be able to see only the broken pieces of your life. But Jesus says, "I can do something with those broken pieces. I want you to work with Me. I want you to bring something strong out of it. Bring Me the broken pieces of your life."

The Great Physician is the God of a new creation. He not only heals, He re-creates. He creates something out of nothing.

Once Jesus visited a very sick patient in the town of Capernaum. She was a 12-year-old girl, the daughter of the head of the synagogue. Jesus arrived at her house to the loud wails of mourners. The child had passed away.

Jesus asked the mourners to leave the scene. Then He took the child by the hand and said, "Talitha, cumi," meaning, "Little girl, I say to you, arise." Immediately the girl arose, and walked. The patient might be dead, but the Great Physician could still help. He was the Creator. He was the God of new beginnings.

He is the God of new beginnings. That was His message to Sardis 2,000 years ago, and it is His message to you today. He says, "Trust Me. Commit your life to Me. Bring to Me what's left, and I will make something wonderful out of your life."

October 4

FROM DEATH TO LIFE

Remember therefore how you have received and heard; hold fast and repent. Rev. 3:3.

Our Lord's diagnosis for the church at Sardis is "You have a name that you are alive, but you are dead." This is a pretty grim diagnosis. You are supposed to be alive. You have the name Christian, but you are spiritually dead.

When a patient is dead most physicians stop working. They stop the medication and turn off the life support. It's time to call the morgue.

But Jesus Christ is no ordinary physician. With Jesus, there is still hope, even when the patient seems beyond help. He can work even when the situation seems helpless. He is life itself. He is the author and originator of life. What encouragement! He can still give life to the spiritually dead today. The breath of His Spirit still inspires life.

A remarkable parable in Ezekiel portrays God's life-giving power. The prophet Ezekiel looks out over a valley full of dead men's bones. God asks a seemingly ridiculous question, "Can these bones live?" (Eze. 37:3). The prophet responds, "O Lord God, You know." In other words, "Why are You asking me, Lord? I have no idea."

But God commands the prophet to preach to the bones. God promises, "Behold, O My people, I will open your graves and cause you to come up from your graves. . . . I will put My Spirit in you, and you shall live" (Eze. 37:12-14).

Miracle of miracles, the dead are brought to life. God gives the same message to the dead church at Sardis: "I can make you, alive again. Allow Me to breathe My Spirit into you, and you will live."

Perhaps you feel that you've come to the end of the line today. Perhaps you find yourself in a desert place. Let me urge you to catch this message from the Great Physician. It's a message for us when hope seems to be gone.

The Creator says, "Give Me your shattered life. I can create something beautiful out of it. I will make all things new. Remember what you have received. I have done so much for you in the past, and I am not through yet. Give Me the opportunity to do something special for you."

Give God what remains today. Do it right now. Lift up the little that you have to Him, and He will create something glorious out of it. Let Him mold your life into something beautiful.

October 5

JESUS SEES THE GOOD

You have a few names even in Sardis who have not defiled their garments; and they shall walk with Me in white, for they are worthy. Rev. 3:4.

Let's look at one more message the Great Physician gave to the people in Sardis, the place of the dead. We find it here in Revelation 3:4, 5: "You have a few names even in Sardis who have not defiled their garments; and they shall walk with Me in white, for they are worthy. He who overcomes shall be clothed in white garments, . . . I will confess his name before My Father and before His angels."

Now, here is a word of encouragement. Even in a group that seemed dead, Jesus points out people who have stood tall. "Not defiled their garments" was a way of saying they haven't compromised or given up their faith.

Jesus focused on those good people. And then He promised great things to all who joined them. Jesus wanted to confess their names, to say good things about them, before His heavenly Father. He wanted a vast group of overcomers. Later in the book of Revelation, we see visions of that great multitude dressed in white.

This is the plan of the Great Physician, who asks us to give Him the broken pieces of our lives. This Great Physician promises to create a wonderful community out of a few who stand tall. He is the God of new beginnings.

God created a new beginning at a crucial point in history. The church of Sardis also represents the church during the Reformation.

As century after century passed and God's truth was repressed, faithful men and women of God came forward to champion His cause. Truth long lost sight of would shine brightly again. God raised up the Reformers. The Waldensians copied the Scriptures by hand. From their mountain hideouts in northern Italy and southern France, they sent young men and women throughout Europe to share God's Word. In Bohemia John Huss, along with his friend Jerome, made obedience to God his motto. German Reformer Martin Luther recaptured the truth of "salvation by grace alone." John and Charles Wesley initiated a powerful revival in England, emphasizing holiness and growth in grace.

The "Sardis" period of the Reformation in the 1500s and 1600s brought many neglected Bible truths to light. Biblical tenets such as baptism by immersion, the second coming of Christ, and obedience to God's law were embraced by Christians everywhere.

God breathed new life into His church, and it lived. He can do the same for you. Has your spiritual life waned? Have compromises crept in? Has faith given way to doubt? Has a warm experience with God become cold?

Let God do His wonderful work in you today. He will bring a new vibrancy into your Christian experience. He did it for a group of faithful believers in Sardis, and He will do it for you.

October 6

JESUS STILL OPENS DOORS, PART 1

See, I have set before you an open door, and no one can shut it. Rev. 3:8.

Ancient Philadelphia was located at the foot of Mount Tmolus, 25 miles southeast of Sardis, on the road to Colossae. The city was founded by Attalus II Philadelphus of Pergamum. He named it Philadelphia, "brotherly love," as an indication of loyalty to his elder brother. In A.D. 17 an earthquake destroyed Philadelphia. Emperor Tiberius rebuilt it into an impressive place. Its beauty inspired ancient writers to refer to it as Little Athens.

Let's look at the message John penned at Patmos for believers in Philadelphia, found in Revelation 3. It is one of the most encouraging of the letters to the seven churches, but first, here is the diagnosis. Jesus gives us a clue as to what was ailing believers in Philadelphia. He says, "I know that you have little strength, yet you have kept my word and have not denied my name" (Rev. 3:8, NIV).

"You have little strength." Christians in Philadelphia had grown weak. But notice the diagnosis. Believers there weren't in danger of imminent death, as was the church at Sardis. These people *wanted* to serve God. They had kept Christ's word; they had not denied Him.

But the Great Physician saw that they had little strength. They were suffering from a confidence problem. They felt intimidated.

We see that a little more clearly in the next verse. Jesus said, "I will make those who are of the synagogue of Satan, who claim to be Jews though they are not, but are liars—I will make them come and fall down at your feet and acknowledge that I have loved you" (verse 9, NIV).

What a promise. "The ones who are threatening you will bow before you. Those intimidating you will acknowledge My power, and your persecutors will acknowledge My greatness." What a God!

Let's look again at His letter to the church in Philadelphia. Jesus continues, "These are the words of him who is holy and true, who holds the key of David. What he opens no one can shut, and what he shuts no one can open. I know your deeds. See, I have placed before you an open door that no one can shut. I know that you have little strength" (verses 7, 8, NIV).

I have set before you an open door. That's the truth Jesus wants these people to grasp. He repeats it. He emphasizes it. Look for the open door.

If you feel intimidated—look for an open door.

If you feel isolated—look for an open door.

If you feel weak and discouraged—look for an open door.

Don't just look at the problem. Don't just look at the obstacle. Don't just look at the enemy. God is creating a way out. This is the message Jesus gives to people with little spiritual strength. It is a message of encouragement from the Great Physician. He is making a promise to each of us. In every situation, no matter how dark or desperate, He will open a door for you. He will find a solution.

JESUS STILL OPENS DOORS, PART 2

Behold, I am coming quickly! Rev. 3:11.

The church of Philadelphia actually represents a particular period in church history, a period of spiritual awakening in the 1700s and 1800s. Printing presses were producing Bibles by the thousands. Mission societies sent workers around the world. There was a revival of interest in the books of Daniel and Revelation, a renewed interest in prophecy. The Spirit moved on people's hearts. There was a great expectation that the coming of Jesus was near. All of this opened doors for the proclamation of the gospel throughout the world.

In 1844 a large group of believers concluded that Jesus Christ would return October 22 of that year. Many had given away all their possessions. They were ready for the kingdom of Christ to interrupt human history.

They waited all day. They prayed into the night. By October 23 they'd fallen into despair. Had it all been a terrible mistake? Many felt that God had let them down. After all, they'd studied the prophecies so carefully and prayerfully. They'd been so earnest.

But the heavens were a blank. Christ hadn't appeared. They'd become the butt of jokes. Their confidence was shattered.

A few began to look at the prophecies and promises of the Bible from a different perspective. They began to try to see a bigger picture. And the promise in Revelation of an "open door" caught their eye (Rev. 3:8).

This group, later called Adventists, discovered wonderful truths about Christ's ministry in the heavenly sanctuary. They got a clearer picture of how He stands as our mediator, our high priest before the Father, and how the prophecies they had looked at pointed to this.

So they were able to move out of bitter disappointment and into a brighter hope, a deeper appreciation of the saving work of Jesus Christ. That became an open door for them. The church at Philadelphia is the church of the open door. Scripture says that at unique times in church history God opens unusual doors. God set an open door before the church at Philadelphia, a door no human being could shut.

Today Christ is opening doors all over the world for the spread of the Adventist message, the good news that He is Lord of all and will soon return.

It has been my privilege to see thousands and thousands respond to this message in major cities on every continent. The response to the Spirit's call is overwhelming. He has created a spiritual momentum that nothing can stop.

JESUS STILL OPENS DOORS, PART 3

Because you have kept My command to persevere, I also will keep you from the hour of trial which shall come upon the whole world. Rev. 3:10.

When trials dominate our lives, our Lord invites us to keep looking for the open door. It's important to persevere. Christ is stronger than any power that can rise up against us. No one can shut a door that He opens.

A beggar wailing by the side of the road had been shut up in blindness from the day of his birth, but Jesus stopped and touched his eyes. Jesus opened the door, and a whole new world opened up for this man. It was a door no one else could open.

Eleven disciples closeted themselves in an upper room, despairing over the loss of their Master, fearing for their lives, their confidence shattered. But a resurrected Christ appeared to them.

Those men walked out to boldly bear witness to what they'd seen and heard and to turn the world upside down. They passed through a door no one else could open, and no one else could shut.

That's what the Great Physician does. He sends you a message when you feel that you have no strength, when your confidence is gone. He promises to open a door for you, whatever the circumstances. And look at the doors He has opened! Look at the lives He has changed! Look at the opportunities He gives you. Look at the possibilities before you.

The psalmist sings, "They looked to Him and were radiant, and their faces were not ashamed" (Ps. 34:5). When we focus on our problems, they become larger than life. When we focus on Jesus, He becomes larger than life.

Don't let all the problems overwhelm you. Don't let all the obstacles dominate your vision. Determine that you will find God's open door. Determine that you will keep looking, keep persevering until you see that light breaking through the door that only Christ can open.

CONQUERING COMPLACENCY

So then, because you are lukewarm, and neither cold nor hot, I will vomit you out of My mouth. Rev. 3:16.

There is not much left today, but Laodicea must have been quite a city. It is off the beaten path, and few tourists visit the site today. Very little excavation has been done. In its prime Laodicea was home to nearly 150,000 people. It was an important trade center of Asia Minor, an imperial city famous for the glossy black wool manufactured there.

Laodicea was an extremely wealthy banking center. When it was destroyed by an earthquake in A.D. 60, its citizens refused financial help from Rome to rebuild the city. The proud Laodiceans erected it out of their own resources. The city was also advanced in the healing arts. Its medical practitioners developed a well-known salve for the eyes.

Revelation's message to Laodicea reached this prosperous place toward the end of the first century. The letter addresses a spiritual problem that afflicts almost all of us at one time or another.

The letter begins with Christ's diagnosis of the problem. He says, "I know your works, that you are neither cold nor hot. I could wish you were cold or hot. So then because you are lukewarm, and neither cold nor hot, I will vomit you out of My mouth" (Rev. 3:15, 16).

Jesus uses a metaphor to describe a spiritual problem. Lukewarm water is neither hot nor cold. It's not hot enough to provide a good bath. It's not cold enough to be good drinking water. It's something you instinctively spew out of your mouth.

What is the Doctor talking about? Complacency, indifference? The Laodiceans weren't hot. They didn't have a spiritual fire in their bellies; they didn't have a passion for knowing God.

But they weren't cold, either. They hadn't rejected God. They weren't exploring the alternative. They were lukewarm. They had just enough spiritual life to make them comfortable, but not enough to move them anywhere. They couldn't be inspired as saints. They couldn't be converted as sinners.

What is the real answer to spiritual complacency? How do you rise out of spiritual lethargy? You begin by taking a step in faith.

Stretch past your comfortable boundaries. Set aside a specific time each day for prayer. Choose a book of the Bible and read it through. Commit passages of Scripture to memory. Take on a new witnessing challenge in the name of Jesus. You break out of spiritual complacency by taking some definite action that stretches you to the limits. What spiritual challenge will you accept today?

October 10

THE PERIL OF SELF-SUFFICIENCY

Because you say, "I am rich, have become wealthy, and have need of nothing"—and do not know that you are wretched, miserable, poor, blind, and naked—I counsel you to buy from Me. Rev. 3:17, 18.

Spiritual self-sufficiency is extremely dangerous. People who are self-sufficient feel they have everything under control. They are not conscious of any problem. They think everything is all right when it's not. That was Laodicea's problem.

In Revelation 3 we can see that Jesus went a little deeper with His diagnosis. He said, "Because you say, 'I am rich, have become wealthy, and have need of nothing'—and do not know that you are wretched, miserable, poor, blind, and naked" (Rev. 3:17).

"I am rich . . . and have need of nothing." That's how the Laodiceans felt. Evidently Christians in the city were part of the general prosperity. They weren't being discriminated against. They weren't suffering persecution.

That was good news. But the Laodiceans weren't excited about the gospel. It didn't move them. The good news of Jesus Christ had become old news. Materialism dulled their spiritual senses. The busyness of everyday life neutralized their spiritual values.

At first glance, being comfortable doesn't seem like such a bad thing, and certainly not a dangerous thing. What's wrong with having your needs met? What's wrong with being financially secure? What's wrong with being happy with what you have?

The answer is nothing at all, *except* when you're poor, blind, and naked—and don't know it! The problem comes when you're starving inside, but you think you're full. It comes when you're blind inside, but you think you see.

Christ invites, "Anoint your eyes with eye salve, that you may see" (verse 18). In the New Testament it is the Holy Spirit who opens our eyes, who enlightens our minds. It is the Holy Spirit who helps us understand and convicts us of truth.

It is easy to develop blind spots to defects in our characters. The Holy Spirit is the one who can help us see what is really deep inside our own hearts.

Why not ask the Spirit to "guide you into all truth" (John 16:13)? The truth about your attitude, the truth about hidden sins in your own heart, the truth about enslaving habits—why not ask the Holy Spirit to reveal these things to you and set you free today?

October 11

AT THE DOOR

Behold, I stand at the door and knock. If anyone hears My voice and opens the door, I will come in to him and dine with him, and he with Me. Rev. 3:20.

This letter is particularly important because Laodicea represents the church of today. It completes God's description of His people throughout history. The word Laodicea means "a people judged." This is the church just before the Second Coming. It is the church of the judgment hour. Unfortunately, Laodiceans are lukewarm or complacent. Living in the most exciting time in the history of the world, they fail to grasp the urgency of the moment. They fail to understand the significance of the hour.

Christ's last church, Laodicea, stands poised on the verge of eternity. Yet she sleeps comfortably in lukewarm complacency. She lives in earth's final hours but fails to recognize the significance of the time she is living in.

Christ stands knocking on the door of Laodicea's heart. He appeals to her to awaken, to seize the opportunity of the moment and proclaim His Word.

What remedy is there for spiritual lethargy? The Great Physician recommends that Laodiceans go out and buy three things.

First of all, buy gold (Rev. 3:18). What does this mean? We find a very similar phrase in Peter's writings: "That the genuineness of your faith, being much more precious than gold" (1 Peter 1:7). Peter relates the testing of faith to gold tried in the fire. Faith is that priceless commodity that is worth investing in. Developing a trust relationship with God is the essence of all genuine spirituality. It is the gold currency of Christianity. Jesus is saying, "Wake up—you are desperately poor without faith."

Next the Great Physician prescribes "white garments" (Rev. 3:18). In the New Testament white garments are symbols of righteousness or a right standing with God. Sinful human beings are made righteous through the unblemished garments of Christ's righteousness. His righteousness transforms our characters.

Last, the Great Physician encourages us to buy eye salve so we can see our need. The Holy Spirit's eye salve helps us see ourselves as we are, and to see Jesus as He is.

Christ's remedy is powerful. He urges us to develop genuine faith, a personal experience with Him, and the ability to see through the Spirit's eyes. We are all spiritually poor, blind, and naked, but He longs to enrich us, clothe us, and give us sight. All we need is found in Jesus.

October 12

FELLOWSHIP WITH CHRIST

To him who overcomes I will grant to sit with Me on My throne, as I also overcame and sat down with My Father on His throne. Rev. 3:21.

Christ's remedy is more powerful than our complacency, more potent than our self-sufficiency. Christ's remedy penetrates into the depths of our souls. A living relationship with Him through faith is the gold currency of our Christian experience. His righteousness is all-sufficient to cover our darkest sins and blot out our vilest deformities.

The eye salve of His Spirit cures our spiritual blindness so we can see Jesus in all of His loveliness. And there is one more fact you need to know about Christ's prescription. He says, "Behold, I stand at the door and knock. If anyone hears My voice and opens the door, I will come in to him and dine with him, and he with Me" (Rev. 3:20).

Here's good news indeed. This physician makes house calls! He doesn't just advertise His great prescription; He brings it to us. He's standing at our door, waiting to be let in.

It's as if this Healer could bring an entire health spa right to our door. He brings the goods that will cure us. He brings the gold, the white raiment, and the eye salve to our doorstep. He longs to enter our lives and fellowship with us. Our Lord longs to have a close, intimate relationship with us, just like two close friends sitting down at supper sharing their inner lives together.

Isn't it time you opened the door, time you sat down and had a talk with Jesus? Isn't it time you had a meal of fellowship with Him? You've invested your life in so many things. How about investing in the relationship that counts the most, the relationship that can energize your sleepy soul?

Christ is waiting. Christ is knocking. Christ is appealing.

It's up to you to invite Him in. Have the messages to the seven churches spoken to your heart? Why not pray this prayer with me:

"Dear Father, we come to You because a spiritual slumber has overtaken us, because we've lost that fire in our belly. And so we want to take that first step of faith right now. We need Your gold for our poverty. We need Your white garment for our nakedness. We need Your eye salve for our blindness. And so we open wide the doors of our hearts right now. Please come in. Please make Yourself at home. Please make Yourself our Savior. Amen."

October 13

DISCOVERING OUR ROOTS

For You created all things, and by Your will they exist and were created. Rev. 4:11.

Alex Haley spent more than a decade tracing his roots on three continents. He patched together bits and pieces of his family history as passed down through the centuries by word of mouth, census records, and family wills.

In time he discovered that in the year 1767 his ancestor had been kidnapped on the Gambia River in Africa, transported on a British slave ship to Annapolis, Maryland, and in 1768 sold to John Waller, of Richmond, Virginia.

Alex Haley's story of his search for his roots sent millions of others on an intense search for their own identity. Genealogical study has become exceedingly popular.

What are my roots? What are yours? Even Haley's roots go deeper than his research revealed. Through Jesus, the late Mr. Haley was not just the descendant of a slave—he was a son of God.

Our identity has its roots in the origin of life. Revelation reveals an amazing heavenly scene. Heavenly beings are praising God in the throne room of the universe. Their song of praise echoes throughout the heavens: "You are worthy, O Lord, to receive glory and honor and power; for You created all things, and by Your will they exist and were created" (Rev. 4:11).

We are not some genetic accident. We are not some freak of nature. We are children of God, fashioned by a loving Creator. "For in Him we live and move and have our being" (Acts 17:28).

Life is a gift from God. Every breath, every heartbeat, every second of life flows from the heart of a gracious Father. We did not create ourselves. We did not will ourselves into existence. We exist by the will of God, who has a plan for our lives.

Today we can praise Him for the gift of life. We can praise Him as our loving Creator and kind Father. We are not homeless orphans or shackled slaves. We are children of God, and no one in this world can take that away from us.

A MOMENT DIVINELY FORETOLD

Who keep the commandments of God and have the testimony of Jesus Christ. Rev. 12:17.

In the desert wastes of Bechuanaland, South Africa, lived a man named Sukuba. A member of a nomadic people, he lived an isolated life. One winter night he crept into his shelter and retired for the evening.

Suddenly the night became brighter than day. A shining being appeared to him and told him to find "the people of the Book." He must find a people who worshiped God. What did it mean? How could he read a book?

Sukuba's language contained clicks and guttural sounds quite unlike the language of many other African tribes. It had never been rendered in writing. "The Shining One," as Sukuba called the angel that appeared to him, said, "The Book talks. You will be able to read it." Sukuba set out with his family, traveling by foot for many days. One night the shining one appeared again and told Sukuba he must find "the Sabbathkeeping church and Pastor Moye." Pastor Moye would have a Book, and also "four brown books that are really nine."

The next day Sukuba prayed that God would give him a sign to lead him on his journey. When he did, a cloud appeared in the sky. For seven days Sukuba followed it. It disappeared over a village. There Sukuba asked for Pastor Moye and was quickly directed to his home.

After Sukuba told his story in the local dialect, Pastor Moye brought out his worn Bible. "That is it!" Sukuba exclaimed. "That is it! But where are the four books that are really nine?"

Years before, Ellen White had written nine volumes called *Testimonies for the Church,* which were later combined into four books. Sukuba's search was over. He had found the people of the Book, a Sabbathkeeping people, a people blessed with the prophetic gift.

Revelation identifies God's end-time people as keeping God's commands and having the gift of prophecy. Revelation 12:17 declares: "And the dragon was enraged with the woman, and he went to make war with the rest of her offspring, who keep the commandments of God and have the testimony of Jesus Christ."

The devil hates the bride of Christ, God's church. Throughout the centuries he has waged war upon her. In this passage John identifies God's last-day people as those who "keep the commandments of God and have the testimony of Jesus."

Testimony means a "witness." God's church is guided by a "witness from Jesus." That's precisely what a prophet is. Through the centuries God's prophets have borne witness for Him. John was a witness from Jesus. This is why the angel declared, "The testimony of Jesus is the spirit of prophecy" (Rev. 19:10). Based on Revelation 12:17, at the end of time God would raise up a Christ-centered, commandment-keeping movement guided by the Spirit of Prophecy. As Seventh-day Adventists we humbly believe that we are a divine fulfillment of Revelation's prediction, and that God is still providentially leading millions like Sukuba into this movement.

October 15

GOD'S PROPHETIC GIFT

So that you come short in no gift, eagerly waiting for the revelation of our Lord Jesus Christ. 1 Cor. 1:7.

In the early days of the Adventist movement a popular Protestant preacher challenged James White with a question. "Don't you Adventists believe in the Bible and the Bible only? If you do, why do you have a so-called prophet in your church?"

James White responded, "We Adventists accept all of the Bible, even those parts which speak about the gift of prophecy. To reject the gift of prophecy is to deny those Bible passages which promise God would raise up the 'gift' in our day." The apostle Paul would have heartily agreed. "Do not quench the Spirit. Do not despise prophecies" (1 Thess. 5:19, 20). In Ephesians 4:8 Paul adds that when the Savior ascended on high, He "gave gifts to men." The apostle lists one of those gifts as the gift of prophecy.

In December 1844, 17-year-old Ellen Harmon received her first vision. She saw the Adventist people traveling an elevated road to heaven, with a brilliant light illuminating the pathway.

What an encouragement this message was to this small and scattered group of believers, which would later be known as Seventh-day Adventists.

From 1844 until her death in 1915 Ellen White received more than 2,000 prophetic visions and dreams, wrote more than 25 books, and lectured to tens of thousands on three continents. With amazing accuracy and insight, she wrote on such subjects as education, nutrition, the life of Christ, practical godliness, world conditions, general health, medical practice, the coming world crisis, and many others.

In his book *California, Romantic and Beautiful,* George Wharton James wrote about Ellen White, who had lived her last years in California. James said: "This remarkable woman, also, though almost entirely self-educated, has written and published more books and in more languages, which circulate to a greater extent than the written works of any woman of history" (p. 320).

God has given the gift of prophecy to His people so we will prosper physically, mentally, and spiritually. His promise to us today is "Believe His prophets, and you shall prosper" (2 Chron. 20:20).

Do you cherish God's prophetic gift? Do you accept it as a gift from a loving Lord who wants you to draw closer to Him daily? Accepting God's special gift to His church today will bring you heaven's true prosperity.

October 16

HE NEVER PASSES US BY

But a certain Samaritan, as he journeyed, came where he was. And when he saw him, he had compassion. Luke 10:33.

Ann Landers told an interesting story in one of her columns. A man outside a Western city waited 11 hours after his car broke down for somebody to stop and help him.

The man was just a few miles out of town when his car engine stalled. He stepped out and attempted to flag down passersby. The cars hurried on, traveling 60 or 70 miles per hour on the freeway. Not one person stopped. It was a terribly cold night. At last the weary traveler gave up hope. The suicide note he left on his car windshield read, "I have been waiting for 11 long hours for somebody to stop. I can't stand the cold any longer. They just kept passing me by." So he ended it all.

There are times in all of our lives when it appears everyone just seems to pass us by. No one seems to really care. Jesus told a story to encourage us during the times we feel desperately alone.

A beaten, bruised, battered merchant lay bloodied on the road to Jericho. A priest, returning from his Temple duties in Jerusalem to his home in Jericho, merely glanced at the groaning man as he passed by. He was too holy to be helpful. A Levite, another religious man, approached. The Levite gazed at the suffering man and evaluated the risk involved. The thieves who robbed the dying man might rob him. He might be putting his life on the line. He too passed by the suffering man.

Finally a Samaritan, one of another race, drew near. The Scripture says he "came where he was" (Luke 10:33).

Jesus always comes where we are. He enters into our heartache. He understands our needs. The Samaritan had compassion on the man, bandaged his wounds, and carried him to a place of safety.

Jesus draws near in our times of grief. He cradles us in His arms and binds up our wounds. He ministers to our needs. He heals our hurts. He makes every provision necessary to get us going again. Others may pass us by, but He never will. He hears our pleas for help. He sees our pain. He knows all about our suffering. And best of all, He does not leave us alone. When we need Him most He is there.

October 17

HEALING THE WOUNDS

For I will restore health to you and heal you of your wounds. Jer. 30:17.

Harold Hughes had never been there much for his two young girls. He had the usual reasons. His trucking business ate up almost all his time. When he wasn't on the road he was often out entertaining business associates.

But one problem in particular kept Harold physically and emotionally absent from his family. He was an alcoholic. When his wife, Eva, tried to talk to him about it, he would blow up. Sometimes his girls hid in the closet when he came home. Finally Eva and the children left the house. This shocked him into making a solemn promise. He swore, before a judge, that he wouldn't touch liquor for a year. His family returned.

A few weeks later Harold traveled to a truckers' meeting in Iowa. One morning he woke up in a Des Moines hotel and noticed vomit in the bathroom. He didn't even remember his night of drinking. But one more promise had gone down the drain.

Things went from bad to worse. One night Harold decided to end it all with a 12-gauge shotgun in a bathtub. Before he pulled the trigger, though, he thought he'd best explain to God why he was doing this.

That prayer proved the turning point of his life. Harold confessed himself a failure, a hopeless drunk, and asked for forgiveness. That night Christ came into his life. God the Father was very present, driving out the emptiness and self-hatred, filling him with joy. Harold submitted himself to the discipline and discipleship of Christ.

Daily he sought God in prayer and studied God's Word. God fulfilled His promise: "For I will restore health to you and heal you of your wounds" (Jer. 30:17).

God restored Harold's physical, mental, emotional, and spiritual health. Things gradually began to change in his life. Not all of the changes came at once, but Harold was moving in the right direction. His marriage improved. His relationship with his children improved. And his own sense of self-worth improved.

Harold Hughes became a distinguished United States senator and the governor of Iowa. He would receive many public honors, but his most important moment was the night he committed himself totally to Jesus.

Jesus invites us to come to Him with all of life's challenges. He is fully capable of handling them. Why not bring Him the biggest challenge you face today and let Him handle it?

October 18

THERE STOOD A LAMB

The Lamb slain from the foundation of the world. Rev. 13:8.

A story from the early Jamestown settlement gives us a beautiful picture of grace. It's the story of Pocahontas and John Smith—the real story.

Tensions between the Colonists and the Indians who occupied the land kept mounting. John Smith, a courageous leader of the settlers, tried to negotiate peace with the Native American chief Powhatan.

But one day, during an Indian ceremony, Smith was seized by warriors who forced his head down on some rocks. They raised their clubs as if to kill him.

Suddenly the chief's favorite daughter, a young girl named Pocahontas, rushed from the crowd and laid herself over the captive. She offered her life in exchange for Smith's. The execution was halted.

Two days later Smith was astonished to learn that he'd been adopted as the chief's honored son.

Pocahontas eventually fell in love with and married an English farmer named John Rolfe. He was a Christian man of kindness and integrity. Pocahontas soon adopted the Christian faith, becoming a believer in the Lamb of God who takes away the sin of the world.

Pocahontas understood sacrifice, what it means to give yourself away.

Giving yourself away is the essence of Christianity. Heaven's central theme is sacrifice. When the exiled apostle John gazed into heaven in prophetic vision he beheld "a Lamb as though it had been slain" (Rev. 5:6).

The Lamb is mentioned nearly 30 times in the book of Revelation. From this world's origin to its glorious conclusion, the love story of the dying Lamb is the headline story. Jesus is the "Lamb slain from the foundation of the world" (Rev. 13:8). One day we shall rejoice at the marriage supper of the Lamb (Rev. 19:7).

His sacrifice, His death, His love wins our hearts. His was the supreme sacrifice, and all we can do is fall at His feet and give our hearts away. Without Jesus' sacrifice we are condemned to eternal death; with it we are assured of eternal life.

October 19

LET FREEDOM RING!

He has sent Me . . . to proclaim liberty to the captives. Isa. 61:1.

On a cool winter day in February 1832 a young theological student rested in his dormitory room at Andover Seminary in Andover, Massachusetts. Samuel Francis Smith leafed through a sheaf of German songs for children, given to him by his friend, the famed hymn writer and composer Lowell Mason. The sun set in the western sky, painting the horizon with strokes of deep purplish-red.

Smith lay on his bed relaxing. A strenuous day of study had left him exhausted. It was a relief to spend a few quiet moments going over the music his friend had sent him.

As he hummed over one tune after another, one melody above all others gripped his attention. He hummed it again and again. He glanced at the words at the bottom of the page. His knowledge of German told him the words were patriotic, but they did not appeal to him. They lacked the inspirational quality of all enduring music. Samuel decided to write his own words. He found a scrap of paper and began to write. On that scrap of paper, in the simple room of a university student, a song that would move millions was born. The words flowed freely. Samuel's pen had a hard time keeping up with his mind. It was as though some divine hand was guiding him as he wrote:

"My country, 'tis of thee,
Sweet land of liberty,
Of thee I sing.
Land where my fathers died!
Land of the Pilgrim's pride!
From every mountainside,
Let freedom ring!"

There is a yearning deep within the hearts of people everywhere for freedom. Shackled with the bond of totalitarianism, they long to sing, "Sweet land of liberty." Imprisoned for the beliefs of conscience, they cry out, "Let freedom ring."

There is another kind of tyranny. It is the tyrannical spirit of the evil one who takes control of all who yield to his alluring temptations. The apostle Paul pens an eternal truth when he declares, "Do you not know that to whom you present yourselves slaves to obey, you are that one's slaves whom you obey?" (Rom. 6:16).

Satan holds us in bondage. When we yield to sin, it controls us. It dominates us. It shackles us. It finds us. It imprisons our souls.

Only Jesus can set us free. When He cried "It is finished" on Calvary, He declared victory over sin's shackles. From Calvary's mountain Jesus shouts, "Let freedom ring." In Jesus there is true freedom. In Jesus there is real liberty. In Him the chains that bind us are loosed, and we are free indeed.

October 20

SEEING WITH GOD'S EYES

Blessed are your eyes for they see, and your ears for they hear. Matt. 13:16.

The New Testament urges us again and again to look at people with God's eyes. We are invited to see people in a new way.

The apostle Paul affirms this in 2 Corinthians 5. He writes about Jesus dying for the whole world, for every human being (verses 14, 15). He writes about the difference that sacrifice makes, how we must look at people through Christ's love. "Therefore, from now on, we regard no one according to the flesh. . . . If anyone is in Christ, he is a new creation; old things have passed away; behold, all things have become new" (verses 16, 17).

Christ gives us a whole new way of looking at people. We don't regard our neighbor according to the flesh, according to externals. We don't focus on the imperfections, the frailty, the things that might put us off. We now look at this individual as someone for whom Christ died. Do you know what that means? It means this individual has infinite value, infinite worth.

Looking at people with the eyes of grace. That's what matters. That's what makes a difference in this world. We're not just caught up in the packaging. We're looking at what's inside.

We focus on what people can become—not with the right cheekbones, not with the right color of eyes, but with the right heart that God puts inside us.

What a difference that would make today.

It would make a difference on the job. There are people in your workplace who have so much to give, but who are kept in the corner, just because of appearances.

It would make a difference in your marriage. We need to be valued by those closest to us, and we need to be valued most for what's inside us.

And it would make an enormous difference for our kids. They need to grow up knowing that they are valued for what's inside them, for their potential, for their character. So much in the world of teens tells them the opposite. They are ranked by looks and by performance. They want so desperately to be accepted, to be popular. But popularity so often is determined by superficial, external things.

Character counts with God. God looks at the purity of our motives. He looks at the sincerity of our heart. He looks at the honesty of purpose in our lives. When we see with God's eyes we too will look beyond all of the surface. We will look not merely at what people do but at the purity of their purpose. We will see the worth in everyone. We will cherish those closest to us. After all, they were created in God's image and redeemed by His blood.

October 21

EYES OF GRACE

The eyes of your understanding being enlightened; that you may know what is the hope of His calling, what are the riches of the glory of His inheritance in the saints. Eph. 1:18.

An online auction in the fall of 1999 captured the media's attention. The Los Angeles *Times* ran a feature story on it. It wasn't an auction of classic jewelry, sports cars, or vintage music. It was an auction of the eggs of eight of the world's most gorgeous models, eggs that when fertilized could become beautiful babies.

Here is the story. A California fashion photographer had acquired the rights to the models' eggs. Interested couples could view the models on the photographers' Web site. The photographer knew he could auction their eggs at quite a high price. The bids began at $15,000 and were to go as high as $150,000.

Our society looks at externals. It values good looks. When you really think about it, an auction like this places value on human beings based on how outwardly beautiful they are. It implies that those who are not as beautiful are not as valuable. It is the opposite of what the New Testament teaches.

Perhaps you don't realize it, but your heavenly Father has placed an enormous value on you. But He didn't set a price on you based on your looks, or your bank account, or your position at work.

God looked at your heart. He looked at your heart when He gave up His one and only Son, and He was willing to pay an infinite price for you.

Peter wrote, "You were not redeemed with corruptible things, like silver or gold, . . . but with the precious blood of Christ, as of a lamb without blemish and without spot" (1 Peter 1:18, 19).

God placed an infinite price on you when Jesus laid down His life for you. He did that because He looked inside you. He saw something redeemable. He saw someone who could become a child of God. He saw someone who could become a new creation.

Just remember that. Remember that when you are reacting to other people. Remember that God has placed an infinite value on you. Look at others in the way God has chosen to look at you. See their potential. See what really matters most. God has placed an incalculable worth on you. He values you more than you can possibly imagine, and He values you for who you are, not how you look. This should fill our hearts with encouragement today.

October 22

DEALING WITH DEATH

So when this corruptible has put on incorruption, and this mortal has put on immortality, then shall be brought to pass the saying that is written: "Death is swallowed up in victory." 1 Cor. 15:54.

Actress Kari Coleman pretended to be a psychic-medium for an appearance on a variety show. She studied certain techniques and practiced giving readings. After her performance Kari said, "I can't believe how vulnerable people make themselves. It's disturbing."

Kari felt especially guilty about deceiving a man whose mother had died. She caught up with him after the show and confessed tearfully that it had all been a hoax. His mother hadn't really given messages. To Kari's astonishment, the man didn't seem angry or upset. He was happy to have had the experience, even if it was an illusion.

Kari has concluded that people's obsession with mediums is unhealthy. "Until you deal with the finality of death," she says, "you can't move on. If you truly thought that there was a human being who could talk to your dead child, you'd remain stuck on that. You have to have closure."

The Bible presents a picture of death that blends finality with incredible hope. In Scripture there is closure up to a point. Death is a sleep (John 11:11-14). The dead cannot communicate with the living (Job 7:9, 10). Between the dead and the living there is a "great gulf fixed" (Luke 16:26).

But death is not the end of the road. The grave is not a dark night without a morning. Christians never say goodbye for the last time, for there will be a glorious reunion on resurrection morning. "For the Lord Himself shall descend from heaven with a shout, with the voice of an archangel, and with the trumpet of God. And the dead in Christ will rise first. Then we who are alive and remain shall be caught up together with them in the clouds to meet the Lord in the air" (1 Thess. 4:16, 17).

The Christian hope is in the coming of our Lord. Sickness and suffering will not have the last word; Jesus will. Disaster and death will not triumph; Jesus will.

In the catacombs beneath Rome, second-century Christians wrote on their loved ones' tombs, "Goodbye, my love, until the morning."

A bright morning is coming in which all God's children will be caught up to meet Him in the sky. On that day we shall have final closure "when death is swallowed up in victory" (1 Cor. 15:54).

October 23

MAGIC VERSUS THE WORD

For Your word has given me life. Ps. 119:50.

Karen Winterburn made a very faulty assumption, that everything supernatural must be good. As a teenager she had studied the Bible intently. But later Karen began dabbling in the occult. People around her kept telling her it was part of her spiritual journey. It seemed rather romantic. She was exploring a whole new world.

Eventually Karen became a professional astrologer. She counseled people and taught at conferences. She practiced divination, using numerology, I Ching, and tarot cards. She developed a specialty as a "trance medium."

Parapsychologists even conducted experiments with Karen while she was in her trance. Under hypnosis, she could discuss subatomic physics and biofeedback problems in detail—subjects she knew little about. Karen seemed to have tapped into a higher consciousness. She was deep in the world of magic.

And yet Karen felt empty. All this was supposed to bring her closer to god-consciousness, or at least to an awareness of the god within her. But she felt further removed from any meaningful relationship with God. In fact, Karen felt removed from any genuine spiritual life.

She was trying to fill a void deep inside her, but she found herself simply bowing down to a succession of gods that came along—Hindu gods, Greek gods, Egyptian gods, Chaldean gods.

She kept asking, "Are you the one?" And they all answered, "Yes." But each one left her spiritually numb.

After years of this, Karen finally confronted a hard truth. She wrote, "It became increasingly clear to me that spiritual growth was not something I'd been enhancing, but preventing. For three months I forced myself to face this issue. Over the years I'd had many interesting spiritual experiences, but there had been no spiritual growth. I realized I had been going around in circles and was no closer to the truth now than when I first started searching for it."

There is a source of spiritual growth that is solid. It presents substance, not mystery. It may not appear as spectacular, but it is much more permanent. It is not as sensational, but it is much more spiritually challenging. There is a depth of spiritual experience in the study of God's Word. The same Holy Spirit who inspired the Bible inspires us as we study it. The Christ who spoke then speaks now. The Sermon on the Mount, His parables and miracles all echo through the centuries. They still touch our hearts. They still transform our lives. They still radically change us inside.

The apostle James puts it well when he declares, "Receive with meekness the implanted word, which is able to save your souls" (James 1:21). Growth in grace through God's Word requires discipline, but in the long run it provides a spiritual strength that lasts.

October 24

THE SABBATH AND SELF-WORTH

Hallow My Sabbaths, and they will be a sign between Me and you, that you may know that I am the Lord your God. Eze. 20:20.

A story is told of that terrible time when countless people were sent to Nazi concentration camps. At the train terminal in one of the death camps, the SS officers began separating able-bodied men from the women and children.

One father there was a member of a royal family. He realized with a start that he might never see his son again. So he knelt down beside the boy and held him by the shoulders. "Michael," he said, "no matter what happens, I want you always to remember one thing. You're special; you're the son of a king."

Soon, father and son were separated by the soldiers. They were marched off to different sections of the camp. The two never saw each other again.

Michael learned much later that his father had perished in a gas chamber. He had to go out alone and try to make his way in the world. But his father's last words would always stay with him: "You're the son of a king." Michael determined that, whatever came, he would behave like the son of a king.

The Sabbath is an important message from our heavenly Father, a sign that declares: "You are a child of the King of the universe. I claim you as My own."

The Sabbath speaks of the God who created us. It leads us back to our origins. Each Sabbath we are reminded we are not cosmic orphans. We are not abandoned street urchins. We are children of the Creator.

Since He created us, He values us. Since He made us, He is interested in us. Everything that concerns us concerns Him. The things that trouble us trouble Him. When we are hurt, He is hurt. As Isaiah the prophet puts it: "In all their affliction He was afflicted" (Isa. 63:9).

Why? Simply because He created us. He is a loving Father who cares about His children. If God values me that much, shouldn't I value myself? If God treasures me more than I can imagine, shouldn't my heart be filled with encouragement today?

I am His and He is mine, and with that I am content. My heart overflows with joy in the certain knowledge that I am a child of the King of the universe.

October 25

OPEN HEARTS HEAL

O Corinthians! We have spoken openly to you, our heart is wide open. 2 Cor. 6:11.

One day Frederick II, king of Prussia, inspected a prison in Berlin. One after another the prisoners vigorously protested their innocence. Each claimed to have been wrongfully accused. Only one prisoner remained silent. So Frederick asked him, "You, there! Why are you here?"

"Armed robbery, Your Majesty."

"Are you guilty?"

"Yes indeed. I deserve my punishment."

The king summoned the warden. "Guard," he commanded, "release this guilty wretch at once. I'll not have him in this prison corrupting all these fine, innocent people."

When we are honest about our faults, God's grace can heal them.

The wise man states, "He who covers his sin will not prosper" (Prov.

28:13). It is futile to try to hide our sins from God, for "all things are naked and open to the eyes of Him to whom we must give account" (Heb. 4:13).

Open hearts heal. Confession is therapeutic. When in deep sorrow for our sins we honestly confess them to God, He works a miracle of grace upon our hearts. He forgives our sin and begins a process of healing inside us. Our confession prepares the way for God to do something special in our hearts. The results of sin—guilt, condemnation, fear, anger, resentment, and a multitude of other negative emotions—destroy the beautiful person we really are.

When we are open before God, we give Him permission to do His wonderful work inside us. He lances the boil of bitterness and drains the pus of resentment. He purges the poison. He strips away negative emotions so we can really be the people we were made to be.

Will you come before Him today with an honest heart and open confession? Will you be transparent before God? You will be glad you did, for open hearts heal.

October 26

HIS LOVE ABSORBS OUR HURT

By this we know love, because He laid down His life for us. 1 John 3:16.

A young man named Don was having the time of his life. At least that's what it looked like on the outside. He'd gone out with quite a string of attractive girlfriends. Other men looked at him enviously. But inside, Don was miserable. He was falling apart. His dating had become compulsive. He found himself using one woman after another just to get out of his own depression. When he felt down, he had to have some female reassurance.

Don knew he wasn't being fair with his partners. He'd been raised in a very strict home. Often he repented and promised God he would change his ways, but the pattern continued. Finally Don visited a Christian counselor who used spiritual and biblical principles in his work. Don just wanted to change the vicious cycle of his behavior. He wanted a formula to change his destructive habits. But slowly he realized that there was a reason he had these serious bouts of depression.

Behind Don's depression was an emptiness, an inability to absorb love in a healthy way. And so he was compelled, again and again, to try to get love in unhealthy ways. Don wasn't able to get a handle on his destructive behavior until he faced the brokenness inside, until he began to understand what God's unconditional love is all about.

The apostle John understood that love. With a pen dipped in the love of God, he wrote, "Behold what manner of love the Father has bestowed on us, that we should be called children of God" (1 John 3:1). Our love-starved hearts find love in Him. Our craving for love is satisfied in Him.

Some of us have been fortunate enough to come from families in which love was freely expressed. Others of us come from loveless backgrounds or dysfunctional homes—homes where love wasn't expressed much at all, or only in inappropriate ways. Whatever your background, God makes up the love deficit. Let these encouraging passages from 1 John sink into your heart: "By this we know love, because He laid down His life for us" (1 John 3:16). "In this the love of God was manifested toward us, that God has sent His only begotten Son into the world, that we might live through Him" (1 John 4:9). "And we have known and believed the love that God has for us. God is love" (verse 16).

Today live in God's love. Consciously say, "God loves me, and His love fills my heart. In Him I am complete." Allow His love to fill you up today.

October 27

TELL YOURSELF THE TRUTH

Blessed be the God and Father of our Lord Jesus Christ, who has blessed us with every spiritual blessing in the heavenly places in Christ. Eph. 1:3.

Conducting an It Is Written evangelistic series in São Paulo, Brazil, I met a woman named Anna who believed her life was worthless. She was attractive, intelligent, and outgoing, but extremely depressed.

On her twenty-third birthday she decided to take her own life. Before ending it all, she wrote letters to her family and her close friends, and she even wrote a letter to God.

Miraculously, at the very time she was writing these letters, the telephone rang. The person calling had dialed a wrong number, but he immediately sensed Anna's distress. He began to gently encourage her and present her with hope. Then he invited her to some evangelistic meetings I was holding. Anna came desiring a new life and longing to be healed from her brokenness. She came longing for the pain and hurt within to go away.

Anna sat spellbound as I talked about how, in Christ, we're valuable; in Christ we're loved; in Christ we're accepted; in Christ we can be made whole. Anna confronted her self-talk. She confronted the lies swirling around in her head. She accepted the truth that in Christ's eyes she was valuable. The lie that had imprisoned her unraveled.

The truth, of course, was obvious enough. But it had to sink in. The Holy Spirit impressed her with reality. God made that impression real in her mind, and His light shone in her heart. This was the beginning of healing for Anna.

Here is the thought that changed her thinking: "He [Christ] made us accepted in the Beloved" (Eph. 1:6). If we are accepted, we are not rejected. If the Father accepts me through Jesus, then I can accept myself. When we accept Jesus by faith we reside in His righteousness. The Father accepts us as He does His own Son. All of Christ's good works and His righteous living are credited to our account. "There is therefore no condemnation to those who are in Christ Jesus" (Rom. 8:1).

The Father will not condemn His own Son. Through Christ we are as truly accepted by the Father as if we were His own Son. He welcomes us. He embraces us. He reassures us. He accepts us. He loves us. Eternal life is ours! Heaven is our home.

Through Christ our future is bright. He accepts us, so we can accept ourselves now and through all eternity. If He values us that much, we can value ourselves. When negative self-talk floods your mind, tell yourself the truth. You are accepted and valued by God! In the end, that's what really matters.

October 28

KNOWING GOD, PART 1

And this is eternal life, that they may know You, the only true God, and Jesus Christ whom You have sent. John 17:3.

The essence of eternal life is knowing God. The real joy of eternity is not mansion building, it is relationship building. Fellowship with God is the deepest and most satisfying of all relationships.

God longs for an intimate relationship with us. Our eternal friendship with God will be an extension of the relationship we have begun here. Throughout all eternity we will discover more of the beauty of His character, the matchless charms of His love, and the enormous reservoir of His grace.

This relationship with God energizes our entire Christian experience and prepares us for eternity. Ellen White wrote, "Walk continually in the light of God. Meditate day and night upon His character. Then you will see His beauty and rejoice in His goodness. Your heart will glow with a sense of His love. You will be uplifted as if borne by everlasting arms. With the power and light that God imparts, you can comprehend more and accomplish more than you ever deemed possible" (*The Ministry of Healing*, p. 514).

Knowing God, meditating on His character, dwelling on His love, we become everything God created us to be. In fellowship with God we reach our full potential. In touch with the Creator we receive His power. In our relationship with Jesus, His grace reigns in our hearts and overflows into our lives.

Christianity is not merely a set of rules; it is a radical relationship. Throughout eternity we will seek to know our Lord more. The more we know Him, the more we will admire Him. We will joyfully exclaim with the Shulammite woman, "I am my beloved's, and his desire is toward me" (S. of Sol. 7:10).

There is no sweeter fellowship than knowing Jesus. There is no greater satisfaction than friendship with our Lord. There is no greater love than that which unites our hearts with His.

God has given us a little taste of His love here as an appetizer, to stimulate our desire for eternity. The more we become acquainted with Him, the more we desire to know Him better. Knowing Him, the kingdom of heaven dwells within our hearts already.

October 29

KNOWING GOD, PART 2

May my meditation be sweet to Him; I will be glad in the Lord. Ps. 104:34.

The story is told of an elderly European man who visited America for the first time in the late 1800s. When he returned home after his lengthy stay his friends asked him what impressed him most. His unusual answer startled them when he responded, "The Americans keep moving, moving, moving. They are always moving. Even when they sit down, they have a chair that moves them back and forth." This, of course, was the rocking chair.

In our complex world of tight schedules, pressurized deadlines, production and sales quotas, and mass media communication, life itself seems a whirl. We too are a society that is moving, moving, moving.

Maybe it is time to pause, to take a deep breath and evaluate our priorities, assessing what matters most. Maybe it is time to stop running and listen to God's voice.

A. W. Tozer prayed, "Lord, teach me to listen. The times are noisy, and my ears are weary with a thousand raucous sounds which continuously assault them. Give me the spirit of the boy Samuel when he said to Thee, 'Speak, for Your servant hears'" (1 Sam. 3:9).

"Let me hear Thee speaking to my heart. Let me get used to the sound of Thy voice, that its tones may be familiar when the sounds of the earth die away, and the only sound will be the speaking of Thy voice."

This prayer can become a reality in our lives. Why not begin making it real in your life today?

Take a walk alone. Develop the art of praying while you are walking, then be silent and listen for the voice of God. Look at the stars. Sit by the ocean. Walk in the woods. Wander through a park. Tune in to God's voice.

Or get up a little earlier and meditate upon the Psalms and hear God speaking to you. Maybe you are a "night person" who gears up in the evening. If so, find a quiet spot in the house after everyone has gone to bed, and slowly peruse Scripture and let God speak.

It is in these reflective moments that God seems nearest and our souls connect. Why not let your soul connect today? Find that place in God's heart where your soul can find home.

October 30

THE ANSWER MAN

If any of you lacks wisdom, let him ask of God, who gives to all liberally and without reproach, and it will be given to him. James 1:5.

Cecil Adams is quite an "answer man." He answers questions from readers in a syndicated newspaper column called The Straight Dope. Cecil manages to get to the bottom of a remarkable range of mysteries.

For example, someone wanted to know, "Do I get better gas mileage with the air conditioner on or with the windows open?" So Adams ran some tests. It was a dead heat. Turning off the air conditioner and opening the windows didn't save on gas because it increased drag.

Another inquirer wrote, "If a baby was born on the moon and lived there 20 years, would he be able to cope with earth's gravity if he were brought to earth?" Answer: "The moon person's muscular system would probably be too weak to deal with earth's gravity."

And someone else asked, "How long could a man live on bread alone?" Answer: "Three to six months. If he had water, too."

Adams is proclaimed as the world's smartest human being. He advertises: "All major mysteries of the cosmos succinctly explained."

An explanation of all mysteries! The idea has quite an appeal, doesn't it? Cecil Adams can network with biologists and chemists and physicists to answer many of life's little curiosities.

But what about the *real* mysteries of life? How can I find peace of mind? How can I be the person I really want to be? How can I be free from guilt? How can my marriage reach its full potential? Where can we find guidance when making major decisions? How can we know what job or career to pursue? How can we decide whether to move or stay put?

There is One who provides solid answers for our perplexing questions. He longs to guide us to make the best decisions possible. We can make David's prayer ours: "Hear my prayer, O Lord, give ear to my supplications! In Your faithfulness answer me" (Ps. 143:1).

God is faithful. He will never let us down. He is eager to give us direction. He is the real "answer man."

God's wisdom is infinite, and He is eager to share His wisdom with us. There is nothing He would rather do than have the privilege of guiding our lives. He will never manipulate our decisions or force us to accept His wisdom. But He is there waiting patiently to answer the deepest questions of our hearts.

October 31

THE DAY THE WAR ENDS

These will make war with the Lamb, and the Lamb will overcome them, for He is Lord of lords and King of kings; and those who are with Him are called, chosen, and faithful. Rev. 17:14.

A German private on the western front named Hans would always remember the day World War II ended for him. It was June 6, 1944. Hans had seen years of fighting as part of Hitler's proud, apparently invincible army. But now he felt like an old man.

Hans and his comrades had expected an invasion for weeks. They were dug in on the long German line of defense, along the coast of Normandy.

Reports started coming over the wireless. Parachutists had landed here. Gliders had come in there. Landing craft were approaching.

In the middle of this turmoil, Hans got orders to take a reconnaissance patrol toward the coast. He gathered several infantrymen and prepared to set off.

But just then a British tank roared up and opened fire. Everyone scattered. Hans hid in some bushes and then tried to make his way back to German lines, but he was captured by British paratroopers and moved toward the beach.

When the sun rose the next morning, Hans saw something that quickly changed his outlook as a prisoner of war. Spread over the ocean was an invasion fleet that stretched to the horizon, ship beside ship without a break. And down on the beaches Hans saw troops, weapons, tanks, munitions, and vehicles unloading in a steady stream. There seemed no end of it!

Who could resist such an onslaught? Hans breathed a sign of relief and told himself he was a lucky man. Clearly on D-Day, 1944, there was only one side to be on, the side of that Allied armada pouring into Europe.

Do you ever get the feeling that you've been part of a war, some prolonged conflict in your personal life? Do you ever feel worn down by the suffering that just seems to go on and on in our world?

The book of Revelation describes the glorious day when God's victorious armies will descend from the sky and the war will end.

Revelation 17:14 describes the forces of hell as making war with the Lamb and declares, "The Lamb will overcome them." Revelation 19 adds, "I saw heaven opened, and behold, a white horse. And He who sat on him was called Faithful and True, and in righteousness He judges and makes war" (verse 11).

No power on earth or in hell can stand against the armies of God. All the forces of evil are powerless in His presence. One day soon the great war will be over. Our Lord will reign forever as King of kings and Lord of lords. His righteousness, His plan, His truth will conquer.

DO YOU HEAR VOICES?

Everyone who is of the truth hears My voice. John 18:37.

Pastor Bob Oltoff is a counselor in Thousand Oaks, California. Bob tells a fascinating story about a woman facing deep scars from her past.

"I had a woman come into my office who was really suffering from depression," Bob says. "The more I talked with her, the more I saw how trapped she was in her past. After we looked into her background a little bit, I set up three chairs—one for her to use as she shared her feelings, another for her to use as she looked at what she was saying to herself, and a third for her to use as we examined what God's Word says about it. After she shared her feelings, she moved to the chair in which she discussed her negative self-talk.

"When we looked at the negative things she was playing back, I asked her, 'Where do these tapes come from?' And she was able to name different people, parents, teachers, and friends from the past who were the source of these negative ideas. Then she moved to the last chair, and she looked at what God's Word says about these things. 'Is that what God is saying to you?' I asked, referring to her negative self-talk. I could see her eyes just light up as she said, 'No! That isn't what God would say. God would say, "I love you."' "

What kind of voices do you hear? Are they negative voices from the past, voices of guilt and condemnation, fear and doubt? You can be certain that any voice that tears you down without giving you hope is the voice of the evil one.

Satan leaves us broken and bruised, with every door shut, but Jesus heals and encourages us. When Jesus speaks to us, even in rebuke, He always opens a door of hope. He says, "I will heal their backsliding, I will love them freely" (Hosea 14:4). Jesus' love flows from His heart to heal our hurts. He is the one who "heals the brokenhearted and binds up their wounds" (Ps. 147:3).

Listen for His voice. It is the voice of hope, of encouragement and cheer, the voice that lifts us up. It is the voice of a loving Savior who really cares. If you open your heart, you will hear His encouraging words today. If you will really listen, you will hear His words of hope.

RELYING ON GOD INSTEAD OF A CREDIT CARD

Honor the Lord with your possessions, and with the firstfruits of all your increase. Prov. 3:9.

Scott and Kathy Nelson once struggled over a very large burden of debt. Like many families, their debt had sort of sneaked up on them. But unlike many couples, the Nelsons found a way to eliminate all of their nonmortgage debt, and they did it rather quickly.

Although Scott had a good salary, the higher his income became, the more the family's debt load increased. The Nelsons thought they were raising their standard of living, but they were getting deeper into the red. At one point they had $60,000 in nonmortgage debt. They were drowning in it. Between student loans, a new car, credit cards, and weekly household expenses, their debts were building up fast.

When what was happening finally dawned on them, Kathy asked God to help them out of their dilemma. She started reading the book of Proverbs, a book with much to say about financial principles. Kathy read a chapter every day of the month. She and Scott began applying heaven's financial principles to their lives. They put God first. They made sure they were tithing honestly. As they put God first their debt began to go down. God impressed both of them to live by a budget, not by their whims.

Scott and Kathy pulled a basic budget off the Internet. They discovered guidelines of finance from a good Christian counselor and began cutting expenses. They paid down their credit cards first, to eliminate excessive interest charges.

Within two years they were debt-free. Kathy enthusiastically commented on their experience. She said, "The biggest blessing we have found in being out of debt is that it gives us the freedom to be generous. There is a lot of satisfaction in that. Those who refresh others will be refreshed themselves."

Following God's financial principles is the path to lasting financial freedom. When we sacrifice to place Him first, He pledges to care for our needs. Our Lord declares, "Seek first the kingdom of God and His righteousness, and all these things shall be added to you" (Matt. 6:33). The key to financial security is placing God first, not our own desires. Debt follows when we are consumed with our own wants, but following God's desires leads to financial stability.

Before any significant purchase, honestly ask, "Lord, is this what You desire me to do?" How can you know whether it is or isn't? If it is a nonessential item that leads you further into debt, it certainly isn't. If you are in serious debt and can get along without it, it certainly isn't. Be honest. Listen for God's voice. Present the issue before Him, then make the most informed decision possible.

November 3

GOD STILL WORKS MIRACLES, PART 1

Evening and morning and at noon I will pray, and cry aloud, and He shall hear my voice. Ps. 55:17.

In January of 1999 our It Is Written evangelistic team and production crew flew to the Philippines to conduct an evangelistic series. Our meetings were scheduled to take place at the Philippine International Convention Center and be transmitted via satellite throughout the Pacific Rim.

We were concerned that the satellite transmission equipment might not arrive on time. We praised God when we learned our equipment had arrived the Tuesday before our meetings were to begin. It was then that a serious problem surfaced.

All of our equipment was held up in customs subject to a $335,000 bond. The customs officials were adamant. Unless we paid $335,000, the goods would not be released.

All of our efforts to negotiate the equipment's release failed. Time was running out. Our production coordinator talked with numerous customs officials. The story was always the same. Without the payment, no goods.

We didn't have the money. Meanwhile, hundreds of churches, with tens of thousands of people, eagerly anticipated hearing God's Word Friday evening. What options did we have? Our staff prayed earnestly. We met in little prayer groups, claiming God's promises to find a way when there is no way.

Providentially we discovered that the Philippine ambassador to New Guinea was a Seventh-day Adventist. If he were in the country, he could possibly help us.

As God would have it, Ambassador Ben Tejano was in Manila and eager to help. He appealed directly to the then president of the Philippines, Joseph Estrada. President Estrada signed an executive order stating, "Immediately release all goods and transmission equipment of the Seventh-day Adventist Church at no charge."

Within a few hours our equipment was released. Our evangelistic meetings began on time. Tens of thousands heard God's end-time message of love and truth.

God still works miracles. He still answers prayer.

When we are at our wits' end, He isn't. When human solutions to our problems have run out, divine solutions have not. When we don't know what to do, He knows just what is necessary. Without a doubt, we can still depend upon Him to respond when we ask.

November 4

GOD STILL WORKS MIRACLES, PART 2

Is anything too hard for the Lord? Gen. 18:14.

On January 17, 1999, during It Is Written's Acts 2000 satellite evangelistic series, I was invited to officiate at a unique baptism in the Philippine National Prison. An Adventist lay couple dedicated their lives to studying the Bible with these prisoners. They have been ministering in the prison for the last quarter of a century. There is an Adventist church within the prison walls of more than 400 members. God's grace reaches into surprising places. God's love breaks the hardest hearts. God's light still penetrates the darkness.

Nothing is too hard for God. In the Philippine National Prison I met hard-core criminals totally transformed by God's grace. They were changed men. Their lives were different. They were freer in prison than on the streets. They were no longer imprisoned by drugs, alcohol, illicit sex, and tobacco. They were no longer slaves to their cravings. They were no longer victims of their uncontrollable passions. They were truly free in Christ.

As the locked gates of the prison opened, a group of Seventh-day Adventist prisoners surrounded me for my protection. We embraced as brothers. They were just as righteous in God's sight through Jesus Christ as I was. I was no more saved than they were.

As they ushered me into the modest church sanctuary, I was captured by the prison quartet that was singing:

"Let's sing a happy song.
Let's sing about Jesus.
With a smile on your face you can
Change the human race.
Let's sing a happy song. Let's sing
About Jesus."

The entire quartet were murderers from death's row. Yet they radiated Christ's amazing love. They were forgiven and changed by His amazing grace.

I had the joy of baptizing 46 of those prisoners that day. Twenty-two of the candidates came from death row.

God still reveals His power. God still manifests His hand. God still works miracles on human hearts.

Whatever challenges you face today, His power is for you.

November 5

LIVING THE LIFE

And let us not grow weary while doing good, for in due season we shall reap if we do not lose heart. Gal. 6:9.

Late one night a father received the one phone call that parents dread the most, the one we all pray never comes.

It was the highway patrol. A vehicle carrying four teenagers had spun out of control at high speed and rammed into a barrier. All the passengers had been killed. The officer on the phone said, "We believe your daughter may have been one of the victims."

Ashen-faced, the father drove to the hospital to identify the body of his beautiful girl, snuffed out in the prime of life. As he sat there in the emergency room with his head in his hands, grieving and shocked, he heard a police officer mention that alcohol was probably the culprit in this accident. Several broken whiskey bottles had been found in the wreckage beside the mangled bodies.

Now the father had a focus for his frenzied anguish. He rose up in a rage and threatened to kill whoever had provided the four young people with liquor. He would find the guilty party, whatever it took!

Back home, overwhelmed by grief and rage, he stumbled into the kitchen and opened the cupboard where he kept his own supply of alcohol. There he found a note in his daughter's handwriting. His heart leaped to his throat. The note read, "Dad, we're taking along some of your liquor—I know you won't mind."

The people around us absorb how we live much more than what we say. Our lifestyle influences them more than our words. Our walk impacts them more than our talk. When our life is consistent with our words, it makes a difference in the lives of others.

Jesus' words had such an impact because His teachings were consistent with how He lived. His life matched His words. The crowds could utter, "No man ever spoke like this Man!" (John 7:46) because there was never a man who lived like He lived. There was no gap between what Jesus said and how He lived.

Skeptics may debate an idea, but they cannot deny God's power in the awesome testimony of a changed life. When those closest to us see Christ's love revealed in all our actions, they too will stand in awe of how great He is.

November 6

CONVERSION MAKES A DIFFERENCE!

And have put on the new man who is renewed in knowledge according to the image of Him who created him. Col. 3:10.

A tall, muscular youth named Chuck showed up one day at the home of Pat, a fellow member of a gang called the Rubes. Pat was alone, and Chuck asked quickly, "You ready?"

"Ready for what?"

"To rob the bakery at Fourth and Elm," Chuck replied, grinning.

Weeks before, the two had planned to "knock off the joint" as soon as Pat could get around on his bad leg. He'd been shot while robbing a house. Hesitantly Pat began to explain. "Chuck, a few days ago something happened to me."

"What happened?"

"I got saved."

"Saved from what?"

"I accepted Christ as my Savior." Pat blurted out his story about church, an altar call, confession and forgiveness, and new peace as God's child.

Chuck looked out the window for a moment, and then back at his buddy. "OK, so now you're saved. Big deal! Come on, let's go rob that bakery!"

"So you're saved. Big deal!" Chuck's response is all too true for too many people. What difference does conversion make? Conversion, big deal!

Claiming to be born again has very little to do with genuine conversion. A genuine commitment to Christ leads to an authentic Christianity that makes a radical difference. Old habits are changed. Old attitudes are transformed. Old thought patterns are renewed.

By faith we accept that the old person was nailed to the cross with Christ. The old person died. By faith we believe that when Christ was resurrected we too were made alive in Him. We now live new lives through the power of the resurrected Christ. "But now having been set free from sin, and having become slaves of God, you have your fruit to holiness, and the end, everlasting life" (Rom. 6:22).

Genuine conversion does make a difference. If there is no difference, there is no conversion. If there is no difference, we may claim to be born again, but we are merely deceiving ourselves. Christ offers much more than a superficial modification of our old habits and patterns; He offers a complete transformation. And He offers it to you right now.

November 7

GOD IN THE SEWERS

Therefore we do not lose heart. Even though our outward man is perishing, yet the inward man is being renewed day by day. 2 Cor. 4:16.

Let me tell you about a friend named Milton Schustek. He pastored in Czechoslovakia during the years of Soviet domination and religious oppression.

When the Communists took over his country, Schustek wanted to be free to minister to his Sabbathkeeping congregation in Prague. But the Communists had other ideas. They were determined to send all ministers to labor camps.

Milton knew they wanted to send him as far away from his congregation as possible, to the coal mines in the north. But he figured out a way that he might be able to stay close to his pastoral work in the city. There was one job nobody wanted—to clean out the sewers. Nobody wanted to climb into those narrow filthy culverts, hundreds of feet under the city streets.

Milton decided to go see the Communist officials about that job. But first he got down on his knees and prayed. "Jesus," he said, "I want to worship You every Sabbath. Please help me keep Your law and be faithful to You."

Milton was ushered in to see the local official. He said, "I understand you want to ship me to the mines to work. Let me tell you something. My grandfather worked in the mines, and my father worked in mines, and I am willing to work in whatever mine you send me to. But I have a suggestion. You need someone to do the worst job you have. I know about it. It is climbing down into those sewers, and I am willing to do the job. Why don't you assign me to clean the sewer pipes of Prague? I'd be happy to do it." The Communist official agreed to give him the job.

I will never forget the look on Milton's face when he told me this story. He admitted it was a very tough job, very dark and lonely. "But every day was worth it," he said, "because I could worship God with my congregation each Sabbath."

God has His faithful people in every age. They are lights shining in a dark place.

Milton Schustek was willing to serve God at any cost. God took care of him, and He will take care of you, too. God works miracles for those who trust Him. When in faith we take hold of His strength, miraculous doors open. He opened them for Milton Schustek, and He will open them for you.

We will never see God work miracles in our lives if we live lives of careless compromise. Compromising denies God the privilege of working a miracle to deliver us from our dilemma. Stand firm, don't lose heart, and watch God open doors.

November 8

DREAMS IN OUR DAY

And it shall come to pass afterward that I will pour out My Spirit on all flesh; your sons and your daughters shall prophesy. Joel 2:28.

Recently a team of four Adventists trekked through the jungle trails and swollen rivers of the central Philippines. They entered a completely isolated area inaccessible by motor vehicle. The people were animists who worshiped objects of nature.

After hiking through the jungle for eight hours, they came to a village. What they found amazed them. They found a building already erected for the worship of God. A villager had dreamed of a man dressed in white linen with shining shoes who said, "Build a big house for God and worship Him." The man in the dream also said some people would be arriving who would teach "Bible truth." Another villager dreamed of a man telling her that the coming visitors were good people.

The four Adventists began teaching about Jesus Christ and His gospel. The villagers accepted the message warmly. Soon there were 24 baptized believers to fill that "big house for God." Deep into the jungles of the island of Mindoro, the Olangan tribe had been untouchable. But today they are accepting the gospel.

God prepared the way. Angelic visitors descended from the throne room of the universe to the dense jungles of the Philippines. The Spirit opened hard hearts.

Skepticism has no place for the miraculous. The cynic dismisses the divine. But to reject miracles because they are unscientific is to deny the authenticity of Scripture.

Consider God's use of visions and dreams. God spoke to the Old Testament prophets regularly through dreams. Joseph and Daniel, Isaiah and Jeremiah, Jacob and Ezekiel each received special messages from God through dreams. The entire book of Revelation is the result of a God-given vision.

Once again, in our generation, we can expect God to reveal His will through visions and dreams. Just as He led the apostle Peter to Cornelius through a dream, He will lead honest-hearted seekers to His truth through dreams today. Of course, dreams are not a substitute for Bible truth. Any purported message from God that contradicts Scripture is blatantly false. But God does use dreams on occasion. He has unusual ways of finishing His work, and those ways may surprise us. He will do anything He can to reach His lost children.

November 9

SONGS IN THE NIGHT

But no one says, "Where is God my Maker, who gives songs in the night." Job 35:10.

His name was Juliek. Nobel Peace Prize-winning author Elie Wiesel met him on the way to a Nazi death camp. He and hundreds of other Jews were forced into a barracks for three days in the town of Gleiwitz. Jammed tightly into a room, many smothered to death. The sheer mass of human bodies simply cut off sources of air.

Among these twisted bodies, Elie noticed young, emaciated Juliek, clutching a violin to his chest. Somehow Juliek managed to hang on to the instrument, mile after mile through snowstorms, on the forced death march to Gleiwitz.

Now he struggled to free his limbs. Crammed among hundreds of the dead and dying, he slowly drew his bow across the strings. Juliek began to play a piece from a Beethoven concerto. A beautiful melody arose, pure and eerie in that horrible room.

In the darkness Elie heard only those sounds of the violin. Elie felt as if Juliek's soul were in the bow, as if his whole life were gliding on the strings. Elie would always remember the youth's pale, sad face as he said a tender, gracious farewell to his audience of dying men.

That night Elie fell asleep to Beethoven's concerto. In the morning he saw Juliek slumped over nearby, dead. Beside him lay his violin, broken and trampled.

But the song remained. Juliek's final melody still rose above the horrors of that death march. Not even Nazi cruelty could suffocate its gentle winsomeness. Juliek's song echoed the beauty of another world. It made an eloquent statement: There's something beyond this suffering and inhumanity.

There is a song that wafts its way from earth to heaven, a song of a better world. In the midst of suffering, sorrow, and sickness, there is a song. A song of home, a song of heaven, a song of eternity. God gives us songs in the night, sweet melodies that lift our hearts from what is to what will be.

Today let the thought of heaven give you a reason to sing. Let the music of another world cheer your heart. Let the tune of eternity inspire your spirit. Heaven's chorus sings of a land where there are no more tears, pain, sickness, suffering, war, or death. Join with all of heaven today and let your heart rejoice.

November 10

GOD'S ANSWER MAY NOT BE OURS

Hear my prayer, O Lord, give ear to my supplications! In Your faithfulness answer me, and in Your righteousness. Ps. 143:1.

Gary Habermas, chair of the Philosophy Department at Liberty University, is a thinking man. He's also a praying man. He kept a record of his prayer requests during the 1980s. After he witnessed a remarkable series of God's providence and healing, he had to conclude that personal prayer works.

When his 87-year-old grandmother became deathly ill, he engaged in some serious prayer at her bedside. To his great joy, she recovered.

Later Debbie, his wife of 23 years, was diagnosed with stomach cancer. He prayed again, even more earnestly. When Debbie died, it seemed that Gary's prayer hadn't been answered.

But before she passed away, Debbie whispered to her husband, "God spoke to me three words—I love you."

Debbie had doubted God's love all her life. But now Gary realized she was as sure of God's love as she was of his.

Gary experienced an intense grief—and a deep gratitude. He'd learned something about another kind of healing, emotional healing. These are his words: "I trust God to have a good answer to my prayers. That's not the same as knowing what the answer is."

Gary Habermas refused to remain rigid. He didn't demand that God answer his prayer only one way. He didn't become bitter. As a result, he saw something beautiful in the comfort of divine love.

Prayer is dangerous when we use it to back God into a corner. When we demand a precise answer, in a precise way, at a precise time, we play God. The One who loves us most knows best how to answer our prayers. Every sincere prayer will be answered, but it may not be the answer we are looking for. Mature Christians trust God to answer their prayers in the way His infinite wisdom sees best.

God's solution and ours may be dramatically different. "'For My thoughts are not your thoughts, nor are your ways My ways,' says the Lord" (Isa. 55:8).

God's love is limitless. His wisdom is infinite, His power unparalleled. We can trust His limitless love to move His infinite wisdom to impart His unparalleled power to answer our prayers in the way He knows best.

November 11

SOMEONE TO HOLD ON TO

When you pass through the waters, I will be with you; and through the rivers, they shall not overflow you. Isa. 43:2.

In the summer of 1993 the annual "Crucifix at the River" festival began in the Philippines. Crowds gathered at a little town north of Manila for nine days of festivities. But what began as a colorful religious spectacle ended in tragedy.

More than 300 worshipers crowded on the three barges of a shrine that was to float down the river. The shrine carried a three-tiered altar and wooden crucifix. Unfortunately, as the shrine drifted downstream people began to swim out to try to climb on board the already packed shrine. Marshals did their best to toss people back into the water, but more and more people climbed on, until the overloaded shrine began to sink. People panicked. The current had grown swifter, and the barges keeled over. More than 300 people drowned.

What a graphic illustration of what happens when we cling to the wrong thing.

These people's religious boat sank. In a time of crisis it could not sustain them. They were simply clinging to the wrong thing in the name of religion. They needed something or someone to cling to who would not let them down.

Is it possible that we too are like them? When we cling to our own opinions rather than God's Word, sooner or later we will sink in the murky waters of temptation. If we hold on to the notion that somehow God will wave some magic wand and save us while we are openly disobedient, we will be disappointed in the end. We deceive ourselves into thinking that no matter how we treat our bodies, God is going to preserve our health miraculously. We think God will supply our needs, but we squander our earnings, clinging to an emotional raft that will not sustain us.

Only one thing can sustain us in the end—a relationship with God. A personal, intimate relationship with the Creator of the universe.

The One who walked on water and pulled Peter out of the overpowering waves will deliver us when the waters of trial seem overwhelming. We are secure in His grip. He will never let us go.

November 12

THE GOD OF THE UNEXPECTED

The wind blows where it wishes, and you hear the sound of it, but cannot tell where it comes from and where it goes. So is everyone who is born of the Spirit. John 3:8.

A young lawyer named Charles didn't expect to meet this Person when he began studying the Bible. He was just trying to find out more about Jesus Christ.

Ever since his conversion, he had spent the hours after work in his office praying and reading Scripture. He was getting to know God personally, and it was exciting. He hadn't before imagined that this was possible.

One evening he had such a wonderful time in the Word that it seemed he was talking with Christ face to face. He felt deeply moved. And then it happened. Here are Charles's own words:

"Without any expectations of it, without ever having the thought in my mind that there was anything for me, the Holy Spirit descended upon me in a manner that seemed to go through me, body and soul. . . . It seemed like the very breath of God."

There are times the Spirit surprises us. God does not always announce when He will show up. He often uses a variety of ways to touch us in deep ways. I have been profoundly moved while singing a simple hymn. A prayer, the reading of a text, a pastor's sermon have all touched me at different times.

But for me there is little that moves me the way quietly meditating on Scripture does. God often uses His Word to speak to my soul. As I read His Word, His voice is clear. I am inspired, encouraged, and uplifted. I am convicted of my sin and compelled to renew my commitment to Him.

His Word energizes my soul. It encourages my heart and gives me new hope and joy.

There are times I read God's Word listlessly. Nothing seems to be happening. The words seem to have little impact. But then, invariably, it happens. The words seem to leap off the page. My heart is thrilled. My soul is stirred. My life is touched in unusual ways. God is speaking. He has the message I need most for that very moment. I am enraptured in His love and surrounded by His presence, and I don't want the moment to end.

Let God surprise you today as you spend time with Him in His Word. Let the Word be the channel of heaven's infinite blessings.

November 13

OVERWHELMED WITH GOD'S LOVE

O God, You are more awesome than Your holy places. The God of Israel is He who gives strength and power to His people. Ps. 68:35.

Dwight L. Moody was having a wonderful conversation with God one day while walking the busy streets of New York City. He had asked God to fill him with the Holy Spirit.

Moody found it difficult to find words to describe what happened next. But he wrote this: "I can only say that God revealed Himself to me, and I had such an experience of His love that I had to ask Him to stay His hand."

Moody was overwhelmed with this quality, this sense of God's love. As a result, he found great power. Returning to work, he preached the same sermons he'd always preached, and yet there was a difference. Now "hundreds were converted."

Moody wrote: "I would not now be placed back where I was before that blessed experience if you should give me all the world."

God longs to do much more for us than we can possibly imagine. Often we live well below our privileges. We pick up a few spiritual crumbs here and there when we could feast at the banquet table of His love.

The psalmist states it well: "You open your hand and satisfy the desire of every living thing" (Ps. 145:16). God's hand is open. He offers unimaginable spiritual blessings. He longs for us to be full of His love, His Holy Spirit, His power. When we seek Him with all our heart, He will pour out the abundance of His Spirit.

"If you then, being evil, know how to give good gifts to your children, how much more will your heavenly Father give the Holy Spirit to those who ask Him!" (Luke 11:13).

The Holy Spirit is the personal presence of Christ that energizes the soul. The Holy Spirit is the third person of the Godhead, who brings life-giving power into our lives. He is the personal representative of our Lord, who brings vitality to our Christian experience. The Holy Spirit convicts us of sin, reveals God's truth, and leads us into service.

Seek His presence today and, like Dwight L. Moody, experience the fullness of His presence. Be satisfied with nothing less than the infilling of the Holy Spirit in your life. Ask God for it. Open your heart to receive it, and claim the gift by faith.

November 14

PEACE IS A GIFT

Peace I leave with you, My peace I give to you. John 14:27.

Lorenzo Dow went through a period of soul-searching. He wanted a relationship with God. He wanted to be filled with the Spirit. And finally, God inspired him, "Believe the blessing now." That is, "Believe that you've received it."

That proved a breakthrough for Lorenzo. He said, "A gentle running peace filled my soul."

Before, Lorenzo had bounced often between ecstasy and melancholy. He was often discouraged. But now Lorenzo began to experience what he called a "simple, sweet, running peace from day to day, so that prosperity or adversity didn't produce the ups and downs as formerly; but my soul is more like the ocean, while the bottom is still calm."

Lorenzo Dow was filled with the Spirit. And he was filled with the quality of peace. He became a powerful man of God.

Peace is not an attribute we strive for. It is not a state of mind we achieve through some meditative state. Peace is a gift God offers. We receive it by faith. When we open our hearts to the Spirit, the Spirit brings peace.

Scripture calls the Holy Spirit our Comforter. The New Testament word is *paraclete.* It means "one who stands alongside." He is the one who holds us up and supports us, encourages us, steadies us, and gives us peace.

Peace is a state of calm assurance. It is the result of trust, of knowing that someone much greater than we are is in control. Peace is the opposite of worry.

Worry projects the worst possible scenario on the screen of our minds. Peace trusts that God will work to accomplish His good in every situation. The apostle Paul declares, "He [Jesus] Himself is our peace" (Eph. 2:14). Jesus is the "Prince of Peace" (Isa. 9:6). Receiving Him, we receive peace. And when we are at peace with God, we "cannot be made miserable" (*Testimonies,* vol. 5, p. 488).

The old hymn states it well: "Peace! peace! wonderful peace, coming down from the Father above; sweep over my spirit forever, I pray, in fathomless billows of love." Today open your heart to receive heaven's Dove of Peace. Accept His gift of peace. It is yours for the asking.

EXPERIENCE GOD'S PEACE

He is the Rock, His work is perfect. Deut. 32:4.

A story is told about a young man who took a hike through the English countryside. He began climbing a hill and looked down on a peaceful landscape the Master Artist must have painted.

But suddenly the wind picked up, clouds thickened overhead, lightning flashed, and the sky opened up with a downpour. The young man scrambled for cover, but the few trees on the hill offered little protection. He was getting soaked to the bone. The lightning seemed to be striking very close.

Then he spotted a rock outcrop jutting out near the hilltop. He ran over to it and spied a split in the rock, a cleft. It was just big enough for him to wedge his way in. The rock thrust out above him, offering complete shelter from the rain.

As he dried out, waiting for the storm to pass, the young man remembered lessons he'd learned about God as a child, lessons about how the heavenly Father hides us in the shelter of His hands.

Back home, he began to write down some lyrics. "Rock of Ages, cleft for me, let me hide myself in Thee." "Rock of Ages" became one of the most beloved hymns of all time.

In the storms of life peace comes from the Solid Rock. In Him there is true rest. A calm assurance floods our souls. Secure in Him, our troubled hearts find peace and our restless longings cease.

Throughout Scripture Christ is the solid rock we can depend on. He is the immovable stone we can count on, the impenetrable fortress protecting us from the enemy. He is our firm foundation in the storms of life.

This rock imagery is particularly rich in the Psalms. Psalm 31:3 declares: "For You are my rock and my fortress." Psalm 94:22 adds: "But the Lord has been my defense, and my God the rock of my refuge." In Psalm 61:2, the psalmist cries out, "When my heart is overwhelmed, lead me to the rock that is higher than I."

He is our shelter. Our protection. Our defense. He is our peace.

"Rock of Ages, cleft for me, let me hide myself in Thee."

THE JOY OF JESUS

These things I have spoken to you, that My joy may remain in you, and that your joy may be full. John 15:11.

Jacob Knapp began to seek God intently. He'd struggled with guilt for some time. One day he realized that Jesus Christ had indeed removed this load of guilt. Knapp rose from his knees and looked up to heaven gratefully.

And then it happened. It seemed as if Jesus were descending toward him with open, welcoming arms.

These are Jacob's words: "My soul leaped within me, and I broke . . . into singing praises to the blessed Savior. The sweet melodies of the birds seemed to make harmony with the songs. The sun shone with a luster not its own. The majestic trees appeared to bow in sweet submission. All nature smiled, and everything, animate and inanimate, praised God with a voice (though unheard before) too loud and too plain to be misunderstood."

This experience set the tone for Jacob's ministry. It was a defining moment in his life. He discovered Christianity was not merely something to believe in, but someone to love. Christianity is much more than a belief system. It is a heart experience with God. This experience with God makes all the difference.

A marriage without love is bondage. A couple may live together but be miles apart emotionally. Going through the motions of marriage, staying together for the kids, they each feel trapped.

Our religious experience may be very much the same. It is possible to feel trapped in rigid rules. Religion may degenerate to obligation, to "should haves" and "oughts." Love changes it all. A relationship with God fills our hearts with warmth, love, and praise. In Christ our hearts sing. Through Him duty becomes a delight. Sacrifice becomes a pleasure. His commands become doorways to happiness.

Jacob Knapp's ministry won more than 100,000 people to Christ. You may not have the dramatic conversion experience Jacob had. Maybe you should not expect it. But you can have an intimate relationship with Jesus that fills your life with His love. Filled with this love, you can go out and change your world, as Jacob did his.

TO BE HEAVENLY-MINDED

Set your mind on things above, not on things on the earth. Col. 3:2.

The story is told of a family who lived in a wilderness home on the bleak New England shore. It was a home of their own making, with furniture carved out by their own hands. There were two grown children. One of them was a young doctor who was almost constantly away from home, visiting the little towns and isolated settlements along the coast. The other was a lonely girl about 20.

Each evening she would steal away in the quiet of the nearby wooded sections, without the family knowing just where she went, to have her devotions alone in nature's retreat. Always she would sing:

"When softly falls the twilight hour,
O'er moor and mountain, field and flow'r,
How sweet to leave a world of care,
And lift to heav'n the voice of prayer."

One evening as she enjoyed her meditation, and just as she had completed the first two lines of her little song, a stranger crept up behind her, struck her on the head, and fled. She dropped to the ground, unconscious. When the evening meal was served, the girl was missing. Her family and friends frantically searched for her. They found her unconscious. She remained unconscious for several days. The doctor brother was called, and an operation was planned to remove the pressure on her brain.

When she at last regained consciousness, her lips began to move, and she finished the song so abruptly interrupted a few days before: "How sweet to leave a world of care, and lift to heav'n the voice of prayer."

When God's people arise from their graves at Jesus' glorious return, their thought patterns will continue in the direction they were set on earth. The apostle Paul talks about those who "set their minds on the things of the flesh" and "those who live according to the Spirit" (Rom. 8:5). Paul writes, "For to be carnally minded is death, but to be spiritually minded is life and peace" (verse 6).

If we cultivate spiritual thoughts here, our minds will be filled with spiritual thoughts throughout eternity. The process begun here will continue there. We cannot expect a spiritual mind-set in heaven if we have a carnal mind-set on earth. For the committed Christian, heavenly-mindedness begins right now.

A GOD OF NEW BEGINNINGS

Do not remember the former things, nor consider the things of old. Behold, I will do a new thing, now it shall spring forth. Isa. 43:18, 19.

Frank Deford was devastated by the death of his daughter, Alexandra. Cystic fibrosis had claimed her life at the age of 8.

Several months after the funeral the question of adoption came up. Perhaps the Defords could adopt another girl. Chris, their son, thought it was a great idea. But Frank was reluctant. Giving some needy child a home was certainly a good thing, but Frank just couldn't think of bringing in some stranger to take Alexandra's place. It seemed terribly unfair. No one could ever replace her in their home.

But then one evening Frank's wife remarked, "You know, if we wanted to get a baby, we could probably never get one in the States. It would have to come from some faraway country."

Yes, Frank understood that. Then his wife asked, "Do you remember Alexandra's prayer? Remember the part she made up herself and said every night?" Yes, Frank remembered. His daughter had always prayed, "And, God, please take care of our country, and bring some of the poor to our country."

Tears came to Frank's eyes. Now he understood. Adopting another girl wouldn't replace Alexandra, but it would answer her prayer.

Within a few months the Defords welcomed into their home a precious girl from the Philippines. Now they could go on, rebuilding their lives. A child's idealism had moved them to action. Frank later wrote, "We'll just have to start up again and go on from here. But thank you very much, Alexandra, because we do have a great deal to work with since you came our way."

We can either get stuck in the pain of the past or move on to new beginnings. New beginnings do not ignore or erase the past, but they take us beyond its devastating hurt. They lead us out of its destructive bondage. The past is a teacher, but it is not our master. Someone has aptly said, "You can never run forward looking backward."

Each morning God invites us to have a new beginning. "Through the Lord's mercies we are not consumed, because His compassions fail not. They are new every morning; great is Your faithfulness" (Lam. 3:22, 23).

Frank Deford and his wife made a new start. Their adopted daughter didn't replace Alexandra, but she did bring them incredible new joy. They discovered God's "compassion does not fail," His mercies are "new every morning." They could exclaim "great is Your faithfulness."

We can discover this God of new beginnings in our lives too. We can move on from the mistakes of our past. We can begin again. Let today be your day of new beginnings.

November 19

UNBOUNDING LOVE

Love never fails. 1 Cor. 13:8.

A newspaper columnist once asked readers to send in their favorite love letter for a Valentine's Day column. A woman named Gloria sent one she'd received from Ralph Illion in 1944, when he was a sailor, stationed in the Pacific. He wrote: "Dear Gloria:

"It's about time I introduced myself. We haven't met, yet I have heard so much about you. I must confess I have fallen in love. This confession might come as a shock, since you know nothing about me except what other people have told you. Don't take them too seriously. I'm really not a bad guy once you get to know me. And my feelings for you will never change as long as I live.

"I hope this makes the proper impression and you won't think me too bold. Send me a picture. Please keep my love for you locked in your heart, to be opened only when I call for it in person."

Well, Ralph made it back from the Pacific, and he was able to meet Gloria face to face: a healthy, lively baby girl, his precious daughter. And, yes, they did fall in love.

Gloria is a grown woman now. But she still cherishes that love letter she received from her dad at the tender age of 3 months. It's a father's gift of love, a lasting legacy, words that still burn in her heart.

Another Father, whom we have never seen, loves us with an incredible love. The prophet Isaiah speaks with assurance when he says, "You, O Lord, are our Father; our Redeemer from everlasting is Your name" (Isa. 63:16).

His Word is a love letter. It constantly reminds us of His care. It reveals the heart of a Father's love.

Just as Ralph Illion longed to be with his daughter, the heart of an infinite God longs to be with us. He is lonely for our love. He will never be content unless we are with Him throughout all eternity. There is a place in His heart only for us. Daily He reminds us of His love. One day He will reassure us of His awesome, infinite care when, with a warm embrace, He smiles and says, "It's time—time now to go home."

THE KINDNESS QUOTIENT

Be kind one to another. Eph. 4:32.

Hundreds of academic professionals gathered to honor a man who had earned a Nobel Prize in science. During the preliminary ceremonies his wife waited backstage with the wives of other men who would be honored also. The wife of the Nobel Prize winner didn't seem particularly excited. The other women asked her why.

"How can I be happy with a husband like that?" she asked, and went on to describe a rather pathetic home life.

Immediately the other women chimed in. "Why, that's my story exactly." All had the same experience of neglect and abuse.

While cameras flashed on the stage and dignitaries gave admiring speeches, a very different story was unveiled backstage. Those closest to the honorees could only describe a common misery.

It is one thing to be right. It is another thing to be nice. It is possible to have a high IQ, but a very low KQ.

KQ stands for the kindness quotient. It has to do with our interpersonal relations. Success in life results not simply from how smart we are, but from how we treat other people. The kindness factor makes all the difference.

Kindness is one of God's attractive attributes. He is "gracious and merciful, slow to anger, abundant in kindness" (Neh. 9:17).

The psalmist asserts, "His merciful kindness is great toward us" (Ps. 117:2).

Kindness looks for opportunities to do others good. It delights in making others happy. Kindness is not demanding; it is giving. Think of what the atmosphere in our homes would be like if we all were a little kinder. Think of what the workplace would be like if we were a little kinder. Think of what our schools, our churches, and our committees would be like if we were a little kinder.

Kindness produces kindness. The people around us often reflect back the attitudes we project toward them. They are like mirrors imaging what we are.

The little girl was on target who one night prayed, "Lord, help all the bad people to be good, and help all the good people to be kind."

Why not think of someone you can perform an act of kindness for today?

THE ONE WE GREATLY ADMIRE

When He comes, in that Day, to be glorified in His saints and to be admired among all those who believe. 2 Thess. 1:10.

Columbia University psychologists discovered something quite remarkable in a 1968 study. Over a period of time, a research team dropped specially identified wallets on various streets in lower Manhattan. They then kept track of how many of the wallets were returned to their owners. After weeks of checking, the researchers discovered that about 45 percent of those finding the wallets returned them within a couple of days.

But then something unusual happened. Not a single one of the wallets dropped on June 5 was returned. On that day a young man named Sirhan Sirhan fired a bullet at Robert F. Kennedy. Within hours the entire nation heard the news that he was dead.

The researchers realized that this tragic news had somehow damaged whatever social bonds had inspired people to return those wallets. Further studies established that the hearing of bad news consistently lessened people's willingness to help others. They also revealed that good news concerning some helpful citizen or heroic deed actually made people behave more cooperatively.

People are motivated to do good by positive ideals. The best within us is brought out by the heroic acts of others. When we see kindness modeled, we are more likely to be kind.

Looking to Jesus, we discover everything we long to become. All of the kindness, compassion, and goodness we crave resides in Christ. Journeying with Him through the cobblestone streets of Jerusalem, we watch Him forgive a woman caught in the very act of adultery. We listen to His words, "Neither do I condemn you; go and sin no more" (John 8:11).

We are amazed as He touches the eyes of the blind and unstops the ears of the deaf. His sensitivity toward others overwhelms us. He sits children on His lap, feeds a hungry crowd, and drives devils out of a demon-possessed man.

Concerned about the host's embarrassment at a Galilean wedding feast, He works a miracle. Conscious of the small yet vitally important things in life, He prepares breakfast for Peter before explaining the things of eternity. What a model, what a hero, what an ideal. Looking at Jesus' positive example, we are changed, transformed, and renewed. We become like Him, whom we most admire.

LEADING BY EXAMPLE

Brethren, join in following my example, and note those who so walk, as you have us for a pattern. Phil. 3:17.

Catherine Marshall remembers her father, Pastor John Wood, as the man who led her to Christ. When Catherine was a young girl, the Father who ruled from heaven seemed rather fearful. She heard a lot about giving her life to this God, but the idea of spending all her time praying, reading the Bible, and talking about God didn't appeal to her at all.

But her father on earth did. She was sure that he loved her. When she had progressed in her piano lessons enough to play simple hymns, Dad would sometimes allow her to serve as pianist in church.

Catherine Marshall wrote, "Thus early I was given a sure sense of self-worth, the recognition of my individuality. . . . These are securities that parents can give their children only through their actions."

And it was by his actions that Pastor John Wood showed how accessible and gracious the Father in heaven could be. He would often take Catherine along when visiting his parishioners. One of her favorite stories was of her dad's visit to railyards near their home in Keyser, West Virginia. He wanted to speak with a new member of his congregation.

Pastor Wood found this man hard at work in an enormous railroad roundhouse. The pastor reached out to greet him, but the man said, apologetically, "Can't shake hands with you, Pastor. My hands are too grimy."

With hardly a pause John Wood bent to the ground and rubbed his palms in the coal soot. "How about it now?" Smiling, he stretched out an equalized hand.

John Wood didn't just tell his daughter about God, he showed Him to her. She wrote, "All along God had meant for the love of my earthly father to be a pattern of my heavenly Father and to show me the way to make a connection with Him."

Jesus came to earth to reveal the Father's love. Some things cannot be described; they must be shown. The greatest testimony to our loving Father is the example of that love, lived out day by day, in the lives of His followers. The most powerful example of the genuineness of Christianity is the way we live.

Catherine Marshall's father and countless other moms and dads passed Christianity's flaming torch of truth to the next generation. Through the example of their godly lives, God calls us to do the same today.

RECOUNTING GOD'S BLESSINGS, PART 1

The blessing of the Lord makes one rich, and He adds no sorrow with it. Prov. 10:22.

The Pilgrims celebrated the first American Thanksgiving during the second winter they spent in the New World. In a real sense it was a strange Thanksgiving, for there wasn't much to be thankful for. That first dreadful winter had killed nearly half of the members of the Plymouth Colony. Almost no family was spared the loss of a loved one.

But new hope grew up in the summer of 1621. An abundant corn harvest brought rejoicing. Governor William Bradford decreed that a day be set aside for feasting and prayer to show the gratitude of the Colonists that they were still alive.

The women of the colony spent days preparing for the feast. Foods were boiled and baked and roasted. Even the children were kept busy turning roasts on rods in front of an open fire. At a time of national tragedy the Colonists looked at what they had, not at what they had lost. Although they wept at the death of their loved ones, their faith led them to rejoice at God's amazing goodness.

Thanksgiving points us to the good things we have. It lifts us above loss. It speaks to us of a God who meets our needs. It rejoices at the blessings that God has given.

Thanksgiving is not merely a day; it's a state of mind. Thanksgiving is not a once-a-year event; it's a daily attitude.

Simply practicing thanksgiving all day long makes a difference. An attitude of gratitude or thanksgiving transforms health-destroying stress to life-transforming joy.

Motivational author Melody Beattie writes: "Gratitude unlocks the fullness of life. It turns what we have into enough, and more. It turns denial into acceptance, chaos to order, confusion to clarity. It can turn a meal into a feast, a house into a home, a stranger into a friend. Gratitude makes sense of our past, brings peace for today, and creates a vision for tomorrow."

The grateful heart sees life through new eyes. Rather than complaining about what it lacks, the grateful heart celebrates what it has.

Why not make a list of the blessings God has given you? Write down 10 things you are thankful for today. Reading your list will leave you more thankful than before.

RECOUNTING GOD'S BLESSINGS, PART 2

Let us come before His presence with thanksgiving. Ps. 95:2.

Have you ever wondered how some people possess such remarkable inner strength? They seem to have an incredible ability to deal with adversity.

What made Russian Nobel Prize winner Aleksandr Solzhenitsyn find such freedom, even in the horrible circumstances of a Russian prison? What made Victor Frankl survive three years in a concentration camp where the average life expectancy was 90 days? How did Corrie ten Boom come out of the Ravensbrück prison camp unscathed? The answer lies in one word: "Gratitude." Solzhenitsyn, Frankl, and ten Boom all developed the spirit of thankfulness for what they had. They thanked God for every breath, for every day of life, for the smile of an inmate, for every cup of water, for every morsel of food. This attitude of gratitude lifted them above their dismal surroundings. It took them to another level.

How do we develop this "attitude of gratitude"? It's one thing to observe others who have it. It's quite another to have it ourselves.

Let's go back 2,000 years to a Roman prison. Here we find a prisoner named Paul who not only survived in a surrounding of dank misery, but thrived. Let's discover his secret of dealing with the enormous stress of his own life.

Reading the letter to the Philippians, penned in a dark, damp Roman dungeon, we're immediately amazed. The apostle is not resentful; he's grateful. He's not complaining; he's rejoicing. He's discovered joy in the midst of life's trials. He's thankful in the midst of life's adversities.

Paul writes, "I rejoice, yes, and will rejoice" (Phil. 1:18). "I am glad and rejoice with you all" (Phil. 2:17). "Rejoice in the Lord always. Again I will say, rejoice" (Phil. 4:4). "But I rejoiced in the Lord greatly" (verse 10).

This certainly doesn't sound like a man who's in prison. It sounds like somebody who's enjoying his life to the fullest. It doesn't sound like someone separated from his family and friends, but someone surrounded by love. It doesn't sound like someone who's experienced one of life's greatest tragedies; it sounds like a man who's certain of triumph.

The apostle Paul tapped into a source of spiritual power far greater than himself. He was able to rejoice because he discovered the Source of all joy. He was at peace because he discovered the Source of peace. He was thankful because he found the One who is the source of all thanksgiving. In Christ we can be thankful today, tomorrow, and forever.

COMPLIMENTS MAKE A DIFFERENCE

A word fitly spoken is like apples of gold in settings of silver. Prov. 25:11.

A young wife named Sandra slumped in her pastor's office. She began to pour out a long, painful story about her husband. He treated her with contempt, Sandra explained. Nothing she did pleased him. Each day she dreaded the moment he returned home from work.

Sandra was a beautiful young woman, but her sense of rejection had turned her into a defeated, tense, frigid wife. And the more she felt of her husband's disdain, the less motivated she became to please him. Sandra was trapped in a vicious cycle. The pastor decided he'd better have a visit with Sandra's husband, Joe. This man was astounded to hear that he was the cause of his wife's depression. Like most men, he didn't understand how well his wife could read his attitude toward her.

The pastor came up with one specific suggestion: "Select 10 positive qualities in your wife," he said, "and thank God for them. Thank God twice a day, in the morning and on the way home from work."

That didn't seem very difficult, so Joe agreed. He began thanking God for the things he liked about Sandra. And before long, she actually began to change before his eyes. She became more cheerful, more positive, more affectionate. Joe continued to be thankful for her, and Sandra grew in self-respect and motivation.

After some time the pastor asked Joe if he had memorized his list of 10 positive qualities. The husband replied happily, "I not only have it memorized, but I'm finding new things in her to be grateful for every day."

Positive words produce positive actions. Negative words produce negative actions. Affirmation brings out the best in us, but criticism brings out the worst.

The wise man said, "Anxiety in the heart of man causes depression, but a good word makes it glad" (Prov. 12:25). "A word spoken in due season, how good it is!" (Prov. 15:23).

Compliments have unusual power to change the entire atmosphere of the home, the classroom, or the workplace. Jesus was a master at giving compliments. People were amazed at the "gracious words" that flowed out of His mouth (Luke 4:22). To a questioning scribe, He responded, "You are not far from the kingdom of God." He encouraged a woman caught in adultery with "Where are your condemners?" "Neither do I condemn you; go, and sin no more." Of the centurion, the Savior said, "I have not found such faith, not even in Israel."

What are you grateful for in your husband or wife? your son or your daughter? your brother or sister? your friends, classmates, or working associates? Tell them. Don't be afraid to compliment the people around you and watch the difference it makes.

November 26

LOST AT BIRTH

Therefore, brethren, having boldness to enter the Holiest by the blood of Jesus. Heb. 10:19.

The year was 1979. On a trip into Mexico, 13-year-old Efren de Loa became ill. A local hospital treated his symptoms, but his condition failed to improve. The boy's anxious family took him home to the United States. Doctors at Oakland Children's Hospital diagnosed Efren's illness as aplastic anemia, a rare and possibly fatal disease. The boy's best hope was a compatible donor, preferably a close member of his family. His parents and seven brothers and sisters took the tests to see if they were suitable donors.

Then came the surprise. Not only did their blood fail to match—tests clearly revealed that Efren was not even a biological member of the family!

His mother realized immediately what had happened. The day she brought Efren home from the Mexicali hospital, she had been standing in line with the baby in a bassinet beside her, waiting to be discharged. While her attention was occupied at the registrar's counter, a hurried nurse came along and placed a second baby in the bassinet.

When Mrs. De Loa turned from the counter, there was a moment of confusion. Two babies. Both boys, born on the same day. No name tags. Both wrapped in identical hospital linen. Which baby was hers?

Then the other mother came along. The two of them stood in silence gazing into the bassinet, wondering. "I think this one is mine," Mrs. De Loa concluded. The other woman agreed, and the two of them parted, never to meet again. Or so they thought. Suddenly now, 13 years later, it became very important to find the other family. Efren's life depended upon it.

Mexicali's major newspaper ran the story, giving the few details Mrs. De Loa could remember. After five days Efren's biological family came forward. The two mothers embraced—and each of them met their real boys, whom they had never seen all those years. And thanks to the matching blood provided by Efren's biological family, he now had a new lease on life.

They were lost at birth. It was only through their blood that their true identities were discovered and they took their rightful place in their real family.

What a parable of human nature. We too were lost at birth. Born in a sinful world, we were doomed to death, unrighteous, unholy, separated from God.

Our true identity is revealed through the shed blood of Christ. In Scripture blood symbolizes life (Lev. 17:10-14). Through Christ's shed blood God establishes a new covenant (Matt. 26:27, 28). We are no longer strangers, but adopted into God's family (Eph. 2:13). The shed blood of Christ provides the legal basis for us to be called children of God (verse 19). Through the blood we are redeemed, forgiven, and set free, and we will one day be restored to His presence (Acts 20:28; Rom. 5:9; Rev. 12:10, 11; Col. 1:19, 20).

Cleansed by the blood of Christ, heaven's most precious gift, we can have absolute confidence that we are children of God. Without a doubt, here is something to rejoice about.

November 27

COURAGE AT THE CROSS

Christ has redeemed us from the curse of the law, having become a curse for us (for it is written, "Cursed is everyone who hangs on a tree"). Gal. 3:13.

On May 21, 1946, in Los Alamos, New Mexico, a daring young Canadian scientist named Louis Slotin was carrying out delicate experiments with uranium. He was helping prepare for the second atomic bomb test, to be carried out in the waters of the South Pacific. Slotin needed to determine exactly the amount of U-235 necessary for a chain reaction. Scientists call it a "critical mass."

Slowly he pushed together two hemispheres of uranium. Then, just as the material became critical, he pushed them apart with an ordinary screwdriver, instantly stopping a chain reaction. He did this many times.

But on this day, just as the mass became critical, Slotin's screwdriver slipped! Instantly the room was filled with a dazzling bluish haze. Other scientists present jumped back in horror. But instead of ducking and perhaps saving himself, Slotin tore the two hemispheres apart with his bare hands. The chain reaction was interrupted.

By this instant, self-forgetful act of courage, Slotin saved the lives of seven other persons in the room. He realized that he himself had been exposed to a lethal dose of radiation, but he retained his presence of mind. He shouted to his colleagues to stand exactly where they had been at the moment of the accident. He then drew on a blackboard a sketch of everyone's relative position. That would enable doctors later to discover the degree of radiation each man had absorbed.

A few moments later Slotin stood by a roadside, waiting with another scientist for the car that would rush them both to a hospital.

Quietly Slotin assured his companion, "You'll come through all right, but I haven't the faintest chance myself." That proved only too true. Nine days later Louis Slotin died in agony.

One bore the full radiation of sin's destructive power for us. He pulled the "hemispheres of sin" apart with His own bare hands. He experienced the enormity of sin's curse.

When the cynical priests chided, "He saved others; Himself He cannot save" (Matt. 27:42), they spoke an eternal truth. Jesus made a conscious decision to experience the awful pain and destructive power of sin to save us. All that sin does, it did to Jesus on the cross. All that sin is, it was to Jesus on the cross. All that sin means, it meant to Jesus on the cross. He willingly accepted its full consequences, its complete penalty, and its final results.

We will never totally understand what this means, but we can appreciate Jesus' self-forgetful act of courage. As Louis Slotin reassured his companions, Jesus reassures us, "You will come through all right."

November 28

THE GOD WHO REVEALS HIMSELF

I will heal them and reveal to them the abundance of peace and truth. Jer. 33:6.

Sundar Singh had always been sensitive and spiritually inclined. But when this Hindu teenager's mother died, he became very bitter.

Sundar began to make trouble at the mission school he attended, mocking and bullying those who professed Christianity. He was filled with anger about life, and yet still felt a need to somehow find God. One night his turmoil turned to desperation, and he cried out, "O God, if there is a God, reveal Thyself before I die." Sundar planned to commit suicide unless he received an answer.

This intense young man stayed up all night, praying and waiting. In the early morning, as he was saying his final prayer, a bright cloud of light suddenly filled the room. Out of this brightness came the face and figure of Jesus. Sundar wasn't expecting Jesus—Krishna perhaps, but not Jesus.

The youth heard his visitor ask, "How long will you persecute Me? I have come to save you. . . . I am the Way."

Sundar fell at the figure's feet, and the vision faded. But he had received his answer. That Sunday Sundar became a dedicated believer and later India's greatest Christian evangelist. The bright vision led to a powerful witness for Christ.

Sundar's experience is strikingly similar to the apostle Paul's when Jesus stopped him in his tracks on the Damascus road. God may not always reveal Himself to us as dramatically as He did to Paul or Sundar Singh. He rarely reveals Himself in spectacular ways. But He will always reveal Himself to us if we seek Him with a sincere heart.

God is not playing hide-and-seek with us. No matter how much we long to know Him, He longs to reveal Himself more. God speaks in a variety of ways. He shows up in the most unexpected places.

Isolated and feeling defeated, Moses met God in a burning bush in the Midian desert. Fleeing for his life, Elijah found God in a remote cave. Daniel's friends Shadrach, Meshach, and Abednego discovered Him in the raging inferno of a fiery furnace. David saw God's handiwork in the majesty of the heavens, as all nature spoke to the shepherd-king of an all-powerful, loving Creator. Matthew met Jesus while collecting taxes. Peter met Him while mending fishing nets. Nicodemus met Him at night, and a Samaritan woman met Him at noon.

Keep your eyes open. Be ready to hear His voice. Open your heart to His love. Be prepared. You too will meet Him this day in unexpected places. He will reveal Himself in ways you cannot imagine.

November 29

NEVER PART AGAIN!

They shall be the descendants of the blessed of the Lord. Isa. 65:23.

Tina sat in the hospital at 3:00 a.m., listening to her father's painful gasps. This was the man who'd changed her diapers and taught her to ride a bike. He'd been a dock worker most of his life, but now cancer had reduced him to a frail, disoriented fragment of himself.

Dad was dying. He couldn't fight any longer.

Tina thought she could just go on with her life after the funeral. But nothing was quite the same. She was haunted by the parent who wasn't there. A scent of Old Spice aftershave or a beloved Sinatra song prompted waves of tears. Tina says, "I know I'm an adult and I'm supposed to be strong, but there are some days I feel like I'm 4 years old, and all I want is my dad."

There is a haunting emptiness when we are separated from those we love. There is a sense of loneliness that no one else but those closest to us can fill.

Losing our closest relationships through death is devastating. Mothers and fathers who have experienced the tragic death of their children long to see them again. Widows and widowers long to embrace their spouse once more. Ask a teenager who's lost a dad to cancer, or let a college student speak whose best friend has just been killed by a drunk driver, and they will tell you how much they long to see the one they loved.

Scripture promises these glad reunions. Our Lord has the keys of the grave and death (Rev. 1:18). He will "make all things new" (Rev. 21:5). There will be a glad reunion day!

Our loved ones are not gone forever. The grave doesn't swallow them up. We have not lost them. They rest in Jesus, where they can never be lost. They await the glorious resurrection, where together with us they will meet Him in the sky.

Death does bring a haunting loneliness. It creates an aching void. The promise of the resurrection eases the pain and gives us hope again. It points to a time when we'll never part again.

November 30

AN ETERNAL FORTUNE

O God, You know my foolishness; and my sins are not hidden from You. Ps. 69:5.

Years ago, in one of the crowded cities of India, a speeding taxi struck a street urchin. A government official who witnessed the accident rushed the badly injured boy to a nearby hospital, where he gradually recovered.

Every day the official and his wife visited their young friend, becoming quite fond of him. Since he had no family, they decided to adopt him. Upon his release from the hospital, they joyfully brought him to their mansion as one of their own family.

Every day the mother brought her son back to the hospital to get his bandages changed. One morning she found herself especially busy and asked the boy if he could go by himself. "Of course," he replied proudly, "I know my way around this city." The mother gave him a dollar and a quarter to pay the doctor, and, with a smile and a kiss, bade him farewell.

The boy set off for the hospital. Then, just as he turned the corner, a temptation crossed his mind. He stopped, opened his hand, and stared at the shining coins. Never before had he held so much money. Why did he have to give them to the doctor?

For a minute he stood there thinking. Then the decision was made. Clutching his coins, the boy raced down the street, never to be seen again.

The father he abandoned had considerable wealth. All his other children were university graduates who eventually held high positions in government and business. He had planned to give his new son every advantage, even making him an heir to the family fortune. But the little fellow threw it all away for $1.25.

There are times we too give up so much for so little. We clutch the coins of disobedience and flee down the street of sensual pleasure. We leave behind an eternal fortune for a few earthly trinkets. We choose the earthly over the heavenly, the here over the hereafter, the present over the eternal. All the while our heavenly Father longs with a broken heart to give us so much more.

We are heirs to the family fortune. Let's never forget it.

CHANGED THINKING PRODUCES CHANGED BEHAVIOR

As he thinks in his heart, so is he. Prov. 23:7.

Two psychologists completed a 16-year study of the criminally insane that surprised a lot of people. Samuel Yochelson first sought to learn the difference between criminals who were mentally ill and those who weren't. After four years he reluctantly concluded that there was no real difference.

What he and his colleagues did discover was a common thinking pattern shared by all types of criminals. Whites and Blacks, the rich and the poor, college graduates and grade school dropouts, ghetto dwellers and suburban homeowners—all habitually thought in certain ways. They exhibited intense fears, pervasive anger, low self-esteem, a thirst for power, and incessant lying.

The psychologists devised a unique program of treatment for these people. They ignored the criminal's unfortunate past and concentrated on their present destructive habits of thought. The men in the study were made acutely aware of moral standards, and through repetition and discipline were educated in new thinking patterns. They kept a daily record of their thoughts and discussed their progress in regular sessions.

The results amazed experts. Men with long criminal records actually learned to become honest and responsible—not through any outward coercion, but because their thoughts had changed.

Conversion involves a change in our thinking. Our natures are fallen. Deep within we are naturally evil. Our hearts are corrupt. This may seem too harsh an assessment of human nature, but it is the biblical one. Jeremiah 17:9 attests to this human predicament with the words "The heart is deceitful above all things and desperately wicked." Paul adds, "There is none who does good, no, not one" (Rom. 3:12). When we surrender our lives to Christ, He miraculously changes us from within by the power of His Holy Spirit. One of the ways God does this is by changing our thought patterns. Things we once loved we now hate. Things we once hated we now love.

God changes our thinking though His Word.

Meditating upon His Word, we replace evil with good. Reflecting upon Scripture, we change our thoughts. Focused upon Jesus, we become like the one we so greatly admire. We do not change our thought patterns by trying to rid our minds of evil thoughts. We change our thought patterns by replacing evil with good. Fill your mind with pure thoughts of heaven today.

December 2

WHEN GOD INTERVENES

You have been a shelter for me, a strong tower from the enemy. Ps. 61:3.

One night a Los Angeles journalist decided to take a shortcut home. She began walking up a steep unlit path. Before long she heard steps behind her, moving faster and faster. Suddenly a stranger jumped her and began strangling her with her own scarf.

At that moment, miles away, the woman's mother woke from a deep sleep. She had a gnawing fear that something terrible was about to happen to her eldest daughter.

The mother immediately knelt by her bed and began to pray. She talked earnestly with God for 15 minutes, seeking His protection for her daughter. After she was assured that her prayer had been answered, she climbed back into bed and fell asleep again.

Back on the rocky path, the assailant suddenly stopped. The woman saw him cock his head for a moment, as if listening to something. Then he fled down the hill.

This woman and her mother are sure that God showed Himself as a faithful rescuer because of that prayer.

It's important to realize that the devoted mother wasn't praying to a God far off. She was familiar with His voice. She knew Him well enough to know that He had answered. She knew Him well enough to trust in His protection.

When that good woman knelt by her bed, that strong power was very close indeed.

In the battle between good and evil, prayer is a mighty weapon in the hand of the believer. Through prayer the forces of hell are beaten back. Ellen White writes that God will do, in answer to the prayer of faith, that which He would not do if we did not thus ask (see *The Great Controversy,* p. 525).

When this faithful mother prayed, our Lord commissioned mighty angels to beat back her daughter's assailant. The powerful influence of the Holy Spirit convicted him to flee. But . . . how do we explain the painful reality that some Christians are robbed, raped, and murdered? Is it all lack of faith? Was no one praying for them?

On this planet in rebellion bad things do happen to good people. In ways we don't fully understand, God does use heartache, disaster, and suffering to draw us closer to Him. He even uses evil that He was in no way responsible for to accomplish His long-term purposes. Also, God respects the freedom of choice of those who may harm us and does not always intervene. Sometimes in the larger scheme of things, He allows evil to run its course.

Is this difficult to understand? Certainly! But we can still trust Him. We can still keep believing. We can still keep reaching out to Him. We can still keep praying, knowing that He does intervene. He does deliver. He does answer. He will not let us down, and what we don't yet understand, He Himself will explain one day in eternity.

December 3

EAT YOUR PRUNES OR ELSE!

As the Father loved Me, I also have loved you. John 15:9.

A little boy in Aberdeen, Scotland, was not a great fan of prunes, despite his mother's frequent encouragement about how good they were for him. One evening she served prunes for dessert, and the boy rebelled.

Mother pleaded. Mother coaxed. But the boy remained tight-lipped, arms folded stiffly in front of him. Finally in her exasperation she said, "God will be angry if you don't eat those prunes!" Still the boy refused, and he was sent off to bed.

Mother tucked him in, frowning solemnly, and went downstairs. Suddenly a violent thunderstorm broke out. Lightning flashed against the windows, thunder ripped through the sky, and rain pelted the roof. The mother crept upstairs and peeked into her little boy's bedroom, expecting to see him in bed. Instead, the lad had gone over to the window. Staring out at the angry storm, he muttered, "Such a fuss to make over those ugly prunes."

We may smile at the boy's comments, chuckling at his lack of understanding of God. Yet it is altogether likely that we struggle with the very same issue. Even committed Christians may cling to the false notion that their sins make God angry.

This view of God is rooted in fear, not love. When our Christian experience is based on fear, there is very little genuine joy and dynamic spiritual power in our Christian lives.

Another way of approaching the Christian life makes all the difference. The Scripture teaches, "God is love" (1 John 4:8). "I have loved you with an everlasting love" (Jer. 31:3). "Every good gift and every perfect gift is from above" (James 1:17).

God is good, does good, and desires only good for us. Our sins do not make God angry. They deeply hurt Him. He is not mad at us when we sin. His heart is broken, because sin is self-destructive. We are destroying ourselves. We fail to experience the "abundant life" He offers (John 10:10).

The greatest motivation in living a godly life is the sense that a loving God who has given His life for us is hurt when we turn from that love to some cheap, sinful pleasure. Like a loving parent He is deeply pained when we bring grief upon ourselves through disobedience. His only desire for us is genuine lasting happiness.

If His love cannot keep us faithful, nothing can.

December 4

WHEN LOVE OVERFLOWS

Beloved, if God so loved us, we also ought to love one another. 1 John 4:11.

It is impossible to genuinely love God without loving the people God brings into your life every day. When God places His love in our hearts, it overflows to the people around us.

Christian author, Corrie ten Boom, describes how this love flowed out of the life of her own mother. Mrs. ten Boom was the kind of person who lived to serve. Her hands were always busy knitting sweaters for orphans, baking bread for the homeless, or making birthday gifts. This woman was known and loved by people throughout her Dutch town of Haarlem.

But then a massive stroke left Mrs. ten Boom partially paralyzed. She could utter only three words: "yes," "no," and "Corrie." It appeared her deeds of love had come to an end.

This seemingly helpless woman, however, found a way to communicate. Every morning the ten Boom daughters sat their mother in a comfortable chair by the front window so she could watch the busy street outside. And she began to communicate. They began a system much like 20 questions.

When Mrs. ten Boom saw someone special, she called out, "Corrie!"

"What is it, Mama? Are you thinking of someone?"

Mother would reply with an enthusiastic "yes." Then her daughter continued the questioning. Was it the person's birthday? Did the person seem to have some special need? Did they appear discouraged? Once Corrie had some idea of her mother's intentions, she wrote a note of encouragement and hope to the person her mother pointed out. Then she guided Mother's stiff fingers to sign her name.

For the last three years of her life, this woman sat at her window and continued ministering to the people outside. Not even paralysis could stop her service of love.

This kind of service of love can make a difference in our neighborhoods and communities. It can make a difference in our churches. Love revealed in compassionate deeds, kind words, and unselfish actions does make a difference.

Heaven's love overflowed from the life of Jesus, and He changed the world. When heaven's love flows from our lives, we, too, will change our world.

December 5

TITHE SYMBOLIZES TOTAL COMMITMENT

And you shall remember the Lord your God, for it is He who gives you power to get wealth. Deut. 8:18.

A certain man in a country overseas was studying the Bible, and his friends became alarmed at his enthusiasm.

"Don't you know," they warned him, "that if you become involved with that church they will take 10 percent of your income?"

It sounded serious. But wisely he went directly to the pastor of the church in question to learn the truth. He put the question straight. Would the church take 10 percent of his income?

The pastor gave a unique answer—one that sounded a little like compulsion, which of course God never uses. But I think you will agree that he made his point. This is what he said:

"Yes, it is true that the church will ask you to be faithful to God in your tithe. But that is not all. You will be called upon for offerings in addition to your tithe. And that is not all. You have children. The church will encourage you to put them in a Christian school. And that costs money. Then the church will encourage you to send them to a Christian college. And that costs still more. And even that is not all. The day may come when the church will ask you to send your boy or girl to Africa, or somewhere like that. It could be that you would never see your child again. The Lord does not ask only 10 percent. The Lord asks everything you have!"

Yes, God asks everything we have. But in the light of what He has done for us, in the light of what Calvary cost Him, is it too much to ask? How can we offer Him less?

Tithing is much more than money. Faithfulness in tithe reveals our loyalty to God. One of the reasons God confronts us with specific tests in our Christian life is to deepen our faith. Our faith grows at the point of a test. When there is no test, there is no growth.

Abraham's faith grew when God asked him to offer up Isaac. Daniel's faith grew in Nebuchadnezzar's banquet hall. Joseph's faith grew in Pharaoh's prison. Isolated and alone herding his sheep and fighting off bears, David's faith grew. Elijah's faith blossomed on Mount Carmel before 450 prophets of Baal.

Throughout the centuries the great heroes of faith were challenged to grow at the point of a test.

If you have not been a faithful steward of the finances God has entrusted to you, why not commit your finances to Him today? As you face this financial test your faith will grow.

December 6

DISCERNING THE SIGNS

You know how to discern the face of the sky, but you cannot discern the signs of the times. Matt. 16:3.

The history books record that World War II began officially on September 1, 1939. The first shots were actually fired six days earlier.

Hitler originally planned to launch an attack on Poland August 26. The evening before, several combat units were poised to strike. But last-minute political developments forced Hilter to postpone the invasion. Each of the combat units had to be contacted by radio and called home. But one unit could not be reached.

At 12:01 a.m. on the originally appointed day, August 26, a unit led by Lieutenant Herzner moved out and captured a railway station at the town of Mosty, taking a few Polish prisoners. When Herzner telephoned in his report, he was told that he'd jumped the gun. On orders, he released his prisoners and returned to Germany.

Now, this snafu should have made Hitler's intentions plain. But incredibly enough, the Polish government missed the sign. They let the incident pass without notice. And when the Nazis swept into the country on September 1, the Poles were still taken by surprise.

We don't want to miss the signs of God's final invasion of human history. We don't want to be surprised by Christ's second coming.

Although numerous signs speak loudly, Jesus gives one in Matthew 24 as His final sign. He declares, "This gospel of the kingdom will be preached in all the world as a witness to all the nations, and then the end will come" (Matt. 24:14).

I am convinced that Jesus is fulfilling His promise. This prophecy is being fulfilled. Now impenetrable areas are being touched by the gospel. Thousands of Global Mission pioneers are taking the gospel to unentered territories. Mass media is making an impact. Adventist radio and television programs teach millions weekly. *It Is Written* is now broadcasting in nine languages in 130 countries of the world, including 200 million Arabic-speaking people in 12 countries of the Middle East. In March 1994 Adventist World Radio began a powerful new broadcast from two 250-kilowatt transmitters in the republic of Slovakia, covering all of Central and Eastern Africa, India, and the Middle East with the good news of Jesus Christ.

Another powerful transmitter on the island of Guam sends radio programming over Asia, including much of China. The Adventist Media Center in Tula, Russia, produces programs in 16 different languages daily. These are just a few of the ways God is using to finish His work. Indeed, this gospel of the kingdom is being preached to the world.

One thing is certain. God is winding things up, and we don't want to miss it.

December 7

THE HOUSE GOD BUILT

On this rock I will build My church, and the gates of Hades shall not prevail against it. Matt. 16:18.

In 1850 architect Sir Joseph Paxton submitted his design for the building that would house London's Great Exhibition of 1851. Paxton conjured up a building of gigantic dimensions that would have nothing heavy or clumsy about it. He imagined a structure that would produce the effect of lightness, even weightlessness.

The problem was, there was no way to construct such a building at the time. Large structures required massive walls to support them. There seemed no way to create the graceful, airy building Paxton had in mind.

But then he remembered a certain plant he'd worked with as a gardener, the royal water lily. The floating leaves of this lily are huge, up to six feet in diameter, and very thin, yet in spite of this, they're quite stable. They achieve this stability by a complicated strutting on the underside. Ribs radiate from the center of the leaf outward, splitting into many branches.

The royal water lily gave Paxton the key to making his architectural dream come true. He used a few main struts connected by many small ribs in his design. The result: the Crystal Palace, a tremendous success. It proved a great turning point in architecture. The bold skyscrapers of steel and glass we see all around us today date back to that graceful, airy Crystal Palace, and yes, back to the remarkable design of the royal water lily.

The Lord constructed another magnificent edifice, His church. "Wisdom has built her house, she has hewn out her seven pillars" (Prov. 9:1). Divine wisdom has built God's church on seven basic teachings. These scriptural doctrines are the struts that support the structure of truth God has established. They are the divine, eternal verities. Although many ribs connect to these main struts (doctrines), these seven are the "pillars" of support. They are all centered in Christ, and all of Scripture revolves around them.

These seven eternal truths are the foundation of God's revelation throughout history. They are identifying marks of God's last-day church.

1. Scripture (John 17:17)
2. Salvation (John 3:16)
3. Second Coming (John 14:1-3)
4. Sabbath (John 14:15)
5. State of the Dead (John 11:11-26)
6. Sanctuary (John 17:4, 11, 24)
7. Holy Spirit and the Spirit of Prophecy (John 14:15-17)

Christ in His Word, Christ's grace flowing from Calvary's cross, Christ returning, Christ the source of all true rest and peace, Christ the resurrection and the life, Christ alive imparting power from heaven's sanctuary, Christ imparting the gifts of the Spirit to empower His church on earth to finish the work. These are heaven's eternal truths, and all the powers of hell cannot destroy them.

December 8

OUR DISAPPOINTMENTS ARE NOT GOD'S

He said to me, "You must prophesy again about many peoples, nations, tongues, and kings." Rev. 10:11.

Have you ever gone through a time of great disappointment, of personal defeat? Our disappointments may not look the same to God. He can make something great out of something terrible. He is the God of new beginnings who turns tragedy into triumph.

The disciples went through the greatest disappointment of their lives.

Wouldn't you be devestated if the one you pinned your hopes on was executed on a cross, if the one you believed to be the world's Messiah was dead?

Did the Old Testament Messianic prophecies predict the death of Jesus? Could the disciples have known? Could they have been prepared? Certainly! They misunderstood the Old Testament predictions. They thought the Messiah would usher in a kingdom of glory. They did not anticipate a kingdom of grace.

Out of the disappointment of A.D. 31, God raised up the Christian church. The outpouring of the Holy Spirit on the day of Pentecost empowered the church to carry the gospel to the far-reaching corners of the world.

Fast-forward 1,800 years. A small band of believers studied the prophecies of Daniel and Revelation. They concluded that Jesus was coming and coming soon. Their numbers swelled into the tens of thousands. Scores of genuine conversions attest to the Spirit-incited power of their message.

As they traced the prophecies of Daniel, based on the 2300-year prophecy of Daniel 8:14, they concluded Christ would come October 22, 1844. These early Adventists waited for His return with great anticipation. When He did not appear, they were crushed. John the revelator described their experience when he foretold that they would take the little book (Daniel) out of the angel's hand and eat it (study it), and it would be sweet in their mouth but bitter in their stomach (see Rev. 10:9-11).

Those prophecies once so sweet in their experience seemed terribly bitter in their stomachs. The sweetness of discovery was gone. The bitterness of disillusionment threatened to snuff out their faith.

The hour of their disappointment was the hour of God's appointment. Like their first-century counterparts, these believers misunderstood the nature of the prophecy. Jesus appeared on time in heaven's sanctuary, in His final phase of ministry, to finish His work on earth.

From heaven's sanctuary He once again poured out His Spirit to raise up the Advent movement to complete the task of preaching His everlasting gospel.

Both the New Testament church and the Advent movement were raised up out of disappointment. What happened to these people so bitterly disappointed? They grew into a mighty missionary movement, proclaiming God's final message.

Our Lord delights in turning tragedy to triumph. Let Him turn your disappointments into something wonderful today.

TWO THOUSAND YEARS AND STILL COUNTING

For yet a little while, and He who is coming will come and will not tarry. Heb. 10:37.

The young pastor's questions surprised me. They reflected doubt, revealing an inner sense of uncertainty. They were honest questions, not cynical, but they were doubts nonetheless. He asked, "Do you still believe Jesus is coming soon? Haven't Adventists preached the coming of Jesus for more than 150 years? Wouldn't you agree that His coming might be 500 years, 750 years, or 1,000 years away? Does it make any difference at all?"

These questions demand sensible answers. It is true that Seventh-day Adventists have anticipated the coming of Jesus for more than 150 years. It is also true that we did not originate the idea of the Second Coming. We are not the first generation to look for a speedy return of our Lord.

When Jesus ascended to heaven, His own disciples anticipated that He would return quickly. They did not imagine that there would be a 2,000-year delay. After the apostle Paul's first letter to the church at Thessalonica, early Christians believed Christ was coming in their lifetime. They were excited about an imminent return of our Lord. The apostle wrote Second Thessalonians to put the coming of Christ in perspective. He warned them of events that would transpire beforehand.

The great lines of prophecy have always traced events culminating before the coming of Jesus. The central question, then, is one of timeline prophecy. Where are we in light of the prophecies of Daniel and Revelation?

In Daniel 2 the kingdoms of gold, silver, brass, and iron have faded into the dust heaps of history. Babylon, Media-Persia, Greece, and Rome are now gone. The empire of Rome has been divided. The next event is the rock that smites the image. The four beasts of Daniel 7 representing these same four world-dominating powers are gone. The lion, the bear, the leopard, and the dragon are demolished. The 10 horns representing the divided kingdom of Rome have given way to the rise of the little horn, a religious political power in the Papacy. The 2300 evenings and mornings, or years, of Daniel have met their fulfillment in 1844 and the beginning of Jesus' final phase of ministry in the heavenly sanctuary.

Revelation's seven churches, representing seven epochs of church history, have met their fulfillment, culminating in lukewarm Laodicea. The seven seals have unfolded, and the seven trumpets have sounded down through the centuries.

All of the great epochs of prophecy have been fulfilled. We do not know when Christ will come. We cannot define how near is near or how soon is soon, but with absolute confidence we can exclaim that fulfilled prophecy proclaims His coming *is* near.

December 10

FINDING FELLOWSHIP IN GOD'S SPIRITUAL FAMILY

I bow my knees to the Father of our Lord Jesus Christ, from whom the whole family in heaven and earth is named. Eph. 3:14, 15.

I admire the way a Virginia woman named Dorothy Redford created a family celebration out of a very unpromising past. In researching her genealogy she discovered a bill of sale in a county courthouse showing that her earliest known ancestor, Elay Littlejohn, and eight children had been sold as slaves to the owner of Somerset Plantation in North Carolina. Dorothy began combing through documents from Somerset and discovered for the first time the network of names that were her extended family. She decided to have a family reunion.

In September 1986 Somerset Place Plantation, now a state historical site, witnessed a homecoming unique in American history. The descendants of the slaves who once labored on that North Carolina plantation came together to touch their roots. There was a concert of spirituals, an exhibition of African dances, and the reenactment of a slave wedding. But the highlight of that event was simply the delight of mutual discovery, of finding that they sprang from a common past.

The Somerset reunion proved an unforgettable event. Dorothy Redford took the time to make that memory. In effect, she took the time to create a whole new family.

In a very real sense we too were all slaves. Sin is a very harsh taskmaster. It keeps us in bondage, destroying our potential. Liberated in Christ, we join a whole new family. We come from different backgrounds, but we are joined together by a common past and a common deliverance into a new spiritual community—the church.

A gospel song by Bill and Gloria Gaither states this eternal truth well: "You may notice we say brother and sister 'round here, it's because we are a family, and these folks are so dear. When one has a heartache we all shed a tear . . ."

We all long for connectedness, for family, for home. The church is God's family. It may not be a perfect family, but it is His. It provides nurture, security, and togetherness in our fragmented world. It offers us the sense of community we so crave. The church is a place for mutual understanding, bearing one another's burdens, listening to each other's joys and sorrows, and meeting one another's needs.

Just as each part of the body is part of the whole, each member of the church is united through Christ. In one church God has created a whole new family. Rejoice today that you are part of the family of God.

December 11

BE READY

You also be ready, for the Son of Man is coming at an hour you do not expect. Matt. 24:44.

An eighteenth-century English novel tells of a small Welsh town in which for 500 years the people all had gathered in the village church Christmas Eve to pray and sing. Shortly before midnight they lit candles and lanterns and sang carols.

It is a magnificent scene. The church is decorated festively for the occasion. Sounds of "Silent Night, Holy Night" and "O Come, All Ye Faithful" punctuate the air. The procession leaves the church minutes before the clock strikes 12:00. They walk down a country path several miles to an old country shack.

There they set up a manger scene. In simple piety they kneel and pray. Their hymns warm the chilly December air. Everyone in town capable of walking is there. Young and old, educated and uneducated, rich and poor are all there.

For centuries they have done this, and a fascinating myth has risen—that if all the town's citizens are praying with perfect faith, right then on Christmas Eve the second coming of Christ will occur.

In the story one of the main characters is asked, "Do you believe He will come this Christmas Eve?" "No," he answers, shaking his head sadly. "No, I don't." "Then why do you go each year?" "Ah," he says, smiling. "What if I were the only one who wasn't there when it happened?"

What a response. This old man speaks words of amazing wisdom. In essence he says, "I don't know when Jesus will come, but I know this, when He comes I want to be ready. I don't want to miss the event. I don't want to be home sleeping at midnight, only to be startled that He has come."

An early Adventist preacher was noted as saying, "The only way to be ready when Jesus comes is to get ready and stay ready." Readiness for the coming of Jesus is not something we achieve at the end of the Christian life. It is something we experience today in Christ.

Is there anything in your life that would keep you from being ready for the coming of the Lord? Are there attitudes or habits in your life that stand between you and Him? Have you fully committed your life to Christ? Are you anticipating His soon return with incredible joy? Is there something in your life you need to deal with now, something that you sense you cannot put off any longer?

Jesus and an old Welsh man speak. They both say, "Be ready."

December 12

WHY CULTS ATTRACT

False christs and false prophets will rise and show great signs and wonders to deceive, if possible, even the elect. Matt. 24:24.

In March 1997, 39 members of the Heaven's Gate cult produced a farewell video and then took their own lives. They believed that trailing the Hale-Bopp comet was a spacecraft coming to take them to the "next level." The victims were found with purple cloths over their heads and shoulders.

In trying to identify the 39 bodies, police set up a toll-free number for relatives to call. In 24 hours they fielded calls from more than 1,500 anguished relatives who had been out of contact with their loved ones for months or even years.

Cults are everywhere, proclaiming that they have messages from God, seeking to control the mind, deceiving those who would believe. There are Bible-based cults, UFO cults, satanist cults, New Age cults, and Eastern cults.

Why do cults flourish? What is their magnetism? What attracts people to their often bizarre ideas? The answer is complex, but one aspect is obvious. Cults attract people looking for certainty. In a world filled with doubts, cults provide definition. They leave little room for doubt. Things are either black or white, right or wrong. There is no middle ground. Cult leaders may be mistaken, but they are certain. They may teach absolute falsehood, but they are certain of what they teach.

God's answer to the challenge of the cults is scriptural certainty.

Luke wrote to Theophilus "that [he might] know the certainty of those things in which [he was] instructed" (Luke 1:4). Jesus emphatically stated, "Your word is truth" (John 17:17). The apostle Paul claimed, "All scripture is given by inspiration of God, and is profitable for doctrine" (2 Tim. 3:16).

The Bible is not filled with myths or allegories. It is filled with absolute, divine authority. The authority of Scripture is central in the life of each believer. Scripture is the governing influence of our lives. When we reject the Scripture's authority, we open ourselves to delusion.

The uncertain, skeptical twenty-first-century mind is ripe for the certainty and definiteness cults offer. God offers us something much better, the absolute truth of His Word. To neglect scriptural truth is to prepare our minds for a deceptive cult delusion.

December 13

THE CHOICE IS YOURS

Wheover desires, let him take the water of life freely. Rev. 22:17.

Cult leaders are charismatic individuals who focus attention on themselves. They become more of a source for truth than God's Word, making it difficult for cult members to separate what they say from what God says.

Heaven's Gate cult leader Marshall Applewhite believed that he and his coleader, Bonnie Lu Nettles, came from an "evolutionary level above human bodies." Applewhite believed that he'd been temporarily placed in a human body to show people how to get to "the next evolutionary level."

Applewhite went further. In September 1995 he issued an online statement entitled "Undercover 'Jesus' Surfaces Before Departure." Applewhite began to refer to himself as Jesus. He claimed he was a messenger from God, just like Jesus, on the same level with Jesus.

The leader of the Solar Temple cult did the same thing. Luc Joret believed he was a manifestation of Christ. He managed to persuade people that through death they could journey to a new life on the star Sirius. Nearly 100 Solar Temple members have committed suicide over the past few years to take that so-called journey.

Jim Jones and David Koresh took on Messiah-like qualities for their followers. Cults flourish when people surrender their individuality and their right to make moral decisions. The essence of Christianity is the ability to choose. Sometimes we make good decisions. At other times we make poor decisions, but through all of our decisions we grow. When we surrender our moral decision-making process to anyone else, we fail to grow spiritually.

Spiritual growth demands choices. A significant part of being created in God's image is our individual accountability before God. The Bible begins with God's giving our first parents the incredible choice at the tree in the Garden of Eden. It ends with God's giving all humanity a choice with the amazing words "And the Spirit and the bride say, 'Come!' And let him who hears say, 'Come!' And let him who thirsts come. Whoever desires, let him take the water of life freely" (Rev. 22:17). *Whoever desires* is also translated "whoever chooses." The book of Revelation concludes with God appealing to our choice. We are responsible for our decisions.

We surrender our ability to choose at the risk of eternal loss. Today God calls us to place our wills on the side of right.

December 14

UNDER HIS WINGS

He shall cover you with His feathers, and under His wings you shall take refuge. Ps. 91:4.

Mayerly Sanchez is the leader for the Colombia Children's Movement for Peace. She grew up in a community rampant with crime and violence near Bogota, Colombia. Mayerly is a positive force for peace in an area torn apart by conflict. She knows her work for peace could easily get her killed by the drug lords or the high profile criminal gang leaders in her community. But she continues her efforts for peace without fear.

Recently she said, "God is the one taking care of us. To work and speak of peace here is not very safe, but He is always with us. . . . We take refuge in Him."

Fear paralysis. It cripples us. God invites us to look away from our fears to His powerful promises. He is our security. He is our refuge.

In the most beautiful and meaningful language of Scripture, God describes what He longs to do for every one of His children on earth when the plagues fall. "He shall cover you with His feathers, and under His wings you shall take refuge" (Ps. 91:4).

Only in eternity will we really understand God's protecting power. I am convinced that my life could have been snuffed out numerous times if it were not for God's protection. God protects us in ways we cannot know until the day we meet Him face to face.

Ellen White wrote, "The omnipotent power of the Holy Spirit is the defense of every contrite soul. Not one that in penitence and faith has claimed His protection will Christ permit to pass under the enemy's power" (*The Desire of Ages*, p. 490).

This promise is for us. In Christ we are secure. In Christ we are safe. In Christ all fear is banished. "The Saviour is by the side of His tempted and tried ones. With Him there can be no such thing as failure, loss, impossibility, or defeat; we can do all things through Him who strengthens us" *(ibid.)*.

When you are assaulted by the enemy, fix your mind on your almighty deliverer. He has never failed one dependent, trusting soul and He certainly will not fail you. He is our refuge, our serenity, our divine protector. In Him we are safe today, tomorrow, and forever.

December 15

WE SHALL MEET IN HEAVEN

If we hope for what we do not see, we eagerly wait for it with perseverance. Rom. 8:25.

Charlotte Collyer had a hope to cling to, even as she sorrowed over the loss of her husband on board the *Titanic.*

Writing to her mother-in-law, she wrote, "Sometimes I feel we lived too much for each other, that is why I've lost him. But mother, we shall meet him in heaven. When that band played 'Nearer, My God, to Thee,' I know he thought of you and me, for we both loved that hymn."

Charlotte was recalling the brave band members on the *Titanic* who kept playing that hymn, even as the great ship tilted up and began sliding into the Atlantic. In the midst of all the panic and confusion and cries of distress, their instruments raised a hope on that deck, a great hope of coming to God. And that's what Charlotte was holding on to in her darkest hour. The thought of meeting her beloved in heaven, seeing him face to face, was her comfort.

Melody Homer clings to this same hope as well. Her husband, Leroy, died in the fiery crash of United Flight No. 93, near Shanksville, Pennsylvania, on September 11, 2001. Rather than harbor bitterness against her husband's murderers, Melody holds on to the hope of the Second Coming. When I interviewed her in her New Jersey home, she said with a quiet confidence, "I know I have not seen Leroy for the last time. One day we will be caught up together to meet Jesus in the sky."

Melody's faith spoke to my heart during that interview. Her courage encouraged me. She was extremely realistic about the pain her husband's untimely death caused her. She was equally realistic about the hope that beat in her heart about the coming of Jesus.

Death is not a final goodbye. It is only a brief pause. It is God's prelude to eternity. Without the hope of resurrection, death would be a tragic ending. With it we await a new beginning.

The hope that burns within our hearts is the glorious hope of being reunited with our loved ones again at the coming of Christ. This hope gives us courage to face today and a thousand tomorrows. It dries our tears and points us to another time and place, where our eager expectation gives way to His glorious reality.

December 16

AN AMAZING AWAKENING

As for me, I will see Your face in righteousness; I shall be satisfied when I awake in Your likeness. Ps. 17:15.

Growing up in the early 1900s, Magda was a happy child. She did well in high school, receiving honors as both a scholar and an athlete. But in 1918, while working as a secretary, she contracted sleeping sickness. Magda recovered after a few months, but then, in 1923, she started showing signs of Parkinson's and slipped into a state of limbo that lasted 45 years. The woman spent her days in institutions, sitting in a wheelchair, motionless, expressionless, apparently oblivious to anything happening around her. Those who provided nursing care regarded her as a hopeless case.

In June of 1969 Dr. Oliver Sacks began administering a newly developed drug called L-DOPA to a few survivors of sleeping sickness. Magda gradually awakened. First she found her voice again, then she began writing a few sentences. Soon she was able to feed herself and walk a bit. And then a whole person blossomed, where there had been only a shell. Dr. Sacks wrote that Magda "showed an intelligence, a charm and a humor, which had been almost totally concealed by her disease."

Magda recalled happily her childhood in Vienna and talked nostalgically about school excursions and family holidays. But she did not remain trapped in the past. Somehow this courageous woman found the strength to cope with the 45-year gap in her life. She renewed emotional ties with her daughters and sons-in-law. She discovered her grandchildren and enjoyed visits with many other relatives who came to see the miracle of Magda restored to reality.

What an incredible awaking! This is the hope God offers to each of us even now, no matter how long or deep our slumber in sin has been.

There will be another awakening when the kingdom of God shines down on this planet. We will look up with joy and ascend with Christ. We need not remain trapped in the tragedies of life in a sinful world, unable to bridge the unimaginable gap between life as we've known it and the life God wants to give us today. Job put it this way: "So man lies down and does not rise. Till the heavens are no more, they will not awake nor be roused from their sleep" (Job 14:12).

Unlike the awakening from sleeping sickness, we won't wake up and suddenly find ourselves old. We will wake up and find ourselves young again, with new bodies recreated like the resurrected body of Christ. "Our lowly body" will be "conformed to His glorious body" (Phil. 3:21).

Place your life in His hands with the solid assurance that if you die before His return, you will awake to see the splendor of His coming.

December 17

WHEN JOY IS FULL

In Your presence is fullness of joy. Ps. 16:11.

When the great Russian writer Maxim Gorky visited the United States, he was taken to Coney Island one weekend. His hosts took him on all kinds of thrill rides. Walking through the excited holiday crowds, they showed him museums of freaks, palaces of jugglers, and theaters with dancing girls. They thought they were giving this distinguished author the time of his life.

At the end of what seemed like a perfect day, they asked Gorky how he'd liked it.

The writer was silent for a moment. Then he said, "What a sad people you must be!"

Gorky was right. Any society that bases its very existence on the "cheap thrills" of the moment must be a sad society indeed.

Jesus offers something so much better for us. He declared, "I have come that they may have life, and that they may have it more abundantly" (John 10:10). The original New Testament word for "more abundantly" is the word "superabundance." Jesus offers a life of superabundance.

The psalmist adds, "No good thing will He withhold from those who walk uprightly" (Ps. 84:11). Pleasures will run dry very quickly. God's abundance is never ending. "You are complete in Him" (Col. 2:10). He offers us "pleasures forevermore" (Ps. 16:11). He satisfies "the desires of every living thing" (Ps. 145:16). Happiness comes from knowing and doing God's will (see John 13:17).

There is no greater joy than knowing that we are in the center of God's will. There is no greater happiness than knowing we are pleasing God. There is no greater satisfaction than the genuine satisfaction that comes from sharing His love with some other human being.

The happiness Jesus gives us is lasting. It's not like soap bubbles that burst in the breeze. The joy Jesus gives us is genuine. It is not some cheap imitation sold at a high price.

Make Jesus the center of your joy today. He will give you a sense of inner completeness, which will continue until the day He comes to take you home.

December 18

LISTENING TO HIS VOICE

My sheep hear My voice, and I know them, and they follow Me. John 10:27.

Thomas Edison had just completed his latest invention, the phonograph, and a famous reporter, Henry Stanley, visited his laboratory to see it demonstrated. Stanley was amazed as he heard a man's voice emerge somehow from the little box. He was struck by the possibilities of this phonograph and asked, "Mr. Edison, if you could hear the voice of any famous person throughout the history of the world, whose voice would you prefer to hear?"

"Napoleon," Edison answered quickly.

But Stanley had someone else in mind. He replied, "I should like to hear the voice of our Savior."

Obviously our Lord does not speak to us through Thomas Edison's phonograph. How does Jesus speak to us? There are four prime ways He communicates His will to us.

First, Jesus speaks to us through His Word. As we open the pages of Scripture our Lord is talking to us. He impresses us through the teachings of the Bible. He reveals His will through Scripture. To fail to read His Word or to read it only occasionally is to miss wonderful opportunities to hear His voice. The same God who inspired the Bible still inspires those who read its pages. The same God who spoke *to* the prophets still speaks *through* the prophets.

Second, Jesus speaks to us through His Holy Spirit. He convicts our hearts of sin. He lifts our spirits with some encouraging thought. He impresses our minds with creative ideas. In quiet meditation we hear Him speak through the Spirit. When we fail to reflect, we miss opportunities to hear Him speak.

Third, Jesus speaks to us through the providences of life. If we are observant, there will be times God opens and shuts doors. There will be times God will impress us through some event or answered prayer. If we have ears to hear, we will hear Him speaking to us personally through all of our life's experiences.

Fourth, Jesus speaks to us through other people. Often in life God impresses our family and friends to give us wisdom we may not have on our own. If we are sensitive to His voice, we will hear Him speak through the counsel of godly friends.

Today listen for his voice in His Word. Hear Him speak to your heart through His Spirit. Open your ears to discern the meaning of His providence. And listen to the wise counsel of godly people.

December 19

LEFT OUT IN THE COLD

And this will be the sign to you: You will find a Babe wrapped in swaddling cloths, lying in a manger. Luke 2:12.

It was cold, bone-chilling cold. The wind howled, and the snow fell heavily. It was Christmas Eve in 1952 in a remote village in Korea. Only a few people were on the streets completing those last-minute chores before Christmas. One lone woman in her early 20s slowly trudged down the street. Every step was labored. It was difficult for her to make much headway at all against the driving wind. She was nine months pregnant, and the baby was due that very night. She had no family. The young woman had become pregnant by an American GI. Now she was alone, all alone, with no place to deliver the baby. She remembered a kind missionary across town. Suddenly thoughts raced through her mind. *If only I can get to the missionary's house in time, I can deliver my baby there.*

Crossing a bridge to the other side of town, she recognized the telltale signs that the baby was about to be born. Stumbling down the hill to the riverbed, she found shelter under the bridge. There, in the freezing cold, this young Korean woman delivered a beautiful baby boy. Throughout the night she wrapped him in her own clothing to keep him warm.

Early Christmas morning as the missionary pastor was crossing the bridge, he heard the cries of the newborn baby. Quickly, he rushed to help. To his amazement, he found the mother frozen to death, but the baby boy, wrapped in her clothing, was doing quite well.

The missionary immediately reported the scene to the authorities. Since the boy had no father, the pastor eventually adopted him. As the years passed, father and son became inseparable friends. Ten years later, on Christmas Eve in 1962, the father told his adopted son about the incredible sacrifice of his loving mother. The boy was deeply moved.

On Christmas morning, when Dad quietly entered the boy's room to wake him up, he found the boy's bed empty. He searched the house but couldn't find him. As the boy's father looked out the window, he saw footprints in the snow. He hastily followed them to the bridge where the boy had been born 10 years before. There, to his absolute astonishment, the father saw the boy standing under the bridge—barefoot, stripped to the waist, shivering in the snow—crying. The father rushed to the son's side and threw his arms around the boy. The boy looked up through tear-stained eyes and said, "Dad, I wanted to know what Mama felt like in the cold that night long ago when she died for me."

Jesus wanted to know what it's like to be lonely, tired, rejected, sorrowful, hurt, and bruised, so He plunged into this cold, cruel, calloused world. He took the full brunt of Satan's viciousness. Jesus experienced a level of physical pain, emotional trauma, psychological distress, and spiritual agony that we can never imagine. The words of the prophet Isaiah ring with relevance, "Unto us a child was born." All Jesus experienced was for us. He knows. He understands. He empathizes. He is concerned. He drew near. He shivered in the cold world with us.

Come to Him with all your heartache, tears, and sorrow. He knows what you are going through right now and is by your side to help.

December 20

RENEGADE RELATIVES

And she will bring forth a Son, and you shall call His name Jesus, for He will save His people from their sins. Matt. 1:21.

As you look over your family tree, are there some branches that kind of embarrass you? Do you have some renegade relatives who give the family a bad name? Jesus did. When you trace the lineage of Jesus through Joseph as recorded in Matthew 1, you discover some amazing things. Jacob the deceiver is listed there. Tamar, Judah's daughter-in-law, is mentioned. She pretended to be a harlot, deceived her father-in-law, and gave birth to twins by him. David, the murderer and adulterer, is part of Jesus' genealogy, as is Rahab, the harlot. What a list! What a family tree! Why do you think Matthew's gospel lists them? Do genealogies simply take up space?

I think there is a good reason. Jesus is the Savior of all people. His grace reaches all. His mercy is for all. His salvation knows no limits. His power knows no bounds.

Jesus' genealogy speaks eloquently of a Christ who is mighty to save. There is hope for each one of us as we consider Jesus' unusual genealogy. "Every son and daughter of Adam may understand that our Creator is the friend of sinners. For in every doctrine of grace, every promise of joy, every deed of love, every divine attraction presented in the Saviour's life on earth, we see 'God with us'" (*The Desire of Ages,* p. 24).

Do you have some relatives who don't know Jesus? Are you grieving over some son or daughter who has turned their back on the faith of their childhood? Take courage! Let your heart be renewed with hope. Our Lord promises, "And they shall come back from the land of the enemy. There is hope in your future, says the Lord, that your children shall come back to their own border" (Jer. 31:16, 17). The ones we might think are the most hopeless, our Lord can reach. Even the hardest hearts are not beyond His reach. If you have any doubt, reread His own genealogy. If He reached some of those scoundrels, He can reach your renegade relatives, too.

December 21

STANDING BY YOUR CONVICTIONS

Finally, my brethren, be strong in the Lord and in the power of His might. Eph. 6:10.

Martin Luther grew up in a religious world that was basically terrified of God. Christians especially feared purgatory, where it was thought souls must spend years being cleansed of every sin before entering heaven.

Luther was taught that indulgences could be purchased that guaranteed a shorter time in purgatory. Quite a business had grown up around the buying and selling of indulgences.

But Martin Luther began studying the Bible for himself. Paul's letter to the Romans impressed him greatly. He learned of the free grace of God, which justifies sinners. And Luther concluded that God's mercy cannot be bought or sold. He rejoiced that although "all have sinned and fall short of the glory of God," we are "justified freely by His grace through the redemption that is in Christ Jesus" (Rom. 3:23, 24).

Luther could have gone along with the crowd and lived a nice quiet life as a monk. But his conscience wouldn't let him sit by and see God's grace distorted. He had to make a stand.

And he did. He stood alone before Charles, the holy Roman emperor, and before princes and lords and powerful church officials at the Diet of Worms. These men demanded that he publicly recant his teachings.

But Luther courageously replied, "Unless I am convicted by Scripture and plain reason . . . I do not accept the authority of popes and councils. . . . My conscience is captive to the Word of God. I cannot and I will not recant anything, for to go against conscience is neither right nor safe. Here

I stand. I cannot do otherwise. God help me. Amen."

These words ensured the success of the Reformation. One man was willing to bear witness against religious practices that distorted the gospel. All of Christendom seemed to accept indulgences, but Luther could stand alone and say no. Why? Because his conscience was captive to the Word of God.

One man standing by his convictions rocked the world. God moved a whole generation through his courage. God can change your world if you are willing to stand upon the principles of His Word. God calls for principled men and women of courage who do not fade into the background at the opposition of the majority. God's "world changers" know what they believe, stand for what they believe, and share what they believe, because of their love for the One in whom they believed.

December 22

PEACE ON EARTH! GOODWILL TO ALL!

Glory to God in the highest, and on earth peace, good will toward men! Luke 2:14.

The casualties on both sides were high. The shelling was intense. Heavy bombardment from the artillery lasted all day. The ground shook from the incessant pounding of the Axis' aircraft. The Allied forces responded with a firefight of their own. Rival armies faced each other across the trenches.

Joe, an 18-year-old American GI, leaned back against the earthen wall of his freshly dug trench, exhausted. The sun was setting. Another day had passed, and he was still alive. It was Christmas Eve, 1943. Thoughts of home flooded into his mind . . . Mom, Dad . . . his brother, Tom . . . his sister, Alice . . . freshly baked apple pie . . . homemade raisin cookies . . . roast turkey . . . colorfully wrapped presents . . . the Christmas tree . . . smiles . . . hugs . . . logs burning in the fireplace . . . hot chocolate . . . peace.

But in this nightmare called war, death stared him in the face. Peace and goodwill were only figments of his imagination.

The battlefield was quiet now. The air was crisp and clear. The stars twinkled in a moonlit sky. Then he heard it. Could it really be singing? Were his ears deceiving him this Christmas Eve? Was this some kind of subtle trap?

The sounds of Christmas carols gladdened the night air. Although the words were German, the tune was unmistakable. "Silent night, holy night,

All is calm, all is bright; Round yon virgin mother and Child!"

A few hundred yards away German soldiers sang Christmas carols in full view. Slowly, cautiously at first, Joe pulled himself out of his foxhole. His heart was touched. His emotions were stirred. Suddenly he couldn't restrain himself any longer. Spontaneously he too began singing.

"Silent night, holy night, All is calm, all is bright." His American colleagues joined in the singing. Soon voices that a few hours earlier had shouted the curses of war now echoed a chorus of praise. The two opposing sides approached each other. They shook hands and embraced. They laughed, they sang. For one night they were brothers. They shared a common humanity.

The fighting stopped. The bombing ceased. The mortars were silent on that Christmas Eve. For a brief moment enemies became friends. The peace of Christmas united, even if only for a few brief moments, two opposing armies.

If God did it then, why can't He do it now? If God did it there, He can certainly do it here. Christmas can be a time of peacemaking. A time of goodwill, a time of oneness for all. Let the Prince of Peace fill your heart this Christmas, and become an instrument of His peace to all around you today.

December 23

PLASTERED ACROSS THE SKY

The angel said to them, do not be afraid, for behold, I bring you good tidings of great joy which will be to all people. Luke 2:10.

Benjamin Franklin once had a problem somewhat similar to that of many parents today. He was trying to teach his farmer neighbors how to grow better crops, but they weren't listening. They probably thought the incurable experimenter was crazy. Franklin had discovered that plaster sown in the fields actually helped things grow. But when he told other farmers about this, they scoffed. So Franklin dropped the subject and said no more about it.

But the following spring he planted a section of wheat near a well-traveled pathway. First he traced some letters in the soil with his finger and sprinkled plaster into them. Then he sowed seed over the whole plot of ground. After a few weeks the green stalks shot up, and those passing by began to see a pattern, more and more defined in the grass. Finally the tallest, greenest stalks clearly spelled out a message on the field, which finally persuaded Franklin's stubborn neighbors of the usefulness of humble plaster.

When God wanted to convince His stubborn children of His amazing love, He plastered the message across the sky. Angels visited humble

Bethlehem shepherds with a message too plain to be misunderstood. They sung of "good tidings" of "great joy" which shall be "to all people." And today we too sing, "Hark! the herald angels sing, 'Glory to the newborn King.'" Throughout the centuries, God's spokespersons the prophets were ridiculed, mocked, slandered, and persecuted. When His people failed to listen to those He sent, God did something radical. He sent His own Son.

There are some things you cannot explain, for they must be demonstrated. God's love is like that. It can never be explained, but it can be revealed. God's love is revealed in Jesus' leaving the magnificent splendor of heaven to be born in a dung-filled stable among donkeys and cows on a chilly Bethlehem night. God's love is revealed in Jesus' leaving the adoration and praise of the angels to experience the wrath of Herod. His love was shown as He experienced the ridicule of the religious leaders, the poverty of humble Galileans, the condemnation of a common criminal, misunderstanding from His own family, and denial by His own disciples. On a blood-stained cross God plastered love across the face of a lost planet. He revealed the lengths He would go in order to save us. There is no sacrifice He would not make. There is no price He would not pay. There is nothing He would not give to redeem us.

Heaven gave its all. Heaven gave its best. Heaven gave all it had. Now that's why the angels sing, "Glory to God in the highest," and with them we will sing all through eternity.

December 24

A GIFT FOR THE GIVER

When they had opened their treasures, they presented gifts to Him: gold, frankincense, and myrrh. Matt. 2:11.

When Jesus was born, the people of His day had three reactions to His birth. The scribes and Pharisees were indifferent. They hardly knew what was happening. What a tragedy to be indifferent to the Savior of the world!

Sadly, there are some religious people who are indifferent to Christ this Christmas. Christ still gets lost in the busyness of the season. He gets covered up under the Christmas tree in the neatly wrapped presents. He is hidden in the rush of it all. He's crowded out with office parties, luncheons, and a multitude of other Christmas engagements.

There were some who opposed Him then, and there are those who oppose Him now. Herod and the Roman soldiers were threatened by the prospect of this newborn King. They were threatened by the potential challenge of His rulership. Herod passed a decree that every Hebrew child under 2 years old be murdered. He would not risk his throne.

There are people today, this Christmas season, who will not relinquish the throne of their hearts. They battle and struggle, fighting to maintain control.

There was still a third reaction to Jesus. Three kings from the East brought Him gifts. The Wise Men fell at His feet in adoring worship. Wise men and women still worship Him today.

Matthew's Gospel describes it like this. "When they had opened their treasures, they presented gifts to Him: gold, frankincense, and myrrh" (Matt. 2:11).

Gold is a gift for a king. It represents all of our material possessions. We come to Jesus in adoring worship, holding nothing back. Everything we have is a gift from Jesus. At Christmas we acknowledge, "Lord, all my possessions are Yours. You are my King of kings."

Frankincense is a gift for a priest. It was used by the priests in the ancient sanctuary. At Christmas we come kneeling, declaring, "Jesus, You are my Priest. You intercede for me. You are my Intercessor. You present Your perfect righteousness before all of heaven, in the place of my utter failure. Lord, all of my worship is Yours."

Myrrh is a gift for one who is ready to die. It is an ointment used in ancient burial services. At Christmas we come acknowledging, "Jesus, You are my dying Savior. You are the innocent Baby who was born and my righteous Redeemer who died for me."

Today, rejoice! It's a time to celebrate!

Accept Him as your Savior. Approach Him as your Priest. Acknowledge Him as your King.

December 25

A BIRTH TO CELEBRATE

Rejoice, highly favored one, the Lord is with you. Luke 1:28.

There is no more exciting event in a married couple's life than the birth of their first child. My wife and I were 25 years old when our daughter Debbie was born.

I was so certain the baby would be a girl, I bought a cute little bright—and I mean bright—red dress. You can only imagine our baby girl with a newborn's reddish complexion in that bright-red dress. She lit up the entire hospital.

To say that Teenie and I were excited about the birth of our firstborn is an understatement. To say we prepared for the event is a further understatement!

We read every child-training book we could get our hands on. We attended natural childbirth classes together. We picked out colors for the new arrival's room. We painted the room pink. We bought a crib, baby clothes, and toys. When Debbie was born, we were ready.

God was excited about the birth of His Son too. Angel choruses announced His arrival. Shepherds and Wise Men heralded His birth. The voices of prophecies centuries old proclaimed the birth of the Messiah.

Isaiah the prophet predicted the Christ child would be born of a virgin (Isa. 7:14). Jacob said He would be of the lineage of Judah (Gen. 49:10). The prophet Micah declared that the Messiah would be born in Bethlehem (Micah 5:2). Heaven did everything it could to prepare the world for the Savior's birth.

This was no ordinary birth. Jesus was supernaturally conceived by the Holy Spirit in Mary's womb. This was no ordinary child. Jesus was the divine Son of God dwelling in human flesh, the divine-human Christ.

The angel announced Jesus' mission to Joseph. "She will bring forth a Son, and you shall call His name Jesus, for He will save His people from their sins" (Matt. 1:21).

His mission was clearly defined by heaven—to save His people from their sins.

The baby born in Bethlehem's manger is your Savior and mine. The Christmas season is a time to celebrate and rejoice. It's a time to praise. We were not left alone in the depths of our sin. In the darkness of our rebellion, there is a light. Imprisoned in sin's bondage, there is hope.

We can rejoice. In the baby born in Bethlehem's manger God has sent us an undeniable message of His love. He will fill your life with joy and rejoicing this Christmas season.

December 26

CHRISTMAS PEACE

Glory to God in the highest, and on earth peace, good will toward men! Luke 2:14.

Senator John McCain spent five and a half years as a prisoner of war in Hanoi during the Vietnam War. He and many other pilots endured terrible suffering. But there came a day, McCain remembers clearly, when they were able to rise above the abuse and isolation.

It was Christmas Eve, 1971. A few days earlier McCain had been given a Bible for just a few moments. He furiously copied down as many verses of the Christmas story as he could before a guard approached and took the book away.

On this special night the prisoners had decided to have their own Christmas service. They began with the Lord's Prayer and then sang Christmas carols. McCain read a portion of Luke's Gospel in between each hymn.

The men were nervous and stilted at first. They remembered the time about a year earlier when the guards had burst in on their secret church service and began beating the three men who were leading out in prayers. They were dragged away to solitary confinement. The rest of them were shut up in 3' x 5' cells for 11 months.

But still the prisoners wanted to sing on this night. And so they began, " 'O come, all ye faithful, joyful and triumphant.' " They sang barely above a whisper, their eyes glancing anxiously at the barred windows.

As the service progressed, the prisoners grew bolder. Their voices lifted a little higher until they filled the cell with "Hark! the Herald Angels Sing" and "It Came Upon the Midnight Clear."

Some of the men were too sick to stand, but others propped them up on a platform and placed blankets around their trembling shoulders. All wanted to join in the songs that now seemed to make them indeed joyful and triumphant.

When they came to "Silent Night," tears rolled down their unshaven faces. John McCain later wrote, "Suddenly we were 2,000 years and a half a world away in a village called Bethlehem. And neither war, nor torture, nor imprisonment had dimmed the hope born on that silent night so long before.

"We had forgotten our wounds, our hunger, our pain. We raised prayers of thanks for the Christ child, for our families and home. There was an absolutely exquisite feeling that our burdens had been lifted."

As we open our hearts to Him the Christ child will give us His peace too. He will lift our burdens. The problems of life will fade into insignificance in the light of His glorious love. The Christ who was born in Bethlehem 2,000 years ago longs to be reborn in our hearts today. Just as He turned a North Vietnamese prison into a place of love, He longs to fill your home with love today.

AUTHENTIC CHRISTIANITY HAS AN IMPACT

The Word became flesh and dwelt among us, and we beheld His glory, the glory as of the only begotten of the Father, full of grace and truth. John 1:14.

In a Romanian prison in the early 1950s two men confronted each other. One was a self-assured, intelligent, tough young lieutenant named Grecu. He was a dedicated Communist, confident that he was building a better world.

The other man was a young Lutheran pastor named Richard Wurmbrand. He was weak and pale. On his face were the heavy shadows of a man who had endured much torture and deprivation.

Grecu had interrogated the pastor for several days. Then he forced him to write a supposed confession of crimes against the state.

Pastor Wurmbrand had to make a confession, so he confessed that he had been sharing the good news about Jesus Christ by tapping in code on prison walls. Wurmbrand also confessed, "I am a disciple of Christ who has given us love for our enemies. I understand them and pray for their conversion so that they will become my brothers in faith."

After a half hour Grecu returned, swinging his truncheon. He had been beating prisoners. He picked up the paper and began to read. After a while he put his truncheon aside. At the end Grecu looked up at the pastor with troubled eyes and said, "Mr. Wurmbrand, why do you say you love me? This is one of your Christian commandments that no one can keep. I couldn't love someone who shut me up for years alone, who starved and beat me."

Wurmbrand shared more about what he had seen and heard of Jesus. The lieutenant had thought he would always be an atheist, but when the prisoner talked about what he had experienced, God seemed very real. Grecu saw Christ in Richard Wurmbrand's life and could not resist the power of divine love. He too became a believer.

The Christmas season speaks of God through Christ dwelling in human flesh. God became man to give us a glimpse of what He is really like. God didn't merely send us a love letter to tell us what He was like; He came to show us.

Jesus desires to reveal Himself to the world again through us. He longs to dwell in weak, frail human flesh again. He wants to demonstrate to a callous world the glory of His grace through His followers. He touched Grecu, an atheist Communist lieutenant, through a humble Lutheran pastor, Richard Wurmbrand.

This Christmas God longs to be born in your heart anew. He longs to love through you. Will you allow Him to be born again in the manger of your heart this Christmas?

December 28

THE BREATH OF GOD

How can this servant of my lord talk with you, my lord? As for me, no strength remains in me now, nor is any breath left within me. Dan. 10:17.

Dr. Drummond was a physician who found himself rather skeptical about what he heard about Ellen White. At one point he even declared that he could hypnotize her and give her a vision. One day Ellen White was caught up in a vision in Drummond's presence. He stepped forward and checked out her physical condition. After a bit he turned pale. "She doesn't breathe!" he exclaimed. His examination convinced this physician that the visions were from God.

Sometimes the visions of Ellen White lasted for hours, sometimes for only a few minutes. But the physical phenomena surrounding her visions gave evidence that they were supernatural.

There are physical tests that accompany the manifestation of the genuine "gift of prophecy" that give evidence to its authenticity. One of these is the "breath test." The word inspiration means "God-breathed." Since God is breathing through the prophet, communicating His will, the prophet does not have human breath while in vision. Daniel describes his experience in vision with the words "No strength remains in me now, nor is any breath left within me" (Dan. 10:17).

We discover something significant in Scripture about the way God communicates with His prophets. He speaks directly, as He did with Moses. He speaks through visions, and He speaks through dreams.

Only three ways. And the favorite methods used in the psychic arts—astrology, palmistry, crystal gazing, contacting the supposed spirits of the dead, witchcraft—are not found among them. God's Word is clear: "If there is a prophet among you, I, the Lord, make Myself known to him in a vision; I speak to him in a dream" (Num. 12:6).

A genuine prophet speaks for God. His or her messages are "God-breathed," for they come from God Himself. The genuine prophet is testifying for Jesus, revealing what Jesus has shown in vision.

To ignore the inspired messages God gives through the gift of prophecy is to reject the testimony of Jesus Himself. We can praise God that He has thought enough of us to raise up the modern-day gift of prophecy in His last-day church. This gift of prophecy through the writings of Ellen White provides inspiration and guidance for our lives today. Why not begin the new year reading a few pages of that classic *The Desire of Ages* each day. You will never regret it.

December 29

THE SPIRIT'S FRUITAGE

By their fruits you will know them. Matt. 7:20.

Look at the world impact of the Seventh-day Adventist Church worldwide. Let's consider one area only—health care. As a result of God's messages through Ellen White, the church has established more than 500 hospitals, dispensaries, and clinics throughout the world. Some years ago a millionaire named Charles Kettering received treatment at one of these hospitals. He was so impressed with the caring service he received that he gave $10 million to start a new Adventist-operated hospital near his home in Ohio.

The world-famous medical center at Loma Linda University was established as a direct result of Ellen White's visions. At first the Council on Medical Education tried to persuade the new medical college not to apply for accreditation. An adequate staff wasn't really available. The school insisted, however, and was given the lowest rating of "C." It wasn't long, however, before the school received full accreditation and its graduates were welcomed everywhere with the highest "A" rating.

In recent years the United States government has sent the Loma Linda heart team to various countries on goodwill tours. The medical center has become one of the most advanced heart-transplant facilities in the world. Its proton beam cancer treatment is world-renowned. Loma Linda University Medical Center is on the cutting edge of scientific medical research.

The Disney Corporation turned to Seventh-day Adventists to establish the hospital of the future in their ultramodern, high-tech community in Celebration, Florida.

Although the Adventist wholistic approach to health is biblically based, Ellen White urged church leaders to establish hospitals around the world to minister to the whole person. Her vision of whole-person healthcare has become a standard in the industry, though it was new in her day.

One of the fruits of Ellen White's visions is a worldwide health-care system ministering to hundreds of thousands. There are millions whose lives have been saved and are healthy today because of Seventh-day Adventist hospitals.

Millennia ago Jehoshaphat admonished Judah, "Believe His prophets and you shall prosper" (2 Chron. 20:20). His words echo down the ages. They speak to us today. When the church heeds God's Word through the gift of prophecy, it prospers. When we listen to the voice of God speaking to us in the prophetic gift, we prosper. We neglect the gift of prophecy at our own peril.

December 30

POWER TO HELP

Be strong in battle! Even so, God shall make you fall before the enemy; for God has power to help and to overthrow. 2 Chron. 25:8.

Ed was a Christian, but he had a serious smoking problem. He was addicted, smoking almost two packs a day for 20 years. One day Ed asked me for help to overcome smoking. I spent time with him, explaining how Jesus worked miracles throughout the New Testament. We talked about people whose cases appeared hopeless but who were miraculously healed.

I finally asked Ed to bring all of his cigarettes and lay them on the floor. We knelt together, and I encouraged him to offer a simple prayer in faith, believing that God would deliver him. His prayer, one of the weakest I have ever heard, went something like this: "Oh, dear Jesus, I can't quit. You know I can't quit. I am so weak, Lord. Tobacco has a grip on me, and I can't give it up."

I couldn't take it anymore. I shook him as he prayed. I said, "Stop praying like that!" He looked up at me and said, "Pastor, what did you say?" I said, "Don't pray anymore. You're going to be worse after you pray than you were before." He'd never heard a preacher talk to him like that before. I said, "Look, you're convincing yourself that you can't quit smoking, but Jesus says in Matthew 7:7, 8: 'Ask, and it will be given to you; seek, and you will find; knock, and it will be opened to you. For everyone who asks receives, and he who seeks finds, and to him who knocks it will be opened.' "

I told Ed, "Get down on your knees and tell God, 'I know I'm weak, but You're strong, God. You've got almighty power. You touched blind eyes, and they were opened. You touched deaf ears, and they were unstopped. Lord, Your power is greater than tobacco.'

"Ed, your problem is that you think tobacco is greater than Jesus, but you need to tell Jesus you believe that His power is greater. Please pray your prayer over again right now."

He bowed his head and prayed, "Dear Jesus, I'm so weak, but You're strong. You're almighty. You can deliver me, Lord. I may have a craving, but You're greater than that craving. I may want to run out and get some tobacco, but You're greater than that, Lord. Please deliver me."

Ed was delivered by the grace of God! And you too can be delivered.

Is there some habit that enslaves you? Is there some sin that keeps you in bondage? Accept God's promises by faith. Believe that He has the power to deliver you. Surrender that specific sin to Jesus. Claim victory over it in Jesus' all-powerful name and expect a miracle.

You can become a new you this new year, for God will find some way to deliver you from your enslaving habits.

December 31

REJOICE ALWAYS

Rejoice always. . . . In everything give thanks. 1 Thess. 5:16, 17.

A thankful heart produces positive emotions. These positive emotions produce healthful chemical by-products that are life-giving. Even in prison the apostle Paul radiated a thankful spirit. He knew that God, who is always in control, would strengthen him to cope.

Here's an eternal truth the apostle shares with us from a Roman prison. "I can do all things through Christ who strengthens me" (Phil. 4:13).

As a prisoner in Rome, Paul had lost his reputation. His enemies maligned his character. He'd lost his freedom. He was confined to a Roman cell or placed under house arrest. His health was failing.

Throughout his ministry, he was stoned. He was fiercely beaten. He walked for miles with little food. He experienced shipwreck. He battled a raging storm for survival for three days. He was often near death. Still, in all of life's experiences, the apostle's faith was strong. His faith kept growing in the tough times. The almighty power of the living God strengthened him.

God's power is more than adequate for all of the tragedies of life. Here's something to be incredibly thankful about. We can face every one of Satan's assaults, every one of his attacks, and each of his temptations through the power of the almighty Son of God who strengthens, empowers, and delivers us. When people are strengthened by God's Spirit, they have thankful hearts even in difficult times.

The apostle Paul lived his life by three fundamental principles:

One: God is in control.

Two: God will strengthen me to cope.

Three: God will supply all of my needs.

What's troubling you today? Do you feel the need of loving affection? Are you lonely? Do you have financial needs? Is your health failing? Are you struggling with some overpowering temptation? Do you have an inner yearning for purpose in your life? Are you looking for a sense of guidance?

Why not bring all your needs to the Creator of the universe today? Why not claim His wonderful promise "My God shall supply all your need" (Phil. 4:19) ?

You can rejoice today. Your heart can be filled with thanksgiving. You have something to be grateful for. A loving God knows your needs. He has committed all the resources of heaven to meeting them. What have you been thankful for during this past year? Why not determine to live a life of thanksgiving this coming year?